ERNST KALTENBRUNNER

ERNST KALTENBRUNNER
Ideological Soldier of the Third Reich

by Peter R. Black

Princeton University Press
Princeton, New Jersey

Copyright © 1984 by Princeton University Press
Published by Princeton University Press, 41 William Street,
Princeton, New Jersey 08540
In the United Kingdom: Princeton University Press,
Guildford, Surrey

All Rights Reserved
Library of Congress Cataloging in Publication Data will be
found on the last printed page of this book

ISBN 0-691-05397-9

This book has been composed in Linotron Electra

Clothbound editions of Princeton University Press books
are printed on acid-free paper, and binding materials are chosen
for strength and durability. Paperbacks, although satisfactory
for personal collections, are not usually suitable
for library rebinding

Printed in the United States of America
by Princeton University Press
Princeton, New Jersey

To Mary

Contents

Acknowledgments

THIS study could not have been completed without the help of numerous individuals and institutions. An overall expression of gratitude is due to the faculties and staffs of the History Department at the University of Wisconsin, the History Department and Graduate School at Columbia University, the German Academic Exchange Service, the Memorial Foundation for Jewish Culture, and Princeton University Press for the general educational background, and for financial, production and editorial assistance that made possible both my research and, ultimately, the appearance of this book.

The individuals to whom I am indebted are too numerous to mention in full here. Thanks are due to: Dr. John Mendelsohn, Robert Wolfe, and the staff of the Modern Military Records Branch and the Microfilm Reading Room of the National Archives; Marek Web and the staff at the YIVO Institute for Jewish Research in New York City; Hermann Weiss and the staff at the Institut für Zeitgeschichte in Munich; Dr. Harry Slapnicka and Dr. Hans Sturmberger of the Upper Austrian Provincial Archives in Linz; Dr. Fritz Mayrhofer and Richard Bart of the Linz City Archives; Dr. Gerhard Botz of the University at Salzburg; Peter Kammerstätter of the Institute for Modern and Contemporary History at the University in Linz; Dr. Herbert Steiner and the staff of the Dokumentationsarchiv des österreichischen Widerstandes in Vienna; Dr. Lorenz Mikoletzky, Dr. Isabella Ackerl, and the staff of the Allgemeines Verwaltungsarchiv in Vienna; the late Dr. Ludwig Jedlicka, Dr. Gerhard Jagschitz, and Dr. Anton Staudinger of the Austrian Institut für Zeitgeschichte in Vienna; Dr. Hanne Marschall, Archive Adviser Elisabeth Kinder, and the staff at the Bundesarchiv in Koblenz; the staff at the Berlin Document Center in West Berlin; Dr. Gerhard Wiebeck of Munich; Police Inspector Alois Mayrhuber, and retired mailman Alphons Gaisberger of Alt Aussee; Nikolaus, Graf Revetera of Helfenberg; and many others.

I also wish to acknowledge my debt to the individuals who provided me with written or verbal information pertaining to Kaltenbrunner with the proviso that none of these individuals can be held responsible for the opinions and interpretations presented in this study. My thanks go to: the late Alfred Eduard Frauenfeld; the late Albrecht Gaiswinkler; Dr. Heinrich Gleissner; Otto Holzinger; Dr. Wilhelm Höttl; Elisabeth Kaltenbrunner; the late Dr. Roland Kaltenbrunner; the late Dr. Werner Kaltenbrunner; Dr. Ernst Koref; Dr. Irmfried Latzel-Lasser; Robert E. Matteson; Karl Moser; Franz Peterseil; Otto Picha; Wilhelm Pöschl; Sebastian Radauschl; Alfred Rodenbücher; Hans

Christian Seiler; Leopold Tavs; Dr. Erich Thanner; and Father Trunkel of the Roman Catholic parish office in Alt Aussee. A special debt of thanks is due to Dr. Hansjörg Kaltenbrunner and to his wife, Lotte Kaltenbrunner.

Without the remarkable blend of perceptive criticism and emotional encouragement offered me by Dr. Istvan Deak of Columbia University, I could not have completed this study. Dr. Robert O. Paxton of Columbia University, Dr. Vojtech Mastny of the Johns Hopkins School of International Affairs, and Dr. Charles Sydnor of Longwood College also offered their time, support and valuable suggestions for improving the manuscript. My dear friend Katherina Zimmer did me the invaluable service of wading through my ponderous early drafts with an eye to factual data, style, and consistency. To Dr. Robert Koehl of the University of Wisconsin I am grateful for the idea of a Kaltenbrunner biography and for a basic training in the history and source material of the Nazi regime. Special thanks are due to R. Miriam Brokaw of Princeton University Press, who believed that my Kaltenbrunner manuscript was publishable and sold the idea to the Press, and to Robert Brown of the Press for his expert editorial assistance in transforming the manuscript into a book. I am very grateful to Judy Marwell and Pat McCoy for their invaluable assistance in preparing the manuscript for publication. My parents, Adelaide and Sidney Black, provided me with much needed emotional, financial and, at key times, editorial support. Finally, I wish to thank my wife, Mary, who, through her enduring patience and constant support, lightened considerably the lonely burden of research and writing.

None of the persons or institutions mentioned in these pages can be held accountable for opinions, interpretations, and errors of fact contained in this book; for these the author alone is responsible.

Note on Sources, Style, and Citations

In the process of gathering research material for this study, I have relied to some extent on sources in private hands; these had neither been used previously nor catalogued in any way. They consist of records made available to me by Kaltenbrunner's son, Dr. Hansjörg Kaltenbrunner, and other members of Kaltenbrunner's family as well as the records of personal interviews and correspondence that I conducted and carried on.

For purposes of citation, the records made available by Kaltenbrunner's family have been divided into three groups. The first two comprise the documents that I saw on my first visit to Dr. Hansjörg Kaltenbrunner in Gramastetten on the weekend of 25-27 March 1977. Those documents that were photocopied for me (and copies of which are in my possession) are cited as belonging to the "Kaltenbrunner File." They include Kaltenbrunner's prison "memoir," written for his children, and his correspondence with his lawyer, Dr. Kurt Kauffmann. The documents that were not photocopied and that include such items as Hugo Kaltenbrunner's birth certificate and Gymnasium report cards have been cited as belonging to the "Kaltenbrunner Family Records." For a full list of the items used from these collections, the reader may consult the Bibliography.

In December 1977, nine months after my first visit to Dr. Hansjörg Kaltenbrunner, Kaltenbrunner's brother Roland died as the result of a stroke. In his papers, Dr. Hansjörg Kaltenbrunner found a few items of interest, which he photocopied and sent on to me in New York. In citing these documents, I have grouped them under the heading "Nachlass Roland Kaltenbrunner." A full list of the items used from this collection can be found in the Bibliography. The original documents from all three groups are in the possession of Dr. Hansjörg Kaltenbrunner in Gramastetten.

Two types of interviews were conducted. One group was taped and transcribed; the other was not. In each citation, the name of the person interviewed, the place of the interview, and the date of the interview appear in that order. If an interview was taped and transcribed, the page of the transcript follows: e.g., Interview with Dr. Wilhelm Höttl, Bad Aussee, 14 and 15 April 1977, Höttl Tape, p. 15. Second references to such interviews appear in the following form: Höttl Tape, p. 15.

I have used the following abbreviations in the footnotes:

AVA   Allgemeines Verwaltungsarchiv, Vienna

BA   Bundesarchiv, Koblenz

BDC   Berlin Document Center, West Berlin

DGFP   *Documents on German Foreign Policy, 1918-1945.* Washington: U.S. Government Printing Office, 1949-1958

DöW   Dokumentationsarchiv des österreichischen Widerstandes

EPD   Eichmann Prosecution Documents. Gathered by the Israeli police for the Eichmann trial in Jerusalem. Copies on file at the Munich Institut für Zeitgeschichte

IfZ   Institut für Zeitgeschichte

IMT   International Military Tribunal, *The Trial of the Major War Criminals.* Nuremberg: Secretariat of the International Military Tribunal, 1947-1949

NA   National Archives, Washington, D.C.

NCA   Office of U.S. Chief of Counsel for the Prosecution of Axis Criminality, *Nazi Conspiracy and Aggression.* Washington: U.S. Government Printing Office, 1946-1948

NPA   Neues Politisches Archiv, Vienna

OÖLA   Oberösterreichisches Landesarchiv

SS-HO   SS Hang Ordner, on file at the Berlin Document Center

TWC   Nuremberg Military Tribunals, *Trials of War Criminals.* Washington: U.S. Government Printing Office, 1949-1954

VfZ   *Vierteljahrshefte für Zeitgeschichte*

German words, terms, ranks, and office names appearing in the text have been translated wherever it was possible and meaningful to do so. German words and Nazi ranks that would lose their meaning and significance if translated remain in the original German. Where the German names of offices and positions lent themselves to translation, the original German follows in parentheses after their mention; thereafter these names appear in English only.

I have generally tried to avoid the use of German acronyms; the following eleven appear in the text:

HA-Orpo   *Hauptamt Ordnungspolizei* (Main Office Regular Police)

HSSPF   *Höherer SS- und Polizeiführer* (higher SS and police leader)

OKH   *Oberkommando des Heeres* (High Command of the Army)

OKW   *Oberkommando der Wehrmacht* (High Command of the Armed Forces)

RKFDV   *Reichskommissar für die Festigung deutschen Volkstums* (Reich Commissar for the Strengthening of German Nationhood)

RSHA   *Reichssicherheitshauptamt* (Reich Main Office for Security)

RuSHA   *Rasse- und Siedlungshauptamt* (Race and Settlement Main Office)

SA   *Sturmabteilungen* (Storm Detachments)

SD   *Sicherheitsdienst* (Security Service)

SOEG   *Südosteuropa-Gesellschaft* (Southeast Europe Society)

SS   *Schutzstaffel* (Protection Squads)

WVHA   *Wirtschafts- und Verwaltungshauptamt* (Economic and Administrative Main Office)

I would like to make one final point about the reliability of the source material used in this study. Wherever possible, I have tried to anchor the narrative in contemporary documentation. Nevertheless, as is often the case when writing a biography, I have had to rely at times on self-serving trial testimony and the reminiscences of participants or contemporary observers called forth decades after the events analyzed in this book. For example, as an accurate historical source, the testimony of Kaltenbrunner (or that of his colleagues, Neubacher, Seyss-Inquart, Rainer, etc.) at the Nuremberg Trial is highly suspect, given his (and their) efforts to avoid retribution by the victorious Allies. Equally suspect are many of the Nuremberg affidavits offered into evidence by a prosecution staff eager for speedy convictions. Another example is the memory of Wilhelm Höttl, who was a member of the underground Austrian SD and later the chief of the Hungary and Italy desks of the SD foreign intelligence office and whose memoirs and willingness to be interviewed have been exploited repeatedly by scholars and journalists. When I interviewed Höttl in 1977, I found him to be the source of much interesting information, some of which, however, could not be verified either through contemporary documentation or through other witnesses. Occasionally, upon closer questioning, Höttl would reveal that an incident which he had just related as though he had experienced it, had been told to him by an individual who was no longer alive. In many cases, the surviving documentation does not support his speculations or reveals some of his anecdotes to be inaccurate. Such weaknesses are present in the reminiscences of other contemporaries, both former Nazis like Otto Holzinger and anti-Nazis like Ernst Koref and Otto Picha.

Despite the questionable reliability of such sources, they occasionally fill important gaps in the contemporary documentation. Though Kaltenbrunner's "Memoir" to his children is self-serving and completely unreliable in reference to his political activity and beliefs, it provides us with most of what we know about Kaltenbrunner's childhood and can be corroborated in part by the reminiscences of Kaltenbrunner's brother Werner. Despite the weaknesses of Höttl's evidence, his descriptions of infighting in the RSHA and some of his anecdotes concerning the abortive peace negotiations in 1944-1945 are made more credible by corroborative evidence from other sources (Höttl's evidence on events in Austria before 1938 is more difficult to test as to its reliability). Thus, while I have relied to some extent on such sources, I believe that I have tried to handle them with the caution that they require.

ERNST KALTENBRUNNER

Introduction

OF THE twenty-one German leaders who stood before the International Military Tribunal in 1945 to account for crimes committed by the Nazi regime, few inspired more revulsion and contempt than Ernst Kaltenbrunner, former chief of the Reich Main Office for Security (*Reichssicherheitshauptamt*, RSHA). Austrian by birth, Kaltenbrunner had joined the Austrian Nazi Party in 1930 and the SS (*Schutzstaffel*) a year later. In 1937, he emerged as chief of the Austrian underground SS; after the annexation of Austria in 1938, he was appointed higher SS and police leader (*Höherer SS- und Polizeiführer*, HSSPF) in Vienna. In January 1943, he was summoned to Berlin by *Reichsführer* SS Heinrich Himmler to succeed Reinhard Heydrich as chief of the RSHA. In this position, he directed the operations of the Secret State Police (*Geheime Staatspolizei*, Gestapo), the Criminal Police (*Kriminalpolizei*, Kripo), and the Security Service (*Sicherheitsdienst*, SD). These operations included the deportation of the European Jews and Gypsies to extermination camps, the murder and mistreatment of prisoners of war and the civilian populations of occupied Europe, and the suppression of the 20. July 1944 revolt against Hitler. In view of Heydrich's assassination in 1942 and Himmler's suicide in 1945, the Allies chose Kaltenbrunner to represent the SS on the dock at Nuremberg.

In the light of the evidence and proceedings at the trial, Kaltenbrunner appears almost inhuman.[1] The revelation of shocking crimes committed by the SS could not but fashion an image of its ranking representative as an insensitive murderer, a callous super-criminal whose actions placed him beyond the human pale. His weeping fits before the trial and his cynical denials of responsibility on the stand made him appear more loathsome as a coward who would not accept responsibility for his actions. Even in comparison to his fellow defendants, he seemed particularly unappealing. Author Evelyn Waugh summed it up most succinctly when, observing the defendants from the spectators' gallery, he noted that "only Kaltenbrunner looked an obvious criminal."[2]

Yet, in contrast to most of the other defendants, very little was known about Kaltenbrunner's personality, background, or career. Unlike Göring or Hess, Ribbentrop or Rosenberg, Frank or Streicher, Kaltenbrunner had risen

---

[1] International Military Tribunal, *The Trial of the Major War Criminals*, 42 volumes (Nuremberg, Germany: Secretariat of the International Military Tribunal, 1947-1949).

[2] *The Diaries of Evelyn Waugh*, ed. Michael Davie (Boston-Toronto: Little, Brown & Co., 1976), p. 646.

to prominence only in 1943. He left no memoirs, diaries, or speeches that might have broken through the facade of his personality. Documents produced at Nuremberg linked him to revolting crimes, but their terse, flat wording revealed no sense of the person who signed them. One of the other defendants later remarked that perhaps only a novelist could "conjure up" a profile of Kaltenbrunner, but that even he could never "depict the whole truth."[3]

Despite his unsavory reputation and perhaps because of this dearth of information, Kaltenbrunner has received little attention as a historical or human figure. Trained observers in the Nuremberg prison registered their personal revulsion, but then turned their attention to other SS figures whom they found more interesting, more cooperative, or more easily typed in psychological terms.[4] Fascinated by the personalities of Heydrich and Himmler, former RSHA figures have much less to say about Kaltenbrunner.[5] He has also received insufficient treatment in academic literature. François Bayle virtually ignores the Austrian SS leader in his series of profiles on higher- and middle-level SS officers. Likewise Joachim Fest left Kaltenbrunner off the "face" of the Third Reich.[6] Systematic analyses of the SS mention him in passing or not at all, while more general histories of the organization have written him off as a "second-rater" who landed on the higher levels of the Nazi regime through a series of flukes.[7]

Existing analyses of Kaltenbrunner vary sharply on the question of whether his Nuremberg image is the real and correct one. Former SD officer Wilhelm Höttl, writing under a pseudonym in 1950, argued that the Allies exaggerated Kaltenbrunner's actual influence in the field of Nazi war crimes.

---

[3] Hans Fritzsche, *The Sword in the Scales* (London: Allan Wingate, 1953), p. 187.

[4] G. M. Gilbert, *Nuremberg Diary* (New York: Signet, 1961), pp. 234-244; Gilbert, *The Psychology of Dictatorship* (New York: Ronald Press, 1950), pp. 240-261; Douglas M. Kelley, *22 Cells in Nuremberg: A Psychiatrist Examines the Nazi War Criminals* (New York: Greenberg, 1947), pp. 133-137.

[5] Walter Hagen, *Die geheime Front: Organisation, Personen und Aktionen des deutschen Geheimdienstes* (Linz-Vienna: Nibelungen Verlag, 1950); Walter Schellenberg, *Hitler's Secret Service* (New York: Pyramid, 1971); Heinrich Orb, *Nationalsozialismus: 13 Jahre Machtrausch* (Olten: Verlag Otto Walter, 1945).

[6] François Bayle, *Psychologie et Ethique du National-Socialisme: Etude anthropologique des dirigeants SS* (Paris: Presses Universitaires de France, 1953); Joachim Fest, *The Face of the Third Reich: Portraits of the Nazi Leadership* (New York: Pantheon, 1970).

[7] The former include: Helmut Krausnick et al., *Anatomy of the SS State* (New York: Walker & Co., 1968); Ermenhild Neusüss-Hunkel, *Die SS* (Hannover-Frankfurt: Norddeutsche Verlagsanstalt, 1956); Karl O. Paetel, "Die SS: Ein Beitrag zur Soziologie des Nationalsozialismus," *VfZ*, 2 (January 1954), 1-33. Examples of the latter are: Heinz Höhne, *The Order of the Death's Head: The Story of Hitler's SS* (New York: Ballantine, 1971), especially pp. 624-625; Gerald Reitlinger, *The SS: Alibi of a Nation, 1922-1945* (New York: Viking, 1968), pp. 236-238.

According to Höttl, Kaltenbrunner owed his career to chance. He became chief of the Austrian SS in 1937 because the Austrian police had arrested all his predecessors. In 1938 he "automatically" became HSSPF in Vienna, a position that had "almost exclusively representative significance." Following Höttl's version, Kaltenbrunner's appointment to the RSHA was a "great surprise" to his contemporaries since he had neither the "police experience" nor the "personal connections" to do the job. Therefore, the activities of the Gestapo and the Kripo interested him only superficially; he was concerned primarily with the SD, that is, the intelligence service. Though he knew that Germany would lose the war, his personal attachment to Hitler blinded him to all reason until it was too late.[8]

Two scholarly analyses of Kaltenbrunner do not contradict so much as ignore the Höttl thesis. Both essays formed parts of larger works on several or all of the Nuremberg defendants—one from a historical and one from a clinical perspective.[9] Dependent on sources and materials produced just before and during the Nuremberg Trial, each effort resulted in a predictable confirmation of the Nuremberg picture. Eugene Davidson concluded that Kaltenbrunner was "at bottom . . . a cold and ruthless killer who gladly did without any legal forms if the renunciation meant fewer Jews or Slavs, fewer Goebbelses or Goerings [i.e., personal rivals]." Florence Miale and Michael Selzer commented on Kaltenbrunner's suspiciousness, insensitivity, crude primitiveness, and "manipulative opportunism"; and then described him as an "undeveloped creature" who was "adapted to the bottom [i.e., of the ocean]."[10] While such conclusions accurately reflect the research on which they were based, they reveal little of Kaltenbrunner's motivations and virtually nothing of his background. Why did Kaltenbrunner become a murderer? What political, social, and intellectual factors inhibited the development of his personality or blocked his ability to feel emotions? The Nuremberg materials provide but incomplete answers.

In his unpublished doctoral dissertation Wendell Houston has provided a more sophisticated analysis of Kaltenbrunner.[11] Houston relied heavily on Nuremberg documents and information from Wilhelm Höttl, and applied the results of his research to theories regarding the "authoritarian-totalitarian

[8] Hagen, *Geheime Front*, pp. 82-84.

[9] Eugene Davidson, *The Trial of the Germans: An Account of the Twenty-two Defendants Before the International Military Tribunal at Nuremberg* (New York: Collier, 1972), pp. 315-328; Florence R. Miale and Michael Selzer, *The Nuremberg Mind: The Psychology of the Nazi Leaders* (New York: Quadrangle, 1975), pp. 111-125.

[10] Davidson, *Trial*, p. 327; Miale and Selzer, *Mind*, pp. 124-125.

[11] Wendell Robert Houston, "Ernst Kaltenbrunner: A Study of an Austrian SS and Police Leader," doctoral dissertation, Rice University, 1972.

personality" and the "banality of evil."[12] This synthesis resulted in the portrait of a somewhat incompetent "run-of-the-mill chap" saddled with a "dominant-submissive personality," who, by a combination of circumstances beyond his control, rose to a position in which his need to obey made a mass-murderer out of him. Kaltenbrunner, Houston concludes, was "simply an example of the horrible banality of evil."[13]

However well a list of Kaltenbrunner's crimes as depicted in the Nuremberg documents combines with Höttl's apologia of 1950 to fit a banality thesis, the resulting picture does not fully satisfy. Lacking access to family documents and Austrian police archives, Houston could offer only an outline of Kaltenbrunner's formative years and a vague picture of his role and that of the Austrian SS in the Austrian National Socialist underground movement. He assumed that the political, intellectual, and social factors which shaped Kaltenbrunner's entry into politics dated from 1929-1930 or, at the very earliest, from 1918. Can we, however, explain Kaltenbrunner's attraction to Nazism and his later willingness to commit mass murder in its name merely as a reaction to the difficult economic, social, and psychological conditions of the 1920s and 1930s? Many Austrians of Kaltenbrunner's background faced these same conditions and worse. Not all went over to the Austrian Nazis; still fewer joined the SS. Finally, only a handful rose to high office in the SS and participated in Nazi occupation and racial policies. Would not a thorough investigation of how political, social, and intellectual currents in Habsburg society (into which, after all, Kaltenbrunner was born) interacted with specific influences in Kaltenbrunner's own childhood and young adulthood lead to a deeper understanding of the foundations for his receptivity to Nazi modes of thought and action? Moreover, what, if any, specific influences strengthened those foundations in the turbulent years after 1918? Can conclusions drawn about Kaltenbrunner's background help to explain the striking participation of Austrians and other borderland Germans in the execution of Nazi policies? Finally, can we speak of Kaltenbrunner's personality and motivations in terms that go beyond oversimplified theories of demonic criminality and the banality of evil?

One purpose of this study will be to test the possibility that specific political, intellectual, and social influences operating in conjunction with but independently of the general crisis that faced most Austrians in the interwar years helped form Kaltenbrunner's political personality and laid the groundwork for an "ideological commitment" to the National Socialist movement.

---

[12] See T. W. Adorno et al., *The Authoritarian Personality* (New York: Harper & Brothers, 1950); Hannah Arendt, *The Origins of Totalitarianism*, 2nd ed. (New York: Meridan, 1958); Arendt, *Eichmann in Jerusalem: A Report on the Banality of Evil*, rev. ed. (New York: Viking, 1969); Fest, *Face*.

[13] Houston, "Kaltenbrunner," pp. 33-36, 52-53, 84-85, 152-155, 187-190.

Hannah Arendt defined "ideology" as the "logic of an idea" and postulated that ideologies propose to explain the world—past, present, and future—by a single *idée fixe*. Once defined, the idea itself becomes secondary in importance to the fact that all phenomena in the world—past, present, and future—can be explained in its terms.[14] Race was the Nazi *idée fixe*—the inequality of and struggle between the races. One can reasonably expect the identification and analysis of Kaltenbrunner's social and cultural origins to reveal those elements that prepared him first to embrace the Nazi ideology and then to live by its tenets. In addition, such an endeavor would afford a clearer understanding of the motivation behind his actions as chief of the RSHA and permit some new conclusions about his behavior as a prisoner at Nuremberg.

On the other hand, Kaltenbrunner's spectacular career success invites speculation on how political power was acquired and maintained in Nazi Germany. The existing thesis—that Kaltenbrunner became chief of the Austrian SS through a fluke in 1937, that he became HSSPF in Vienna "automatically" in 1938, and that he was appointed chief of the RSHA in 1943 as a weak replacement for Heydrich[15]—seems dubious in view of both the style of Nazi politics and the structure and purpose of the SS-Police apparatus. The statement that the Nazi regime did not conform in actuality to the rational, monolithic format depicted by the prosecution at Nuremberg and by some early students of the phenomenon[16] has become a cliché. Based on archival materials and memoir literature, dependable scholarship has since revealed that the "absolute, total Führer State was not in the least a well-reasoned apparatus, not in the least a rational system, but rather a maze of privileges and political connections, fields of competence and authorizations, and finally a battle of all against all, which at the time was described by the wonderful phrase 'Nazi war games.' "[17] Joseph Nyomarkay has shown how Hitler's "charismatic legitimacy" formed the "only point of cohesion in the otherwise heterogeneous Nazi movement." Dietrich Orlow and Wolfgang Horn have demonstrated how Hitler's personalized and cosmic definition of leadership encouraged factionalism, but prevented the latter from

---

[14] Arendt, *Totalitarianism*, pp. 468-474.

[15] Houston, "Kaltenbrunner," pp. 52-53, 77-78, 83-84; Höhne, SS, p. 624; Reitlinger, SS, p. 237; Hagen, *Geheime Front*, p. 82.

[16] See, for example, Franz Neumann, *Behemoth: The Stucture and Practice of National Socialism, 1933-1944* (Toronto–New York–London: Oxford University Press, 1944); Eugen Kogon, *Der SS-Staat: Das System der deutschen Konzentrationslager* (Frankfurt am Main: Verlag der Frankfurter Hefte, 1946), especially pp. 26, 33.

[17] Hans Buchheim, *SS und Polizei im NS-Staat* (Duisdorf: Selbstverlag der Studiengesellschaft für Zeitprobleme, 1964), pp. 16-17.

tearing the movement apart before it achieved power.[18] In his study of the Nazi regime at the central and local levels, Edward Peterson has traced the limits of Hitler's power and interest in the day-to-day workings of the Reich bureaucracy and how the implementation or sabotage of measures depended on the political acumen of central and local officials both in gaining support or securing indifference from above and in blocking the ambitions of personal/political rivals.[19] Using this setting, Heinz Höhne and Gerald Reitlinger have punctured the myth that the SS was either monolithic and rational in structure or possessed of unlimited power vis-à-vis the organs of Party, State, and *Wehrmacht*.[20] Indeed, Dietrich Orlow and Robert Koehl have described the Nazi system of warring factions, unhampered by defined legal or institutional constraints and cemented together by personal loyalties, as the "rebirth of a type of feudalism" or "Nazi neo-feudalism."[21]

Given such a political atmosphere, it is reasonable to assume that Kaltenbrunner had to maneuver and struggle to attain and maintain positions of power at each stage of his SS career. In such a heterogeneous and often disorganized system, the success or failure of his efforts depended not only on his ideological commitment, but also on his personal relationships with politically influential superiors: his loyalty to them and his ability to earn their patronage through services rendered despite obstacles presented by rival personalities and factions.

One should not, however, accept the feudalism metaphor too readily; for, with its implication of decentralization and the lack of a basic consensus on domestic and foreign-policy issues, the image of "neo-feudalism" obscures the fact that Hitler's basic ideological aims—unleashing the war, conquering Lebensraum in the east, and exterminating inferior and unwanted life—were not hampered in any significant way by the incessant struggle for personal power. In studying Kaltenbrunner's career, one must heed Robert Koehl's warning against an overemphasis on the "interpretative disintegration of the SS into the many fragments which composed it."[22] Himmler and his top

---

[18] Joseph Nyomarkay, *Charisma and Factionalism in the Nazi Party* (Minneapolis: University of Minnesota Press, 1967); Dietrich Orlow, *The History of the Nazi Party, 1919-1933* (Pittsburgh: University of Pittsburgh Press, 1969); Wolfgang Horn, *Führerideologie und Parteiorganisation in der NSDAP, 1919-1933* (Düsseldorf: Droste Verlag, 1972).

[19] Edward N. Peterson, *The Limits of Hitler's Power* (Princeton, New Jersey: Princeton University Press, 1969). See also Dietrich Orlow, *The History of the Nazi Party, 1933-1945* (Pittsburgh: University of Pittsburgh Press, 1973).

[20] Höhne, *SS*; Reitlinger, *SS*.

[21] Dietrich Orlow, *The Nazis in the Balkans: A Case Study of Totalitarian Politics* (Pittsburgh: University of Pittsburgh Press, 1968), p. 21; Robert Koehl, "Feudal Aspects of National Socialism," *American Political Science Review*, 54 (December 1960), 431.

[22] Robert Koehl, "The Character of the Nazi SS," *Journal of Modern History*, 34 (September 1962), 283.

advisers had a vision of what SS should represent and how it should function; therefore, an understanding of the purpose and functions of the SS-Police system will provide a suitable framework for understanding Kaltenbrunner's career. Responsible scholars have already laid the foundation. Hans Buchheim and Ermenhild Neusüss-Hunkel have sorted out the purposes and functions of the SS and its various offices.[23] Buchheim has also provided historians with an excellent analysis of the role of the HSSPF. George Browder has depicted the development of the Security Police and the SD up to and through their amalgamation into the RSHA in 1939. Robert Koehl has offered an account of the relationship between ideology and improvisation in another SS main office.[24] By reaching an understanding of the HSSPF and the RSHA in the context of the SS apparatus I wish to offer a new explanation of Kaltenbrunner's rise to power in 1943.

The most significant part of Kaltenbrunner's career remains his tenure at the RSHA from 1943 to 1945. How did this provincial SS leader succeed in the struggle for power within and outside the SS? How much control did he exert in the RSHA? How did the latter fare under his leadership against state and party rivals? By studying how Kaltenbrunner gained and wielded personal power, one can arrive at some conclusions about the acquisition and maintenance of personal power in the Third Reich. George Browder has commented that our assessment of Kaltenbrunner's role in the RSHA should hardly be left at the level of the Nuremberg judgment.[25] One aim of this study is to fill this lacuna in the research.

This study has two purposes. On the one hand, I seek to reveal the man behind the "monster" whom observers at Nuremberg found so abhorrent. This I propose to do by studying the social, cultural, and psychological roots and later manifestations of Kaltenbrunner's commitment to National Socialism. On the other hand, drawing upon the concept of "charismatic legitimacy" that was so intrinsic to ideological commitment in Nazi Germany, and the style of personal politics as practiced in the Third Reich, I propose to use an analysis of Kaltenbrunner's career as a means for arriving at a tentative theory of how successful political careers were made in the Third Reich.

There is one final motivation for the study of a man such as Ernst Kal-

[23] Hans Buchheim, "The SS—Instrument of Domination," in Krausnick, *Anatomy*, pp. 129-301; Buchheim "The Position of the SS in the Third Reich," in *Republic to Reich*, ed. Hajo Holborn (New York: Pantheon, 1972), pp. 251-297; Neusüss-Hunkel, *SS*.

[24] Hans Buchheim, "Die Höheren SS- und Polizeiführer," *VfZ*, 11 (October 1963), 362-391; George Clark Browder, "Sipo and SD, 1931-1940: Formation of an Instrument of Power," doctoral dissertation, University of Wisconsin, 1968; Robert Koehl, *RKFDV: German Resettlement and Population Policy, 1939-1945* (Cambridge: Harvard University Press, 1957).

[25] Browder, "Sipo and SD," p. 376.

tenbrunner. Can he safely be categorized either as an "unhealthy" and "abnormal" individual or as the characteristic product of German society, a phenomenon so distant from the "solid American citizen" that he need be of no concern except as a historical or medical curiosity?[26] Or must one go to the other extreme and search for "banal evil-doers" under every bed?[27] I hope that a "humanization" of this callous creature of the Nazi system will, if not provide answers, at least provoke more thought on these questions.

[26] Miale and Selzer, *Mind*, pp. 268, 270, 297-298.
[27] Stanley Milgram, *Obedience to Authority: An Experimental View* (New York: Harper & Row, 1974).

CHAPTER I

The Austrian Roots of Ideological Commitment

THE FOUNDATIONS of Kaltenbrunner's ideological outlook can be traced to the economic, social, intellectual, and psychological crisis confronting middle-class German citizens in the Habsburg Monarchy during the last decades of the nineteenth century. They lie in the response of the German-Austrian nationalist student movement to that crisis, a response whose radical, racist pan-German ideology not only triumphed among German nationalist students at the Habsburg universities, but gradually spread beyond academic walls to influence wide sections of the Monarchy's German citizenry. Central to this pan-German ideology was an intense emotional desire for a racially homogeneous and unified German state, purged of all elements believed to be responsible for impeding the foundation of such a state: liberalism, capitalism, Marxian socialism, Catholicism, Slavic nationalism, and last, though far from least, "international Jewry." To understand the social, cultural, and psychological milieu into which Kaltenbrunner was born and in which he matured, it is essential to examine the sources and manifestations of the ideology propagated by the Austrian student radicals: Austrian pan-Germanism. For Austrian pan-Germanism had among its most ardent followers Kaltenbrunner's father, Hugo, and later, under drastically changed conditions, Ernst Kaltenbrunner himself.

Austrian pan-Germanism evolved from the interaction of German *völkisch* nationalism with specific political, economic, and social currents in the Habsburg Monarchy after the Compromise of 1867.[1] Völkisch nationalism rested on the twin pillars of unity and purity; its ideal was a unified German national state purified of "foreign" influences. Early in the nineteenth century, German Romantic nationalists, reacting with righteous anger to the Napoleonic occupation of Central Europe and with deep despair to the political chaos and disunity in Germany, postulated that, despite unfavorable appearances, Germans were nonetheless united by an invisible, internal bond most accurately described as a national "soul." The idea of this mystical cementing force, expressed in the term V*olk*, had its roots in Herder's theory that nationality was defined by a common ethnic-cultural heritage expressed

[1] In 1867, the Austrian Empire was converted into a Dual Monarchy in which Cisleithanian Austria and the Kingdom of Hungary became equal partners.

11

in a common language.[2] However, German Romantic nationalists ignored Herder's belief that each "nation," regardless of size or political-economic status, had a unique and valuable contribution to make toward the development of human civilization. Germans, they postulated, had a special, historically defined mission to impart the benefits of their vibrant culture to the decadent West and the barbaric East.

However firm their convictions regarding German uniqueness and superiority might have been, the Romantic nationalists were nevertheless tormented by the fear that, unless guaranteed protection and opportunities for "natural development" by the existence of a strong, united Reich-state, German culture would not be able to withstand the corrosive influence of "French" cosmopolitanism and abstract legalism. Their insistence on German superiority was thus joined with visions of apocalyptic disaster for German and world civilization. Within a context of political disunity and military defeat, such visions lent a sense of cosmic urgency to an emerging obsession with ethnic unity and purity expressed in the demand that German language and culture be protected from "cosmopolitan" influences. Thus, three elements—the concept of mystical national unity implied in the term *Volk*, the belief in intrinsic German cultural superiority, and the cataclysmic vision of a choice between salvation through unity and purity on one hand and irreversible human degeneration on the other—laid the groundwork for what was later known as völkisch thought, which in turn became the touchstone of pan-German ideology.

In the Restoration Era (1815-1848), joint repression by the Central European monarchies temporarily linked German nationalism and political liberalism in such a way as to obscure the former's anti-Western aspects. Before the foundation of a German national state under Prussian auspices in 1871, liberals and nationalists in Germany envisioned pan-German union as "a single political state, a Greater Germany embracing all German-speaking states and provinces in Central Europe, with a liberal constitution and a government reflecting equally the traditions of all parts of the country."[3] Such visions were shattered by the failure of the Frankfurt Parliament in 1848; Bismarck's demonstration of 1866-1871—that liberal institutions were less essential to German unification than were conservative power politics— swept away the debris. For nationalists and liberals in Germany, Bismarck's

---

[2] Herder's ideas are presented in his *Ideen zur Philosophie der Geschichte der Menschheit*, 3 vols. (Leipzig: F. A. Brockhaus, 1869). For a definition of the term *Volk*, see George Mosse, *The Crisis of German Ideology: Intellectual Origins of the Third Reich* (New York: Grosset & Dunlap, 1964), p. 4.

[3] Andrew G. Whiteside, *The Socialism of Fools: Georg Ritter von Schönerer and Austrian Pan-Germanism* (Berkeley–Los Angeles: University of California Press, 1975), p. 1.

"little German" (*kleindeutsch*) solution of 1871 marked the culmination of their sixty-year quest for German national unity.[4]

Excluded from the Bismarckian state, the Germans of Habsburg Austria continued to yearn for the creation of a single German Reich. While German-Austrian Liberals set aside for the distant future their vision of a liberal, federal, *grossdeutsch* union (i.e., a union of all the former territories of the Holy Roman Empire with Vienna as its capital) and concentrated for the present on consolidating German rule over an empire that—as of 1867— had ceased to be a German state, a small but vocal minority of German-Austrians accepted Bismarck's creation as a first step toward the establishment of an all-inclusive pan-German union. They advocated the dissolution of the Habsburg Monarchy and the incorporation of its German-speaking provinces into the German Reich. Because they accepted the Bismarckian pattern of unification, they came to be known as Austrian kleindeutsch nationalists.[5] Austrian kleindeutsch nationalism fathered Austrian pan-Germanism: it was revolutionary in aim in that it called for a disruption of the Bismarckian order through the dissolution of the Habsburg Monarchy and extremist in method in that, following what its adherents believed to be Bismarck's example, it glorified violence as the basis of political action.[6]

Kleindeutsch nationalism developed and spread among the German-Austrian middle and lower-middle classes during the last decades of the nineteenth century for three likely reasons: national pride evoked by the foundation of the German Empire; the dissolution of the sixty-year bond between Austrian Liberalism and German nationalism; and Habsburg concessions to the demands of the Empire's Slavic minorities for political autonomy, equal economic opportunity, and linguistic rights. These factors combined to evoke

---

[4] Ibid., pp. 1-2

[5] In Germany during the nineteenth century, the kleindeutsch solution to the problem of German unity was understood to mean the establishment of a German national state within the boundaries fixed by Bismarck in 1871. In Austria between 1867 and 1914, kleindeutsch union meant the incorporation of the German-speaking provinces of the Habsburg Monarchy into a German Empire ruled from Berlin. Conversely, grossdeutsch union was understood by Austrians to represent a German national state whose boundaries followed those of the Holy Roman Empire and in which Vienna would be recognized as the political, economic, and cultural center.

[6] Whiteside, *Socialism*, pp. 2-5, 12-16; Paul Molisch, *Geschichte der deutschnationalen Bewegung in Österreich von ihren Anfängen bis zum Zerfall der Monarchie* (Jena: Verlag von Gustav Fischer, 1926), p. 72. General histories of the Habsburg Monarchy during the last century of its existence are the following: Arthur J. May, *The Habsburg Monarchy: 1867-1914* (New York: Norton, 1968); A.J.P. Taylor, *The Habsburg Monarchy, 1809-1918: A History of the Austrian Empire and Austria-Hungary* (New York: Harper Torch, 1965); C. A. Macartney, *The Habsburg Empire, 1790-1918* (New York: Macmillan, 1969); Robert A. Kann, *A History of the Habsburg Empire, 1526-1918* (Berkeley–Los Angeles–London: University of California Press, 1977).

among nationally conscious German-Austrians the feeling that, under the Habsburg system, the empire was being gradually "de-Germanized."[7]

While the National Liberals in the German Reich enthusiastically supported the new German state, the Austrian Liberal Party, which dominated parliamentary life in Cisleithanian Austria from the establishment of the Dual Monarchy in 1867 until 1879, failed (despite valiant efforts) to lend the Habsburg state a sense of German national mission. The Liberals' claim to protect German national interests was blurred by their aversion to the Prussian-Conservative structure of the German Reich and their identification with Emperor Francis Joseph. Moreover, the new ostentation represented by Liberal politics obscured a slow but steady economic growth throughout the Monarchy and aroused fear and envy among those sections of the middle and lower-middle classes who did not benefit so directly from Liberal fiscal and social policies. The wave of financial speculation which led to the stock market crash of 1873 convinced many that the Liberals were in politics for the purpose of self-enrichment.[8] In such an atmosphere, kleindeutsch nationalism flourished.

Far more crucial to the spread of Austrian kleindeutsch nationalism were the efforts of the Habsburgs to reach political compromises with their non-German subjects. When Emperor Frances Joseph dismissed the Liberal Auersperg cabinet in 1879, a coalition of Czechs, Poles, German clericalists, and conservatives under the leadership of Count Edward Taaffe came to power. Known as the "Iron Ring," the Taaffe government sought to win Slavic support for the Monarchy by offering political autonomy, linguistic parity, and equal economic opportunity. German nationalists detested such concessions, fearing that if promulgated they would undermine German dominance in Austrian politics, economics, and culture. Though Taaffe fell in 1893, a similar coalition under the Polish Count Kasimir Badeni formed a government in 1896. In an effort to placate the Czechs, Badeni issued two language ordinances that required knowledge of *both* German and Czech for entry into state service—regardless of position—in Bohemia and Moravia. Strict enforcement of the decrees would have placed Bohemian and Moravian Germans at a disadvantage in the competition for state employment since, though virtually all educated Czechs spoke and wrote German,

---

[7] The term "de-Germanization" is from H. Gordon Skilling, "Austrian Origins of National Socialism," *University of Toronto Quarterly*, 10 (July 1941), 482.

[8] For a general account of Austria under Liberal rule, see May, *Habsburg Monarchy*, pp. 46-69; Macartney, *Habsburg Empire*, pp. 569-585, 603-611. On the slow and steady growth of the Austrian economy, see Nachum Th. Gross, "Die Stellung der Habsburgermonarchie in der Weltwirtschaft," in *Die Habsburgermonarchie 1848-1918*, Vol. I: *Die wirtschaftliche Entwicklung*, Alois Brusatti, editor (Vienna: Verlag der österreichischen Akademie der Wissenschaften, 1973), pp. 27-28.

few Germans had bothered to learn Czech. Though the decrees were re-
scinded after "the most fearful nationalist struggle known since the inception
of the constitutional regime," German fears of a "Slavization" of Austria
were thoroughly aroused.[9]

Beyond hatred for the Slavs and contempt for the Liberals, Austrian kleindeutsch nationalism was intensely anticlerical. The Catholic hierarchy had
resolutely supported the Habsburg dynasty in its antinationalist stand throughout
the nineteenth century. Conservative clerics rejected Herder's concept of the
nation-state and presented their faith as a universalist doctrine, transcending
political borders and cultural-linguistic differences. Loyal to the Empire and
sensitive to political and doctrinal policy emanating from the Vatican, German-
Austrian clerics found spiritual and political allies among non-German
Catholics in their struggle against liberalism and German nationalism.

Anticlerical feeling was particularly strong in the universities, where German nationalists perceived the Church to be an obstacle not only to political
unification but also to the development of a unified national consciousness.
They felt that Catholic mistrust of Protestant North Germany obstructed the
formation of a political union, and that clerical influence over education
stifled the development of a will toward national unity among Austrian youth.

After the foundation of the German Reich at the expense of two Catholic
powers (France and Austria), animosity between German nationalists and
Austrian Catholics deepened. Bismarck's vicious persecution of German Catholicism during the 1870s hardly served to inspire support among Austrian
Catholic leaders for a closer relationship with the Reich. The latter identified
their interests ever more closely with the Habsburg multinational state and
welcomed Poles, Czechs, Slovenes, and Italians as allies against pan-German
nationalists. Both Taaffe and Badeni were supported by the clerical hierarchy.[10]

However, Austrian kleindeutsch nationalists, or, as they were later called,
Austrian pan-Germans, came to see such obstacles to German unity as a
mere front for the "real" opponent of Germandom: the Jew. Anti-Semitism
in Germany and Austria had its roots in medieval religious prejudice, but
its modern foundation lay in an anti-Western naturalist trend within German Romantic nationalist thought.[11] Some German Romantic nationalists

[9] On the policies and composition of the Iron Ring, see May, *Habsburg Monarchy*, pp. 193-
226; William A. Jenks, *Austria under the Iron Ring* (Charlottesville: University Press of Virginia, 1965). On the Badeni decrees and the uproar that followed, see Whiteside, *Socialism*,
pp. 160-187; Molisch, *Bewegung*, pp. 190-191; May, *Habsburg Monarchy*, pp. 325-328. The
term "Slavization" is from Skilling, "Austrian Origins," p. 483.

[10] Whiteside, *Socialism*, p. 207; May, *Habsburg Monarchy*, pp. 194, 322-325.

[11] Raul Hilberg, *The Destruction of the European Jews* (Chicago: Quadrangle, 1967), pp. 1-
17; P.G.L. Pulzer, *The Rise of Political Anti-Semitism in Germany and Austria* (New York:
John Wiley & Sons, 1964).

had deemed the French revolutionary tradition, with its emphasis on urban political predominance, individual liberty, and the power of reason, inapplicable to German conditions. Casting their eyes nostalgically to an idealized vision of the medieval German Reich in which a hierarchical social structure was stabilized by the close relationship of each of its estates (*Stände*) to the land, these Romantics idolized the peasant who lived from the produce of the land, the village artisan who provided the peasant with self-produced finished goods, and the medieval lord-hero who protected both with his military strength and wise counsel. These types were perceived as genuine manifestations of "German" culture and society.[12]

Many of these Romantics who glorified rural life as natural, pure, and dignified abhorred urban existence as soulless, deceitful, and dehumanizing. Though they had little criticism for the mythical vision of the medieval city, characterized by harmonious interaction of the classes, they condemned the modern city for tearing man from his natural roots in the soil, forcing him to depend on an "artificial" monetary system to fulfill his basic needs. Equally despised as outgrowths of modern urban influence were the uniform legal code and the written constitution. Many Romantic nationalists rejected the idea that social and economic relationships could be regulated by a "lifeless" piece of paper and clung passionately to what they labeled "German law," a vague mixture of tribal and medieval social and economic codes which, having evolved "naturally" from existing social relationships and economic needs, were "alive" or "organic." Collectively designated "Roman law" to underline their "alien" (i.e., French/Latin) origins, uniform legal codes and constitutions guaranteeing civic equality were vilified by some Romantics as tools used deceitfully by urban financiers to disrupt man's relationship to the soil, to replace an ideal pastoral economy with a corrupt system dominated by money. Civic equality broke down formerly distinct social categories, creating a social mobility that dislodged the individual from his time-honored place in the community. Rendered rootless, modern man ceased to appreciate the virtues of hard but fruitful labor, and hungered for worthless money and empty power. Glorification of the noble peasant, hatred of the city, and awareness of the "distinction" between Roman law and German law are all themes that appear in Ernst Kaltenbrunner's memoir-letter to his children.[13]

To eliminate these cosmopolitan, "French" elements that uprooted and obscured the "inner reality" of the German soul, some German Romantic nationalists called for a national revolution against the evils of modern society: capitalism, industrialization, urbanization, constitutional law, individ-

---

[12] Pulzer, *Anti-Semitism*, pp. 33-36; Mosse, *Crisis*, pp. 16-17.

[13] E. Kaltenbrunner, "Memoir," Nuremberg, July–August 1946, pp. 5-6, 7-11, 22, 23, Kaltenbrunner File. For an explanation of the traditional Romantic aversion to urban influence, see Pulzer, *Anti-Semitism*, pp. 33-48, 65-67.

ual liberty, and civic equality. Later, during the last decades of the nineteenth century, German nationalists, drawing on Romantic stereotypes, identified the Jew as the prime beneficiary of these trends.

Whereas Romantic nationalists had viewed the presence of individual Jews in Germany as no danger to the Volk, demanding only that Jews discard their "Jewishness" and become "good Germans,"[14] their preconception of what characterized a genuine member of the Volk and the lingering survival of medieval restrictions on the Jewish population of Central Europe made it unlikely that the Jew could ever fit into their idealized German society. The advent of racial nationalism in the late nineteenth century made assimilation impossible.

Before 1848, most Austrian Jews lived on the estates of the landed aristocracy, where many were engaged in small-scale finance, estate management, and domestic handicraft industry. They were forbidden to own land, were subject to a special tax, and were barred from entry into the civil service and the legal profession. A privileged few, who were permitted access to the Empire's major cities, entered and often excelled in those fields open to them: banking, finance, handicraft industries (textiles and leather), journalism, art, literature, and medicine.

Full emancipation of Austrian Jewry was guaranteed in the Liberal constitution of 1867. After this date, Jewish migrants from Bohemia-Moravia and Hungary helped to swell the population of Vienna. Between 1857 and 1890, the number of Viennese Jews leaped from 6,217 to 99,444, while the population of the city as a whole did not quite double.[15] Already well established in banking and industry, Jews increased their numbers and influence in the liberal professions and began to compete with non-Jews in previously forbidden spheres such as law and the civil service.

Surviving medieval stereotypes and Romantic hostility to urban and "foreign" influences combined to render the Jews a particular anathema to Austrian kleindeutsch nationalists. Forbidden until 1867 to own land, the Jews had not been identified with an idealized rural existence extolled as the essence of the German soul. Prominent in finance, they were associated with big urban and international capital, the rule of money, and the implementation of Roman law. Due to the association of some Jewish intellectuals with the cause of urban labor, Jews were made responsible in general for the growth of internationalist, Marxian socialism. Jewish preponderance in journalism, literature, and the fine arts appeared to symbolize a "Judaization"

---

[14] According to Pulzer (*Anti-Semitism*, pp. 226-227), such attitudes persisted in Germany even after the foundation of the German national state.

[15] In 1857, the Viennese Jews accounted for 1.3% of the city's population; in 1890, before the administrative expansion of the city's boundaries, they accounted for 12% of the population. See ibid., p. 10.

of German-Austrian culture. Finally, the coincidence of Jewish emancipation with the triumph of Liberalism and constitutional government, with the exclusion of German-Austria from the German national state, and with the dislocation of the traditional social structure caused by the economic and social policies and developments of the late nineteenth century gave rise to a feeling that the Jews had perfidiously concocted the "un-German" system of 1867 to advance their own interests. Most restricted under the old Habsburg autocracy, the Jews had gained the most by the legal, social, and economic reforms of Dualism and thus aroused the envy and hatred of those who were dissatisfied with the system.

Völkisch thought rendered the exclusion of Jews from the German Volk irrevocable when its adherents began to define nationality by race. In the mid-nineteenth century, a romantic nostalgia for the medieval social order and newly established concepts of evolutionary science combined to produce a theory that racial purity influenced the rise and fall of civilizations. Writing in the 1850s, Count Joseph Arthur de Gobineau, a French diplomat, expressed the pessimistic view that mankind, having violated the principle of racial segregation, had embarked upon an irreversible descent into mongrel barbarism. Gobineau extolled the Aryan race as the purest of contemporary races, but pointed out that it too had been bastardized by racial integration.[16]

In the late nineteenth century, völkisch thinkers in Germany and Austria revived Gobineau's concepts of racial inequality and Aryan superiority and, by applying them to a pseudoscientific version of Darwinian evolutionary theory, lent them a positivistic dynamism. They rejected Gobineau's pessimism and predicted a future evolution of the Aryan race toward perfection, provided that it was kept pure of "foreign blood." A model example of this kind of thinking was Houston Stewart Chamberlain's concept of cosmic struggle between the Germanic, or Aryan, race and the "Asiatic" Jews. His *Grundlagen des XIX. Jahrhunderts* (1900) depicted an embattled Aryan race, defending Western culture against the Jews. The conflict was absolute; one race, the weaker, would perish. Chamberlain's pseudo-scholarship lent völkisch thought a contemporary, scientific air; it also contributed to the hysterical tone that increasingly colored völkisch literature.[17]

By 1900, Austrian pan-German nationalism and anti-Semitism had become synonymous. Drawing upon Romantic conceptions of the true nature of the Volk, pan-Germans stereotyped the Jew as the very essence of anti-

---

[16] Gobineau's ideas were expressed in his *Essai sur l'inégalité des races humaines* (1853). For his influence, see *Gobineau: Selected Political Writings*, ed. Michael D. Biddiss (London: Jonathan Cape, 1970); Arendt, *Totalitarianism*, pp. 170-175; Mosse, *Crisis*, p. 90; Helmut Krausnick, "The Persecution of the Jews," in Krausnick, *SS State*, p. 4.

[17] Mosse, *Crisis*, pp. 93-98. See also George Mosse, *Toward the Final Solution: A History of European Racism* (New York: Harper & Row, 1980), pp. 105-107.

Germanness, attributed to his influence the liberal and "antinational" policies of the Habsburg regime, and declared him incapable by ancestry of modifying his urge to annihilate German culture. Germans in Austria were particularly sensitive about their national identity in a multinational state that was not only modernizing its economic and social structure, but also appeared, in doing so, to be sacrificing German interests to Slavs, "antinational" Catholics, and international socialists. Consequently, many of them developed a strong susceptibility to the virulent, racial anti-Semitism and the obsession with racial purity propagated by the völkisch nationalists.

The impact of Austrian kleindeutsch nationalism, anti-Semitism, and anticlericalism on growing national and social tensions created by the slow and often painful evolution of Cisleithanian Austria toward an economically modernized yet politically supranational state gave rise to a political mass movement. Based in the German-Austrian middle and lower-middle classes, this was the Pan-German Party (Alldeutsche Partei), which was inspired by the personality of Georg Ritter von Schönerer.[18] Introduced to Austrian kleindeutsch ideas through contacts with university circles and well aware of the grievances of the German middle and lower-middle classes against the Habsburg system, Schönerer fused this national and social discontent into a dynamic political movement that became instrumental in exposing broad sections of the German-Austrian population to Austrian pan-German ideas. As a völkisch historian, writing in the 1920s, remarked, "Schönerer's greatest merit in reference to the German-National movement lay not in the development of new ideas or in the assertion of new political aims, but rather in the absorption and dissemination of existing ideas."[19]

Convinced that the Habsburgs were deliberately undermining the German position in Austria, Schönerer advocated that the German provinces of the Empire be incorporated into the German Reich, whose rulers he uncritically admired. Moreover, he was instrumental in bringing the "racial principle," which had already found wide acceptance inside the universities, onto the street and in gaining mass support for it. Originally indifferent to the idea of race—Schönerer had launched his political career as a Liberal—he came to adopt it as the sole criterion for defining German nationality. In 1883, he wrote, "We shall never agree . . . to recognize a Jew as a German because

[18] Two biographical works on Schönerer, one critical and one uncritical, are: Whiteside, *Socialism*; Eduard Herwig Pichl, *Georg Schönerer und die Entwicklung des Alldeutschtums in der Ostmark*, 6 vols. (Oldenburg-Berlin: Gerhard Stalling, 1938). See also Carl E. Schorske, *Fin-de-Siècle Vienna: Politics and Culture* (New York: Alfred A. Knopf, 1980), pp. 116-133. For Schönerer as a precursor of National Socialism, see F. L. Carsten, *Fascist Movements in Austria: From Schönerer to Hitler* (London–Beverly Hills: Sage, 1977), pp. 9-29; Bruce F. Pauley, *Hitler and the Forgotten Nazis: A History of Austrian National Socialism* (Chapel Hill: University of North Carolina Press, 1981), pp. 18-24.

[19] Molisch, *Bewegung*, p. 151.

he speaks German or even because he behaves as a German nationalist, or to strive for, even to approve, any mixture of Germans with Jews."[20]

Schönerer's pan-Germanism was also bitterly anticlerical. In attacking the Church, Schönerer hoped not only to weaken the Monarchy's strongest pillar, but also to demonstrate to Berlin that German-Austrians would not promote Catholic interests in a united German state. In 1898, he issued a *Los von Rom* manifesto, in which he called upon German-Austrians to convert to Lutheranism and warned that the "clerical spirit of intrigue" was "influencing the whole of public life in Austria more than ever before, with dangerous effects on the free exercise of the German people's national powers in a way which is justly causing anxiety to every German." Urging Germans to break with the "un-German" Roman Church, Schönerer hinted darkly at an alliance of "Slavic insolence" and "Roman lust for power" committed to "annihilate Germandom in this Empire which has been built upon German foundations."[21]

The nationalist uproar occasioned by the Badeni language ordinances in 1897 and the success of the Pan-German Party in the *Reichsrat* elections of 1901 marked the high tide of overt pan-German agitation in Habsburg Austria. Austrian pan-Germanism appealed in its nationalism to academics, professionals, and students, for whom national unity was a matter of cultural survival. Its vague social program was anticapitalistic in tone and thus appealed to artisans and peasants who sought an alternative to the liberal, industrial society of the modern world. Anti-Slavic feeling attracted workers, bureaucrats, and university graduates, who were beginning to face stiff Czech and Slovene competition for jobs.[22] Appealing to all was the very essence of Austrian pan-Germanism: its emotional radicalism, its contemptuous rejection of liberal society, and its creed that violent struggle was more rewarding and more effective than political compromise.

Though the Pan-German Party splintered and declined after the electoral success of 1901 and Schönerer was already a forgotten man a decade later,[23] German-Austrians remained susceptible to pan-German ideas, which exploited their economic, social, and cultural anxieties to propagate an uncompromising doctrine of national unity based on the racist principle. Austrian pan-Germans attributed the prolonged absence of German unity to a conspiracy of enemies whose purposes were served by persistent disunity.

---

[20] Quoted in Skilling, "Austrian Origins," pp. 486-487.

[21] *Los von Rom* Manifesto, 16 November 1898, in Pulzer, *Anti-Semitism*, pp. 343-344.

[22] Whiteside, *Socialism*, pp. 335-336, n. 28; Pulzer, *Anti-Semitism*, p. 151; Ferdinand Burschofsky, *Beiträge zur Geschichte der Deutsch-Nationalen Arbeiterbewegung*, Vol. II (Hohenstadt: Im Selbstverlag, 1907), p. 5; Andrew Whiteside, *Austrian National Socialism Before 1918* (The Hague: Martinus Nijhoff, 1962), p. 38.

[23] This development is analyzed in Whiteside, *Socialism*, pp. 225-242, 263-284, 317-325.

Masterminding this malicious plot was the Jewish "nation," which threatened Germandom from the east (directing the westward push of the Slavic "flood"), from the west (importing liberalism, Roman law, and financial capitalism), and from within (exploiting the civil rights granted to its members by law to gain a commanding position in Austrian economic and cultural life, to destroy the principles of national identity and private property through Marxian Socialism, and to bastardize the German race biologically by sexually defiling it).[24] Chief pawns of the Jewish arch-enemy within the Austrian context were the Habsburg dynasty and the Catholic Church, for they (1) did not recognize the significance of the racial question; (2) were committed to the survival of the multinational state and the permanent division of the German nation; (3) tolerated civic equality, thus enabling Jews to infiltrate German society further; and (4) encouraged Slavic "insolence" by granting linguistic and national concessions to the minorities of the Empire. Pan-Germans warned that unless these influences were eliminated from German society, German culture and, ultimately, the German race itself would be destroyed.

Austrian pan-Germanism left another legacy: the concept that political conflict reflected biological-racial struggle. Violence was a natural form of political agitation that would result either in total victory or in total annihilation. Enemies of the German Volk had to be mercilessly destroyed at all levels—political, economic, cultural, and racial—for compromise was equated with defeat and hence the destruction of the German nation.

The relevance of Austrian pan-Germanism for the foundations of Kaltenbrunner's ideological commitment to National Socialism lies in its uncritical acceptance by the German nationalist student movement in Austria, which profoundly influenced the formative political and intellectual development of Kaltenbrunner's father Hugo and Kaltenbrunner himself. Nowhere in Habsburg Austria was commitment to pan-German ideas more consistent and more uncompromising than among members of the nationalist student fraternities, or *Burschenschaften*.[25] The Burschenschaft idea had always been

---

[24] On the role of sex-envy in Austrian anti-Semitism, see Pulzer, *Anti-Semitism*, pp. 60-61. For a good example of it, see Adolf Hitler, *Mein Kampf*, trans. Ralph Mannheim (Boston: Houghton Mifflin, 1943), p. 325.

[25] Histories of the Austrian student fraternities, individually and as a group, tend to reflect the bias of their authors, themselves mostly ex-fraternity students. Some of the individual histories are: Karl Becke, *Die Wiener Burschenschaft Albia: 1870 bis 1930* (Vienna: F. Hammann, 1930); Ferdinand Bilger, *Die Wiener Burschenschaft Silesia von 1860 bis 1870 und ihre Bedeutung für die Anfänge der deutschnationalen Bewegung in Österreich* (Heidelberg: Karl Winters, 1911); Kurt Knoll, *Geschichte der Wiener Burschenschaft Oppavia*, 2 vols. (Vienna: Reinholt, 1934); Wilhelm Klauser, *Geschichte der Grazer akademischen Burschenschaft Stiria* (Graz: Styria, 1912); *Festschrift zum 60. jährigen Stiftungsfest der Grazer akademischen Burschenschaft "Arminia": 1868-1928* (Graz: Verlag der Grazer akademischen Burschenschaft "Arminia," n.d.);

closely associated with the concept of national unity. Founded on 12 June 1815 at the university in Jena, the first German Burschenschaft welcomed to its ranks all German students who shared the common goal of a unified German state, regardless of status, citizenship, or regional affiliation. Its members swore to cultivate cultural purity in speech, literature, and dress and to sacrifice their lives in the battle for the sacred goal of union. No less vigilant on the "internal" front, they aimed to eliminate all "foreign" influences from university life. The mood of the Wartburg festival (1817), at which antinationalist and foreign books were hurled onto a huge bonfire, reflected the students' obsessive concern with cultural purity.[26]

The revolutionary nationalism of the Burschenschaft spread from Jena via Prague to Vienna and Graz in the months following the Wartburg festival. In 1819, however, the nationalist student societies in Austria were suppressed by Prince Metternich. This reactionary pressure effected a temporary moderation of the xenophobic, antiliberal trend in German-Austrian student politics; when nationalist student societies reappeared briefly during the revolutions of 1848, their leaders hailed the French revolution of that year as the harbinger of a new national democratic era.[27] Yet, for those students who valued national unity more than individual liberty, the failure of the 1848 politicians to achieve the national goal rendered their liberal methods suspect. Conversely, Bismarck's solution by "blood and iron" recalled the glory of the War of Liberation in 1813; the adoption of constitutional government by the defeated Habsburgs in 1867 seemed pale and unexciting in comparison. Though a majority of German-Austrian students remained loyal to Vienna, a small but active minority rejected the multinational state as inimical to German national interests and blamed Habsburgs, Catholics, and Jews for its establishment. Refusing to accept the "un-völkisch" settlement of 1866-1871 as final, they looked to the Hohenzollerns to complete the job that Bismarck had begun. These students and certain of their pro-

Klaus-Eckart Ehrlicher and Reinhart Leitinger, *1868-1968, Ein Hort deutschen Fühlens: Die Grazer akademische Burschenschaft Arminia im Wandel der Zeiten* (Radkersburg: Grenzland-druckerei Ernst Huallenz, 1970). A summary of Burschenschaft ideals and practices is given in Whiteside, *Socialism*, pp. 43-63. Other general, but biased, works are: Paul Molisch, *Politische Geschichte der deutschen Hochschulen in Österreich von 1848 bis 1918*, 2nd ed. (Vienna-Leipzig: Wilhelm Braumüller, 1939); Kurt Knoll, *Die Geschichte der wehrhaften Vereine deutscher Studenten in der Ostmark* (Vienna: Reinholt, 1924); Oskar Scheuer, *Die geschichtliche Entwicklung des deutschen Studententums in Österreich* (Vienna: Schemann, 1910).

[26] For a discussion of the völkisch elements in the ideology of the early Burschenschaft, see Hans Kohn, *The Mind of Germany: The Education of a Nation* (New York: Harper Torch, 1965), pp. 81-98; Mosse, *Crisis*, p. 5; Whiteside, *Socialism*, pp. 43-44; Walter Laqueur, *Young Germany: A History of the German Youth Movement* (London: Routledge & Kegan Paul, 1962), p. 8.

[27] Mosse, *Crisis*, pp. 191-192.

fessors were the original Austrian kleindeutsch nationalists whose ideas influenced Schönerer and, through him, broad sections of the nonacademic German-Austrian community.[28] The growing pan-German vogue then facilitated the triumph of Austrian kleindeutsch ideas in the German-Austrian nationalist fraternities. This process was gradual, spanning the years between the reemergence of the Burschenschaften in the 1860s and culminating in the exclusion of Jewish students from German nationalist fraternity life in the late 1880s. By 1893, the year in which Hugo Kaltenbrunner was chosen for membership in the Graz Burschenschaft "Arminia," the process was complete.

At the time of its foundation in November 1865, the Vienna Burschenschaft Arminia, like most fraternities and nationalist clubs founded before the Austro-Prussian war of 1866, was grossdeutsch (i.e., favored a Vienna-based German state with borders corresponding to those of the Holy Roman Empire) in politics and "progressive" on the question of the traditional student dueling ritual.[29] Although Austrian kleindeutsch ideas were gaining popularity when members of the Viennese organization aided students in Graz to form a sister chapter of Arminia on October 29, 1868, the Graz Arminia was initially committed to a liberal German national state. Its purpose, as stated in its statutes, was "to prepare its members through academic . . . political and moral [sittlich] education for vigorous activity in favor of the liberal [freiheitlich] union of Germany, to promote student interests in every field, and to guide its members toward intimate friendships."[30] Graz "Armines" cherished the motto, "Freedom, Honor, Fatherland" (Freiheit,

[28] Molisch, Bewegung, pp. 91-92; Whiteside, Socialism, pp. 48, 51-53, 62-63, 308-313.

[29] Dueling had been a traditional pastime of German students since the early modern era. The German Burschenschaft of 1815 forbade the duel as a barbaric relic of the Middle Ages. Those student societies which retained the ritual after that date were "conservative," whereas nondueling organizations came to be known as "progressive." Waffentragende Burschenschaften were those permitted by the university authorities to wear and display their dueling sabers. While only a small minority of students belonged to the nationalist Burschenschaften and clubs, almost all Austrian students, German and non-German, belonged to some kind of student society. Among the dueling organizations were, in addition to the Burschenschaften—which tended to be middle class, radical, and nationalist in politics—the traditional groups, called Korps, which were socially aristocratic, politically conservative, and pro-Habsburg. Nondueling clubs at the universities ranged from extreme nationalist to pro-Habsburg. For social and political distinctions between the various student groups, see Whiteside, Socialism, pp. 45-47. For analogous groupings in Germany, see Konrad H. Jarausch, Students, Society and Politics in Imperial Germany: The Rise of Academic Illiberalism (Princeton: Princeton University Press, 1982), pp. 244-261.

[30] Ehrlicher and Leitinger, Hort, p. 19. See ibid., pp. 16-18, on the Austrian grossdeutsch politics of the Viennese Arminia, of which the later Radical Liberal and founder of the Austrian Social Democratic Workers' Party, Viktor Adler, had been a member. See also William J. McGrath, "Student Radicalism in Vienna," Journal of Contemporary History, Vol. vi: Education and Social Structure in the 20th Century (New York: Harper Torch, 1967), p. 187.

Ehre, Vaterland); the black-red and gold that they bore on their sashes symbolized the liberal flavor of the pre-1848 Burschenschaft.[31]

Bismarck's success in creating a united German state and the growing antiliberal vogue in Habsburg Austria combined to increase the influence of Austrian kleindeutsch nationalism in the fraternities, a development that in turn induced the Habsburg police to crack down on ultranationalist and Prussophile activities at the universities. In response to this pressure, the nationalist fraternities moved onto a more "conservative" track. Observing the risks of overt political activity but also citing the need to "defend" the honor of both the fraternity and its individual members, younger "foxes"[32] called for the reinstitution of the traditional dueling ritual, upon which the Habsburg rulers and especially the Catholic Church frowned (since the *Korps* had never ceased to duel during the Liberal era, their practices represented more an attachment to tradition than a political statement against the Habsburg system). Though antidueling sentiment remained dominant for a time, in 1883, Arminia, under pressure from its own foxes and from other nationalist Burschenschaften which had already become "conservative," adopted the dueling ritual as the prime medium to "develop strength of character and personal courage."[33]

[31] Ehrlicher and Leitinger, *Hort*, pp. 16-18, 26-27.

[32] The *Fuchs* of the Burschenschaft corresponds to the pledge in American fraternity life.

[33] Ehrlicher and Leitinger, *Hort*, pp. 47-49, 102. A challenge to duel was usually a response to a real or imagined insult to one's personal honor or to the honor of a fraternity. In the former case, only the maligned and his opponent would duel; in the latter, three or four members of the maligned fraternity would duel an equal number of opponents in single combat. The contest, known as a *Hatz* (literally, a hunt involving the use of dogs trained to follow the prey by sight rather than by scent, i.e., coursing), was normally fought with dull blades, though especially serious insults called for sharp sabers or even pistols. In Austria, participants were allowed to wear eye guards; Reich German dueling ritual permitted the use of nose guards as well. During the contest, the body was held motionless; only the saber arm up to the shoulder joint could be moved. Victory was achieved by drawing blood (*einen Abfuhr teilen*), after which collective or individual honor was restored regardless of defeat if the loser did not flinch or cry out as the blade parted his skin. Fraternity students wore their facial scars as proud symbols of their manhood, for most fraternity duels were less a response to a serious insult than an opportunity to demonstrate one's personal courage. Questions of who could duel whom, and what constituted an insult worthy of challenge, were known as *Commentfragen* and were decided by leaders in each fraternity. The right to accept or give out a challenge, *Satisfaktionsfähigkeit* ("the ability to give satisfaction"), was limited to those deemed "worthy" of it. Austrian Burschenschaft dueling procedures were explained to the author by the late Dr. Werner Kaltenbrunner, who, like his brother Ernst, was a member of the Arminia in Graz in the 1920s (interview with Dr. Werner Kaltenbrunner, Vöcklabruck, 25 March 1977), and Dr. Hansjörg Kaltenbrunner, Ernst Kaltenbrunner's son, who for a short time in the 1950s was a member of the Vienna Albia (conversation with Dr. Hansjörg Kaltenbrunner, Gramastetten, 25 March 1977). For dueling terms, see Ehrlicher and Leitinger, *Hort*, passim.; *Festschrift Arminia*, passim.; Whiteside, *Socialism*, p. 46; Jarausch, *Students*, p. 261.

Simultaneously, the fraternities moved to exclude Jews from their ranks. Preoccupied with a need to "cleanse" the universities of "foreign influence," Austrian kleindeutsch radicals demanded that Jews be banned from the fraternities as a symbol of dedication to the German national cause. During this period, the nationalist student groups repeatedly provoked anti-Semitic riots, which, as the Zionist students began to retaliate, were "unparalleled in intensity."[34] In 1878, the Vienna Libertas became the first Austrian fraternity to adopt the racial principle, decreeing that, for membership purposes, "Jews cannot be considered as Germans, and not even when they are baptized." Reluctant to relinquish German-speaking allies, even Jewish ones, in feuds with Italian and Slovene students, Graz fraternities hesitated to adopt statutes barring Jews from membership. In 1886, however, the Graz Arminia fell in with the new trend and excluded Jews from its ranks. Social contact with Jews was henceforth strictly forbidden to all members. By 1890, virtually all German nationalist student organizations in Austria had followed suit.[35]

Further insult was added by the cruel and petty way in which Jews were excluded from fraternity life altogether. During the 1880s, they were gradually denied the right to seek satisfaction in duels on the grounds that they had no honor worthy of defending. A typically vicious example of fraternity thinking on this matter was a resolution of the *Waidhofener Verband*, an umbrella organization for dueling fraternities in Germany and Austria, passed in 1896:[36]

> In full appreciation of the fact that there exists between Aryans and Jews such a deep moral and psychic difference, and that our qualities have suffered so much through Jewish mischief, in full consideration of the many proofs which the Jewish student has also given of his lack of honor and character and since he is completely void of honor according to our German concepts, today's conference . . . resolves: "No satisfaction is to be given to a Jew with any weapon, as he is unworthy of it."

Exclusion from even this negative participation in the German national movement dealt a cruel blow to the ideals of individual German nationalists of Jewish ancestry.[37]

[34] Jarausch, *Students*, p. 415.

[35] On Vienna Libertas, see Pulzer, *Anti-Semitism*, p. 253. On Arminia's exclusion of Jews, see Ehrlicher and Leitinger, *Hort*, pp. 57-59. On exclusion of Jews from all nationalist fraternities by 1890, see Molisch, *Hochschulen*, p. 121; Pulzer, *Anti-Semitism*, p. 253.

[36] Pulzer, *Anti-Semitism*, p. 253.

[37] Many Austrian Jews who later rose to world renown had been ardent German nationalists during their student years. Among them were Viktor Adler, Sigmund Freud, Heinrich Friedjung, Gustav Mahler, and Arthur Schnitzler. Theodor Herzl, the father of modern Zionism, had been a member of the Vienna Albia. See McGrath, "Student Radicalism," p. 195.

Like other nationalist fraternities, the Graz Arminia also cultivated a strong anti-Habsburg and anticlerical bias. Habsburg Austria was depicted as a decadent welfare state, run for the benefit of "foreigners" but paid for by Germans. Conversely, Armines lauded Wilhelmine Germany as the epitome of "social, economic and scientific progress . . . and victorious power." On account of its close identification with the Habsburg state, the Catholic Church also came under attack; initial enthusiasm for the Los von Rom movement reflected the animosity between nationalist and Catholic students. The latter, however, were better able than the Jews to assert their ideals owing to their greater numbers and the political support they received from the Habsburg state. Just as the Church used the Christian Social movement to challenge pan-Germanism on the streets and in the voting booths, it sponsored a Catholic, pro-Habsburg Burschenschaft, the Graz chapter of which was called the *Carolina Verband* (CV), to check pan-German influence in the universities.[38]

During the period when student nationalism and anti-Semitism were reaching their high tide and Schönerer's pan-Germanism was enjoying its greatest influence, Hugo Kaltenbrunner, then a law student, was an active member of the Graz Burschenschaft Arminia and served as one of its officers.[39] With his fraternity brothers, he participated in the celebration of Bismarck's eightieth birthday in the spring of 1895 and was involved in fraternity demonstrations against the state-sponsored commemoration of the millennial anniversary of the Hungarian Crown in 1896.[40] When he received his law degree in 1898, the Badeni ordinances were on the way to the dustbin, and Schönerer was preparing his Pan-German Party for its greatest electoral success.

Hugo Kaltenbrunner did not remain uninfluenced by pan-German sentiment. He took fraternity life quite seriously and gained a reputation as a stickler for dueling protocol. Later, as a lawyer and father, he never tired of reminiscing about the "good old student days."[41] Though available evidence would refute the suggestion that he indoctrinated his children, his fraternity ideals, reflecting pan-German attitudes of the late nineteenth century, per-

[38] Ehrlicher and Leitinger, *Hort*, pp. 70, 97-98.

[39] Each Burschenschaft elected four to six officers (*Charge*) each semester. These were: president (*Senior*), treasurer (*Sackelwart*), secretary (*Schriftwart*), dueling master (*Fechtwart*), master of ceremonies and judge (*Sang-kneip und Strafwart*), and master of initiation ceremonies (*Fuchsmajor*). Though elected democratically, officers exercised virtually complete control over the social and political activities of each fraternity brother. Hugo Kaltenbrunner served as dueling master in the winter semesters 1895/1896 and 1896/1897. During the summer semester of 1896, he was Arminia's president. See *Festschrift Arminia*, pp. 55-57.

[40] On Arminia's involvement in such demonstrations, see Ehrlicher and Leitinger, *Hort*, pp. 92, 94-96.

[41] W. Kaltenbrunner interview, Vöcklabruck, 25 March 1977.

meated the atmosphere of his household, where they might be adopted by his son, the young, impressionable Ernst Kaltenbrunner. Before discussing the effect of this paternal influence on Ernst Kaltenbrunner, it seems appropriate to delve into his ancestral origins and early childhood.

On 4 October 1903, less than three years after Schönerer had declared war on "international Jewry, international Catholicism, and the international house of Habsburg" in his Basic Program of 1901,[42] Ernst Kaltenbrunner was born in Ried, the industrial capital of the Upper Austrian Innviertel. His ancestors had been master craftsmen in the small Upper Austrian village of Micheldorf. There his great-great-great-grandfather, Wolfgang Adam Kaltenbrunner (1738-1806), had owned a scythe smithy. Listed by occupation as a *buergerlicher Sensenwerksbesitzer* (owner of the town scythe smithy), Wolfgang Adam acquired middle-class wealth along with middle-class status. Kaltenbrunner himself underlined this point, writing that, as a result of an export trade in agricultural tools, the smithy "not only brought about a certain prosperity, but also conveyed middle-class status [*bürgerliches Ansehen*]."[43]

Wolfgang Adam's grandson, Carl Adam Kaltenbrunner, was the first in the family to break into the professional middle class, earning not only fame as a local poet but also respect and status as assistant director of the Imperial State Printing Office in Vienna. Carl Adam's literary exercises reflected both his enthusiastic German nationalism and his strong regional patriotism, which his great-grandson Ernst was to share. His letters to his son, Karl, reveal a strong sense of German national identity, fervent hopes for a "union of the German peoples," and despair at the general political apathy in respect to this goal.[44]

Karl Kaltenbrunner was the first lawyer in the family. Involved in the foundation and management of savings banks in Grieskirchen and Eferding in Upper Austria, he was elected mayor of Eferding in 1889 and served until his retirement twenty years later.[45] With Karl's generation, the Kaltenbrun-

[42] Whiteside, *Socialism*, pp. 215-216.

[43] E. Kaltenbrunner, "Lebenslauf," Nuremberg, 1945, p. 1, F-190, IfZ Munich. On Kaltenbrunner's ancestry, see Carl F. Mistlbacher, "Ahnentafel," Linz, 10 December 1936–13 March 1938, Kaltenbrunner File. In the *Nachlass* of Kaltenbrunner's youngest brother, Roland, is a brief history of the scythe smithy, entitled, "Der obere Absang oder Saganger, später Unterhaindl oder untere Kaltenbrunner Werkstatt genannt, zum Marktgericht Kirchdorf gehörig," 1863.

[44] On Carl Adam Kaltenbrunner's life, see "Der Lebenslauf Carl Adam Kaltenbrunners," Kaltenbrunner File. For examples of his poetry, see Carl Adam Kaltenbrunner, *Aus da Hoamat: Ausgewählte Dichtungen* (Linz: J. Wimmer, 1905). On his nationalism, see also letters of Carl Adam Kaltenbrunner to Karl Kaltenbrunner, 3 and 31 March, 4 and 18 November 1859, 6 March 1860, *Nachlass* Roland Kaltenbrunner.

[45] W. Kaltenbrunner interview, Vöcklabruck, 25 March 1977.

ner family had completed the transition from the traditional artisan class to the respected professional middle class of the nineteenth century. Ernst Kaltenbrunner was the offspring of a deeply rooted provincial family that had achieved a degree of local fame and respect in government, in the legal profession, and even in literature. Moreover, the family's provincial background facilitated the transmission of political and social attitudes through the generations. Upper Austrians generally maintained close cultural ties with Bavaria and, though Christian Social strength was overpowering in the countryside, the urban and semi-urban professional middle class was *national* and anticlerical in outlook.[46]

Hugo Kaltenbrunner was born on 22 August 1875 in Grieskirchen and was baptized a Catholic. At the academic Gymnasia in Salzburg and Linz he was an average student, excelling only in history and gymnastics. After receiving his law degree in the summer of 1898, he served his mandatory year of apprenticeship at the district court in Linz and, after a brief period of employment in the prestigious Jaeger law firm, moved to Ried to join the firm of Dr. Anton Graf. By 1906, he had completed his seven-year stint as a candidate lawyer (Rechtsanwaltsanwärter) and had opened up his own law firm in the small market town of Raab.[47]

Kaltenbrunner's mother, Theresia Elisabeth Utwardy, was born on 7 November 1875. Though of more modest origins than her husband, she had seen more of the world than he. Her grandfather, Josef Utwardy (1805-1876), was a Hungarian of Swabian descent who had brought his leather shop from Nagykanizsa to Eferding in the mid-nineteenth century. Unlike her future husband, Theresia Utwardy had spent much of her life beyond the borders of the Habsburg Monarchy. Her mother died giving birth to her; and she was taken in by a maternal aunt, who lived in Bucharest with her husband. Although she and her aunt spent summers in Eferding, Theresia Utwardy lived the balance of the year in the Romanian capital, where she received a French education.[48]

During her summers in Eferding, Theresia fell in love with the mayor's son, Hugo Kaltenbrunner, whom she had known as a child. Their marriage

---

[46] On the strength of German nationalist political parties in Upper Austria after 1918, see Harry Slapnicka, *Oberösterreich—Zwischen Bürgerkrieg und Anschluss, 1927-1938* (Linz: Oberösterreichischer Landesverlag, 1975), pp. 40, 43-49.

[47] Birth certificate and certificate of baptism for Hugo Kaltenbrunner, Kaltenbrunner Family Records: *Gymnasial-Zeugnisse* for Hugo Kaltenbrunner, Salzburg and Linz, 1885-1893, ibid.; certificate of court service, Presidium of the District Court of Steyr, 1 June 1900, ibid.; certificate of successful completion of state legal examinations, *k.k. Oberlandesgerichtspräsidium*, 24 January 1906, ibid.; Oberösterreichischer Amtskalender, *Der Oberösterreicher: Auskunfts- und Gesellschaftshandbuch, 1907* (Linz: Verlag von Vinzenz Fink, 1906), p. 132; E. Kaltenbrunner, "Memoir," p. 4.

[48] Mistlbacher, "Ahnentafel"; E. Kaltenbrunner, "Memoir," pp. 20-21.

took place on 23 August 1902, and the bride followed her groom to Ried and Raab. Her first years in the provincial atmosphere of the Innviertel were difficult; small-town monotony did not compare favorably with the excitement and culture of the big city. She had hoped to teach her three sons (Ernst, Werner, and Roland) French, but her husband overruled her, insisting that the boys first learn to speak "proper German." After the family moved to Linz in 1918, Theresia Kaltenbrunner was happier; there her command of the French language and her mastery of aristocratic manners earned her the reputation of a *feine Dame*.[49]

Her strongest principle appears to have been devotion to her husband and sons. Ernst was her favorite; she gave him a great deal of attention and often covered for him when he ran afoul of his father. Ernst reciprocated this feeling; much later, he depicted his mother as "dear," but also "selfless," her face evoking images of "warm summers" and "rural landscapes."[50]

In contrast to the close relationship that he enjoyed with his mother, Kaltenbrunner had a distant, less emotional relationship with his father, whom he remembered as "blond" and "handsome" but "overworked," as a man "who was good to us," but who "had many a reason to tan our hides" with the aid of a cane. In general, however, relations between father and son were not bad. Hugo Kaltenbrunner enjoyed lecturing his children on the topics that had interested him most in school—history and geography—and often took them on extended mountain hikes.[51]

Thus, nothing in Kaltenbrunner's ancestral or family background hints at the presence of an abnormal personality prone to criminality, or a social misfit incapable of finding any meaningful connection with the world in which he lived. The Kaltenbrunners viewed themselves—and were viewed by others—as *einwandfrei bürgerlich*, "straightforward members of the solid middle class."[52] In the Habsburg context, Hugo Kaltenbrunner's *deutschnational* outlook was typical of the respectable, German, professional middle-class milieu. Although there is every indication that Kaltenbrunner senior had abandoned the radicalism of his student years, the preoccupations of his youth manifested themselves (as elsewhere in his social and professional class)

[49] Verbal information from Herr Richard Bart, Stadtarchiv, Linz, 31 January 1977. On unhappy early years in Ried and Raab and children speaking proper German, see E. Kaltenbrunner, "Memoir," p. 5; interview with Frau Elisabeth Kaltenbrunner (Kaltenbrunner's widow), Linz, 25 March 1977; W. Kaltenbrunner interview, Vöcklabruck, 25 March 1977.

[50] E. Kaltenbrunner, "Memoir," p. 12. On favorite, see W. Kaltenbrunner interview, Vöcklabruck, 25 March 1977.

[51] E. Kaltenbrunner, "Memoir," pp. 12, 19.

[52] Letter of Dr. Ernst Koref to the author, 9 December 1976. Later a leader in the Austrian Social Democratic Workers' Party, Koref was one of Kaltenbrunner's Gymnasium teachers in Linz.

in moderate form in his beliefs and behavior. These sentiments saturated a new generation that would reach maturity in a radically different setting.

It is possible that Hugo Kaltenbrunner, through his social and occupational integration into Habsburg society, gradually made his peace with Emperor Francis Joseph, but the death of the emperor and the lost war sharpened his yearning for pan-German union. Yet, despite his disappointment with the peace treaties following World War I, his opposition to the Austrian Republic remained moderate. His politics were confined to predictable votes for the postwar, bourgeois Pan-German People's Party (*Grossdeutsche Volkspartei*); and he never approved of Nazi manners and methods. Whatever his thoughts on the value of political violence as a fraternity student, he clearly had little stomach for it as an adult. Yet, like many in the Austrian professional middle classes, he became willing to swallow his distaste for Nazi hooliganism if through its temporary use the desired result—Anschluss—could be attained.[53]

Anti-Semitism was also present in the Kaltenbrunner family. Though pronounced anti-Jewish sentiment was not readily apparent to outsiders, Kaltenbrunner's younger brother recalled that while Kaltenbrunner senior had business relations with individual Jews, he "rejected" all social intercourse with them. Displaying little animosity toward Jews as individuals, he viewed "Jewry" as an "alien body" in the German national organism. Whereas unavoidable business relationships with Jews moderated the harsh stereotypes of the fraternity years for Hugo Kaltenbrunner, his son Ernst inherited the abstractions without the softening influence of personal contact, of which, according to his brother Werner, he had little.[54] Thus, even before 1914, an anti-Semitic "mood" pervaded the Kaltenbrunner family environment.

Of more direct influence was Hugo Kaltenbrunner's antipathy toward the Catholic Church. Upon learning that his son Ernst was taking an active role in the daily mass held at the elementary school in Raab, Kaltenbrunner senior protested furiously. At first Ernst did not understand his father's passion and continued clandestinely to perform his duties as an altar boy. Nevertheless, if his later claims can be believed, young Ernst soon found that the priests "could not communicate any more to me than that which I could decipher for myself; and the picture of the world which I constructed for myself over the years does not stem from them."[55] Since Kaltenbrunner left Raab at the age of nine, it is reasonable to assume that if he indeed had been estranged from Catholicism at this time, the anticlericalism of his father

[53] Verbal information from Dr. Ernst Koref, Linz, 1 February 1977; W. Kaltenbrunner interview, Vöcklabruck, 25 March 1977.

[54] W. Kaltenbrunner interview, Vöcklabruck, 25 March 1977. On Hugo Kaltenbrunner's Jewish clients, verbal information from Herr Richard Bart, Linz, 31 January 1977.

[55] E. Kaltenbrunner, "Memoir," pp. 14, 17-18.

(and perhaps of völkisch-minded elementary-school teachers as well) had some influence on this development.

Kaltenbrunner spent seven years in Raab before departing for Linz to attend the *Realgymnasium*. Looking back on them from his prison cell in Nuremberg, he counted those years among the happiest of his life. Raab was the epitome of a secure, carefully ordered life in which he, the "doctor's son," held a well-defined and respected position. In his memory, the town represented an ideal society, tied to the land and to nature. This relationship created a social and emotional harmony unmarred by the specter of class struggle and the atomizing effect of modern liberal society. Kaltenbrunner later claimed that in Raab he experienced the intimate family and communal ties that "a person needs, should he wish to lead his life within the community and not as an eternal outsider." Here, he "came to feel a love for nature and an interest in the passion and joys of a simple life."[56] With admiration he remembered the stoical endurance of the rural poor, who possessed little more than a strong sense of family solidarity:[57]

> I noticed how many a tired father first conferred with his wife on whether he might go for a jug of beer for supper that evening. I witnessed blows of fate: when a cow became ill or a suckling pig perished, or the hay could not be brought in from the single meadow, because it would not stop raining. . . . I saw too how the old father carefully prepared the planks for his coffin, and while sharpening his scythe asked his neighbor whether he also had dry planks. Death held no horror for them; and they made no fuss about births. Mothers were not long absent from the housework and were inexhaustible in their love for their many children. However much they seemed to have to divide it, each little child had all of their love.

Kaltenbrunner described this intense familial love, happiness, and fortitude as a "great miracle," which he was fortunate to experience in his own family.[58]

Writing in his prison cell in Nuremberg, Kaltenbrunner transferred this image of a poor, rural, and happy family to the social structure of Raab. He remembered how those who owned houses in town remained "closely bound" to their rural roots, "for each had preserved his little plot of land and forest and when harvest time arrived, hay and husks of grain lay in the streets." Each Raaber could thus participate meaningfully in the harvest festival centered around the village brewery. Peasants and townspeople traded their goods in classless harmony: "Cattle and lumber found their buyers and the crafts-

---

[56] Ibid., p. 11; E. Kaltenbrunner, "Lebenslauf," p. 3, F-190, IfZ Munich.
[57] E. Kaltenbrunner, "Memoir," p. 10.
[58] Ibid.

men and shopowners of the village [found] in the peasants their best customers."[59]

Kaltenbrunner's memory at Nuremberg was filled with such idealized childhood experiences: the local theater in Raab with its enthralling peasant and hunting dramas; the magical forest Hannerlholz, where the Kaltenbrunner boys caught snakes, bugs, and frogs and picked strawberries and mushrooms—here Kaltenbrunner had a "setting for all fairy tales."[60] Though they contrast radically with Hitler's depiction of his adolescence in Linz and young adulthood in Vienna, Kaltenbrunner's childhood memories echo Hitler's romantic nostalgia for rural society and peasant values.[61] The belief of both that the peasantry embodied the best of human virtues reflected the primitivistic thinking which Romantic and, later, völkisch nationalists had been preaching for almost a century. As a prisoner in Nuremberg, Kaltenbrunner exhorted his son to return to the land and to imitate the "genuine peasant" in customs and speech, for he (the peasant) "has remained closest in mode, workmanship, thought, and speech to the homeland and is thereby the happiest [of men]."[62]

In 1946, while awaiting sentence in prison, Kaltenbrunner sought for the benefit of his children to convey the traumatic nature of his departure from this rustic paradise in 1913. He missed Raab terribly and later wrote of his father's decision to move the family to Linz in 1918:[63]

> My mother and brothers were delighted to come to the city. I was the only one who mourned for Raab. I often returned during vacations and at harvest time helped several peasants whom I knew. . . . Later, as well, I drove through Raab on the way to Linz from Berlin and was deeply disappointed when many old people no longer recognized me at first glance. I never fully realized that thirty years or more had passed in the meantime, so ensnared in the memory of my childhood years did I remain.

While chief of the RSHA, he often told two of his subordinates that, after the war, he hoped to retire to the land in Upper Austria and to live the simple life of a peasant.[64] This nostalgic sentimentality interacted with a stark brutality to form a peculiar symbiosis in Kaltenbrunner's adult character,

[59] Ibid., p. 7.

[60] Ibid., p. 9.

[61] For Hitler's memories of Austria, see *Mein Kampf*, pp. 5-6, 7-10, 17-65. On Hitler's peasant nostalgia, see pp. 138, 233-234.

[62] E. Kaltenbrunner, "Memoir," p. 22.

[63] Ibid., p. 29.

[64] Affidavit of Wilhelm Waneck, 15 April 1946, Kaltenbrunner-8, IMT XL, p. 341; statement of Wilhelm Höttl, 10 October 1945, 1746-PS, exhibit B, p. 19. Such expressed postwar plans for a "simple life" were characteristic of many top Nazis, including Hitler himself.

that "split personality" of which Joachim Fest has spoken,[65] whereby Kaltenbrunner, as RSHA chief, could request authorization to deport five thousand Jews during the day and yet remain a loving father, husband, comrade, or lover by night.

While at the *Volkschule* in Raab, Kaltenbrunner had shown enough interest in the machinery at the local smithy and brewery to convince his father that he should be prepared for a technical career at the Realgymnasium in Linz. On 12 September 1913, the boy moved into a boardinghouse owned by Frau Bertha Katzer, the widow of a distinguished lawyer. His memories of the following years were not pleasant. Deeply homesick for Raab, he also found his landlady overly strict and stingy.

It is not known whether Kaltenbrunner's experiences during World War I had an effect on his later political development; he offers no clues on this subject. Unlike Himmler or Goebbels,[66] he reveals no hint of a yearning to play war games, though he was proud to hear his father give an impassioned speech to Raab recruits in August 1914. Beyond mentioning that food at the boardinghouse became scarce as the war progressed, Kaltenbrunner has nothing to say about this period.

The end of the war brought the Kaltenbrunner family back together. Kaltenbrunner senior closed his practice in Raab and moved his family to Linz, where he joined the prestigious law firm of Dr. Carl Beurle. The Kaltenbrunner family took an apartment on the Mozartstrasse and Ernst moved back into his father's house.[67]

To one outside observer, little in Kaltenbrunner's appearance and behavior at the Realgymnasium hinted at the later development of his career. To Ernst Koref, one of his teachers, he appeared nondescript, generally pleasant, and well bred; his only distinguishing feature was "a certain self-consciousness in which his handsome and agreeable appearance presumably played a role."[68] One of Kaltenbrunner's roommates at the boardinghouse offers a different picture. He reports that Kaltenbrunner was much more interested in German mythology than in his studies. During discussions (po-

---

[65] Fest, *Face*, p. 302.

[66] On Himmler, see Bradley F. Smith, *Heinrich Himmler: A Nazi in the Making, 1900-1926* (Stanford: Hoover Institution Press, 1971), pp. 47-60; on Goebbels, see Helmut Heiber, *Josef Goebbels* (Munich: Deutscher Taschenbuch Verlag, 1974), pp. 17-18.

[67] E. Kaltenbrunner, "Memoir," pp. 28, 29; E. Kaltenbrunner, "Lebenslauf," pp. 3-4, F-190, IfZ Munich; conversation with Dr. Hansjörg Kaltenbrunner, Gramastetten, 26 March 1977; announcement of Hugo Kaltenbrunner's entry into the Beurle law firm, 1 December 1918, Kaltenbrunner Family Records; *Der Oberösterreicher*, 1919, pp. 177, 316, 317.

[68] Dr. Ernst Koref to the author, 9 December 1976. In assessing Koref's statements, one must be cautioned that Kaltenbrunner later saved his teacher (who was half Jewish) from internment at Dachau, an act for which Koref, despite his personal, political, and ideological distaste for the Nazis, remains grateful to Kaltenbrunner.

litical and otherwise) that often degenerated into "wild scuffles," Kaltenbrunner was possessed by a stubborn fanaticism. Discussion with the lawyer's son served little purpose: "When the point was reached at which one thought oneself to have convinced him, he became obstinate and stuck to his viewpoint, stubbornly and impervious to reason."[69]

Kaltenbrunner may have been "stubborn" about pan-German sentiment, for his roommate came from a solid Christian Social family. It has been noted that secondary schools in Germany and Austria were hotbeds of völkisch nationalism; Hitler, who attended the Realgymnasium in Linz at the turn of the century, paid a glowing tribute to his history teacher for exposing the "anti-German" machinations of the Habsburgs. At the same Realgymnasium, Kaltenbrunner joined the *Penneburschenschaft* "Hohenstaufen." Modeled on the university Burschenschaft, Hohenstaufen displayed a marked pan-German slant; its members directed their hatred at Catholic rivals.[70] Thus, even during his most formative years, Kaltenbrunner identified with an ultranationalist elitist group, whose energies were fueled by hatred of those who did not share the beliefs of its members.

In the summer of 1921, Kaltenbrunner completed his diploma at the Realgymnasium; that autumn he matriculated at the technical university in Graz. He chose Graz under the influence of his father's happy memories, and a technical career because of a romantic desire to enter the Dutch colonial service as an engineer and thus to see the world. Though matriculated in the department of chemistry, he transferred after two years to the law school at the university, from which his father had graduated twenty-five years earlier. He later claimed that his chemistry studies had failed, partly owing to lack of funds—the postwar inflation had allegedly weakened the financial situation of his family to such a degree that his allowance was cut off—which forced him to sell his instruments and to find temporary employment both as a tutor and as a laborer shoveling coal on the night shift at the railroad station, and partly owing to the entreaties of his mother, who begged him to study law with a view to eventually taking over his father's law practice. When the struggling student realized that his father's health was seriously impaired, he complied with his mother's wish. He worked hard and fast, and, to the astonishment of his friends, completed his degree in the summer of 1926.

Such is the story that Kaltenbrunner wrote for the benefit of his children

[69] Herr Wilhelm Pöschl to the author, 24 May 1977. I am grateful to Nikolaus Graf Revetera for his aid in establishing contact with Herr Pöschl.

[70] See Hitler, *Mein Kampf*, pp. 14-15. On Pan-German sentiment in secondary schools, see Mosse, *Crisis*, pp. 267-268. On Hohenstaufen, see W. Kaltenbrunner interview, Vöcklabruck, 25 March 1977. The German noun *Penne* means flophouse and was used as slang for the high school.

and the Nuremberg psychiatrist;[71] but his brother Werner remembered differently. According to Werner, Kaltenbrunner was lured to Graz by the opportunity for companionship offered by Arminia. Far from being a sober, hard-working student, he plunged into a wild life, replete with women and liquor. He had several girlfriends and apparently sustained a relationship with a divorcee for over a year, a liaison that raised some eyebrows in the fraternity. He did not scruple to squander his generous monthly allowance of two hundred Austrian Schillings (approximately $40) and remained in a state of chronic indebtedness; he often asked his brother Werner, who matriculated at the university as a law student in the fall of 1923, to lend him money. Kaltenbrunner senior was irritated by such irresponsible behavior, but Theresia Kaltenbrunner often stood up for her favorite and sometimes sent him a little extra to cover his debts.

Nor can we be certain that Kaltenbrunner's interest in chemistry was serious. According to his brother, he soon discovered that the field required too much time and discipline to accommodate his extracurricular activities, including his politics. Conversely, law was better suited to his life style, for the study of law was traditionally easy in Austria. Finally, Werner Kaltenbrunner labeled his brother's claim to have worked at the railroad station in Graz a "fairy tale."[72]

The real significance of Kaltenbrunner's student experience lies in its confirmation of völkisch preconceptions and prejudices held by his father's generation and aggravated in the context of the postwar Austrian Republic. World War I and its aftermath accelerated those political, social, economic, and intellectual trends that völkisch thinkers had dreaded and condemned for a century: liberalism, parliamentary democracy, monopoly capitalism, urbanization, Marxism, social upheaval, economic dislocation, and, perhaps most important, national disunion, which, it was feared, would hasten cultural disintegration. Gone was the Empire; in its place was a "German-Austrian" region (i.e., including the seven provinces of the later Austrian Republic,

[71] E. Kaltenbrunner, "Memoir," p. 30; E. Kaltenbrunner, "Lebenslauf," p. 4, F-190, IfZ Munich; testimony of Kaltenbrunner, IMT XI, p. 233.

[72] W. Kaltenbrunner interview, Vöcklabruck, 25 March 1977. It is also difficult to pinpoint Hugo Kaltenbrunner's financial distress or illness as factors in his son's decision to change his course of study. Kaltenbrunner senior had had some bad luck shortly after the war in that the government war bonds in which he invested became worthless and the capital proceeds from the sale of the house in Raab were wiped out in the course of the postwar inflation. Nevertheless, both Ernst and Werner Kaltenbrunner received 200 Austrian Schillings (öS) monthly, and, by 1924, Hugo Kaltenbrunner was doing very well: in the following years he generally earned more than his three partners. In 1926 he grossed 28,265.19 öS, 30% of the Beurle law firm's entire income (*Aufteilungslist* of earnings of the firm Beurle-Crippa-Kaltenbrunner-Horzeyschy, Linz, for the years 1924 and 1925, Kaltenbrunner Family Records; *Jahresschlussbilanz* of the Beurle firm, 31 December 1926, ibid.).

the Sudeten German lands and the South Tyrol), which was proclaimed by
its leaders in one and the same breath to be a republic and to be "a constit-
uent part of the German [Weimar] Republic."[73] This proclamation was issued in the firm belief that the postwar settlement would permit the German-
speaking provinces of the defunct Monarchy to join the German Reich; to
realize this goal, even antiliberal, antidemocratic pan-Germans were willing
to accept, at least temporarily, a democratic Republic. Such hopes were
shattered by the Treaties of Versailles (June 1919) and Saint-Germain (September 1919). The treaties forbade the union of Austria and Germany; awarded
to non-German national states political sovereignty over German-speaking
lands—the Sudeten German districts, Southern Styria, Southern Carinthia,
and the South Tyrol;[74] and assigned to the infant Austrian Republic and its
Hungarian neighbor the burden of reparations payments required from the
vanquished Habsburg state. The resulting rage, disappointment, and bitter-
ness were hardly confined to völkisch fanatics; Social Democrats and Christian Socials despised the treaties no less. Henceforth, völkisch nationalists
saw no reason to recognize the parliamentary regime, even on a temporary
basis, for it was linked to the hated peace treaties.

In the elections of February 1919, more than 75 percent of the vote went
to Social Democrats and the Christian Socials; a "black and red" coalition
took over the government and set to work on a constitution. Rooted in the
anticlerical middle class, völkisch nationalists viewed the "priests" (Pfaffen)
and "Bolsheviks" as representatives of international, cosmopolitan movements, each lethal to the interests of the German nation. The radical rhetoric of the Socialist leaders, who, though practicing political compromise,
preached proletarian dictatorship (much to the approval of their militant
rank and file supporters), and the presence in the party hierarchy of numerous Jewish intellectuals,[75] were exploited by those who warned Germans
against the "Judaization" and "Bolshevization" of Austrian political culture.
Brief communist triumphs in Munich and Budapest in 1919 frightened the
Austrian middle classes regardless of political affiliation and were depicted
by pan-German propaganda as steps in a vast Jewish-Bolshevik conspiracy.

---

[73] Stanley Suval, The Anschluss Question in the Weimar Era: A Study of Nationalism in
Germany and Austria, 1918-1932 (Baltimore-London: Johns Hopkins University Press, 1974),
p. 7.

[74] To Czechoslovakia, to the South Slav Kingdom of Serbs, Croats, and Slovenes, and to
Italy, respectively.

[75] A leader of the Revolutionary Socialist underground after the civil war of 1934 has estimated that 80% of the intellectuals who joined the Social Democratic Workers' Party were
Jewish and that Jews accounted for the bulk of the members of the Socialist student organization, the Socialist Jurists' Association, the Viennese branch of the Social Democrtic physicians'
organization, and the editorial staff of the Social Democratic press. See Joseph Buttinger, In
the Twilight of Socialism: A History of the Revolutionary Socialists of Austria (New York: Praeger, 1953), pp. 80-81.

Finally, the spirited defense of the 1920 constitution by the Social Democrats (who had been most influential in drafting it) enabled enemies of the Republic to attribute each economic crisis, each political deadlock, and each financial scandal to the malicious intent of Jews and Socialists, whose support of the constitution allegedly reflected a desire to prolong such chaotic conditions for their own purposes.[76]

The Christian Social Party, on the other hand, was mistrusted for real and suspected ties with the Catholic hierarchy in Rome, for the marked lack of enthusiasm about Anschluss to Germany among its leaders—including its recognized chief, Msgr. Ignaz Seipel—and finally, for the close relationship of the clerical and political hierarchy with Viennese financial and industrial circles, including Jewish financiers and industrialists.[77]

The minority parties in the nationalist "camp"[78] were also compromised in the eyes of more radical völkisch nationalists. From 1922 to 1933, the Pan-German People's Party[79] and the Agrarian League (*Landbund*) made

[76] On the radical rhetoric of the Social Democrats and the fears it aroused, see Alfred Diamant, *Austrian Catholics and the First Republic: Democracy, Capitalism, and the Social Order, 1918-1934* (Princeton: Princeton University Press, 1960), p. 75; Klemens von Klemperer, "Chancellor Seipel and the Crisis of Democracy in Austria," *Journal of Central European Affairs*, 22 (January 1963), 474.

[77] On Christian Social reservations about Anschluss and efforts to create and nourish an Austrian identity, see Walter Goldinger, *Geschichte der Republik Österreich* (Vienna: Verlag für Geschichte und Politik, 1962), p. 71; Suval, *Anschluss Question*, pp. 190-225. On Seipel's views, see Klemens von Klemperer, *Ignaz Seipel: Christian Statesman in a Time of Crisis* (Princeton: Princeton University Press, 1972), pp. 301-306; Diamant, *Catholics*, pp. 106-116.

[78] Adam Wandruszka has labeled *Lager* the three major political groupings in the First Republic—Socialist, Catholic-Conservative, and Nationalist. Each camp represented a Weltanschauung rather than merely a political interest group, and fostered homogeneity among its members. The Socialists enjoyed unchallenged control among the industrial workers in Vienna and in the provincial industrial centers (Graz, Wiener Neustadt, and Linz). The Catholic-Conservative camp and its exponent, the Christian Social Party, drew support from the peasantry and the urban petty bourgeoisie, from clerics and clericalists, and from large industrial and banking interests. The Nationalist camp, the weakest of the three, was supported by urban and rural anti-clerical middle-class elements and had a strong hold on the state bureaucracy and the universities. See Adam Wandruszka, "Österreichs politische Struktur: Die Entwicklung der Parteien und der politischen Bewegungen," in *Geschichte der Republik Österreich*, ed. Heinrich Benedikt (Vienna: Verlag für Geschichte und Politik, 1954), pp. 289-485.

[79] After World War I, the concepts *grossdeutsch* and *kleindeutsch* changed their meaning in the Austrian context. From 1867 to 1918, *grossdeutsch* union implied a German national state encompassing the lands of the Holy Roman Empire and centered in Vienna. After 1918, *grossdeutsch* union came to mean a unification of all Germans in Europe into a single state based on the principle of racial purity. On the other hand, the concept of *kleindeutsch* union (i.e., the union of Germans in the Habsburg lands with a German Reich ruled from Berlin) as it was understood by German nationalists in Austria during the nineteenth century no longer formed part of the Austrian political vocabulary. After 1918, *kleindeutsch* union reverted back to its original, Bismarkian meaning: that is, the German national state founded on the boundaries established in 1871.

common cause with the Christian Socials in forming an anti-Socialist coalition, despite significant differences on the questions of Anschluss and clerical influence in the state.[80] To völkisch fanatics, such compromises with the "system" were tantamount to a betrayal of the German national cause.

Pan-German agitation benefited greatly from the chaotic economic conditions that plagued the First Republic throughout its sixteen-year history. Pro-Anschluss propagandists (Social Democrats as well as pan-Germans) exploited the general belief that rump Austria was "incapable of survival" (*lebensunfähig*) unless included in a larger economic unit. Since most Austrians (even the Christian Socials, who yearned for a Danubian federation) expected the new state to be a temporary phenomenon, few were willing to contribute actively to its economic well-being. Austrian wholesalers, industrialists, bankers, and investors hoarded their assets and awaited the inevitable inclusion of Austria into a larger political-economic unit; many of them firmly believed that "only the Anschluss can change the inconsolable situation of Austrian industry."[81]

Several economic factors lent support to this view. As the Successor States disengaged themselves from the Monarchy and closed their newly established borders, Austria faced severe shortages of coal and basic foodstuffs. Lacking the capital resources necessary to import sufficient supplies to fill the needs of its urban population, Austria depended on Entente aid to avert a genuine threat of mass starvation and disease.[82]

Although this immediate danger had abated by the spring of 1920, it was followed by a catastrophic inflationary spiral that brought Austria's currency to the brink of collapse. The depreciation of the Austrian crown after November 1918 was hastened by the following factors: a drastic decline in exports due to the loss of traditional markets now hidden behind tariff walls erected by the Successor States; an extensive flight of foreign capital from Vienna as investors feared that the Bolshevik revolution in Hungary would spread to Austria; and the burdensome reparations payments determined at Saint-Germain. The threatening collapse of the crown encouraged foreign speculation in Vienna, where the embittered middle classes watched their savings evaporate and their earnings lose their value.[83]

During the winter of 1920-1921, inflation (which washed over Germany with equal force but had less serious effects in Czechoslovakia and Hungary) rose ever higher as the central government printed more crown notes to

---

[80] Diamant, *Catholics*, p. 256.

[81] Suval, *Anschluss Question*, p. 177.

[82] Karl R. Stadler, *The Birth of the Austrian Republic, 1918-1921* (Leiden: A. W. Sijthoff, 1966), p. 163.

[83] Charles A. Gulick, *Austria: From Habsburg to Hitler*, Vol. I: *Labor's Workshop of Democracy* (Berkeley–Los Angeles: University of California Press, 1948), p. 149.

subsidize the import of foodstuffs and raw materials. Social Democratic policy initially encouraged the inflation in part because the workers benefited most from the food subsidies and in part because the party leaders expected it to attract foreign and domestic capital to fuel Austria's stagnating industry. They introduced a special sliding-scale wage system that protected the industrial workers from the worst effects of the fiscal crisis, but which also aggravated class tension; the middle classes believed that the workers and the Socialists were exploiting the crisis for selfish class ends.[84]

By the summer of 1922, it had become apparent that unless drastic fiscal reforms were implemented with the aid of foreign capital, the crown would collapse. Seipel, who had become chancellor in May, was determined to salvage the integrity of the Austrian state regardless of who paid for it. Alternately threatening Anschluss and promising stabilization, he persuaded the League of Nations to intervene. On 4 October 1922, the Geneva Protocols were signed. These stipulated that Austria would receive a loan of 650 million gold crowns from Britain, France, Italy, and Czechoslovakia in return for allowing the League to supervise the impending fiscal reforms. Austria was compelled to offer the revenues from customs dues and the government's tobacco monopoly as collateral and to reaffirm her integrity as an independent state, whose borders the League agreed to guarantee. Christian Socials and moderate pan-Germans supported the Seipel government's acceptance of these conditions; Social Democrats and radical pan-Germans denounced the chancellor as a traitor to the German people.[85]

The dismissal of some 85,000 civil- and public-service employees in accordance with the financial reforms—known collectively as the *Sanierung*—aggravated an already chronic job shortage in the Republic. Contraction of industry due to the disappearance of export markets and raw materials, the demobilization of the army, and cutbacks in the civil service to conform to drastically reduced areas of administration had been major factors in the first wave of unemployment. Layoffs resulting from the Sanierung and the conservative fiscal policies of the Christian Social governments swelled the ranks of the unemployed, whose discontent was a constant source of political instability. Even in 1924-1929, the "prosperous years" of the First Republic, the number of unemployed was more than 10 percent of the labor force.[86]

[84] Ibid., pp. 151, 152-157.

[85] M. Margaret Ball, *Post-War German-Austrian Relations: The Anschluss Movement, 1918-1936* (Stanford: Stanford University Press, 1937), pp. 43-44, 48-50; Gulick, *Austria*, I, pp. 166-167; Karl R. Stadler, *Austria* (New York–Washington: Praeger, 1971), pp. 122-123. On Social Democratic opposition to the Protocols, see Klemperer, *Seipel*, pp. 208-209.

[86] Goldinger, *Österreich*, pp. 119-120. In the last two years of the Sanierung (1924-1926), the number of unemployed in Austria rose from 127,000 to 202,000. See Stadler, *Austria*, p. 123.

Most serious for the future of the Republic was its failure to provide adequate employment for the younger generation (unemployment statistics for the 1920s did not include those just entering the job market), many members of which developed no stake in an independent Austria. Moving into the lower ranks of the established parties and into the numerous paramilitary organizations, these young men helped to radicalize the political camps and to decrease chances for meaningful political compromise.

Political chaos, economic catastrophe, and cultural despair after World War I did not surprise hard-core pan-German fanatics, for they had "predicted" this state of affairs for two generations. They "knew" who the "real" enemy was, how he operated, and what he intended. Rudolf Jung, self-appointed theorist for the Austrian National Socialist German Workers' Party, summed up the völkisch attitude toward the postwar democratic order: "If we summarize, we might say that all international democracy, the alleged ideals of which the major newspapers and the major parties represent and to the banner of which they pledge their allegiance, is nothing other than the political knockout blow of the Jewish spirit and, in the final analysis, serves no purpose other than to establish the world rule of Jewry."[87] Nor were the Nazis alone in decrying the "triumph" of the Jews in Austria. A leading writer in the right wing of the Catholic-Conservative political camp expressed his critique in terms of which, despite a somewhat religious tinge, a völkisch writer could be proud: "This is why the true ruler needs to mask his hideous visage marked as it is by mammon worship, the murder of the Messiah, and the eternal curse of the Almighty. . . . This is the mask of popular sovereignty and republican constitution, and behind it we shall find the invisible, but real, ruler of our miserable Jew republic."[88]

Nowhere in Austria was such sentiment more intense than in the pan-German student movement. World war and revolution had sparked a radicalism in the universities of a type not experienced since the heyday of Schönerer. Pan-German fraternity students had seen in World War I a naked struggle for survival: "it is the existence or nonexistence of the German Reich and a German-dominated Austria that is now at stake."[89] Political instability, economic chaos, and social insecurity in the first postwar years incited a new wave of radicalism and violence in the universities. Defeat in war had been disappointing and all felt betrayed by the politicians who had signed the peace treaties. Economic factors also encouraged völkisch fanaticism on campus. Reduced opportunities for employment and ever stiffer

[87] Rudolf Jung, *Der nationale Sozialismus: Seine Grundlagen, sein Werdegang und seine Ziele*, 3rd ed. (Munich: Deutscher Volksverlag, 1922), p. 53.

[88] Anton Orel, quoted in Diamant, *Catholics*, pp. 144-145.

[89] *Festschrift Arminia*, p. 95.

competition for success in the liberal professions, where many Jews were employed, fanned hatred of the Jew and the foreigner.

The main target of the postwar nationalist student movement was the Jews. It was widely rumored that Jewish students had avoided military service, completed their studies while German students were away at the front, and seized the best opportunities for employment. Pan-Germans charged that Jews already established in academia and the liberal professions were conspiring to assist their conationals in finding lucrative positions at the expense of German students. Student agitators charged that there were simply too many Jewish doctors, journalists, lawyers, professors, and students.[90] Radical anti-Semitism was almost universal in Austrian universities. Assaults on Jewish students (who were derisively called "Jewish brats") were regular, and demands for a quota system strictly limiting the number of Jews admitted to the universities were persistent. Much of the non-Jewish faculty viewed such activities with indifference or even approval.[91]

Though economic and social factors provided rationalizations for and contributed to pan-German dynamism at the universities, psychological factors also played a role. Lewis Feuer has attributed student radicalism in general to displaced generational conflict and has remarked that it tends to wax in eras of "gerontocracy" (i.e., periods dominated by the extensively long rule

---

[90] Ehrlicher and Leitinger, *Hort*, pp. 57-58, 140-141. Figures on Jewish participation in banking, business, and the liberal professions in postwar Austria are revealing. After 1918, most Austrian Jews were concentrated in Vienna, where in 1923 they accounted for 10.8% of the city's population. See Helmut Genschel, *Die Verdrängung der Juden aus der Wirtschaft im Dritten Reich* (Göttingen: Musterschmidt Verlag, 1966), p. 288. Outside Vienna, the Jewish element was negligible, totaling 15,447 persons or 0.32% of the population in 1934 (ibid.). Despite their small numbers in respect to the total population of Austria (191,481 out of 6,760,233 in 1934, or 2.83%), Jews were prominently, sometimes exclusively, represented in business, banking, handicrafts, and the liberal professions. The following figures on Jewish participation in various professions in Vienna have been recorded: advertising (95%), banking (77%), theater (64%), journalism (63%), petrol and oil industry (64%), jewelers (40%), coffeehouse owners (40%), watchmakers (32%), druggists (26%), opticians (22%). See ibid., p. 289. In addition, Jews accounted for 51.6% of Vienna's doctors and dentists, 31% of dental technicians, 62% of lawyers, and 26% of chemists. See Herbert Rosenkranz, "The Anschluss and the Tragedy of Austrian Jewry, 1938-1945" in *The Jews of Austria: Essays on Their Life, History and Destruction*, ed. Josef Fraenkel (London: Vallentine-Mitchell, 1967), p. 480. Particularly significant for the popularity of anti-Semitism in the universities are the figures pertaining to Jewish professors and students. Jews accounted for 23% of university professors (45% in the medical faculty) in the First Republic; and, while no figures for postwar Austria are available, Jews accounted for 33.6% of the students at the university in Vienna and 23.7% at the technical college in 1890. See ibid.; Pulzer, *Anti-Semitism*, p. 12. Given the competition for academic positions and government posts, the presence of such disproportionate numbers of Jews at the universities lent authority to pan-German propaganda, which called first for a *numerus clausus* and ultimately for the elimination of Jews from the universities altogether.

[91] Pulzer, *Anti-Semitism*, p. 308.

of a single generation of politicians) in which the generation in power has been morally discredited—a process that Feuer calls "de-authorization."[92] The older generation of politicians in postwar Austria had clearly been discredited by the peace treaty, the jarring effects of inflation and economic hardship, the diminishing opportunities for employment, and the inability to arrive at a new national symbolism that would give the Austrian state and its survival some meaning for the students. In the light of these failures, the German nationalist students revolted against a society that offered them little hope of social status and economic rewards appropriate to their academic training. They presented themselves as the conscience of the German nation, the purest of the pure, and disdained the "business as usual" attitude of their fathers who, however much they hated the Republic, had had to compromise with the "system," if only to make a living.[93] The students of 1920 differed little in their ideology from those of 1890; their distinctiveness lay in the fact that, unlike their fathers, who found suitable careers in the centuries-old Habsburg Monarchy, they sought careers in a republic whose structure virtually every one of its citizens wished either to destroy or alter in some significant way. The postwar students graduated into an unstable society permeated with the völkisch ideals that they had absorbed during their university years. The paramilitary formations and the postwar authoritarian political parties offered them a stage on which to act out their frustrations and fantasies.[94]

Völkisch radicalism attracted Austrian students because, beyond its emotional attachment to Greater Germany, it offered them a doctrine sufficiently radical in *form* as well as content to permit a revolt against an older generation that, in entering what Erik Erikson has called the "sphere of *Bürger-*

[92] Lewis S. Feuer, *The Conflict of the Generations: The Character and Significance of Student Movements* (New York: Basic Books, 1969), p. 35; see also pp. 3-36. See also the comments of Michael Stephen Steinberg in his study of German students in the Weimar Republic, *Sabers and Brownshirts: The German Students' Path to National Socialism, 1918-1935* (Chicago: University of Chicago Press, 1973), pp. 1-10.

[93] For a similar conclusion in reference to students in the Weimar Republic, see Michael H. Kater, *Studentenschaft und Rechtsradikalismus in Deutschland, 1918-1933: Eine sozialgeschichtliche Studie zur Bildungskrise in der Weimarer Republik* (Hamburg: Hoffmann und Campe Verlag, 1975), pp. 200-201.

[94] Kaltenbrunner himself was fully aware of the differences between his father's time and his own: "Already in my father's time, the Burschenschaft was a bulwark of German character [*Hort deutschen Wesens*] against the little German stubbornness [adherence to the Bismarckian system is meant here] of Austria and all anti-German influences of the multinational state. . . . This had changed by my time, however, for since the world war, the union of all Germans in one state had become the demand of all estates [Stände], indeed nearly all political parties. The understanding that the union would impart economic and cultural strength, would perhaps lead to a just revision of that which was dishonorable in the peace treaties, scarcely needed to be propagated any longer; it had become a public affair." E. Kaltenbrunner, "Memoir," p. 32.

lichkeit," appeared to its successor as having "betrayed youth and idealism and . . . sought refuge in a petty and servile kind of conservatism."[95] Racism enabled them to feel at one with the humble peasant and the industrious craftsman, to submerge themselves in the larger community of the nation without sacrificing either the social status that they believed was their due or the material base which supported that status. They directed their energies toward the negative task of protecting a mythical racial community from "contamination" by a myriad of alien elements, all of which were but manifestations of the Jewish archenemy. Hence it should hardly surprise us that, twenty years later in his cell in Nuremberg, Ernst Kaltenbrunner wrote to his children that he and his fraternity brothers "traced alien influences that corroded morals and culture back to their originators, recognized and checked them in [a state of] anti-Semitic preparedness."[96]

In this explosive atmosphere, the nationalist fraternities put aside their rivalries and formed a loose coalition, known as the *Deutscher Burschenbund* (Association of German Students) on 16 November 1918. The Association was open only to students of Aryan descent and described its purpose as "involvement in völkisch concerns, preservation of the German character of the universities and technical schools, education in völkisch and ethical [values], and economic and professional advancement."[97] During a Burschenschaft outing in the German town of Eisenach in August 1919, German, Austrian, and Sudeten fraternities voted to unite under a single organization called the *Deutsche Burschenschaft* (German Student Society), whose purpose was promotion of pan-German unity and struggle against all enemies of the nation within and outside university walls.[98] Students at Leoben and Graz set to work immediately, forming armed bands to aid the Styrian *Heimatschutz*—a group of spontaneously formed paramilitary units whose original purpose was to protect farms and shops from marauding soldiers as the Austro-Hungarian state dissolved—to beat back Yugoslav troops that were invading southern Styria and Carinthia in the hope of bolstering claims to the Klagenfurt Basin at the coming peace conference. Even after the Yugoslavs had been driven back, all fraternity members in Graz were required to serve in the Student Battalion of the Styrian Heimatschutz, where they were offered military and physical training as well as ideological indoctrination.[99]

[95] Erik H. Erikson, "The Legend of Hitler's Childhood," in Erikson, *Childhood and Society*, 2nd ed. (New York: W. W. Norton, 1963), p. 334.

[96] E. Kaltenbrunner, "Memoir," p. 32.

[97] Ehrlicher and Leitinger, *Hort*, p. 133.

[98] Ibid., p. 136. The 1919 agreement covered only dueling fraternities. Nondueling fraternities and clubs were drawn into the Deutsche Burschenschaft in 1926.

[99] W. Kaltenbrunner interview, Vöcklabruck, 25 March 1977.

Radicalized by war, postwar political disappointment, economic insecurity, and emotional discontent, the major elements of prewar fraternity politics in Graz—pan-German unity, anti-Semitism, racial nationalism, anticlericalism, anti-liberalism, and Slavophobia—remained of decisive influence among the nationalist fraternities in the Styrian capital when Ernst Kaltenbrunner entered Arminia as a "fox" on 3 October 1921. Symbolically, the first activity in which Kaltenbrunner participated as a fraternity member was a joint fraternity obsequy commemorating the passing of Georg Ritter von Schönerer.[100]

Kaltenbrunner was an enthusiastic fraternity brother. A hard drinker and passionate duelist, he gained a reputation among his comrades as a "reliable dueling match" (*verlässliche Partie*) on account of his steady posture and reckless courage with the saber. Beyond the excitement of the student duel (*Mensur*), however, fraternity life offered practical benefits such as inexpensive living quarters and invaluable professional contacts in the civil service and in the free professions (i.e., medicine, law, education, journalism, theater, etc.). It also provided an intimate, communal atmosphere in which the individual could confirm his national identity and simultaneously be part of an elite organization committed to rejecting all compromise on the validity of völkisch ideals.[101]

The fraternity brothers' arrogant elitism was reflected in the size, structure, and self-image of the Burschenschaften. The fraternities were normally small groups (often having as few as ten members) that emphasized an almost familial intimacy by means of secret handshakes and incantations and special pseudonyms (*Kneipnamen*) either plucked from German or Greek mythology or derived from affectionate nicknames. This sense of elite status created a feeling of uniqueness toward other classes of society, expressed in the belief that the fraternities were the "bulwark of German sentiment" (*der Hort deutschen Fühlens*), the only reliable defenders of German culture in a society corrupted by political and personal compromise. Armines were indoctrinated with this elitist consciousness and were urged "to make conscientious use of their student years to acquire the necessary training and the social standing to serve the German nation as leaders."[102] When he graduated, the fraternity brother, now an "old boy" (*alter Herr*), was expected to promote pan-German ideals among his colleagues in his chosen profession and to aid future brothers in furthering their careers. In this way, Burschenschaft fanatics hoped gradually to mold a völkisch nationalist professional class capable of assuming leadership of the nation.

[100] *Festschrift Arminia*, pp. 110, 158.

[101] E. Kaltenbrunner, "Memoir," pp. 31-32; W. Kaltenbrunner interview, Vöcklabruck, 25 March 1977.

[102] Ehrlicher and Leitinger, *Hort*, p. 103.

Interestingly enough, this elitist nationalism was tinged with a strong sense of regional identification. All were pan-German in outlook, but in the Austrian fraternities there developed a feeling that German-Austrians, hardened by direct struggle with non-German nationalities and Jews, could lend a special enthusiasm and expertise to the pan-German cause. Austrian fraternity students were sensitive to disparaging remarks made about them by their German counterparts. Kaltenbrunner's sentimental attachment to Raab did not leave him immune to such feelings. During a fraternity outing in Danzig in the summer of 1924, a certain Greve, member of the Freiburg Burschenschaft "Saxo-Silesia," dropped a "derogatory" remark about the Austrian fraternities in the vicinity of Kaltenbrunner, who represented Arminia at the outing. A scuffle broke out, and Kaltenbrunner insulted both Greve and the latter's fraternity. Greve challenged Kaltenbrunner and Arminia to a duel, which never came off. Nevertheless, Arminia's historians crowed that Kaltenbrunner alone "stood up for the honor of the *ostmärkische* [i.e., Austrian] fraternities."[103]

Fraternity students in general and Kaltenbrunner in particular took pride in their contempt for "everyday politics" (*Tagespolitik*). This by no means indicated withdrawal from political activity within or outside of the university, but rather signified an uncompromising rejection of the postwar order, even on the most temporary basis. The nationalist fraternity students despised the major political parties—even the Pan-Germans—for these parties had accepted the Republic as a pro tempore reality. The Burschenschaftler styled himself the true defender of the German nation from the "alien influences" that the "politicians" were forever allowing to creep into Austrian life through their "compromises." From him, "politics" were practiced by "Blacks," "Reds," Jews (who allegedly controlled both), bourgeois nationalists, and even Nazis (whose admiration for Italy was not shared by Austrian student radicals); he alone would brook no compromise.[104]

[103] *Festschrift Arminia*, p. 119.
[104] E. Kaltenbrunner, Memoir," p. 32. For the concept of the true defender, see Feuer, *Generations*, p. 3. In this context it is interesting to note the antipathy of the fraternity students toward National Socialist student groups. When in the fall of 1924 the Nazi *Völkischsoziale Finkenschaft* (Völkisch-Social Free Students' Organization) sought to influence and infiltrate the fraternities in Graz, fraternity students were appalled by the Nazis' rude manners and lack of reverence for fraternity social convention. In 1928, Arminia historians wrote of the Nazis: "Unfortunately, there were among them only a few idealists who were serious with regard to common goals; the majority was interested solely in fomenting roughhouse politics against the fraternities. Their loathsome methods of fighting and the countermeasures of the fraternities finally achieved the result that the Völkisch-Socials, after only three years of existence, disappeared entirely from the university." See *Festschrift Arminia*, p. 123. Werner Kaltenbrunner confirmed this view, declaring that the Nazis' involvement in specific political issues outside the university reminded fraternity students of the despised political parties, while the Nazis'

Kaltenbrunner rapidly achieved prominent standing in the fraternity organizations. He served for a semester as secretary of the Graz *Vertreterbesprechung* (VB), to which all dueling fraternities at the university and technical college sent their representatives.[105] During the following semester, he represented all Graz fraternities on the statutes committee of the Deutsche Burschenschaft; and for two years he served as committee chairman of the Graz chapter of the Deutscher Burschenbund.[106] In these positions, he helped to plan, organize, and direct hate campaigns against Jewish, Catholic, socialist, and foreign students' organizations, and to enforce political conformity within the nationalist fraternities.

In 1919 Arminia had forbidden its members any activity on behalf of the Christian Social Party. Scuffles between Armines and members of the Catholic Carolina Verband were not infrequent; and Kaltenbrunner himself stood out as a bitter opponent of clerical influence on campus.[107] Nor were legitimists treated any less severely. When, in the autumn of 1922, a student group oriented toward a Habsburg restoration organized a Burschenschaft "Danubia," Arminia joined other fraternities in the demand that the new organization be denied recognition by the university authorities. Though the latter sympathized with the nationalist hotheads, the Christian Social provincial government pressured the rectorate into a formal acknowledgment of Danubia's statutes. The Vertreterbesprechung, however, spitefully denied the legitimists any right of representation and refused to consider any questions of dueling protocol involving their supporters.[108]

Incidents involving Jewish students invariably mobilized nationalist activities at the university. In the fall of 1923, a university lecturer was allegedly insulted and threatened by a group of Jewish students who had resented his anti-Semitic attitude. When the "scandal" broke, the Graz chapter of the Deutscher Burschenbund (of which Kaltenbrunner was the chairman) or-

---

strictly centralized organization seemed analogous to party discipline in nonacademic political life. W. Kaltenbrunner interview, Vöcklabruck, 25 March 1977. Kaltenbrunner himself wrote, "In my time there was no discussion of National Socialism as a political program." E. Kaltenbrunner, "Memoir," p. 35.

[105] The Vertreterbesprechung represented all dueling fraternities in disputes with one another and with the university authorities. Its chairmanship rotated from one fraternity to another each semester and its officers were elected by the incumbent fraternity. In the winter semester 1922/1923, the chairmanship fell to Arminia. See Günter Cerwinka, "Ernst Kaltenbrunner und Südtirol: Zur Gründung einer italienischen Studentengruppe im Jahre 1923 in Graz," *Blätter für Heimatkunde*, 50, Heft 4 (1976), 173; E. Kaltenbrunner, "Memoir," p. 32; W. Kaltenbrunner interview, Vöcklabruck, 25 March 1977.

[106] E. Kaltenbrunner, "Memoir," pp. 32-33; *Festschrift Arminia*, pp. 115, 116, 118, 121; Cerwinka, "Kaltenbrunner," p. 173.

[107] Ehrlicher and Leitinger, *Hort*, p. 162; *Festschrift Arminia*, pp. 125-127; article in *Die deutsche Polizei*, No. 15, 15 May 1943, p. 193, 2938-PS, IMT xxxi, p. 322.

[108] Ehrlicher and Leitinger, *Hort*, pp. 147-148; *Festschrift Arminia*, p. 113.

ganized gangs of student thugs to surround lecture halls and prevent Jewish students from attending their classes until the culprits could be found and punished. After a few days of these strong-arm tactics failed to bring result, the Burschenbund executive committee organized a mass demonstration to protest the very presence of Jews at the university. Distinguished figures from among the faculty, including the rector himself, took part in the demonstration. Although the "perpetrators" were never identified, Arminia historians took satisfaction in the fact that the incident had demonstrated that "professors and students stood united in the struggle against Jewry."[109]

Demonstrations against the enemies of Germandom did not let up. In the fall of 1924, a professor named Leon at the technical college aroused student enmity when he refused to abide by a university decision to permit war veterans to take special, less exacting examinations for their degrees. Student hotheads broke up Leon's first lecture of the semester and ultimately forced the technical college to shut down for several days. In 1925, völkisch radicals protested the appointment of a Jew to the chair of the law faculty; later that year, members of Arminia participated in the occupation of a festival hall in order to prevent a rally of Slovene students from taking place. A celebration commemorating the birthday of Czech President Thomas Masaryk, organized by the Czech population of Graz, met with a similar fate.[110]

Not all of Kaltenbrunner's extracurricular activities at the university in Graz were of such negative character. In 1922, he aided Bulgarian students to found a nationalist club called "Rodina" and was invited by them to become an honorary member. His interest in and fondness for the Bulgarians were genuine. Bulgaria had been the ally of Germany and Austria-Hungary during World War I and the Bulgarians were often praised in Germany for their supposed industrious nature; they had earned a reputation for being the "Prussians" of the Balkans. Kaltenbrunner knew many of the Bulgarian students and kept contact with some of them until the end of World War II.[111]

Students from nations that had opposed Germany in World War I evoked a considerably different response, however. Particularly interesting was Kaltenbrunner's attitude toward an Italian student organization while he was secretary for the Vertreterbesprechung. In the fall of 1922, an Italian student group applied to the university for official recognition of its statutes and for representation in the Vertreterbesprechung. Kaltenbrunner drafted a letter in his own hand to the rector of the university, requesting that recognition of the Italian group be denied. As grounds for this demand, he cited Italian oppression of Germans in the South Tyrol and expressed a remarkable mis-

[109] *Festschrift Arminia*, p. 116.

[110] Ibid., pp. 120-122, 128-129.

[111] *Die deutsche Polizei*, 15 May 1943, 2938-PS, IMT xxxi, p. 322; E. Kaltenbrunner, "Memoir," p. 33; E. Kaltenbrunner, "Lebenslauf," p. 5, F-190, IfZ Munich.

trust of the nature and aims of Italian Fascism, which, despite a similar ideology (which even Hitler had begun to admire), was branded as an arch-enemy with whom no compromise was possible. In light of the "grave national plight of our conationals [who are being] oppressed in the territory ceded to Italy [i.e., the South Tyrol]," Kaltenbrunner declared that the Vertreterbesprechung could not tolerate the formation of an Italian student organization in Graz. It was bad enough that "our enemies acquire at our universities the intellectual implements for the struggle against us"; but any Italian student organization would be committed to promoting "Italian aims [which are] hostile to us." Kaltenbrunner warned that the Vertreterbesprechung had voted unanimously to "resist the establishment of this [Italian] club with all means."[112] Such was the rigid ideological outlook of the Graz fraternities.

The years of violent demonstrations in support of unchanging völkisch myths and ideals within the elitist atmosphere of the university bred or confirmed racial hatred and arrogance among the student radicals. In Austria as well as in Germany, the fraternity student subculture "militated against liberalism, for its ideals of self-education, training practices, and social customs were curiously collectivist, despite their youthful flaunting of authority."[113]

The anti-Semitic, anti-Slavic, and anticlerical prejudices of an older, now more moderate generation were accepted blindly by a new generation of students who found in them an emotional outlet for their fears of losing social status and their apprehensions concerning suitable employment in a state and society believed to be morally and culturally degenerate. By barring Jews, socialists, Catholics, Slavs, and anyone else who might in a weak moment express or feel sympathy for any of these groups from their dueling rites and hence their society, the fraternity students cut themselves off from any contact that might have moderated the harsh stereotypes handed down to them by their fathers. Defense of the "last bulwark" of Germandom—the universities and the academic elite—was supposed to pave the way for a political union of all Germans from which a rejuvenated and thoroughly "Germanized" cultural development was expected to blossom. Unlike their fathers, who had had similar aims in 1890, Kaltenbrunner's contemporaries were not absorbed into a stable society and were thus never required to compromise with one. Losing the intimate world that had sheltered and consoled them as students, many of the new graduates continued to reject the postwar system in its entirety as a basis of political behavior norms and lived "as atomized individuals in a world of self-created political and social

---

[112] Grazer akademische Burschenschaft Arminia [signed Kroneiser and Kaltenbrunner] to the Rectorate of the Karl-Franzens-Universität in Graz, 27 January 1923, Vereinsakten III/58, Universitätsarchiv, Graz, published in Cerwinka, "Kaltenbrunner," pp. 176-177.

[113] Jarausch, Students, p. 409.

disengagement," lacking any real "bond of cohesion with the pluralist society in which they lived."[114]

The foundations of Kaltenbrunner's ideological outlook were rooted in a pan-German nationalist concept which attracted large sections of the educated German-Austrian elite during the last decades of the nineteenth century. Defined by Andrew Whiteside as "Austrian pan-Germanism,"[115] this concept involved a yearning for German national unity expressed in political terms and confined to those possessing "German-Aryan" ancestry. Political unity and racial purity were believed to promise social and economic security and cultural renaissance. As obstacles to the attainment of the utopian goal, Austrian pan-Germans specified those elements that they considered supranational, cosmopolitan, and hence "foreign": liberalism, Marxian Socialism, democracy, constitutional law, Catholicism, Slavic nationalism, the Habsburg dynasty and the multinational state, industrialization and urbanization. Pan-German theology traced these phenomena to the rationalist tradition of the Enlightenment and the French Revolution and isolated a Jewish "enemy" as the chief beneficiary of each. To achieve this, pan-Germans drew upon traditional Romantic stereotypes of the pure and clean "Germanic" individual and society (in which the primacy of ruralism, "natural" economic and social relationships based on idealizations of medieval political, social, and legal realities, and a genuine "inner community" of all members of the nation were emphasized), and of the dark, impure, almost demonic power of evil, personified in the Jew and characterized by the urban culture with which Jews came to be associated (i.e., industrialization, social mobility and change, the market economy and rationalist doctrines of civic equality, and the innate value of human life, regardless of nationality or social status). Pitting the healthy forces of a mythical antiquity against the corrupt forces of modernity, Austrian pan-Germanism proclaimed a "conservative" revolution against the modern world.

Though Austrian pan-Germans claimed to uphold a conservative tradition, their conservativism was illusory. They yearned for the resurrection of a mythical, medieval Reich, but their political-racial concept of that Reich was rooted in a post–French Revolutionary definition of the national state bolstered by the pseudoscientific social Darwinism of the nineteenth century. They bitterly castigated modern economic concepts, but expected their national state to possess the political, military, and economic apparatus to promote effectively German national aims in Central and Eastern Europe. Though they held rationalism and its outgrowth, modern science, in the deepest contempt, they repeatedly referred to the latest scientific ideas to

[114] Orlow, *Nazi Party, 1919-1933*, p. 2.
[115] Whiteside, *Socialism*, pp. 2-3.

support their irrational doctrines. Though they were profoundly antidemocratic, their national state presupposed a plebiscitary democracy and was thus inconceivable without the principle of universal suffrage. In short, though pan-Germans in Austria tried to associate themselves with preservation and resurrection, they in fact urged revolt and destruction; and, although they aimed at a revolt against the liberal, rationalist tradition of the Enlightenment and the French Revolution, their ideas and methods were ironically born out of that very tradition.

Austrian pan-Germanism was conceived behind sheltered university walls; there not only its basic ideological structure but also its emotional tenor were formed. The universities had always been in the forefront of the German nationalist movement, though their ultimate aims and means remained flexible as long as the political structure of Germany and Central Europe remained undefined. After the foundation of a German national state, however, German nationalist students in Austria saw no further justification for the existence of the Habsburg Monarchy, unless perhaps German political control over the state were perpetually secure. Habsburg efforts to compromise with the Slavic minorities between 1878 and 1901 rendered any such guarantee unlikely and facilitated the dissemination of kleindeutsch ideas not only among German-Austrian students, but also—through the medium of Georg von Schönerer—among members of those classes of the German-Austrian population which feared that continuation of the status quo would further undermine their economic well-being, social status, or cultural heritage.

An emotional and single-minded fixation with the racial question, a tendency to classify all opponents as irreconcilable enemies, and a rejection of all compromise as surrender were central to Austrian pan-Germanism and at the same time typical of its university origins. Because they are not yet integrated into nonacademic society at large and thus have neither stake in it nor reason to compromise with it, activist students are prone to radical absolutism in their political ideals and their plans to reconstruct society. They are also wont to believe that they, the educated elite, bear the responsibility to create a just order for the benefit of future generations and that all sacrifices required of contemporary adult society will be justified by the glorious end product. Insecurity about the possibilities of future employment and the accompanying social and financial rewards often lend a sense of urgency to student demands for a regeneration of society. Idealistic moral commitment to a better world which, given the fluid social status of the student activist, has few links to existing political and social realities, and deep anxiety about the future harden political and ideological inflexibility in student movements. Fearing a real or imagined lack of opportunity in contemporary society, student activists create an ideal society that offers a favorable resolution of their own fears and the real or imagined fears of others. Those who would oppose this obviously "just" order are suspected not merely of obstinateness or imperception, but of malicious intent. If the ideal society is to be established, these opponents must be converted, neutralized, or destroyed. In the case of Austrian pan-Germanism, which defined the ideal society as a racially homogeneous community, the enemy's ancestry precluded his conversion; he had to be neutralized or destroyed.

The evidence suggests that Ernst Kaltenbrunner was influenced deeply by the political and social outlook of his father's generation. We know that he remained deeply attached to his family throughout his childhood and adolescence, that he joined a nationalist schoolboy society at the Realgymnasium in Linz, that such societies were neither uncommon nor of insignificant influence during the last years of the Habsburg Monarchy, and, finally, that Kaltenbrunner senior's tales of student exploits were a factor in his son's decision to study at the university in Graz and to seek acceptance into Arminia. It is certain that he enthusiastically endorsed pan-German ideas and methods while a student and fraternity brother. He held key positions not only in Arminia itself, but also in broader organizations representing völkisch students both in Germany and Austria. While he was active in the student movement, virtually every tangible pan-German "enemy" was attacked or defamed in some manner. This personal involvement in the nationalist student movement confirmed foundations of a pan-German ideological outlook acquired from his father and probably reinforced at the Linz Realgymnasium.

Why, however, did Kaltenbrunner take such a radical route? Others certainly did not, for the German nationalist movement attracted only a minority of Austrian students. The answer may lie in a personal identity crisis—common among adolescents in Austria and elsewhere, past and present—dovetailing with a general identity crisis induced by the disintegration of the Central European order. In later life, Kaltenbrunner expressed a deep and almost mournful nostalgia for the secure, ordered existence that he had enjoyed (or thought he had enjoyed) in Raab. There, as the "leader" in the eyes of his two brothers, the favorite of his mother, and the "doctor's son" in the Volksschule, he occupied a unique, much respected and admired position in his family and among his peers.[116] Looking back on Raab "with his child's eyes,"[117] he saw in it a society that enabled him to be "one of the people" without relinquishing the elite position granted him by his family and social background.

[116] W. Kaltenbrunner interview, Vöcklabruck, 25 March 1977; E. Kaltenbrunner, "Memoir," p. 14.
[117] E. Kaltenbrunner, "Memoir," p. 5.

It was difficult for a young man to perceive stable foundations around which he could fashion a secure self-image in a time when the entire Habsburg political and social structure was in a state of collapse. The disintegration of the Habsburg Empire and the foundation of the ill-fated and unwanted Austrian Republic not only erased the familiar signs of the old order, but also hindered the establishment of a new order based on a consensus of the German-Austrian population. Defeat and revolution in 1918-1919 heralded the triumph of those elements which pan-German theology described as destroying the economic prosperity, social tranquillity, racial purity, and moral foundations of the German nation. For a young adult who had been nurtured on pan-German precepts, compromise (i.e., acceptance of the "Jew republic" in return for an illusory Entente blessing of the Anschluss) served no purpose, for the "enemy" had maliciously left Germandom in Austria hopelessly dependent on the League of Nations and "vulnerable" to plutocratic liberal influence from the West, bolshevik influence from the East, and the rule of that enemy which pan-Germanism credited with control over both—the Jew. Anxiety about the future, despair about the present, and yearning for an idyllic, simple past within the context of a general breakdown of traditional values and institutions in the postwar Austrian Republic produced a radical outburst of pan-German sentiment in Kaltenbrunner the Burschenschaftler. The extremism offered by militant Catholicism and Marxian Socialism could not appeal to him, for in the former he had no faith and with the latter, as a nonworker, he would never feel at home. Kaltenbrunner was drawn to pan-Germanism by its offer of a tranquil, secure community rooted in racial homogeneity, and because it represented a group to which he undoubtedly belonged. Given his cultural, intellectual, social, and emotional background, pan-Germanism was Kaltenbrunner's obvious choice in a time of mass craving for a systematic, absolute set of solutions to the complicated problems of modern society.

Having completed his studies with remarkable speed (considering his extracurricular activities), Kaltenbrunner received his law degree in July 1926 and thereupon left Graz for Linz to serve the mandatory first year of his practical legal training as a court apprentice at the Linz District Court.[118] Two points deserve mention at this stage. First, Kaltenbrunner had throughout his life identified himself with a group and as a leader of that group. In Raab, he was a leader to his brothers within the family unit; in Linz, he identified closely with the Penneburschenschaft Hohenstaufen; and in Graz, he identified not only with his own fraternity in a narrow sense, but also with the German nationalist student movement, which he served in a lead-

[118] *Die deutsche Polizei*, 15 May 1943, 2938-PS, IMT XXXI, p. 322; E. Kaltenbrunner, "Memoir," p. 35.

ership capacity. Second, he graduated just as the young Austrian Republic embarked on its first and only year of relative domestic tranquillity. By the summer of 1926, the Sanierung had finally been completed; the near civil war atmosphere produced by the Socialist transit strike of July 1927 and its suppression by the Christian Social government and its extremist paramilitary ally, the *Heimwehr*, was yet a year away. The majority of Austria's population had at least passively accepted the Republic as a temporary reality. Thus, when Kaltenbrunner left the university for adult society, he did not find it conducive to the radical spirit and almost familial intimacy of his university experience. Having shunned "politics" as a fraternity student, he had no interest in joining a political party—not even the Austrian National Socialist Party. He found himself compelled either to accept society for what it was and adapt to it or to continue to reject it categorically and face political and psychological isolation.

There was yet a third alternative: he might seek a new community to replace the fraternity, another artificial society within which he could pursue old goals and ideals, submit to old codes and practices and escape the feeling of loneliness and powerlessness in a cold, atomized, and often unsympathetic world by becoming "part of a bigger and more powerful whole outside of oneself."[119] Now that the foundations of his ideological outlook had been formed, he could seek a medium through which his yearning for security, community, and greatness could be satisfied or at least soothed.

[119] Erich Fromm, *Escape from Freedom* (New York: Avon, 1965), p. 177.

CHAPTER II

Between Heimatschutz *and NSDAP,* *1926-1931*

FOR TWO YEARS after receiving his law degree at the university in Graz, Kaltenbrunner lived without much sense of direction, changing jobs and seeking without success a circle of friends who would share his ideals and pleasures. Only in the late 1920s, as the "times grew more and more active politically,"[1] that is, as the none-too-stable foundations of the Austrian Republic began to crumble under the double strain of political extremism and economic crisis, did Kaltenbrunner discover the type of society in which he felt most comfortable: among people, who, like himself, despised the Republic and sought to overthrow the prosaic lifestyle of the *Systemzeit*.[2] By 1931, he had found in the Austrian National Socialist Workers' Party (NSDAP) and in the Austrian *Schutzstaffel* (SS) a workable medium through which he could express his commitment to the German nation and its salvation from the "enemies" that threatened its existence.

Little is known about Kaltenbrunner in the five years between the Burschenschaft and the SS. He devoted less than two pages of his "memoir" to this period, referring only vaguely to his motives for joining the Nazi Party (he wrote nothing at all about the SS). Nevertheless, it would be helpful to analyze two organizations with which he became affiliated *before* he joined the Nazi movement: the *Deutsch-Völkischer Turnverein* (German-Völkisch Gymnastic Association) and the Upper Austrian *Heimatschutz* (literally, Home Guard). An analysis of these organizations with an eye toward what Kaltenbrunner sought in them would shed light on his motives for joining the Nazis in 1930-1931.

Kaltenbrunner began his term of legal apprenticeship at the Upper Austrian District Court in Linz;[3] but, before the required year had been com-

---

[1] E. Kaltenbrunner, "Memoir," Nuremberg, July-August 1946, p. 38, Kaltenbrunner File.

[2] *System* was a derisive term used by the Nazis to describe the Weimar regime in Germany and both the Republic and the Dollfuss-Schuschnigg dictatorship in Austria. The term implies that the era preceding the Nazi seizure of power was "sterile, lacked dynamism, did not 'move,' and was followed by their [the Nazis'] 'era of the movement.'" See Arendt, *Totalitarianism*, p. 260.

[3] Under Austrian requirements, a newly graduated doctor of jurisprudence had to spend one year as a legal apprentice in a district court and six more years as a candidate lawyer (Rechtsanwaltsanwärter) before he could quality for the state examination, after which, if he passed, he could assume the official title of *Rechtsanwalt* and open his own practice.

pleted, he moved to Salzburg to take a position in the law firm of a Dr. Villas. He later related that although he learned a great deal at the Villas firm, he suffered from a constant sense of inadequacy, from a feeling that he could never offer the firm what it offered him; he felt "like a little goose, taken in tow in the water for the first time." He was unhappy in Salzburg; and rejection by an old girlfriend of his student years probably increased his sense of isolation. Bored and lonely, he yearned for Linz. When in 1928 a position became available in the firm of Dr. Franz Lasser in Linz-Urfahr (just across the Danube from Linz proper), he returned home.[4]

Though more content at the Lasser firm, which catered to the peasants of the Upper Austrian Mühlviertel, Kaltenbrunner remained restless. In a fruitless search for a community of people his own age, he "drifted" into an "unsatisfying tavern life."[5] His efforts to integrate himself into postwar Austrian society proved to be futile. At the university, he had believed his actions to be of great significance for the fate of the nation; but embarking on a career as a provincial lawyer, he found that his legal training counted for more than his political activities. Stripped of an environment where he could sacrifice all for a glorious cause, he was both insecure and bored.

Others shared his sense of tedium, for he slowly found his way into more congenial company. He received his initiation into the "shady political quagmire" through friends whom he found among right-wing gymnastic circles in Linz. Traditionally, most nationalist gymnastic societies in Germany and Austria had been racial pan-German in outlook; as early as 1902, their ranks had been closed to those who were not of "Aryan" descent. After World War I, many nationalist gymnastic associations offered their members rudimentary military training under the guise of "sport" (this practice was also common in Christian and Socialist gymnastic societies). By late 1928, Kaltenbrunner had become affiliated with one of these organizations, the Deutsch-Völkischer Turnverein, which was based in Linz. In the late 1920s, the Turnverein stood close to various right-wing paramilitary formations, including the Austrian Heimwehr; later, in the 1930s, it became a training ground for the illegal Nazi SA and SS.[6]

---

[4] E. Kaltenbrunner, "Memoir," p. 37; *Die deutsche Polizei*, 15 May 1943, p. 193, 2938-PS, IMT xxxi, p. 322; Kaltenbrunner Folder, Poole Team interrogations for the United States State Department, M-679/2, NA; Oberösterreichischer Amtskalender, *Der Oberösterreicher, 1930* (Linz: Wimmer Verlag, 1929), p. 133.

[5] E. Kaltenbrunner, "Memoir," p. 38.

[6] On Kaltenbrunner and gymnastic societies and *Turnverein*, see ibid., p. 38; interview with Otto Picha, Vienna, 26 January 1977. During the 1930s Picha rented an apartment in the building owned and lived in by the family of Elisabeth Eder, Kaltenbrunner's future wife, who, Picha states, met Kaltenbrunner at a Turnverein outing. On gymnastic societies in general, see Carsten, *Fascist Movements*, pp. 37, 39 note 14, 93. Some chilling examples of the gymnasts' anti-Semitism can be found in ibid., pp. 94-95. On contacts to the Heimwehr, see Franz

If the Turnverein attracted Kaltenbrunner, who had never been a sportsman, on account of its völkisch atmosphere, the Heimwehr movement appealed to him because of its anti-Marxist, anti-Semitic, and antidemocratic dynamism. The Heimwehr, or Heimatschutz, was the largest and most significant of the right-wing paramilitary organizations whose violent language and actions repeatedly upset the stability of the Austrian Republic. It grew out of locally organized self-defense units, which had sprung up in the Austrian countryside in the autumn and winter of 1918-1919. The impetus for forming Heimwehr units varied from province to province. In Lower Styria and Carinthia, for instance, units were organized spontaneously to fight the Yugoslavs, who were laying claim to the Klagenfurt Basin. In Linz and Graz, units were organized to combat the Socialist labor movement. In the countryside, local units protected farms and villages from plunder by marauding bands of soldiers returning from the front without supervision. Despite claims of nonpartisanship, the Heimwehr groups quickly adopted an anti-Marxist line that reflected the social and political outlook of their members: peasants, aristocrats, ex-army officers, and nationalist students. Heimwehr leaders maintained that they would defend their native districts not only from foreign invasion, but also from "Red revolution" at home.[7]

Despite a common hatred of Marxism, the Heimwehr leaders could not unify and streamline their groups into a single dynamic movement; no central leadership comparable to that of Hitler in the Nazi Party ever emerged. This was due to personal rivalries and considerable differences in ideology and aims from province to province. For example, the Styrian Heimatschutz was pan-German and völkisch in ideology—its aim was Anschluss. In Upper Austria, however, legitimist trends were discernible in the Heimatschutz, whose goal was Danubian federation. In some provinces (Tyrol and Vorarlberg), the Heimwehr was subsidized by the provincial government; in others (Upper Austria and Styria), it opposed and was mistrusted by the local authorities. Far from a unified mass movement, as was the centrally organized

---

Winkler, *Die Diktatur in Österreich* (Zurich-Leipzig: Orell Füssli Verlag, 1935), p. 31. For an example of cooperation between the Turnverein and the Heimwehr, see Slapnicka, *Bürgerkrieg*, pp. 45-46. On the SA and the SS in the Turnverein, see Sicherheitsdirektor für Oberösterreich [Hammerstein] to management of the Deutsch-Völkischer Turnverein, Sierninghofen, 16 June 1934, Bka-Inneres, 22/Oberösterreich, Box 5111, 339.798/36 (192.589/34), AVA; Landesgendarmeriekommando für Oberösterreich, "Periodische Berichterstattung für die Monate Juli und August 1933," 29 September 1933, ibid., Box 5104, 219.278/33, AVA.

[7] C. Earl Edmondson, *The Heimwehr and Austrian Politics, 1918-1936* (Athens: University of Georgia Press, 1978), pp. 19-25. See also Bruce F. Pauley, *Hahnenschwanz und Hakenkreuz: Der steirische Heimatschutz und der österreichische Nationalsozialismus, 1918-1934* (Vienna: Europa Verlag, 1972), p. 34; Ludwig Jedlicka, "The Austrian Heimwehr," in *Journal of Contemporary History*, Vol. I: *International Fascism, 1920-1945* (New York: Harper Torch, 1966), pp. 128-129; Winkler, *Diktatur*, p. 24.

Austrian Social Democratic formation, known as the *Republikanischer Schutzbund* (Republican Defense Corps), the Heimwehr remained a "federation of provincial associations,"[8] each reflecting specific political and social conditions in its province. Indeed, after 1923, disunity among the leaders and waning fear of a communist revolution led to the Heimwehr's temporary eclipse.

Continued political instability and growing tension between the Social Democrats and the Christian Social ruling coalition under the leadership of Chancellor Ignaz Seipel led to a gradual resurgence of the Heimwehr in the spring of 1927; and the explosive consequences of the Schattendorf acquittals in July of that year catapulted it into the center of the Austrian political stage. On 15 July 1927, a crowd of Social Democrats and their sympathizers set fire to the Palace of Justice in Vienna in protest against the acquittal of two members of a right-wing veterans organization accused of killing two persons during a Republican Defense Corps march in the Burgenland town of Schattendorf. The Viennese police, at the order of police chief Johannes Schober, fired indiscriminately into the crowd as the latter sought to prevent firefighters from saving the palace. Nearly one hundred people were killed. In retaliation, the Social Democratic leadership, which had not instigated or ordered the demonstration, called a one-day general strike and an unlimited transit strike in the hope of bringing the Seipel government down. Seipel thereupon permitted the Heimwehr to assist the Austrian army and police in breaking the strike, a task that Heimwehr units carried out with some savagery and much relish. The "crisis of 15 July" brought about an unexpected surge of Heimwehr power and confidence. Once more, private and public subsidies became available and, while no less a figure than Chancellor Seipel himself lauded the movement as the bulwark of democracy against "undemocratic party rule," the leaders of this "bulwark" speculated on the possibilities of overthrowing the Christian Social regime.[9]

The crisis also brought the first serious attempt to unite the provincial Heimwehr organizations under a single federal leadership (*Bundesführung*).

---

[8] Karl R. Stadler, "Austria," in *European Fascism*, ed. S. J. Woolf (New York: Vintage, 1969), p. 94. On the Heimwehr in the Tyrol and Vorarlberg, see Carsten, *Fascist Movements*, p. 111. On Styria, see Pauley, *Hahnenschwanz*, pp. 42-43; Pauley, "A Case Study in Fascism: The Styrian Heimatschutz and Austrian National Socialism," *Austrian History Yearbook*, 12-13, Part 1 (1976-1977), 255; Josef Hofmann, *Der Pfrimer-Putsch: Der steirische Heimwehrprozess des Jahres 1931* (Vienna-Graz: Stiasny Verlag, 1965), p. 9. On monarchist trends in Upper Austria, see Slapnicka, *Bürgerkrieg*, pp. 18-19. A competent history of the *Heimwehr* in the years 1923 to 1927 is offered by Edmondson, *Heimwehr*, pp. 25-40.

[9] Jedlicka, "Heimwehr," pp. 133-134; Klemperer, *Seipel*, p. 289. On the crisis and its meaning for the *Heimwehr*, see also Edmondson, *Heimwehr*, pp. 44-48; Carsten, *Fascist Movements*, pp. 110-113; Gerhard Botz, *Gewalt in der Politik: Attentate, Zusammenstösse, Putschversuche, Unruhen in Österreich, 1918-1934* (Munich: Wilhelm Fink Verlag, 1976), pp. 141-160.

Tyrolean Heimwehr leader Richard Steidl was elected federal leader (*Bundesführer*) with Dr. Walter Pfrimer, the leader of the völkisch-oriented Styrian Heimatschutz, as his deputy. To accent their growing strength and confidence, the Heimwehr leaders organized a mass march through the working-class neighborhoods of Wiener Neustadt, the stronghold of the Republican Defense Corps. On 7 October 1928, the day of the march, some 19,000 Heimwehr members appeared; two weeks later, another monster demonstration was held in the "Red capital" itself (i.e., Vienna).[10]

The Heimwehr ideology, a jumble of anti-Marxism, anti-Semitism, hatred for democracy, and belief in reorganization of society along corporate lines, was likely to appeal to a former fraternity student and member of the Student Battalion of the Styrian Heimatschutz. But Kaltenbrunner, who came into contact with the Heimwehr through the Deutsch-Völkischer Turnverein, remained aloof from it until the summer of 1929.[11] A reason for this delay may have been the fact that before 1929, the Heimwehr (or Heimatschutz) in Upper Austria had been completely dependent on the bourgeois party leaders based in Linz. Originally a haven for legitimists and advocates of Danubian federation, the Upper Austrian Heimatschutz had early on shown a marked lack of enthusiasm for the idea of Anschluss, that is, union between Austria and Germany. Unlike the Heimwehr in the Tyrol and Salzburg, the Upper Austrian organization initially rejected both arms and money coming from Bavarian paramilitary formations, such as the *Organisation Escherisch*. After the failure of Emperor-King Charles to regain his throne in Hungary in April 1921, the influence of the legitimists declined and more nationalist elements came to the fore.

Further growth of the Upper Austrian Heimatschutz was blocked by the Christian Social–controlled provincial government, whose leaders mistrusted Protestant and "Prussian" Germany and were at best lukewarm to the idea of Anschluss.[12] On 15 September 1925, after long and involved negotiations, the Upper Austrian Heimatschutz was unified under the strict control of the bourgeois bloc (Christian Socials, Pan-Germans, and Agrarian League). Thus,

[10] On Steidl election, see Carsten, *Fascist Movements*, p. 113. On demonstrations, see Hofmann, *Pfrimer-Putsch*, pp. 10-11; Botz, *Gewalt*, pp. 164-166.

[11] E. Kaltenbrunner, "Memoir," p. 38. For a brief summary of the Heimwehr ideology, see Jedlicka, "Heimwehr," passim.; Stadler, "Austria," passim.; Carsten, *Fascist Movements*, pp. 167-173.

[12] In the elections of 1919, the Christian Socials won 63 out of 101 seats in the Upper Austrian provincial assembly. From 1919 to 1925, they held 38 out of 62 seats; in 1925, they won 44 out of 60; and in 1931, 28 out of 48. See Harry Slapnicka, *Oberösterreich, 1917-1977: Karten und Zahlen* (Linz: Oberösterreichischer Landesverlag, 1977), p. 17. On refusal to accept arms and money from Bavaria, see Slapnicka, *Bürgerkrieg*, p. 18; Horst G. W. Nusser, *Konservative Wehrverbände in Bayern, Preussen und Österreich, 1918-1933* (Munich: Nusser Verlag, 1973), pp. 164-165.

in contrast to the Heimwehr in other Austrian provinces, the Upper Austrian organization was intimately tied to the System.[13]

Even after the crisis of 15 July 1927, Christian Social hostility to völkisch trends in the Upper Austrian Heimatschutz retarded the growth of the latter. Indeed, the Heimatschutz seemed so innocuous in the summer of 1928 that Republican Defense Corps leader Julius Deutsch felt obliged to remark at a Social Democratic rally in Linz that Heimwehr influence was on the decline in Upper Austria.[14] Even as late as the autumn of 1929, a police report noted that, although the Heimwehr was experiencing rapid growth, it was viewed by the politicians "as a subsidiary force which would be at the disposal of the legal government if the power of the state or the legal executive should prove insufficient."[15] As one author has phrased it, until the summer of 1929, the Upper Austrian Heimatschutz had "no separate existence, but dangled on the strings of the political parties."[16]

By the summer of 1929, however, more radical, völkisch elements in the Upper Austrian Heimatschutz were gaining the upper hand despite the efforts of the bourgeois politicians to maintain control over the movement. Since the 15 July 1927 crisis, fascist and völkisch ideas had been on the rise in Heimwehr organizations throughout Austria. The demonstration at Wiener Neustadt, for example, had been organized by the radically völkisch Styrian Heimatschutz and had enhanced the prestige of völkisch ideas in the movement at large.[17]

Moreover, not only was the Heimwehr movement growing more radical in tone, it also appeared to be on the verge of taking over the state. As long as Seipel was chancellor, the Heimwehr leaders were content merely to denounce the democratic structure of the state. After his sudden resignation on 3 April 1929, however, they feared that they had lost a protector. When Seipel's successor, Ernst Streer von Streeruwitz, rejected Heimwehr demands to take "drastic measures" to secure the state against "Bolshevism," the Heimwehr leadership initiated a campaign to torpedo the new cabinet. Heimwehr threats to "march on Vienna" did much to achieve this end. On 26 September 1929, Streeruwitz resigned and was succeeded by the police president of Vienna, Johannes Schober. Schober not only enjoyed a repu-

---

[13] The membership of the three-man chairmanship established to lead the Heimwehr in Upper Austria reflected the primacy of the politicians. Chairman was the Christian Social National Assembly deputy Balthasar Gierlinger; the Wels lawyer Dr. Franz Slama (Pan-Germans) and provincial assembly deputy Franz Meier (Agrarian League) served as deputies.

[14] *Linzer Tagblatt*, no. 73, 1928, cited in Slapnicka, *Bürgerkrieg*, p. 25. On the slow development of the Upper Austrian Heimatschutz, see Ernst Rüdiger Starhemberg, *Memoiren* (Vienna-Munich: Amalthea Verlag, 1971), p. 69.

[15] Cited in Carsten, *Fascist Movements*, pp. 130, 139.

[16] Slapnicka, *Bürgerkrieg*, p. 25.

[17] Winkler, *Diktatur*, p. 27.

tation as the "strong man of 15 July"; he also secretly agreed to implement Heimwehr suggestions for an interim dictatorship and constitutional reform by plebiscite.[18]

One factor that clearly induced Kaltenbrunner to join the Heimwehr was the spectacular rise within its ranks of Prince Ernst Rüdiger von Starhemberg, who was elected provincial leader (*Landesführer*) of the Upper Austrian Heimwehr in July 1929.[19] In addition to being the scion of one of Upper Austria's most distinguished noble families and the namesake of Count Ernst Rüdiger von Starhemberg, who defended Vienna against the Turks in 1683, Starhemberg had völkisch nationalist credentials that were beyond reproach. After serving as an officer candidate during World War I, he had joined the Tyrolean Heimwehr while a student at the university in Innsbruck. In 1921, he fought the Poles in Silesia with the *Freikorps Oberland*. Upon his return to Innsbruck, he found the Tyrolean Heimwehr "unimaginative and inert" and moved to Munich in search of more activity. On 9 November 1923, he marched with Hitler and Ludendorff to the Odeonsplatz. He returned to Austria in 1926 and joined the Upper Austrian Heimwehr shortly after the crisis of 15 July. He invested his family fortune in the growth of that organization by forming and financing Jäger battalions. His election as provincial leader of the Upper Austrian Heimwehr represented a victory for the völkisch elements in the movement and a crushing defeat for the provincial Christian Social organization. Young, radical in rhetoric and flashy in personal style, Starhemberg appealed above all to students, young professionals, and nationalist youth; one contemporary described him as the "idol of German nationalist Austria."[20]

When he joined the Heimwehr in the summer of 1929, Kaltenbrunner could not have been subject to severe economic pressure. Unlike many young professionals, he was employed; indeed, he resigned his position at the Lasser firm in order to serve the Heimwehr.[21] Since one cannot speak of the effects of the Great Depression before the autumn of 1929, Kaltenbrunner's primary motives for joining the Heimwehr appear to have been political and emotional. Politically, he applauded the growing völkisch trend in the

[18] The Heimwehr role in these events can be followed in Edmondson, *Heimwehr*, pp. 74-84; Hofmann, *Pfrimer-Putsch*, pp. 13-16; Ernst Streer Ritter von Streeruwitz, *Springflut über Österreich: Erinnerungen, Erlebnisse, und Gedanken aus bewegter Zeit, 1914-1929* (Vienna-Leipzig: Bernina, 1937), pp. 395-396.

[19] Interview with Dr. Werner Kaltenbrunner, Vöcklabruck, 25 March 1977; interview with Elisabeth Kaltenbrunner, Linz, 25 March 1977.

[20] Winkler, *Diktatur*, p. 39. On Starhemberg's election, see Anton von Rintelen, *Erinnerungen an Österreichs Weg: Versailles—Berchtesgaden—Grossdeutschland* (Munich: Verlag F. Bruckmann, 1941), p. 134; Carsten, *Fascist Movements*, pp. 131-132. On Starhemberg's background, see Starhemberg, *Memoiren*, pp. 41-68.

[21] Letter of Dr. Irmfried Latzel-Lasser to the author, 11 January 1977.

Heimwehr and perceived in it a medium through which he could fight the System and contribute to the cause of national and racial unity. Yet, in joining the Heimwehr, he also answered an emotional need. He was a lonely individual, craving companionship. In reference to his future in-laws, he made a particularly revealing remark, one of our few insights into his character: "My whole life long I was ceaselessly in need of love and support, though I let this show as little as possible."[22] His political ideals merged with an emotional need for membership in a community that would offer him the support which he so dearly craved.

Within fifteen months, however, the Heimwehr had disappointed Kaltenbrunner; he lost faith in the ability and desire of its leadership to realize the yearned-for goal of national-racial community. On 18 October 1930, he transferred his hopes to the Austrian Nazi Party; ten months later, he joined the Nazi SS. Years later, he explained to his children that he had left the Heimwehr because its leadership had been "incompetent and politically fickle" and because it "had changed from a nonpartisan, anti-Marxist movement to the political line of the Christian Socials."[23]

Indeed, by the fall of 1930, internal rivalries had caused the Heimwehr movement to splinter. Owing to the failure of its leaders to iron out personal conflicts and to form a consistently coherent policy, the movement lost its dynamism and was hampered in its efforts to block the influence of its rival on the radical right: the National Socialist Party.

Steidl sought to gloss over the fundamental ideological differences within the Heimwehr by means of a unified statement of policy. At a gathering in the Lower Austrian town of Korneuburg on 18 May 1930, he urged the Heimwehr leaders to sign an oath calling for an authoritarian, nationalist leadership, a corporate legislature organized by profession, and a society liberated from Marxism, "western democracy," and class struggle. The plan backfired, however. Vorarlberg Heimwehr leader Otto Ender refused to take the "Korneuburg Oath" on the grounds that it contradicted his oath to the constitution. Carinthian leaders agreed only to sign a watered-down version of the oath, in which the reference to dictatorship was deleted. Starhemberg himself refused to sign, declaring that the text was "really quite unclear and bombastic."[24]

The lack of a single, unified, and völkisch ideology weakened the Heimwehr in the eyes of völkisch nationalists like Kaltenbrunner. The Korneuburg Oath made no reference to Anschluss; on the contrary, its glorification

---

[22] E. Kaltenbrunner, "Memoir," p. 40.

[23] Ibid., p. 38. For dates of entry into the Nazi Party and the SS, see E. Kaltenbrunner SS File, BDC.

[24] Winkler, *Diktatur*, p. 29. The text of the Korneuburg Oath is in Jedlicka, "Heimwehr," pp. 138-139. See also Carsten, *Fascist Movements*, pp. 171-175.

of the state as the "personification of the people" both implied that there was a future for the Austrian state under a Heimwehr dictatorship and reflected the influence of Italian Fascism on Steidl's ideas.[25] Moreover, Starhemberg's political inconsistency was also disappointing, particularly for Kaltenbrunner.[26] Though the prince had condemned Steidl for his increasing dependence on Italian funds and ideas and, exploiting this issue, had usurped the national leadership of the Heimwehr at the Schladming meeting of 2 September 1930, he too had been Mussolini's honored guest in Venice during the previous July, at which time the Italian dictator offered him financial aid and military hardware. Then, in late September 1930, Starhemberg entered the cabinet of Christian Social politician Karl Vaugoin, and, after having promised Pfrimer to prevent new elections by means of coup d'état from above, reorganized the Heimwehr into a political party, the *Heimatblock*, putting forth a list of candidates to run in the elections that he had promised to prevent! Finally, though in October 1930 he negotiated with the National Socialists on a possible electoral alliance for the 9 November elections, he found their demands for subordination to Hitler and parity on the election list unacceptable and resolved to run alone despite the danger that the voting strength of the radical right would be split.[27]

By the fall of 1930, "the confusion within the Heimwehr knew no bounds." While Starhemberg set about organizing a remarkably incompetent electoral campaign, Pfrimer, who had consistently advocated nonpartisanship in electoral politics, alternated between cautious support of the prince and preparations for a putsch. Worse still was the announcement on 15 October 1930 of an electoral alliance between the Christian Socials and Heimwehr leaders Fey (Vienna), Raab (Lower Austria), and Vas (Burgenland).[28] Perhaps it was more than mere coincidence that Kaltenbrunner joined the Nazis three days later.

For the Nazis, despite Kaltenbrunner's disinterest in them as a student, offered that which he had been seeking in the Heimwehr: a völkisch ideology based on the racially "pure" community and aimed at the union of all Germans, the promise of success without compromise, and a charismatic leader

[25] Carsten, *Fascist Movements*, pp. 171-172; Jedlicka, "Heimwehr," p. 139; Edmondson, *Heimwehr*, pp. 97-103.

[26] E. Kaltenbrunner interview, Linz, 25 March 1977; W. Kaltenbrunner interview, Vöcklabruck, 25 March 1977.

[27] On the *Heimatblock*, see Winkler, *Diktatur*, pp. 31-32. On Starhemberg's negotiations with the Nazis, see Starhemberg, *Memoiren*, pp. 87-94; Charles A. Gulick, *Austria: From Habsburg to Hitler*, Vol. II: *Fascism's Subversion of Democracy* (Berkeley–Los Angeles: University of California Press, 1948), pp. 911-912; Hofmann, *Pfrimer-Putsch*, p. 28. On Starhemberg's relationship with Mussolini, see Starhemberg, *Memoiren*, pp. 76-80; Hofmann, *Pfrimer-Putsch*, p. 26.

[28] Winkler, *Diktatur*, p. 32; Hofmann, *Pfrimer-Putsch*, p. 28; Pauley, "Fascism," p. 263.

standing above all factions and lending the movement the appearance of unity. Since the Nazis had no record of cooperation with the System, their attacks on it were more credible. Moreover, they were untainted in respect to relations with the Italian Fascists, regardless of Hitler's overt admiration for Mussolini. Finally, and perhaps most important, the Nazis never wavered in their hostility to the concept of an independent Austrian state.

The Nazis' commitment to Anschluss was a determining factor in Kaltenbrunner's decision to join them. He confessed to his brother and his wife that above all he hoped for the union of Austria and Germany and believed implicitly that such a union would lead to a glorious future for the German nation. To his children, he wrote that he joined the Nazi Party in Linz because he "considered its goal to be good."[29] And if the Anschluss was all important to Kaltenbrunner, it is not difficult to imagine why he deserted the Heimwehr shortly after the announcement of three of its leaders that they would enter a coalition with the "clericalist" and "anti-völkisch" Christian Socials.

Moreover, the Nazis had just scored a tremendous success in the German Reichstag elections of 14 September 1930. From a mere 810,000 votes in the 1928 elections, they jumped to a total of 6,409,600 ballots, thus becoming the second largest party in Germany. Though factional divisions and faulty organization prevented the Nazi momentum from sweeping into Austria in the elections of November 1930 (the Austrian Nazis received but 108,000 votes, less than 3 percent of the total cast), völkisch nationalists in Austria had little reason to doubt that if the movement seized power in Germany, tiny Austria would fall into line.[30]

Economic factors appear to have played at best a secondary role in Kaltenbrunner's decision to join the Nazis. It is difficult to measure the actual effects of the Great Depression on the Kaltenbrunner family; Kaltenbrunner himself wrote that his father's ill health was the real source of financial troubles which the family may have experienced.[31] The situation could not have been desperate, however. Though Kaltenbrunner had left his job in 1929 to join the Heimwehr, his brother Werner had found a position with a law firm in Vöcklabruck and his youngest brother Roland was enjoying fraternity life at the university in Graz.[32] Given Kaltenbrunner's propensity

[29] E. Kaltenbrunner, "Memoir," p. 38; W. Kaltenbrunner interview, Vöcklabruck, 25 March 1977; E. Kaltenbrunner interview, Linz, 25 March 1977.

[30] On German elections, see Alan Bullock, *Hitler: A Study in Tyranny* (New York: Bantam, 1961), p. 128. On Austrian elections, see Carsten, *Fascist Movements*, p. 162. For a history of the Nazi Party in Austria to 1930, see ibid., pp. 31-39, 71-83, 141-166; Pauley, *Forgotten Nazis*, pp. 29-68.

[31] E. Kaltenbrunner, "Memoir," p. 38.

[32] W. Kaltenbrunner interview, Vöcklabruck, 25 March 1977.

to exaggerate economic hardship, one can view his statements in this matter with suspicion. Nevertheless, the *fear* of economic disaster and the firm belief that Austria could not weather the crisis alone might have had their effect on Kaltenbrunner's switch into the Nazi camp.

Although the dramatic Nazi surge in Germany and general economic instability in Austria may have played secondary roles in influencing Kaltenbrunner to go over to the Nazis, Heimwehr ambivalence on the Anschluss question was the decisive factor in his decision. Nor was his desertion atypical for the Upper Austrian Heimwehr: in the summer of 1932, a group of Upper Austrians under Heimatblock provincial leader Heinrich Steinsky broke with Starhemberg when the latter supported the Dollfuss government's decision to accept the Lausanne Loan from the League of Nations, in return for which a reaffirmation of Austria's agreement to renounce Anschluss was required. An Austrian police official noted laconically that the Steinsky group (which placed itself under the authority of the Styrian Heimatschutz) could not have been very large as most of the *Nationalen* in the Upper Austrian Heimwehr had already gone over to the Nazis.[33]

Membership in the Nazi Party was not enough of a commitment for the former fraternity student Ernst Kaltenbrunner. Having decided to join the movement, he wished to "be 100% National Socialist."[34] In the summer of 1931, small SS units were established in the Austrian provincial capitals and were subordinated to the leader of Hitler's bodyguard, SS-*Standartenführer* Josef (Sepp) Dietrich. While at a Nazi Party outing in Munich in early 1931, Kaltenbrunner met Dietrich, who urged him to apply for membership in the Black Order. Kaltenbrunner responded to the offer: on 31 August 1931 he was taken into the SS with the number 13,039.[35]

Kaltenbrunner found in the Nazi movement and the SS what he politically desired and emotionally needed: a world where the ideal of the racial community was prized, where the theory of racial struggle was accepted as an obvious fact, where all doubts about the meaning of existence were swept away. It has been stated that an individual who entered the Nazi Party before the Reichstag elections of 1930—that is, in the absence of terror or material rewards—voluntarily "subjected himself to the social and emotional strait-

[33] Bundespolizeidirektion Linz to Generaldirektion für die öffentliche Sicherheit, 9 September 1932, Bka-Inneres, 22/Oberösterreich, Box 5102, 205.612/32, AVA.

[34] W. Kaltenbrunner interview, Vöcklabruck, 25 March 1977.

[35] E. Kaltenbrunner SS File, BDC; E. Kaltenbrunner interview, Linz, 25 March 1977; letter of Dr. Franz Mayrhofer to the author, 27 April 1977. Mayrhofer was an acquaintance of Kaltenbrunner and a member of the Upper Austrian Nazi Party organization. On establishment of SS units, see Carsten, *Fascist Movements*, p. 204. Basic works on the SS are those by Krausnick, Höhne, Reitlinger, Neusüss-Hunkel, and Paetel (for all of which see Intro., n. 7); and Robert Koehl, "Towards an SS Typology: Social Engineers," *American Journal of Economics and Sociology*, 18 (January 1959), 113-126; and Koehl, "Character of the Nazi SS."

jacket of the totalitarian mind set."[36] That Kaltenbrunner joined the Heimwehr in 1929, seeking what he would find in the Nazi movement a year later, would suggest that he fell into this category. His political background was völkisch pan-German in content and radical in style. He had never accepted the reality of the Austrian Republic and had felt alone and lost in that world until the Heimwehr and, later, the Nazis offered him a reality more to his liking.

The Heimwehr could not compete with the Nazis' ability to maintain a consistent political myth. Though its leaders had proclaimed the Heimwehr to be above political parties, some of them formed an alliance with the "unvölkisch" Christian Socials, while others regrouped the movement into a political party for electoral purposes. Though Heimwehr leaders promised to get rid of the "gentlemen from the Far East [i.e., the Jews]," they were not above receiving funds from Jewish industrialists and bankers. Starhemberg might threaten an "Asiatic" that his head would "roll in the sand," but he could also retract his words with the lame comment that he had not wished to hurt anybody's feelings.[37] Adolf Hitler, who never would have apologized for such a remark, had a better reputation for consistency. Starhemberg never could quite decide whether he wanted to be a National Socialist, a fascist, or a Habsburg legitimist; Hitler, on the other hand, never compromised his ideological outlook for the sake of any but the briefest, most cynical cooperation with the System. In Austria, Starhemberg was willing to be vice-chancellor; in Germany, Hitler would accept nothing less than the chancellorship.

Those who joined the Nazi movement were offered "a specific subjective view of political and social reality, a view that might be termed an extreme form of political myth."[38] Hitler offered those who felt personally overwhelmed by political and social realities during the economic crisis an opportunity to reduce all their misfortunes to the simple formula that German was "good" and Jew "bad," and that if "good" won out over "bad," all would be "good." The Führer promised still more: the certainty of victory, which required only that his followers share his faith in himself as the personification of the "good" marching in time with the inevitable course of history. His basic message was simple: "What counts is will, and if our will is hard and ruthless enough, we can do anything."[39] This fixed concept with its easy answers and simple guidelines of behavior had great appeal for those who,

---

[36] Orlow, *Nazi Party, 1919-1933*, p. 3.

[37] Gulick, *Austria*, II, p. 907. On Jewish support for the Heimwehr, see Franz Borkenau, *Austria and After* (London: Faber & Faber, 1939), p. 106. On gentlemen from the Far East, see Carsten, *Fascist Movements*, p. 121.

[38] Orlow, *Nazi Party, 1919-1933*, p. 3.

[39] Bullock, *Hitler*, p. 127.

for one reason or another, did not wish to face the complicated realities of the postwar world. By accepting the National Socialist creed—or, indeed, any totalitarian creed—one could be "spared the never-ending shocks which real life and real experience deal to human beings and their expectations."[40]

If activism in the Nazi Party attracted the "marginal man"—that is, one who rejects predominant attitudes—[41] we might conclude that Austrians who joined Hitler's movement before its seizure of power in Germany were possessed of a particularly acute sense of "marginality," which in turn contributed to the radical nature of the Austrian Party. In Weimar Germany, the Nazis appeared to be the last hope for saving the state; in Austria, they were the last hope for destroying it. In Germany, the Nazis were able to attract support by identifying their aims with those of traditional German nationalism, while Nazism in Austria implied the annihilation of any Austrian identity beyond nostalgic regional attachments. Such complete rejection of existing political, cultural, and institutional standards attracted a more radical, "marginal" type to the Austrian Nazi Party.

Contrasting German and Austrian political contexts favored radicalism and marginality in those who joined the Austrian Nazi movement in the first years of the Depression. In Weimar Germany, conservative right, Catholic Center, and Social Democratic left seemed paralyzed in the face of the Nazi electoral surge after 1930. A German who went over to the Nazis after the September Reichstag elections could expect to board a bandwagon before which political and physical opposition was crumbling, to join a movement that would sweep into power with a minimum of bloodshed. In Austria, however, Conservative-Catholics and Social Democrats, protected and strengthened by their "camp" mentality, were determined to resist the Nazi thrust, even while they fought one another. Moreover, with the Heimwehr (after 1930) and the Republican Defense Corps, Christian Socials and Social Democrats could hold their own against the Nazis in the streets. Finally, in contrast to the situation in Weimar Germany, the nationalist right in Austria did not hold the reins of power and therefore could not be used as a stepping stone to a pseudolegal seizure of the state apparatus. Nazi activism in Austria carried more professional and sheer physical risk than in Germany; therefore, while the Austrian Nazi Party attracted fewer in numbers,[42] those who did join tended to be more radical in tone and action. After the establish-

[40] Arendt, *Totalitarianism*, p. 353.

[41] Daniel Lerner, "The Nazi Elite," in *World Revolutionary Elites*, ed. Harold D. Lasswell and Daniel Lerner (Cambridge: MIT Press, 1965), p. 288.

[42] In March 1930, the German Nazi Party had 210,000 members out of a population of 60 million; in September 1931, the Austrian Nazis numbered an estimated 15,000 out of a population of 6 million. See Carsten, *Fascist Movements*, p. 191; Karl Dietrich Bracher, *The German Dictatorship* (New York: Praeger, 1970), p. 167.

ment of the Christian Social dictatorship in 1933, this tendency became even more pronounced.

Radicalism and marginality in the Austrian Nazi Party were also enhanced by the borderland psychology of many of its members. Though the Habsburg Empire was gone, the presence of non-German nationalities (Czechs in the cities and in the Upper Austrian countryside; Slovenes in Styria and Carinthia; Hungarians and Croats in Vienna and the Burgenland; Italians in the Tyrol; and, above all, Jews in Vienna) continued to feed the völkisch obsession with national unity and racial purity. Hitler's own racial concept had been fashioned in old Austria; and the anxieties that helped to determine his development had not dissipated. For the Austrian Nazis, Anschluss was meaningless if not racially pure and purity impossible without Anschluss; and the decades-old anxiety about national identity gave the movement a more radical tenor.

For Ernst Kaltenbrunner, this Anschluss became a magic wand which at one stroke would solve the problems of economic (the Depression) and social (class struggle) relationships. When these questions were resolved through political unity and racial purity, a "golden age" of Germanic-Aryan culture could commence. A few hints of Kaltenbrunner's vision of the Anschluss seem to confirm this. Werner Kaltenbrunner recalled that his brother simply "wanted the Anschluss . . . yet did not know what form it should take." A former comrade from the Austrian Nazi underground movement said that, for himself, Kaltenbrunner, and the Austrian National Socialists, the Anschluss was more than merely a political goal; it was a statement of fact, even an article of faith: "With us there were no special interests. For us, Austria was a part of the German Reich, the homeland of the Führer."[43]

In the SS, an individual could find the racial "aristocracy," the "ideological nobility" of the Nazi world. The SS provided a "common internal elitist consciousness" that bound its members in service of the Führer.[44] In theory, it stood above political strife and carried out Hitler's orders without question or protest. This blind loyalty is portrayed in an SS catechism written in 1936:[45]

> Why must we be loyal?
> We must be loyal because we believe, and may
>   never betray our blood. . . .

[43] Interview with Otto Holzinger, Ried im Innkreis, 10 June 1977, Holzinger Tape, pp. 5-6. Holzinger was the leader of the SA in the Upper Austrian town of Schwanenstadt during the 1930s. See also W. Kaltenbrunner interview, Vöcklabruck, 25 March 1977; E. Kaltenbrunner interview, Linz, 25 March 1977.

[44] Ideological nobility, see Höhne, SS, p. 61; internal elitist consciousness, see Neusüss-Hunkel, SS, p. 21.

[45] "Fragen für SS Männer," 1936, T-175/155/2685453-2685467, NA.

Whom must we above all serve?
Our Volk and our Führer, Adolf Hitler. . . .
Why do you obey?
Out of inner conviction, out of belief in Ger-
    many, in the Führer, the Movement, the
    Schutzstaffel, and out of faith.

If Hitler believed himself to be guided by Providence, then the reflection of its light fell upon the SS. As an SS leader, Kaltenbrunner was more than a politician, a lawyer, or a soldier—he was part of the historical process itself.[46] He did not need to "burn all intellectual and spiritual bridges behind him" as did other SS men, for in fact, he had never constructed any meaningful ties to the political, cultural, and intellectual world of the Austrian Republic. In the SS, he found a brotherhood of others who could and would not integrate themselves into a quiet, peaceful, and "moderate" (*zivil*) life.[47] Here, the inability to adjust to postwar society was deemed a virtue and sanctioned by the highest possible authority—i.e., by Providence, or History, via the Führer. Kaltenbrunner had discovered a world where he needed only to obey in order to become part of the historical progression of mankind. He had thus clarified his ideological commitment to the abstract, mythical German nation.

[46] On Hitler's belief that he was the incarnation of a historic myth, see Robert G. L. Waite, *The Psychopathic God: Adolf Hitler* (New York: Signet, 1978), p. 96.

[47] Paetel, "SS," p. 30.

CHAPTER III

The Austrian Nazi Underground, 1931-1938

HAVING clarified his firm ideological commitment to the National Socialist world, Kaltenbrunner displayed a remarkable ability to seize political opportunities to advance his career and his influence in the Austrian Nazi Party. His political acumen served him well in lifting him from obscurity in 1931 to the leadership of the Austrian SS in 1937 and to the position of state secretary for security after the Anschluss in March 1938. This has been attributed to the fact that the leadership of the Austrian SS "fell" to him because all other ranking Austrian SS officers had been arrested by the Austrian police.[1] The situation, however, was too complicated to permit full explanation by such a handy answer, which implies that Kaltenbrunner played no active part in his rise to prominence. It will be my task to place Kaltenbrunner's rise into the context of the faction-ridden Austrian underground scene and to determine how actively he perceived and pursued opportunities for political influence and personal power.

By January 1931, Kaltenbrunner had become active as a district speaker for the Nazi Party in Upper Austria. He threw himself enthusiastically into the campaign for the approaching provincial elections, scheduled for April 1931. On 9 January, he spoke at the "Goldenes Brunnen" in Linz of the "essence and goals of National Socialism." A Nazi newspaper reported that the speech had attracted a "good crowd" and had brought in "donations and new members!" Nine days later, Kaltenbrunner spoke at a Nazi rally in Aigen. Though the Nazis were weak in this tiny hamlet located near Braunau, the *Linzer Volksstimme* proclaimed the rally a huge success, reporting that Kaltenbrunner "spoke . . . with gripping, convincing words for which the otherwise cautious peasants thanked him with heartfelt applause."[2]

[1] Hagen, *Geheime Front*, pp. 82-84; Houston, "Kaltenbrunner," pp. 52-53.
[2] "Vor den oberösterreichischen Landtagswählen," Linzer *Volksstimme*, Jahrgang 9, Folge 4, 24 January 1931, p. 9, Stadtarchiv Linz. See also Kaltenbrunner testimony, IMT XI, p. 233; E. Kaltenbrunner, "Memoir," Nuremberg, July-August 1946, p. 44, Kaltenbrunner File. The Upper Austrian peasants, however, did not translate their "heartfelt applause" into votes. The Nazis did poorly in the April elections, receiving a mere 15,800 votes (3.45%) compared with 12,127 votes (2.79%) in 1925. See Slapnicka, *Oberösterreich, 1917-1977*, p. 16. Kaltenbrunner also appears to have spoken on campaign tours throughout the Reich in 1931 and 1932. Interview with Elisabeth Kaltenbrunner, Linz, 25 March 1977; *Personal-Fragebogen*, signed by Ernst Kaltenbrunner, 30 May 1938, RG-242/290/K02696, NA.

The Upper Austrian SS which Kaltenbrunner had joined in August 1931 formed the *SS-Standarte* (Regiment) 37, which was attached to the *SS-Abschnitt* (Sector) I, based in Munich under the command of SS-Standartenführer Josef (Sepp) Dietrich. In the fall of 1931, the Austrian SS were reorganized into a separate SS-Abschnitt VIII. The Linz *SS-Sturm* (Company) itself was small and insignificant, numbering only fifty members in 1930.[3] In June 1932, former Army Major Ernst Bach, the Bavarian-born Austrian SS leader, purged and reorganized the SS-Standarte 37. The Linz SS was thoroughly regrouped; half its members were expelled as "part-timers and unreliables." At this time, it appears that Kaltenbrunner was appointed chief of the Linz SS-Sturm. An eyewitness recalls his huge, hulking form (Kaltenbrunner stood 6' 4", had a massive head and broad shoulders, and was heavyset at the hips) leading his tiny SS unit through the streets of Linz in honor of Reichstag deputy Hermann Göring and Bavarian Nazi leader Franz Ritter von Epp, both of whom visited Upper Austria in early May 1932.[4]

The Austrian SS never fell under the jurisdiction of the Austrian Nazi Party or the Austrian SA.[5] It was subordinated directly to Reichsführer SS Heinrich Himmler, who at this time was responsible to Reich SA chief of staff Ernst Röhm. Thus, from the outset, the Austrian SS developed a sense of independence vis-à-vis the Party in Austria.

As its primary task, the Linz SS guarded the headquarters of the Austrian Nazi Party, the "Brown House" in Linz.[6] Other tasks included recruitment of new members and protection of Nazi speakers at Party rallies. What this latter task often entailed is evident from the Linz *Volksgarten* riot of May 1932.[7] On 27 May 1932, having accepted a Nazi challenge to debate the

[3] In 1932, the entire Austrian SS was estimated at 2,172 members. Gerhard Jagschitz, *Der Putsch: Die Nationalsozialisten 1934 in Österreich* (Graz-Vienna-Cologne: Verlag Styria, 1976), p. 25.

[4] Conversation with Richard Bart, Linz, 31 January 1977. For the date of the Göring-Epp visit, see Slapnicka, *Bürgerkrieg*, p. 258. On reorganization of Linz and Austrian SS, see report of Bundespolizeidirektion Linz, 18 February 1933, Bka-Inneres, 22/Oberösterreich, Box 5103, 122.341/33, AVA; statistical history of the *Standarten* (Regiments) of the *Allgemeine* SS, compiled by the SS Personnel Chancellery, 21 December 1938, T-175/574/9, 145, 146, NA.

[5] Bundespolizeidirektion Linz to Generaldirektion für die öffentliche Sicherheit, 29 August 1932, Bka-Inneres, 22/Oberösterreich, Box 5102, 203.966/33, AVA.

[6] Ibid. See also report of Bundespolizeidirektion Linz, 18 February 1933, Bka-Inneres, 22/Oberösterreich, Box 5103, 122.341/33, AVA; letter of Hans Christian Seiler to the author, 17 May 1977. Seiler was a member of the Upper Austrian SA.

[7] This account is taken from the following sources: *Linzer Tagblatt*, 17 Jahrgang, nos. 122 and 123, 28 and 29 May 1932, pp. 1, 8, Stadtarchiv, Linz; *Linzer Tagespost*, no. 122, 28 May 1932, p. 4, ibid.; *Linzer Volksstimme*, Jahrgang 10, Folge 23, 4 June 1932, p. 5, ibid.; Seiler letter to the author, 17 May 1977; Bundespolizeidirektion Linz to Staatsanwaltschaft Linz, 1 July 1932, Bka-Inneres, 22/Oberösterreich, 166.246/32, AVA. The author is grateful to Richard Bart for the newspaper sources, to Dr. Gerhard Botz for the police report.

issues at the Linz Volksgarten hall, the Linz Social Democrats turned out in such numbers that the police were compelled to seal off the hall long before the arrival of the Nazis, who had meanwhile assembled in the nearby *Märzenkeller* "to avoid confrontations." At 8:00 P.M., a SS unit of twenty-five men under Kaltenbrunner's command appeared at the Volksgarten with Upper Austrian Gauleiter Andreas Bolek and the scheduled speaker, Gau Secretary Karl Doppelmayr. While Nazi and Socialist leaders negotiated points of protocol, a scuffle broke out (each side, of course, laid the responsibility at the other's door), in the midst of which a beer glass was hurled, shattering over the heads of the SS men. This was the signal for a general melee; glasses, chairs, and tables were hurled onto the podium. Though the police quickly cleared the hall, the riot spilled out onto the street; order was restored only after 11:00 P.M. that evening. Among the several who sustained injuries was Kaltenbrunner himself, who received a gash behind his left ear.

Such time- and energy-consuming activities hampered Kaltenbrunner's effectiveness in his profession. Kaltenbrunner had joined his father's firm in 1932, presumably on account of his father's illness. His brother Werner Kaltenbrunner believed that Ernst gave his father little aid, though relations between the two remained cordial. Wilhelm Höttl, a former subordinate of Kaltenbrunner in the RSHA, maintained that after the Anschluss, Kaltenbrunner senior once expressed to an acquaintance his relief that Ernst had found a position in the Austrian government, for he (Hugo) "did not wish to contemplate what would happen if his son took over the law firm."[8]

One reason why Kaltenbrunner gave little assistance to his father was that he was occupied giving free legal aid to SS men accused of criminal activities. In October 1932, SA Chief of Staff Ernst Röhm appointed legal advisers for the SA and SS in each Gau (*SA- und SS-Gruppenrechtsberater*). Their purpose was to provide immediate and free legal aid to SA and SS men arrested while performing their "duty." Kaltenbrunner was appointed SS legal adviser for SS-Abschnitt VIII. As Röhm had outlined in his decree, Kaltenbrunner's job was to see that the "SA or SS man . . . has the comforting knowledge that he will not stand totally abandoned without effective aid when authorities or courts persecute him."[9] Paul Majora, a Königsberg schoolteacher, and three companions, all members of the Königsberg SS, were able to bask in this comforting knowledge. Majora and his companions, arrested on 7 September 1932 in Linz for illegal entry into Austria, were

---

[8] The acquaintance was the then deputy provincial governor of Austria, Edmund Glaise-Horstenau. Conversation with Dr. Wilhelm Höttl, Bad Aussee, 14 April 1977. See also E. Kaltenbrunner, "Memoir," p. 47; W. Kaltenbrunner interview, Vöcklabruck, 25 March 1977.

[9] Decree of Röhm, "Richtlinien für die Rechtsschutz innerhalb der SA und SS," 7 October 1932, Aktenmappe SA, Ordner 414/415, pp. 165-166, BDC. See also testimony of Kaltenbrunner, IMT xi, p. 234.

wanted by the Prussian authorities for the murder of a Social Democratic newspaper editor in Königsberg on the night after the 31 July Reichstag elections. At first, the Austrians seemed willing to comply with the extradition request of the Prussian state attorney's office; but Kaltenbrunner and Austrian SA Legal Adviser Georg Ettinghausen intervened, arguing that the appeal be rejected on the grounds that the crime, "even if it had been committed by Majora and companions, should be appraised as a political act." The two lawyers won their point; Majora and his friends were released in December 1932. A police report noted that Kaltenbrunner had put the four men up at a guest house in Linz and arranged for their support through Nazi Party funds. On 23 December 1932, Majora and his companions crossed the border into Italy.[10]

Amidst all this political activity, Kaltenbrunner met and fell in love with Elisabeth Eder, the daughter of a well-to-do Linz grocer, Karl Eder. Born in 1908, Elisabeth came from a family whose politics were pan-German in substance but moderate in style. She met Kaltenbrunner in 1930 through a friend and married him four years later.[11]

Meanwhile, events in Austria moved quickly. On 11 July 1931, Hitler appointed a competent organizational leader, Theo Habicht, to assist the floundering *Landesleiter*,[12] Alfred Proksch, in creating order in the Austrian Nazi Party and subordinating its numerous feuding factions to a central authority. As the economic crisis deepened during the early 1930s, the National Socialists scored spectacular electoral successes in Salzburg (May 1931), Vienna, Styria, and Carinthia (April 1932). In Vienna alone, they received 201,000 votes compared to only 27,540 eighteen months earlier, and took fifteen seats on the municipal council from the Christian Socials. In the provinces, gains were made at the expense of the Heimatblock, the Pan-Germans, and the Agrarian League. On 15 May 1933 the Pan-German leaders accepted defeat and concluded a "fighting alliance" with the Nazis.[13]

---

[10] Ettinghausen to Luetgebrune [supreme legal adviser of the SA High Command], 10 October 1932, Luetgebrune Files, T-253/22/1472896-1472897, NA; *Berliner Zeitung am Mittag* (Königsberg), 17 September 1932, ibid., 1472919; Luetgebrune to Professor Freiherr von Gleispach [expert on penal law at the university in Vienna], 15 October 1932, ibid., 1472900-1472903; Kaltenbrunner to Ettinghausen, 4 November 1932, ibid., 1472909; Bundespolizeidirektion Linz to Staatsanwaltschaft Linz, 13 September 1932, Bka-Inneres, 22/Oberösterreich, Box 5102, 209.615/32, AVA; Bundespolizeidirektion Linz to Generaldirektion für die öffentliche Sicherheit, 20 and 24 December 1932, ibid., 209.615/32 (249.969/32 and 251.738/32).

[11] E. Kaltenbrunner, "Memoir," pp. 39-40, 42-44; E. Kaltenbrunner interview, Linz, 25 March 1977.

[12] When the Austrian Nazi Party accepted Hitler as its Führer in 1926, *Gau Österreich* was considered an integral *Land* (province) of the German Reich. Hence, the leader of the Austrian Party received the title *Landesleiter* and his headquarters were known as the *Landesleitung*.

[13] Carsten, *Fascist Movements*, pp. 191, 200-201; Pauley, *Forgotten Nazis*, pp. 69-84. On factional struggle within the Austrian Nazi Party before 1930 and Habicht's success in tempo-

Defeat in Vienna caused panic among the Christian Social leaders, who were determined to prevent or delay new elections that, it was feared, would erase their slim majority in the National Assembly (*Nationalrat*). On 10 May 1932, a cabinet was formed under Engelbert Dollfuss, whose decision to accept the Lausanne Loan from the League of Nations in order to alleviate the worst effects of the economic crisis was carried against the opposition of the Social Democrats and the Pan-Germans by a single vote. The margin was too narrow to permit effective government; and the chancellor was confronted with an unpleasant choice between new elections and a more authoritarian course. Fearing the results of the former, Dollfuss saw a chance to institute the latter on 6 March 1933, when all three National Assembly presidents resigned their seats over a minor issue. Dollfuss suspended the Assembly, instituted rule by emergency decree, and announced (with Heimwehr approval) the establishment of a "new, authoritarian *Ständesstaat*."[14]

The Austrian Nazis, encouraged by the results of the German Reichstag elections of 5 March 1933, sought by a campaign combining diplomatic pressure from Germany and terror tactics within Austria to force the Dollfuss government to permit new elections. Internal pressure on the government took the form of massive propaganda campaigns (films, pamphlets, and demonstrations), deliberately provoked street battles with the Heimwehr and the Republican Defense Corps, stink bomb and gasoline bomb attacks, and assassination attempts. Dollfuss, however, refused to bend under Nazi pressure. When, on 19 June 1933, two Nazis hurled hand grenades at a group of fifty-six "Christian German Gymnasts," in Krems (Lower Austria), the chancellor banned the Nazi Party and all its formations at a specially convoked cabinet session. Habicht and Proksch fled to Munich and the Austrian Nazi Party was driven underground.[15]

Surprised but still confident of Hitler's support and Dollfuss's weakness, Habicht alternately tried to negotiate and terrorize his way into power; but Dollfuss, relying on support from Italy, kept the Austrian Nazis at bay. On 1 May 1934, he instituted a new constitution, which dissolved all political parties, established an authoritarian government of "estates," and created a blanket political organization named the Fatherland Front (*Vaterländische Front*). The establishment of the Front killed Nazi hopes for new elections. When Hitler assured Mussolini on 14 June 1934 in Venice that he had no

---

rarily suppressing it, see Carsten, *Fascist Movements*, pp. 141-166, 215; Pauley, *Forgotten Nazis*, pp. 36-72.

[14] These events can be followed in: Goldinger, *Österreich*, pp. 170-171; Ulrich Eichstädt, *Von Dollfuss zu Hitler: Geschichte des Anschlusses Österreichs, 1933-1938* (Wiesbaden: Franz Steiner Verlag, 1955), pp. 16-17; Jürgen Gehl, *Austria, Germany and the Anschluss, 1931-1938* (London: Oxford University Press, 1963), pp. 42-44, 49-50.

[15] Jagschitz, *Putsch*, pp. 30-31; Pauley, *Forgotten Nazis*, pp. 107-109.

immediate interest in an Anschluss, Dollfuss appeared to be firmly in the saddle.[16]

Even before this, Austrian government pressure on the Nazis had been increasing. In the fall of 1933, "in order to secure suspected persons," the Austrian authorities established several detention camps, the most famous of which were Wöllersdorf (Lower Austria) and Kaisersteinbruch (Upper Austria).[17] In early January 1934, Kaltenbrunner learned that he would be arrested in an impending roundup. He quickly married Elisabeth Eder on 14 January; on the next day, he was arrested and sent to Kaisersteinbruch. To protest inadequate food rations, faulty sanitation facilities, and frequent mishandling of the prisoners by the Heimwehr guards, Kaltenbrunner and several of his fellow inmates organized a hunger strike in April, and demanded that all prisoners be released. State Secretary for Security Ludwig Karwinsky tried to negotiate with the strikers, but in vain; the affair continued until

---

[16] On Habicht policy, see Franz Langoth, *Kampf um Österreich: Erinnerungen eines Politikers* (Wels: Verlag Welsermühl, 1951), pp. 120-163; Dieter Ross, *Hitler und Dollfuss* (Hamburg: Leibnitz Verlag, 1966), passim. On the 1 May 1934 constitution, see Diamant, *Austrian Catholics* (see chap. 1, n. 76) pp. 256-285; Carsten, *Fascist Movements*, pp. 236-240. On the Fatherland Front, see Irmgard Bärnthaler, *Die Vaterländische Front: Geschichte und Organisation* (Vienna-Frankfurt-Zurich: Europa Verlag, 1971). On Hitler and Mussolini in Venice, see Ross, *Hitler*, p. 227.

[17] Austrian persecution of the Nazis was uneven, reaching high points between June 1933 and the civil war of February 1934 and following the Nazi putsch of July 1934. After 1933, government officials, including the police, were forbidden to join the Nazi Party and were subject to dismissal if they did so and were found out. As early as 1932, army personnel were forbidden to join military formations of the Nazi Party. After the Party was banned in June 1933, the Austrian army expelled a large number of soldiers who had belonged to the Party and had refused to resign their memberships. The number of Nazis incarcerated in prisons and detention camps reached a high point after the July 1934 putsch, tapered off slowly during 1935-1936, and then was drastically reduced after the amnesties of September and December 1936. In September 1934, 11,604 Nazis were incarcerated throughout Austria, 4,507 of them in Wöllersdorf. Two months later, the number shrank to 2,450 (1,323 in Wöllersdorf). From March 1935 until September 1936, the number of Nazis in Wöllersdorf hovered around 300, three times the number of Communists and Social Democrats combined, which fluctuated between 50 and 120 from October 1935 to December 1937. The government also persecuted Nazi activity in minor ways—through fines, investigative arrests, revocation of business and professional licenses, etc. After the 11 July 1936 Austro-German treaty, Austrian government persecution of the Nazis became halfhearted, permitting easy Nazi infiltration of the civil service and the police, though penetration of the army was relatively unsuccessful. At no time did persecution of political opponents in Austria reach the intensity achieved in Nazi Germany. For figures on arrests, see Gerhard Jagschitz, "Die Anhaltelager in Österreich," in *Vom Justizpalast zum Heldenplatz: Studien und Dokumentationen, 1927-1938,* ed. Ludwig Jedlicka and Rudolf Neck (Vienna: Druck und Verlag der österreichischen Staatsdruckerei, 1975), p. 149. On government employees, see Jagschitz, *Putsch,* p. 52. On army policy toward the Nazis, see Ludwig Jedlicka, *Ein Heer im Schatten der Parteien: Die militärpolitische Lage Österreichs, 1918-1938* (Graz-Cologne: Verlag Hermann Böhlaus, 1955), pp. 93-94.

Kaltenbrunner and several of his companions, weak from hunger, were evacuated to a hospital and released. Conceding defeat, the government released 90 percent of the Nazi prisoners and shipped the remainder along with most of the Socialist and Communist prisoners to Wöllersdorf. [18]

More significant for Kaltenbrunner's political future was his close relationship with one of his bunkmates at Kaisersteinbruch—the agricultural engineer Anton Reinthaller. Born in 1895 at Mettmach in the Upper Austrian Innviertel, Reinthaller had begun his political career in the Agrarian League and had switched over to the Nazis in 1928. As chief of the agricultural office in the Landesleitung, he ran afoul of Habicht, whose policy of terrorism he opposed on tactical grounds. Habicht tried to expel Reinthaller from the Party in 1933, but the latter's position was secured by his close contacts with Deputy Führer Rudolf Hess and German Minister of Agriculture R. Walther Darré. During the summer of 1933, Reinthaller negotiated with Dollfuss's minister of justice, Kurt von Schuschnigg, in the hope of reaching a peaceful compromise between the Nazis and the government. After his release from Kaisersteinbruch in May 1934, Reinthaller made contact with the fiercely anti-Nazi minister of trade, Friedrich Stockinger. Apparently, he had reached a tentative agreement with Stockinger concerning Nazi participation in the government: on the morning of 25 July 1934, Reinthaller had been on his way to Munich to discuss the agreement with Hess when he heard of the Nazi putsch that made the trip superfluous. [19]

While a prisoner at Kaisersteinbruch, Reinthaller befriended Kaltenbrunner and enlisted the latter's approval of his tactical line. A moderate by temperament, Reinthaller was farsighted enough to realize that the Austrian Nazis alone could not topple the Dollfuss government and that the hands of the German government were tied by Italy's hostile attitude to the Anschluss. Perhaps it was under Reinthaller's influence that Kaltenbrunner refrained from participation in the putsch of 25 July 1934. [20]

On that day, the Viennese SS-Standarte 89, under the command of SS-

[18] On Kaltenbrunner's arrest and the hunger strike, see E. Kaltenbrunner, "Memoir," p. 45; testimony of Kaltenbrunner, IMT XI, pp. 326-327; testimony of Ludwig Karwinsky before the Vienna Supreme Court, 15 October 1945, 3843-PS, IMT XXXIII, pp. 207-210; article in *Die deutsche Polizei*, 15 May 1943, 2938-PS, IMT XXXI, p. 322; letter of Otto Holzinger to the author, 10 May 1977; interview with Otto Holzinger, Ried im Innkreis, 10 June 1977, hereafter Holzinger Tape, pp. 1-4. Though not particularly harsh by the standards of Nazi concentration camps, conditions in Kaisersteinbruch were unusually grim by Austrian standards, particularly with regard to sanitation and mistreatment of prisoners by camp personnel. See Jagschitz, "Anhaltelager," p. 142.

[19] Wolfgang Rosar, *Deutsche Gemeinschaft: Seyss-Inquart und der Anschluss* (Vienna-Frankfurt-Zurich: Europa Verlag, 1971), pp. 73-75; Eichstädt, *Dollfuss*, p. 73; Riehl to Emil Fey [Austrian vice chancellor], 29 January 1934, in Winkler, *Diktatur*, p. 93.

[20] Holzinger Tape, pp. 1-2, 8-9; testimony of Kaltenbrunner, IMT XI, p. 235.

Standartenführer Fridolin Glass and with the knowledge of the Landesleit-ung in Munich, occupied the federal chancellor's office in the hope of forc-ing the Dollfuss government to resign. Unfortunately for the conspirators, most of the cabinet members, having been warned, had departed, and Glass's men killed Dollfuss instead of capturing him. The putsch itself was badly bungled; its leaders were unable to get into the federal chancellor's office and the SA in Vienna refused to support its rival, the SS. In Carinthia, Styria, and Upper Austria, local SS and SA units fought the army and the Heimwehr until 27 July; but the regime, though shaken by Dollfuss's death, prevailed.[21]

The July putsch had two major consequences for the Austrian Nazi Party. First, the fiasco had embarrassed and frightened Hitler. Not only did the international scandal provoked by the murder of Dollfuss jeopardize his plans for German rearmament; it also prompted an enraged Mussolini to rush four Italian divisions to the Brenner Pass in preparation for a conflict that Hitler could not and did not want to fight. To alleviate the crisis, the Führer summoned his former vice-chancellor, Franz von Papen (who, incidentally, had narrowly escaped murder by the SS during the Röhm purge of 30 June 1934), to Bayreuth and appointed him "special ambassador" to Austria with the task of smoothing over relations with Dollfuss's successor, Kurt von Schuschnigg. Papen insisted that Hitler remove Habicht, dissolve the Lan-desleitung in Munich, and forbid agencies of the Reich to interfere in Aus-trian affairs. After some resistance, Hitler agreed. On 3 August, the Führer's deputy, Hess, issued two decrees: the first dissolved the Landesleitung in Munich and entrusted its dissolution to a settlement center (*Abwicklungs-zentrum*) under *SS-Brigadeführer* Alfred Rodenbücher; the second ordered all Reich Nazis to break off contact with the Austrian Party. As Hess ex-plained to émigré Alfred Frauenfeld, the Führer wished to change tactics, to follow a "perfectly legal course" that would bring the Austrian Nazis to power peacefully: "it was now a matter for the Nazis in Austria alone to decide in what form they could build up a purely Austrian party."[22]

Hitler's tacit acceptance of Austrian independence created a situation in which the Austrian Nazi leaders, too weak to topple the Schuschnigg gov-ernment alone and unable to count on German support for terror tactics,

---

[21] For an exhaustive treatment of the putsch, see Jagschitz, *Putsch*. For the Nazi version, see Bericht der Historischen Kommission des Reichsführers SS, *Die Erhebung der österreichischen Nationalsozialisten im Juli 1934*, ed. Fritz Klenner, Hans Oprecht, and Erich Pogats (Vienna-Frankfurt-Zurich: Europa Verlag, 1965).

[22] Hess to Frauenfeld, 21 August 1934, *Documents on German Foreign Policy, 1918-1945* (*DGFP*), Series C, Vol. III (Washington: U.S. Government Printing Office, 1959), no. 173, pp. 352-353; two decrees of Hess, 3 August 1934, Aktenmappe Österreich, Ordner 303, pp. 11, 15, BDC; Franz von Papen, *Memoirs* (New York: E. P. Dutton, 1953), pp. 340-341.

had to advance their cause by seeking some form of working agreement with Schuschnigg. This factor cast those who had previously opposed Habicht's policies into the forefront of the negotiations with the regime.

A second post-putsch development was the temporary disintegration of the underground movement. The old guard of the Austrian Party was either in Germany or in hiding; newer faces, unknown to the regime, appeared in leadership functions. Factional conflicts grew more severe; none of the new leaders had Hitler's endorsement, for that would have constituted an "interference" in Austrian affairs. Finally, Austrian police pressure made communications and cooperation between the Gau organizations more difficult. A Nazi leadership meeting held at Innsbruck in December 1934 reflected the confusion and vindictive bickering rampant within the Austrian Nazi Party. Leaders from the provinces accused their Viennese comrades of having lured them into a mismanaged putsch and demanded a basic reorganization of the movement. SS and SA blamed one another respectively for the instigation or betrayal of the putsch. Many Austrian Nazis were bitter at the Reich Germans for not coming to their aid in July. A Styrian representative went so far as to announce that "an 'Austrian Nazi Party' should be established, if Germany was not in a position to give sufficient aid to her Austrian brothers."[23]

The failure of the putsch and the removal of the old-guard leadership left the field open for Reinthaller's so-called Reconciliation Action (*Befriedigungsaktion*). Reinthaller had excellent connections with the Upper Austrian provincial government through "independent" nationalists such as former Pan-German politician Franz Langoth and military archivist Edmund von Glaise-Horstenau; and, as we have seen, he had talked with Schuschnigg himself in 1933. Thus, when the new chancellor began to explore possibilities of reconciliation with the German nationalist population, he saw the Reinthaller Action as an agreeable prospect.

Reinthaller's basic concept required that the Austrian Nazis manage their own affairs without Reich German aid or influence. He viewed violence as politically inexpedient, favoring instead the creation of a "legal national opposition which is conscious of its responsibility to Volk and State." He proposed to organize all German nationalist forces in Austria into a single "National Opposition" under the direction of the so-called "National Action," a leadership coterie which would insure that the opposition maintained "full independence and autonomy" from German influence. Members of the National Action, representing Nazis, Pan-Germans, Agrarians, and independ-

---

[23] Report of Bundespolizeidirektion Wien [Skubl], 6 January 1935, Bka-Inneres, 22/general, Box 4913, 302.044/35 (301.117/35), AVA. On despair and confusion in the Austrian Nazi Party, see report of Muff [German military attaché in Vienna], 9 August 1934, T-77/900/5653391-5653394, NA.

ents, would publicly reject the use of violence as a means to achieve political ends and would aim at corporate entry into the Fatherland Front as a symbol of their commitment to Austrian independence and self-sufficiency. In return, the Austrian government was expected to cease all police persecution of the National Opposition and to insure "genuine freedom of action on the basis of National Socialist ideals." The National Action also demanded a revision of the 1 May 1934 constitution, confirmation of that revision by plebiscite, and positions of influence in the government. In August 1934, Reinthaller presented his formula to Schuschnigg, predicting internal reconciliation and satisfactory relations between Austria and the German Reich by 1 November 1934.[24]

The emphasis on corporate entry into the Fatherland Front reflected Reinthaller's concern to pull the confused and divided Nazi Party together by legalizing it and its formations. The underground organization would remain at the core of the National Opposition, while "respectable" nationalists would present a legitimate facade for the Austrian authorities.[25]

The significance of the Reconciliation Action for Kaltenbrunner's career lay in the opportunities it provided for making political contacts. In the late summer of 1934, Kaltenbrunner served as Reinthaller's secretary and met moderate nationalists such as Franz Langoth, the former director of security in Upper Austria; Hermann Neubacher, a brilliant economist who had good contacts with Prussian Minister President Hermann Göring; and the Viennese lawyer Arthur Seyss-Inquart, who enjoyed the personal confidence of Schuschnigg himself.[26] These moderates advocated that German unity be achieved in an evolutionary fashion and expected that its accomplishment would modify the harshness of the Nazi regime in Germany through an infusion of the "special Austrian character." Such contacts were to become useful to Kaltenbrunner in the ensuing years.

In the light of Kaltenbrunner's previous and subsequent career, it is likely that his support of Reinthaller was purely tactical. While Reinthaller's moderation was foreign to the former fraternity student and future RSHA chief, Kaltenbrunner recognized the validity of the argument that, given the present political situation, the Nazis in Austria needed a moderate front.

[24] Reinthaller Reconciliation Program, included in report of Prinz zu Erbach [German Embassy in Vienna], 18 October 1934, T-77/900/5653807-5653819, NA. See also Langoth, *Kampf*, pp. 181-207.

[25] German Embassy in Vienna [Prinz zu Erbach] to the German Foreign Office, 18 October 1934, T-77/900/5653798, NA.

[26] W. Kaltenbrunner interview, Vöcklabruck, 25 March 1977; E. Kaltenbrunner interview, Linz, 25 March 1977; testimony of Kaltenbrunner, IMT xi, pp. 234-235; testimony of Seyss-Inquart, IMT xvi, pp. 77-78; testimony of Neubacher, IMT xi, p. 423. On Neubacher, see Harry R. Ritter, "Hermann Neubacher and the Austrian Anschluss Movement, 1918-1940," *Central European History*, 8 (December 1975), 348-369.

Kaltenbrunner's commitment to the underground movement remained firm. While serving as Reinthaller's secretary, it is more than likely that he was clandestinely regrouping the SS-Standarte 37. After the collapse of the July putsch, the Austrian SS was reorganized into an *SS-Oberabschnitt Donau* (Main Sector Danube); the old *SS-Abschnitt* VIII now comprised merely the SS-Standarten 37 (Linz) and 52 (Krems, Lower Austria). In November 1934, the police reported that Upper Austrian SA units were being purged and reorganized under the cloak of the Reinthaller action; Wilhelm Höttl, who later knew Kaltenbrunner well, deems it certain that the latter was doing the same for the SS-Standarte 37. Significantly, a statistical history of the SS-Standarten compiled in 1938 lists Kaltenbrunner as chief of the SS-Standarte 37 after July 1934.[27]

It is hardly surprising, then, that Schuschnigg began to entertain serious doubts about some of Reinthaller's followers. In mid-September 1934, he rejected Reinthaller's plan for corporate entry into the Fatherland Front and demanded that prominent moderates in the National Opposition enter the Front as individuals and work out a genuine compromise. Fearing accusations of betrayal from the underground leaders, Reinthaller refused. Schuschnigg drew the consequences; on 10 October he issued a decree prohibiting the National Action.[28]

Seven months later, in the spring of 1935, Kaltenbrunner was arrested on suspicion of high treason. Accused of spreading Nazi propaganda in the army, he was committed to a military tribunal in Wels. The case collapsed for lack of evidence, however, and Kaltenbrunner was convicted only of membership in the illegal SS. He was sentenced to six months' imprisonment and his license to practice law was revoked.[29] Although many Austrian Nazis who were imprisoned or lost their jobs on account of their illegal activities emigrated to Germany, Kaltenbrunner told an acquaintance in 1935 that Himmler himself had ordered him to remain in Austria. The origins and nature of Kaltenbrunner's relationship to Himmler at this time remain unclear, but the fact that Himmler appointed Kaltenbrunner chief of SS-Abschnitt VIII (Upper and Lower Austria) in the fall of 1935 indicates that

---

[27] Bundespolizeikommissariat Steyr to Generaldirektion für die öffentliche Sicherheit, 11 November 1934, Box 305, 30.514-13/35 (II/N-284/3/34), p. 46, NPA; interview with Dr. Wilhelm Höttl, Bad Aussee, 14 and 15 April 1977, hereafter Höttl Tape, p. 4; statistical history of the Standarten of the Allgemeine SS, compiled by the SS Personnel Chancellery, 21 December 1938, T-175/574/135, 136, 137, 162, NA.

[28] Excerpts of decree of the Federal Chancellor's Office, 10 October 1934, T-77/900/5653806, NA; circular no. 7 of the National Action [signed Franz Schmied] to National Action agents in Lower Austria, 12 October 1934, ibid., 5653820.

[29] *Die deutsche Polizei*, 15 May 1943, 2938-PS, IMT XXXI, p. 322; E. Kaltenbrunner interview, Linz, 25 March 1977; W. Kaltenbrunner interview, Vöcklabruck, 25 March 1977; testimony of Kaltenbrunner, IMT XI, p. 235.

the Reichsführer SS saw in Kaltenbrunner a useful associate for strengthening the position of the SS in Austria even at this early date.[30]

While Kaltenbrunner sat in prison, the illegal underground Nazi apparatus had been undergoing a thorough reorganization, which in turn changed its character. In January 1935, the police reported extensive purges in the SA; apparently the new Standarten were small and autonomous. As opposed to mass demonstrations and terror, Party leaders appeared more concerned with intelligence and infiltration of government organizations. As one authority has put it, "the Nazi Party in Austria was transformed from a mass party into an elite and cadre party."[31]

Factional quarrels continued to hamper the activities of the underground. In the spring of 1935, adherents of two rival groups denounced each other's leaders to the police, and for a brief spell, the movement was again leaderless. A small group of young unknowns from the Carinthian Gau leadership filled the temporary vacuum of power. Hubert Klausner, a former army major, had become Gauleiter in 1933 after extensive arrests had decimated the Carinthian Nazi organization. His adviser in political matters was Friedrich Rainer. Born in 1903 in the tiny Carinthian town of Saint Veit, Rainer had joined the Nazi Party in October 1930. Like Kaltenbrunner, he had studied law at the university in Graz; it is possible that the two men knew one another there. Rainer's task was to keep in touch with all provincial underground organizations; he has been referred to as the "foreign minister" of the Carinthian Gau leadership. In this capacity, he had close contact with Kaltenbrunner.[32]

The contact between Klagenfurt (the Carinthian capital) and the Reich was upheld by the Trieste-born Odilo Globocnik. A timber merchant by profession, Globocnik had contact with SS-Gruppenführer Reinhard Heydrich, the chief of the SD, as early as December 1934. Globocnik was a

---

[30] Letter of Dr. Franz Mayrhofer to the author, 27 April 1977; statistical history of the Standarten of the Allgemeine SS, compiled by the SS Personnel Chancellery, 21 December 1938, T-175/574/137, NA. According to one author, Kaltenbrunner had contact with Himmler as early as 1935. See Slapnicka, *Bürgerkrieg*, p. 197.

[31] Gerhard Jagschitz, "Zwischen Befriedung und Konfrontation: Zur Lage der NSDAP in Österreich 1934 bis 1936," in *Das Juliabkommen von 1936: Vorgeschichte, Hintergründe und Folgen* (Vienna: Verlag für Geschichte und Politik, 1977), p. 169; report of Generaldirektion für die öffentliche Sicherheit, 30 January 1935, Bka-Inneres, 22/general, Box 4914, 302.051/ 35, AVA.

[32] On career of Rainer, see Rainer SS File, BDC. On Kaltenbrunner and Rainer, see Höttl Tape, p. 6; interview with Leopold Tavs (the Gauleiter of Vienna between 1936 and 1938), Vienna, 21 January 1977, Tavs Tape, pp. 1-2; W. Kaltenbrunner interview, Vöcklabruck, 25 March 1977. According to Höttl, Rainer and Kaltenbrunner met through Heydrich. See Höttl-Rosar interview, 11-12 April 1967, Höttl File, IfZ Vienna.

frequent visitor to Munich; between January and October 1934, he traveled to the Bavarian capital no fewer than seven times.[33]

Rainer and Globocnik were among the first in the underground Nazi organization to realize that Hitler really preferred a nonviolent policy regardless of Schuschnigg's reluctance to negotiate with the Nazis. As Rainer later stated, the "Carinthians" proposed "on the one hand to win the population over to the National Socialist idea by means of illegal organizations, which are to be developed on a selective basis, and on the other hand to make use of all political opportunities that might arise."[34] Like Reinthaller, they refused to relinquish control of the illegal organization, but they were willing to conceal its existence behind a smoke screen of "respectable" nationalists and to wait patiently for a change of course in Berlin.

In the summer of 1936, Arthur Seyss-Inquart agreed to represent the overt interests of the Rainer circle, while the latter concealed any information about the illegal organization that Seyss-Inquart did not need to know. Seyss-Inquart's negotiations with Schuschnigg were geared toward the latter's original offer to Reinthaller: that individuals of the National Opposition accept the independence of the Austrian state and be taken into the Fatherland Front as representatives of a German national policy. Rainer and Globocnik deemed this acceptable at least until the Reich grew strong and secure enough to put pressure on the Austrian regime again. The deepening estrangement of Italy from the Western Powers as a result of the war in Ethiopia promised that such hopes would eventually be realized.

Rainer was not only concerned about making contact with the Austrian government via Seyss-Inquart; he also wanted Berlin to endorse his and Seyss-Inquart's efforts. To achieve this, he depended on the embryonic Austrian SD, through which he maintained contact with Himmler, Heydrich, and Göring. The liaison contacts were a small group of students who formed an SD cell at the university in Vienna; Kajetan Mühlmann, an art historian who had good relations with Göring and Heydrich; and Ernst Kaltenbrunner, who linked Rainer to Himmler and Heydrich.[35]

Kaltenbrunner was in an excellent position to present Rainer's case in the Reich by virtue of his position as chief of the SS in Upper and Lower

[33] On Globocnik and Heydrich, see Richard Moschner, *Kärnten—Grenzland im Süden* (Berlin: Junker and Dünnhaupt Verlag, 1940), p. 33. On Globocnik's visits to Munich, see police report on the activities of the Carinthian Nazi Party, 14 May 1935, Box 305, 34.021-13/35, NPA.

[34] Speech of Friedrich Rainer, "Der Nationalsozialismus in Österreich von der Juli-Erhebung des Jahres 1934 bis zur Machtübernahme am 11. März 1938," Klagenfurt, 11 March 1942, 4005-PS, IMT xxxiv, p. 15. See also Rosar, *Seyss-Inquart*, p. 89.

[35] Rosar, *Seyss-Inquart*, p. 92. For a summary of Rainer's aims, see unsigned memorandum (presumably written by Globocnik and hereafter cited as Globocnik Memo), n.d. [May 1938], T-84/16/44272-44276, NA.

Austria. Shortly after the July 1934 putsch, the Austrian SS had been in a state of "complete dissolution." A special commission based in Munich under *SS-Obergruppenführer* Alfred Biegler carried out a thorough purge; some 40 percent of the members were expelled. The survivors were divided into two groups: a "battle troop" numbering some five hundred men and acting as the "front line" of the SS; and a "reserve troop" numbering fifteen hundred and prepared to replace those in the front line who might be arrested or forced to flee to Germany. Three tasks were given to the Austrian SS: (1) to protect individual Nazi leaders; (2) to observe and report on activities of both the underground Nazi Party and the Austrian police and military establishments; and (3) to report on the general moods and attitudes of the Austrian population.[36]

Moreover, the SS in Austria had a unique relationship to authorities in the Reich after July 1934. Though Landesleitung, SA, and Hitler Youth had been cut loose from their Reich counterparts, "the SS alone remained for the future subordinated to the supreme SS command in Berlin, since it was tactically impossible to create a supreme SS command in Austria during the period of illegality."[37] The Austrian police were aware of the special command structure within the SS and the dangers that it presented. A police report of November 1936 noted that "the activity of the SS is all the more dangerous, since it strives by all means to hide and camouflage its organization and activity from the public and because in it are united . . . the most radical and, from the standpoint of the Nazi Party, the most reliable elements."[38]

In order to report to his superiors in the SS, Kaltenbrunner quickly found it convenient to ignore the leader of the Austrian SS, *SS-Oberführer* Karl Taus, who was based in Styria. From his headquarters in Linz, the Upper Austrian SS leader traveled frequently to Germany, often illegally, and reported directly to Himmler, Heydrich, and the chief of the SD foreign intelligence office, SS-Standartenführer Heinz Jost. In the German railroad station at Salzburg, Kaltenbrunner had a contact named Ludwig Hoffmann who arranged for him to return to Austria hidden in the cab of a locomotive. At the border near Passau, he was aided by a criminal police inspector named

---

[36] Report of Generaldirektion für die öffentliche Sicherheit, 14 December 1934, Bka-Inneres, 22/general, Box 4913, 302.044/35 (303.514/35, 301.117/35), AVA. On complete dissolution, see testimony of SS-Sturmführer Ferdinand Schmied in Bundespolizeidirektion Linz to Staatsanwaltschaft Linz, 12 March 1936, Bka-Inneres, 22/Oberösterreich, Box 5112, 317.512/36, AVA.

[37] Report of Bundespolizeidirektion Wien [signed Skubl], 6 January 1935, Bka-Inneres, 22/general, Box 4913, 302.044/35 (301.117/35), AVA.

[38] Generaldirektion für die öffentliche Sicherheit, "Lagebericht über den Monat Oktober 1936," 30 November 1936, ibid., 302.048/36 (G. D. 328.065 St. B.). See also ibid., "Mai 1935," 30 June 1935, 302.048/35 (G. D. 336.279 St. B.).

Meindl. In addition, he could also stow away on a Danube barge docking at Linz en route to Passau.[39] Later, he was able to use his contacts with the Austrian authorities to obtain exit visas.

Nor did Kaltenbrunner go empty-handed to Germany. He often carried with him detailed reports from the Austrian Nazi underground. By the fall of 1936, he was able to bring Himmler photographs of confidential documents on Austrian foreign policy. These were taken by members of the Nazi Security Service (SD) in Vienna, who had a contact in the confidential mail division of the Austrian Foreign Ministry, and they were sent to Germany either by direct courier to Munich or via Kaltenbrunner in Linz. Though the latter actually had little to do with the formation of the SD in Vienna, he appears to have skillfully impressed Himmler with the belief that the Vienna spy network was "his" work.[40]

Kaltenbrunner used his contacts with Heydrich and Himmler to make Rainer and Seyss-Inquart "presentable" in Berlin, while Mühlmann worked on Göring.[41] As the Rainer-Seyss coalition began to achieve results in negotiations with Schuschnigg during 1937, those who had backed it against other factions gained increased prestige in Berlin despite their weak popular backing in the Austrian Nazi underground. Thus Kaltenbrunner's contacts with Berlin increased his value for Rainer and Seyss-Inquart, while his good relations with the latter further strengthened his position in the Reich.

His position in the SS brought Kaltenbrunner other benefits and duties. From 1936 on he received a regular salary from the Austrian Relief Office (*Hilfswerk*) in Berlin on direct orders from Himmler. He also distributed illegal Hilfswerk funds from Germany to various underground leaders in Austria and used these channels to pass on secret orders from the Reich. The Austrian police suspected him of using contacts in Germany to get jobs for Austrian Nazi fugitives.[42] His brother Werner, who had joined a law firm in Vöcklabruck in 1931, arranged for secret meetings between Kalten-

---

[39] Affidavit of Wilhelm Höttl, 10 October 1945, 1746-PS, exhibit B, pp. 8-10; E. Kaltenbrunner interview, Linz, 25 March 1977; letter of Picha to the author, 17 February 1976.

[40] Höttl Tape, p. 5; affidavit of Höttl, 10 October 1945, 1746-PS, exhibit B, p. 10.

[41] Rosar, *Seyss-Inquart*, p. 92.

[42] On Hilfswerk salary, see letter of Alfred Rodenbücher (chief of the Hilfswerk office in Germany from 1935 to 1937) to the author, 13 March 1977; Alfred Persche, "Hauptmann Leopold: Der Abschnitt 1936-1938 der Geschichte der nationalsozialistischen Machtergreifung in Österreich," n.d., 1460/1, DöW. On distribution of funds and finding positions, see police report, 22 May 1937, Box 307, 40.239-13/37, NPA; letter of Picha to the author, 17 February 1976; Kaltenbrunner to Keppler, 3 September 1937, T-120/751/344886, NA. On the purpose and history of the illegal Hilfswerk, see Schmidt-Scharf and Bogner [Nazi Party Reichsleitung], "Revisionsbericht vom 11.11.38 über das illegale Hilfswerk für Österreich," 11 March 1938, Hanns Rauter SS File, BDC. On secret orders from the Reich, see affidavit of Höttl, 10 October 1945, 1746-PS, exhibit B, p. 10.

brunner and the leadership of the Salzburg SS,[43] which enabled Kaltenbrunner to gather intelligence from and pass on orders to the SS organizations in Austria's Alpine provinces.

Fourteen months after his release from prison, in January 1937, Kaltenbrunner was appointed chief of the SS-Oberabschnitt Donau—of the entire Austrian SS.[44] The reason for the appointment must be sought in the secret "Gentlemen's Agreement" appended to the Austro-German Treaty of 11 July 1936.

Largely as a result of efforts by Special Ambassador Franz von Papen, Schuschnigg was prepared to sign a formal agreement with the German Reich in the summer of 1936. The treaty was cordial but vague; in a secret appendix, however, the Austrian chancellor promised concessions to the National Opposition in return for Hitler's public recognition of Austria's independence and renunciation of any right to interfere in her internal affairs. Schuschnigg agreed to reassess Austria's foreign policy "with due consideration for the peaceful aspirations of the foreign policy of the German Reich." This provision in effect ended Austrian independence in foreign affairs. The most significant of Schuschnigg's concessions were a general political amnesty and the oft-disputed clause 11b, which provided that "representatives of the hitherto existing, so-called 'National Opposition' will be called upon to accept political responsibility, whereby it will be a question of individuals who enjoy the personal confidence of the federal chancellor and whose selection the federal chancellor reserves for himself."[45]

In short, Schuschnigg had agreed to take "respectable" nationalists into the Austrian government. This suited Hitler perfectly. He needed peace in Austria until the Reich was strong enough to follow a more aggressive foreign policy, and clause 11b afforded him a lever with which he could pressure Schuschnigg into further concessions when the time was ripe. On 16 July 1936, five days after the treaty was signed, the Führer ordered Rainer and Globocnik, who had come to Berchtesgaden for instructions, to refrain from all illegal activity, and advised them to join the Fatherland Front.[46] Likewise, other German leaders counseled caution to their Austrian followers. In December 1936, an official in the Austrian ministry of defense noted that the Germans were advising the Austrian Nazis "to do all [they could] *to*

---

[43] *Personal-Fragebogen*, signed by Werner Kaltenbrunner, 30 May 1938, RG-242/490/K02738, NA.

[44] Statistical history of the Standarten of the Allgemeine SS, compiled by the SS Personnel Chancellery, 21 December 1938, T-175/574/136, NA; excerpt from the *Völkischer Beobachter* (Vienna), 2 July 1938, E. Kaltenbrunner SS File, BDC.

[45] The text of the Gentlemen's Agreement can be found as Keppler Document 114, TWC XII, pp. 682-685.

[46] Rainer Speech, 4005-PS, IMT XXXIV, pp. 16-17.

prevent all possible actions of the SS, the SA, and the Hitler Youth, and *to maintain order*" (emphasis in the original).[47]

Himmler's sudden concern about arrests of his SS men reflected these changed conditions; he had not forgotten the fiasco of 1934. As early as June 1936, the security director for Upper Austria reported to Vienna that the SS in Vöcklabruck had received orders "to stand well with the authorities, to carry out no actions." In November, a Villach (Carinthia) lawyer wrote to the general secretary of the Fatherland Front that the local SS command had issued strict orders forbidding SS men to bear weapons or to participate in demonstrations or military exercises; punishment for disobedience would be expulsion from the SS. In December, the SS-Standarte 89 in Vienna was ordered to suspend "all actively hostile actions against the ruling oligarchy." One month earlier, the illegal Landesleitung in Vienna issued general orders that all Party, SA, and SS leaders "ruthlessly combat and eliminate all efforts at destruction, instigation [of disturbances], or putsch-making . . . as these [actions] serve powers hostile to Germany."[48] Despite these orders, some SS in Vienna staged an impotent but noisy anticlerical demonstration in late December.[49] Two weeks later, Himmler appointed Kaltenbrunner chief of the Austrian SS.

Though Kaltenbrunner's reputation as an intelligence expert and his good relations with the Carinthians and the moderate nationalists contributed to Himmler's decision, there was a more immediate reason for the appointment: Himmler needed a strong leader able to keep the Austrian SS units from disturbing the peace that Hitler desired in Austria and had endorsed by the treaty of 11 July 1936.

Kaltenbrunner's predecessor, the Styrian-born SS-Oberführer Karl Taus, was apparently not doing the job. Taus was not in jail at the time of Kaltenbrunner's appointment, he was in Germany. At the end of January 1937, Himmler ordered him not to return to Austria.[50] A glance at Taus's post-

[47] Note from the Bundesministerium für Landesverteidigung [signed Dr. Weiser], 30 December 1936, Box 307, 34.575-13/37, NPA.

[48] Sicherheitsdirektor für Oberösterreich [signed Kissling] to Generaldirektion für die öffentliche Sicherheit, 16 June 1936, Bka-Inneres, 22/Oberösterreich, Box 5112, 338.261/36, AVA; Möbius to Zernatto, 23 November 1936, ibid., 22/general, Box 4972, 373.095/36; Standartenbefehl der SS-Standarte 89, appended to report of the Generaldirektion für die öffentliche Sicherheit, 15 December 1936, ibid., 375.199/36; "Weisungen an das gesamte Führerkorps der PO, SA und SS," November 1936, appended to report of the Sicherheitsdirektor für Oberösterreich to the Generaldirektion für die öffentliche Sicherheit, 19 November 1936, ibid., 22/Oberösterreich, Box 5113, 370.560/36.

[49] Notice of Generaldirektion für die öffentliche Sicherheit, 30 December 1936, Box 307, 34.707-13/37, NPA.

[50] Führer der SS-Sammelstelle to the Reichsführer SS, 8 February 1937, Karl Taus SS File, BDC.

1937 record suggests a reason for this. In February 1937, he was assigned to the commander of SS-Oberabschnitt Fulda-Werra. His superior there reported that Taus was a "decent character," but was much too "passive" and "weak"; he needed to show more authority. In 1938, Taus had the dubious distinction of serving as a concentration-camp administrator at Dachau and Buchenwald. SS-Oberführer Hans Loritz, commandant at Dachau, wrote that Taus was "a good comrade, but much too weak." Karl Koch, Taus's superior at Buchenwald, was also disappointed. He remarked that Taus was "vain" and "soft" and warned against employing him in the concentration-camp system, for, once among his "countrymen" (i.e., Austrians), he was incapable of resisting their most passing whims. SS-Obergruppenführer Theodor Eicke, the inspector of the concentration camps, evaluated Taus as "neither qualified nor able to be employed as a responsible SS leader in a concentration camp."[51] It now becomes apparent why Taus was removed; he was simply unable to keep his subordinates in line.

Kaltenbrunner's appointment was, then, not merely a happenstance caused by the arrest of his superiors.[52] Kaltenbrunner was well suited for the position—and not least by his skill in the game of personal politics. His contacts through Rainer to the Carinthians and Seyss-Inquart were excellent. His good relations with Upper Austrian moderates like Reinthaller, Langoth, and Glaise-Horstenau promised potential contacts with the Upper Austrian provincial government, a useful asset in the "atmosphere of 11 July." In addition, he had the reputation of being an expert in intelligence operations, a key function of the SS in Austria. His easy access to Germany assured Himmler and Heydrich that they would receive information on Austrian affairs rapidly and efficiently. Finally, Himmler saw in Kaltenbrunner a personality strong enough to hold the SS units to a nonviolent course; this is the true significance of the label given to Kaltenbrunner by Seyss-Inquart at Nuremberg, "the policeman of 11 July."[53]

As soon as he was appointed chief of the Austrian SS, Kaltenbrunner was thrown into the factional struggle raging within the Nazi Party. After 11 July 1936—as before—standing in the Austrian Nazi underground depended on the endorsement of Hitler; but Hitler refused to choose one rival over the others. He merely set down the basic guidelines that the Austrian Nazis must drop terror tactics and negotiate a settlement with the Schuschnigg regime,

---

[51] Führer des SS-Abschnittes XXX, "Beurteilung über Karl Taus," 12 July 1937, ibid.; Loritz to Eicke, 13 April 1938, ibid.; Karl Koch, "Beurteilung von Karl Taus," 10 June 1938, ibid.; Eicke to Schmitt [SS Personnel Main Office] 14 June 1938, ibid.

[52] Höttl has maintained this consistently. Höttl Tape, p. 7; Hagen, *Geheime Front*, p. 82; Walter Hagen, *Unternehmen Bernhard: Ein historischer Tatsachenbericht über die grösste Geldfälschungsaktion aller Zeiten* (Wels-Starnberg: Verlag Welsermühl, 1955), p. 94.

[53] Testimony of Seyss-Inquart, IMT XVI, p. 78.

and allowed each of the factions to compete for the open line to Schuschnigg. Those Austrian Nazi leaders best able to hold the support of the illegal organizations without losing the contact with the regime would be the most successful from Berlin's standpoint. Amidst the chronic personal and political rivalries exacerbated by Hitler's calculated indifference, four factions took shape.

The first of these was the most radical and at the same time the least influential. Based in the Austrian SA and the Viennese Gau leadership, these radicals rejected compromise with Schuschnigg as treason and advocated continued underground struggle. Hitler's publicly stated desire for peace they took as a purely tactical measure for foreign consumption. They saw any effort to work within the framework of the 11 July treaty as stupidity or betrayal; and their views were expressed by periodic revolts against the central Landesleitung in Vienna.[54] These malcontents received some sympathy but no support from Berlin, where their underground activity was considered injurious to the efforts of the moderates to infiltrate the administration and society of the Schuschnigg regime.

The second and largest faction centered around the Landesleitung in Vienna, which was led by Lower Austrian Gauleiter Josef Leopold. Born in Krems in 1889, Leopold represented the "old fighters" of the Austrian Nazi Party. A captain in World War I, he had joined the Nazis in 1919 and had been the Gauleiter of Lower Austria since 1927. Probably the most popular of the Austrian Nazi leaders, he was a free-wheeling free-booter type, loyal to Hitler, but suspicious of the German Nazi leaders. He had viewed Habicht as an incompetent interloper.[55]

Leopold enjoyed the support of most of the underground Nazi Party organization and was especially strong in his native Lower Austria. His policy resembled that of Reinthaller; he hoped that, as a result of negotiations with Schuschnigg, the "National Front," at the core of which stood the Nazi

[54] On a revolt of the Vienna Gau leadership, see Hans Heinz Dum, "Bericht IV vom 27.II bis 21.III.1937," March 1937, in "Auszüge aus dem bei der Aushebung der illegalen Landesleitung der österr. NSDAP in der Helferstorferstrasse beschlagnahmten Material," 28 July 1937, Box 308, 42.178-13/37, pp. 549-566, NPA; Wolfgang Scholtz [the leader of the revolt] to Papen, 25 June 1938, T-120/751/345040-345053, NA. On a rebellion in Styria, see Hans Heinz Dum to Holzer [Berlin], 11 April 1937, appendix k, "Auszüge . . . ," 28 July 1937, Box 308, 42.178-13/37, NPA. On Upper Austrian SA and SA mistrust of Leopold, see Persche, "Leopold," pp. 64, 82-86, 118-122, 132-133, DöW. On disappointment with the 11 July treaty, see Jagschitz, "Befriedung," p. 187.

[55] On Leopold, see "Hauptmann Leopold—Ein Mensch und eine Mahnung," Österreichischer Beobachter, Jahrgang 2, Folge 38, October 1937, Box 308, 44.936-13/37, p. 636, NPA; Persche, "Leopold," passim., DöW; Ludwig Jedlicka, "Gauleiter Josef Leopold, 1889-1941," in Geschichte und Gesellschaft: Festschrift für Karl R. Stadler zum 60. Geburtstag (Vienna: 1974), pp. 143-161.

Party and its formations, would first be legalized and then incorporated into the Fatherland Front as a block. During talks with Schuschnigg and the Austrian minister of the interior, Odo von Neustädter-Stürmer, in the early months of 1937, Leopold and his advisers concocted a plan for a *Deutsch-Sozialer Volksbund* (German Social League), in which Nazis and nationalists would gather together to make a "positive" contribution to the regime. Schuschnigg, however, had rejected the same type of plan when Reinthaller had advanced it in September 1934, and he would not now change his stance.[56] In March 1937, the Volksbund project collapsed and Schuschnigg gradually cut Leopold out of the negotiations. Firmly believing that he was carrying out Hitler's orders, Leopold embarked on a more violent course in the hope of pressuring the regime to reopen talks on his terms.

A third faction was made up of "moderate" nationalists, men of professional status such as the lawyer Seyss-Inquart, the schoolteacher and Pan-German politician Franz Langoth, the military historian Edmund Glaise-Horstenau, and the former general of the Austro-Hungarian army Karl Bardolff. These individuals stood close to the Austrian Nazi Party but rejected its illegal tactics. Seyss-Inquart was the most articulate of this group. He wished to adhere to the letter of the Gentlemen's Agreement—i.e., to increase völkisch nationalist influence in official policy through the participation of individual nationalists in the government. These plans dovetailed nicely with those of Schuschnigg. The two men established an office known as the Volkspolitisches Referat inside the Fatherland Front, which was to serve a liaison function between the regime and the German nationalist sectors of the Austrian population. Seyss-Inquart hoped that the underground Nazi organization would gradually lose importance in the atmosphere of 11 July, leaving the field open for individuals like himself to bring about a gradual reconciliation in Austria and, ultimately, to fashion some type of federal union with Germany.[57] He was convinced that the illegal apparatus was superfluous, if not harmful, and that his concept was the only peaceful means to achieve the Anschluss.

The fourth faction, the Rainer-Kaltenbrunner group, balanced between Seyss-Inquart and Leopold in policy. Unlike Leopold, Rainer, Globocnik,

[56] Rosar, *Seyss-Inquart*, pp. 108-117. See also Aktenmappe Deutsch-Sozialer Volksbund, Bka-Inneres, 312.387/37, AVA. For Leopold's political aims, see "Memorandum des Hauptmann Leopolds an den Kanzler zur inneren Befriedung Österreichs," n.d. (probably January 1937), Nachlass Seyss-Inquart/1, BA. On negotiations with Schuschnigg, see affidavit of Schuschnigg, 11 November 1945, 2993-PS; Guido Zernatto, *Die Wahrheit über Österreich* (New York: Longmans, Green & Co., 1939), pp. 172-173.

[57] Memorandum of Seyss-Inquart, 10 December 1945, 3425-PS, IMT XXXII, p. 273. See also Rosar, *Seyss-Inquart*, passim. On Schuschnigg's interest in Seyss-Inquart's plans and on the purpose of the *Volkspolitisches Referat*, see Seyss-Inquart to Zernatto, 25 March 1937, Nachlass Seyss-Inquart/1, BA; Rosar, *Seyss-Inquart*, pp. 117-118, 122.

and Kaltenbrunner saw little hope that Schuschnigg would legalize the Nazi apparatus; but, unlike Seyss-Inquart, they refused to neglect the illegal organization. Backed by Himmler and Heydrich through Kaltenbrunner and eventually by Göring through Mühlmann, the Rainer group supported Seyss-Inquart's policy for the purely tactical aim of gaining time for the Reich to rearm. They thus belonged to Seyss-Inquart's "circle." Globocnik later wrote that the Carinthians "built Seyss into the political apparatus" and sought to use him as a front to infiltrate the Schuschnigg regime and to destroy it from within, all the while keeping the Party "pure."[58] How crucial Kaltenbrunner's support was—at least in Globocnik's eyes—is evident from Globocnik's tribute to the SS chief in May 1938:[59]

> This great success [i.e., the Anschluss] was [made] possible on the strength of the [Nazi] movement in Austria; and this can be attributed to the fact that a resolute group of leaders emerged, who correctly grasped the political situation and acted in accordance with this understanding. That this correct concept could succeed is attributable above all to the loyal support of the Schutzstaffel and its leader, Kaltenbrunner. When Rainer and Globocnik and their co-workers were persecuted from all sides, the Schutzstaffel took them into ever closer partnership and bestowed upon them every possible support. The Security Service [SD], which through its excellent intelligence net succeeded in bringing the correct political assessment to light in the Reich, had an outstanding participation in this development.

Why Kaltenbrunner supported the Rainer group becomes apparent from a brief survey of the situation in 1937. Hitler's order that the Austrian Nazis not provoke an international crisis through overtly violent acts left the latter three options: to take the order as a tactical measure for foreign consumption (i.e., Hitler wanted to be disobeyed) and to continue the underground struggle against Schuschnigg with any and all means; to give up the underground organization and enter the Fatherland Front; or to maintain the underground organization in secret, while exploiting whatever political advantages the "respectable" nationalists could wring from Schuschnigg. As we have seen, Rainer opted for the latter solution in the fall of 1936, and he probably kept Kaltenbrunner closely informed.[60] For Kaltenbrunner, the Rainer group was the most logical choice. If he threw in his lot with Leopold, he would lose not only his legitimacy in the eyes of the government, but also his influence in the underground, for to Leopold he was a newcomer. Moreover, Kaltenbrunner had strict orders from Himmler not to involve the SS

---

[58] Globocnik Memo, May 1938, T-84/16/44254, 44258, NA. On Rainer's concept, see Rosar, *Seyss-Inquart*, pp. 89, 185-186; Rainer Speech, 4005-PS, IMT xxxiv, p. 15.

[59] Globocnik Memo, May 1938, T-84/16/44271, NA.

[60] On close relationship between Kaltenbrunner and Rainer, see W. Kaltenbrunner interview, Vöcklabruck, 25 March 1977; Tavs Tape, pp. 1-2; Höttl Tape, p. 6.

in illegal activity; a pro-Leopold policy, especially after the Volksbund project collapsed in March 1937, would mean disobedience. On the other hand, were Kaltenbrunner to renounce the illegal organization and fully support Seyss-Inquart's concept, he would undercut his own base of power, the SS. Cautious support of Seyss-Inquart had distinct advantages, not the least of which was the indulgence of the authorities. Finally, Seyss-Inquart and other moderates opened up contacts with the Schuschnigg regime that might assure Kaltenbrunner of an influential position in the Austrian regime on its evolutionary course toward Anschluss. By supporting Rainer, Kaltenbrunner could please virtually everyone (Hitler, Himmler, Seyss-Inquart, Rainer and, to a certain extent, the Austrian authorities) except Leopold; therefore, adherence to the Seyss-Rainer coalition made good practical politics without compromising ideological commitment.

The evidence indicates that Kaltenbrunner exploited his contacts with the moderates to win a certain amount of official indulgence for his activities. According to one witness, he had friends in the Linz police department. He also appears to have had contact with Upper Austrian Security Director Peter Graf Revetera and possibly with Provincial Governor Heinrich Gleissner. As early as 1935, a German agent reported that in Upper Austria, "thanks to support from officials of the state and organs of the executive, the Nazi Party has succeeded in establishing a sufficient [auskömmlich] relationship between the authorities and the illegal organization." In early December 1935, Revetera told Langoth of his regret that he had to make so many arrests.[61] Austrian SA leader Alfred Persche noted jealously that Kaltenbrunner worked "quite openly and undisturbed." It was rumored in the Landesleitung that the police had been ordered to leave the Austrian SS leader alone. Leopold apparently had Kaltenbrunner watched and remarked to Persche that the SS leader "stood in some kind of relationship with the Austrian government and even meets secretly with ministers close to Schuschnigg."[62]

Though the Landesleitung probably exaggerated the extent of Kaltenbrunner's contact with the authorities, it is nevertheless likely that the SS leader did have some kind of relationship with Revetera. One of Kaltenbrunner's comrades from the Nazi underground believed such contact to have existed. Former Austrian SD man Wilhelm Höttl concurred, remarking that Kaltenbrunner kept Revetera informed of the mood in the underground movement in hopes of encouraging a reconciliation. In the case of Gleissner, the evidence is contradictory. Gleissner had explained to Papen in August 1935

---

[61] Carsten, *Fascist Movements*, p. 299; unsigned memorandum, "Informationen über nationalsozialistische Organisation in Österreich," 2 April 1935, Box 305, 32.901-13/35, pp. 167-169, NPA. On Kaltenbrunner's friends in the Linz police department, see O. Picha interview, Vienna, 26 January 1977.

[62] Persche, "Leopold," pp. 201-202, DöW.

that the Schuschnigg regime could not deal with the Nazis as long as Catholics were persecuted in Germany. Earlier, however, in June 1934, he was reported to have favored a deal between Dollfuss and the Nazis. Finally, Gleissner himself informed this author that he had never had contact with Kaltenbrunner. Yet, in his memoir, Kaltenbrunner wrote of a meeting between Gleissner, Seyss-Inquart, and himself at the Pöstlingberg Hotel in Linz in early March 1938, at which "joint cooperation for the benefit of the Austrian homeland" was discussed.[63] It seems pointless for Kaltenbrunner to have invented the specifics of the episode; perhaps by this time Gleissner was concerned to make his peace with the leaders of the new order. Yet, for lack of solid evidence, the question must remain open.

Contacts with moderates and provincial government personalities served Kaltenbrunner well when he was faced with arrest. In early March 1937, the members of an SS cell uncovered by the police in Vienna confirmed official suspicion that Kaltenbrunner had become the leader of the Austrian SS and that he had participated in a meeting of illegal SS leaders in an Alpine mountain hut in October 1936. When a warrant was issued for his arrest, the SS leader complained to Seyss-Inquart that the authorities must "know" that "for months I have done *nothing more* than to bring my closest compatriots onto the course known to you [Seyss-Inquart], that [course] which you as well as Leopold, Langoth, Jury, and many others have taken" (emphasis in the original). He went on to warn Seyss-Inquart that his (Kaltenbrunner's) arrest "would be seen in our circles as a deliberate obstruction of the reconciliation efforts; and, as a result, all those elements, who in any case view our efforts with mistrust, will gain arguments."[64] Seyss-Inquart appealed to Glaise-Horstenau; Langoth did the same, warning of the possible consequences should Kaltenbrunner be arrested. Langoth remarked that the case had been transferred to the Linz district court and that Revetera himself was kept informed of its progress. He added that "in no case can an arrest of Kaltenbrunner come to pass," for "Kaltenbrunner's case is of very great significance for the reconciliation action."[65] For the moment, Kaltenbrunner was spared arrest and, though finally arrested in May 1937 on suspicion of being the leader of a provincial branch of the illegal Nazi Relief Office,

[63] On Kaltenbrunner and Revetera, see letter of Franz Peterseil to the author, 17 May 1977; Höttl Tape, p. 7. On Kaltenbrunner and Gleissner, see Papen to Hitler, 12 August 1935, NS 10/50, pp. 138-142, BA; unsigned report from OKW files, 18 June 1934, T-77/900/5653170-5653171, NA; letter of Dr. Heinrich Gleissner to the author, 13 December 1976; E. Kaltenbrunner, "Memoir," p. 49.

[64] Kaltenbrunner to Seyss-Inquart, 14 March 1937, Bka-Inneres, Korrespondenz Glaise-Horstenau, Box 39/10, 3152-3157, AVA. On Kaltenbrunner's participation in the SS leaders' meeting, see police report, 22 May 1937, Box 307, 40.239-13/37, pp. 339-340, 347, NPA.

[65] Seyss-Inquart to Glaise-Horstenau, 16 March 1937, Bka-Inneres, Korrespondenz Glaise-Horstenau, Box 39/10, 3152-3157, AVA; Langoth to Glaise-Horstenau, 6 April 1937, ibid.

he could participate once again in illegal underground meetings by early September.[66]

Before the collapse of Leopold's Volksbund project, Kaltenbrunner maintained contact with both Leopold and Rainer. On 28 January 1937, he and Leopold were invited by Himmler to Berlin, where an agreement subordinating the Austrian SS to the Landesleitung was concluded.[67] On the one hand, this satisfied Leopold's vanity, while on the other, Himmler could depend on Kaltenbrunner's personal loyalty and be assured that the SS would follow his strict orders to stay clear of illegal activity, regardless of whether Leopold's reconciliation bid failed. Initially, Kaltenbrunner cooperated with Leopold and appears to have supported the latter against the radicals in the Vienna Gau leadership during the revolt of March 1937.[68]

In the spring of 1937, Leopold and Seyss-Inquart began to struggle for preeminence in the negotiations with the regime. As the rift grew wider, each accused the other of wrecking the negotiations for petty personal ends. Schuschnigg clearly preferred to deal with Seyss-Inquart; in June 1937, he appointed the Viennese lawyer state councilor (*Staatsrat*) with the special task of drawing nationalist elements into the Fatherland Front. Leopold, whose hostility toward Schuschnigg was increasing, sought to keep Seyss-Inquart and the Rainer group under his direct control; but Rainer, Globocnik, and Kaltenbrunner perceived clearly that Seyss-Inquart could promise greater success and instructed Himmler and Heydrich accordingly. How much Kaltenbrunner was willing to defer to Seyss-Inquart is indicated by his statement to the latter at a meeting in Linz in early 1937. Höttl, who was present, recalled how Kaltenbrunner endorsed Seyss-Inquart's policy: "We must act according to the long view, we must go along with the momentum of the times . . . the illegal Party is of secondary importance; it all depends on negotiation tactics and personal confidence." To which Seyss-Inquart replied with the request that Heydrich be informed of this "correct" policy.[69]

[66] On arrest, see police report, 22 May 1937, Box 307, 40.239-13/37, pp. 339-340, 347, NPA. On Kaltenbrunner's return, see Leopold to Hitler, 8 September 1937, NG-3578, NA.

[67] Papen to Hitler, 26 May 1937, DGFP, I, no. 227, pp. 425-427; "Bericht II: Über die Zeit vom 24.I bis 14.II," "Auszüge . . . ," 28 July 1937, Box 308, 42.178-13/37, pp. 543-548, NPA; appendix to Globocnik Memo, T-84/16/44277, NA; Persche, "Leopold," p. 215, DöW.

[68] "Bericht IV vom 27.II bis 21.III. 1937," March 1937, "Auszüge . . . ," 28 July 1937, Box 308, 42.178-13/37, pp. 549-566, NPA. The Austrian police found memoranda pertaining to Leopold's negotiations with Schuschnigg in February 1937 when they searched the SS leader's house two months later. See police report, 22 May 1937, Box 307, 40.239-13/37, pp. 339-340, 347, NPA.

[69] Höttl-Rosar interview, 11-12 April 1967, Höttl File, IfZ Vienna. On hostility between Seyss-Inquart and Leopold, see Eichstädt, *Dollfuss*, pp. 189-218; Gehl, *Austria*, pp. 153-165; Rosar, *Seyss-Inquart*, pp. 117-214. For Leopold's side, see Leopold to Hitler, 22 August 1937, NG-3578, NA. On Seyss-Inquart's appointment, see Schuschnigg to Seyss-Inquart, 16 June

That Kaltenbrunner passed such ideas on to Berlin and received Himmler's support for the Seyss-Inquart line finds some confirmation in a letter
dated 13 April 1937 and addressed to one of Leopold's contact men in Berlin. Uncovered by the Austrian police during a raid on the underground
headquarters of the Landesleitung in the Vienna Helferstorferstrasse on 21
April 1937, the letter informed Leopold's agent that a "letter from Himmler
ha[d] arrived. He [Himmler] is in accord with version I [i.e., of a draft
policy] which comes from Kaltenbrunner."[70]

After lining up with Rainer and Seyss-Inquart, Kaltenbrunner waged a
secret campaign to discredit Leopold in Berlin. In early September 1937, he
reported to SS-Gruppenführer Wilhelm Keppler, whom Hitler had appointed special plenipotentiary for Austrian affairs with the task of mediating
between Leopold and Seyss-Inquart, that the rift in the Austrian Nazi Party
was "unbridgeable" and requested immediate mediation. The situation, Kaltenbrunner explained, was "absolutely deplorable [and] cries for a remedy";
it was feared that the rift between Leopold and Rainer would become public
and split the Party.[71]

Kaltenbrunner took other steps to thwart Leopold's thrusts aimed at Seyss-
Inquart and the Carinthians. When the Landesleiter expelled Globocnik
from the Party for insubordination, Kaltenbrunner announced that Globocnik's status in the SS would be maintained and insisted that Leopold inform
him of such intentions in the future in order to "give me the opportunity to
evaluate whether the personal and political behavior of the individual SS
member and above all his behavior with respect to his honor makes possible
his continued membership in the SS." Furious, Leopold complained directly to Himmler, but in vain; the Reichsführer denied that Kaltenbrunner
had usurped Leopold's authority and admonished Leopold that "a little more
calm and a little less attention to idle chatter would on the whole be useful."[72]

Ultimately, Leopold was helpless against the machinations of the Seyss-
Rainer coalition, for the latter, through Kaltenbrunner and Mühlmann, had
won over Heydrich, Himmler, Göring, and Keppler, while the German
Foreign Office had never had much use for Leopold's Landesleitung. Yet
Hitler, perhaps more out of personal sympathy than tactical considerations,

1937, reproduced in Rosar, Seyss-Inquart, pp. 130-131. On Kaltenbrunner reporting to Himmler and Heydrich, see Radomír Luža, Austro-German Relations in the Anschluss Era (Princeton:
Princeton University Press, 1975), p. 36.

[70] Police report, 22 May 1937, Box 307, 40.239-13/37, pp. 339-340, 347, NPA.

[71] Kaltenbrunner to Keppler, 3 September 1937, T-120/751/344886-344887, NA.

[72] Himmler to Leopold, 18 January 1938, ibid., 344901. On expulsion of Globocnik, see
Kaltenbrunner to Keppler, 3 September 1937, ibid., 344887; Rauscher [Leopold's contact man
in Berlin] to Himmler, 23 September 1937, ibid., 345180-345183; Leopold to Himmler, 8
October 1937, ibid., 345177-345179.

avoided sacking Leopold until the last minute. Only in February 1938, after the Landesleitung had initiated a campaign of violence to discredit Seyss-Inquart, whom Schuschnigg had appointed minister of the interior in accordance with Hitler's demands at Berchtesgaden on 12 February, did Seyss-Inquart's requests and the intrigues of Kaltenbrunner, Rainer, and Globocnik bear full fruit. On 21 February, Leopold and four of his closest followers were summoned to Berlin, stripped of their Party offices, and ordered not to return to Austria. Klausner, the Carinthian Gauleiter, was then summoned, appointed Landesleiter, and ordered to support Seyss-Inquart in every way. The triumph of the Rainer group was complete; and Globocnik took pains to acknowledge Kaltenbrunner's role in that triumph.[73]

Kaltenbrunner was able to impress Berlin not only through his political acumen; he also created for himself an image as an intelligence expert. We have already seen that he passed on to the Reich important documents pertaining to Austrian foreign policy. Though he apparently had had little to do with the establishment of the Vienna SD, he represented their successes as his own in Berlin.[74] In September 1937, he boasted to Keppler that he had "built up a good intelligence network, particularly in Vienna. Our reports are dispatched twice daily via Salzburg and you really have the latest [news] in your hands." He requested Keppler to authorize the establishment of a special relay station for intelligence reports at the headquarters of the SS-Oberabschnitt Süd (Munich), from where they would go directly to Berlin without preliminary evaluation. Clearly, Kaltenbrunner hoped to use this channel to turn Berlin against Leopold, for of the proposed relay station he wrote that he "assumed that, for the moment, this special line is very necessary because the situation within our ranks [i.e., the rivalry between Leopold and Seyss-Inquart] is coming to a head."[75] Whenever Kaltenbrunner experienced technical difficulties, such as when the Upper Austrian police demanded his passport with the intention of canceling his exit visa, he could depend on Seyss-Inquart or Glaise-Horstenau to clear up such matters.[76] In this way, the Austrian SS leader fashioned an image of himself as an intelligence expert, a reputation that would set him on the road to the RSHA.

Kaltenbrunner was surprised by the rapid disintegration of the Austrian state in the late winter of 1938 and played only a minor role in the events of the Anschluss. The final crisis was precipitated in part by the Berchtes-

[73] Globocnik Memo, May 1938, T-84/16/44271, NA. On Leopold's dismissal and Klausner's appointment, see Pauley, *Forgotten Nazis*, pp. 197-201; Carsten, *Fascist Movements*, pp. 317-318; Zernatto, *Wahrheit*, p. 241. From 1938 to 1940, Leopold held an insignificant post at the Nazi Party headquarters in Munich. In 1940, he was taken into the Wehrmacht and held the rank of major when he was killed on the Russian Front in the autumn of 1941.

[74] Höttl Tape, p. 5.

[75] Kaltenbrunner to Keppler, 3 September 1937, T-120/751/344886, NA.

[76] Ibid., 344885. See also Seyss-Inquart to Kaltenbrunner, 14 September 1937, Nachlass Seyss-Inquart/56, BA.

gaden Conference of 12 February 1938, at which Hitler demanded that Schuschnigg grant a general amnesty for all Austrian Nazis, put an end to all political, cultural, and occupational discrimination, take immediate steps to grant the National Opposition legal status within the Fatherland Front, and appoint Seyss-Inquart minister of the interior. Though the latter was duly appointed on 17 February, Seyss-Inquart was already losing control of the Austrian Nazis. After Leopold's removal, Rainer and Klausner organized "victory" demonstrations in order to demoralize the regime. On 22 February, Seyss-Inquart was compelled to plead for calm over the radio; and he urged the Austrian Nazis to be content with a legalized status in the Schuschnigg state.[77] Growing Nazi pressure and anxiety in Schuschnigg's own camp caused by Hitler's failure to refer to the concept of Austrian independence in his Reichstag speech of 20 February finally induced the Austrian chancellor to take a firm stand. In early March, he decided to give the Nazis the plebiscite that they had demanded since 1933; he, however, would provide the wording. The question to be put on the ballot—"Are you for a free, independent, German, Christian, authoritarian Austria?"—was ingeniously calculated to pressure the Nazis either to confirm the Schuschnigg regime or to reject it and be open to charges that they really did not wish to work within the framework of the 11 July 1936 treaty. When informed by Globocnik of the impending plebiscite on the evening of 9 March 1938, Hitler ordered Keppler to force its cancellation.[78]

Kaltenbrunner's role in the Anschluss crisis was relatively minor; he played no part in the political negotiations or the phone conversations through which Göring engineered Schuschnigg's resignation and Seyss-Inquart's appointment as chancellor.[79] On the evening of 11 March 1938, a few hours before Federal President Wilhelm Miklas appointed Seyss-Inquart chancellor, Rainer met with Kaltenbrunner and Austrian SA leader Johann Lukesch at the headquarters of the Nazi Party in the Seitzergasse. Kaltenbrunner had gathered together some 700 SS men, while Lukesch commanded 6,000 SA troopers. Rainer ordered the SS to surround the federal chancellor's office in order to protect it from "armed Reds." Then, with Klausner's approval, he instructed the eight Nazi Gauleiter over the phone to seize power in the

[77] Rosar, *Seyss-Inquart*, p. 228. A copy of the Berchtesgaden Protocol is appended to the Globocnik Memo, T-84/16/44287-44288, NA. See also Gehl, *Austria*, pp. 172-174.

[78] Testimony of Keppler, Case XI before the U.S. Military Tribunal IV, transcripts pp. 12796-12797, International Law Library, Columbia University, New York City; Rainer Speech, 4005-PS, IMT xxxiv, pp. 27-28; Weizsäcker to Ribbentrop, 9 March 1938, *DGFP*, Series D, Vol. 1, No. 339, p. 562. On the text of the plebiscite question, see Zernatto, *Wahrheit*, p. 275.

[79] These events can be followed in Eichstädt, *Dollfuss*, pp. 354-422; Gehl, *Austria*, pp. 182-195; Rosar, *Seyss-Inquart*, pp. 247-298; and Peter R. Black, "The Austrian National Socialists and the Destruction of the Austrian State, 1933-1938," Master's thesis, Columbia University, 1973, pp. 169-215.

provinces with the aid of the SA and the SS. At approximately 10:00 P.M., 50 SS men, commanded by Kaltenbrunner's adjutant, SS-Obersturmführer Felix Rinner, entered the federal chancellor's office with Seyss-Inquart's approval. Three hours later, Miklas gave in to Göring's demand: Seyss-Inquart was authorized to form a cabinet.[80]

Despite later claims that he had sought no political office in National Socialist Austria, Kaltenbrunner was chagrined to find himself excluded from Seyss-Inquart's cabinet list. The reasons for this are unclear: Seyss-Inquart later claimed that he had wanted to reassure Miklas that the new cabinet would be "moderate." Whatever his reasons, he requested the incumbent state secretary for security, Dr. Michael Skubl, who had loyally served both Dollfuss and Schuschnigg, to remain at his post.[81]

Kaltenbrunner, who may already have known that Göring had insisted on his appointment as Skubl's successor,[82] was "vexed to no end." At 12:45 A.M. on 12 March, he spoke to Himmler on the phone and complained that he had not been given official authority to take over the Austrian police, but had been bypassed for Skubl. Kaltenbrunner confessed that this solution appeared to be "somewhat precarious" (etwas brenzlig) and that he "could not yet see his way to that [solution]." Nor could he reach Seyss-Inquart by phone; the latter was conferring with his new cabinet. Himmler curtly reassured Kaltenbrunner and informed him that he (Himmler) would arrive at Vienna's Aspern airport in a few hours.[83]

After his arrival, Himmler informed Skubl through Glaise-Horstenau that Skubl's presence in the cabinet was no longer desired. Skubl resigned on 12 March; after some token resistance, Miklas appointed Kaltenbrunner to succeed him.[84] On the next day, 13 March, the Anschluss law was passed, and Austria became an integral part of the German Reich.

[80] Friedrich Rainer, "Geschichtliche Entscheidungsstunden," 12 March 1939, 4004-PS, IMT xxxiv, pp. 1-3; Order no. 4 of the Reichsführer SS [signed Bomhard], 12 March 1938, File HA-Orpo, R 19/401, pp. 11-13, BA; Rainer Speech, 4005-PS, IMT xxxiv, pp. 35-36; Eichstädt, Dollfuss, pp. 419-420.

[81] Testimony of Skubl, IMT xvi, p. 181; Arthur Seyss-Inquart, "The Austrian Question, 1934-1938," 9 September 1945, 3254-PS, NCA v, p. 987; Langoth, Kampf, p. 234. On Seyss-Inquart's motives, see Seyss-Inquart to Stahlecker, 6 December 1938, Nachlass Seyss-Inquart/60, BA.

[82] Göring testified at Nuremberg that Hitler himself had added Kaltenbrunner's name to the suggested cabinet list. See testimony of Göring, IMT xi, p. 297.

[83] Himmler-Kaltenbrunner telephone conversation, Munich-Vienna, 12:45-12:54 A.M., 12 March 1938, in Heinz Holldack, Was wirklich geschah: Die diplomatischen Hintergründe der deutschen Kriegspolitik (Munich: Nymphenburger Verlagshandlung, 1949), pp. 324-325. On Kaltenbrunner's vexation, see Höttl Tape, p. 11.

[84] Testimony of Skubl, IMT xvi, p. 200; Skubl to Helmut Zeder [a nephew of Skubl's wife] 5 April 1938, Nachlass Seyss-Inquart/3, BA; Miklas to Seyss-Inquart, 12 March 1938, ibid., 60; Miklas to Kaltenbrunner, 12 March 1938, ibid.

There is some evidence that Kaltenbrunner and other Austrian Nazis were not entirely satisfied with the union that was achieved on 13 March 1938, and that they had hoped that Austrian Nazi politicians—not German troops—would bring Austria "home to the Reich." Kaltenbrunner stated to the Nuremberg prison psychiatrist that he had wanted elections in Austria (in which, he was certain, the Nazis would win), after which the new government would seek close economic and political relations with the Reich, but would also "leave broad leeway for [the development] of the unique Austrian character."[85] This was calculated to appeal to the sentiments of his Allied captors; but his widow told this author that while her husband favored the *Gleichschaltung* of Austria with the Third Reich, he believed that the Austrian Nazis should supervise the process. Kaltenbrunner himself later wrote that he and Seyss-Inquart "sincerely" desired to cooperate with Gleissner and the Austrian authorities in a "common effort for the benefit of the Austrian homeland," and that Schuschnigg's plebiscite plans had "made the Reich too impatient."[86] This suggests that Kaltenbrunner, like Seyss-Inquart, Rainer, and Neubacher,[87] would have been willing to delay the Anschluss if that were necessary to permit the Austrian Nazis to be masters of their own fate.

According to Wilhelm Höttl, Kaltenbrunner joined Seyss-Inquart in advocating a "union with the most careful consideration for Austrian peculiarities in the most varied sectors and a gradual process of fusion into the German Reich." The difference was that Seyss-Inquart honestly wished to work with Schuschnigg, while Kaltenbrunner hoped to destroy the System from within and then bring a nazified Austria into the Reich. As for the German invasion, Kaltenbrunner later told Höttl that "I was not so much for it, but our [views] were disregarded."[88]

Years later, Kaltenbrunner lamented the failure of the Reich to exploit Austria's special position as the gateway to Southeastern Europe: "How sincerely I regret that the role of Vienna was unappreciated, that it [Vienna] was subordinated to men who did not understand either [the city] or the Viennese people, who did not permit Austria to demonstrate its importance, and who [executed a] . . . desolate Gleichschaltung." Or: "How the capacity

[85] E. Kaltenbrunner, "Lebenslauf," Nuremberg, 1945, p. 8, File F-190, IfZ Munich.
[86] ". . . ich sass mit ihm [Seyss-Inquart] und dem Landeshauptmann Dr. Heinrich Gleissner im Pöstlingberg Hotel und wir sprachen von einem gemeinsamen Arbeiten zum Wohl der österreichischen Heimat. Wir meinten es aufrichtig, aber schon die nächsten Wochen brachten die Erkenntnis, dass durch eine Abstimmung in verfassungswidrigen Formen aufs Neue der Weg evolutionärer Entwicklung verbaut werden sollte und nun war's dem Reich zu dumm. Es kam der Anschluss unter den bekannten Ereignissen des 11.-13. März 1938." E. Kaltenbrunner, "Memoir," p. 49. See also E. Kaltenbrunner interview, Linz, 25 March 1977.
[87] Ritter, "Neubacher," p. 369.
[88] Höttl Tape, p. 8; affidavit of Höttl, 10 October 1945, 1746-PS, exhibit B, p. 16, NA.

of Vienna, beloved and proven mediator to the Southeast, was squandered and ruined by the appointment of most incapable [persons]." And again: "Vienna should again become the crystallization point for the successor states of old Austria and should stand in close contact with the Reich for the consolidation of economic exigencies."[89]

True, such sentiments were expressed in the loneliness of the Nuremberg prison cell and after the political and physical destruction of Austria by Hitler; yet, the aim that Austrians should rule Austria with relatively little interference from the Reich was not foreign to Kaltenbrunner's closest collaborators. Odilo Globocnik wrote as early as 1938 that "the breakthrough in the struggle for National Socialism does not lie in the revision of boundaries . . . but in the success of the National Socialist will; and with that the acquisition of power in a state which then in its actions spontaneously carries out tasks for the entire nation, aligned with the leadership of the entire nation, [but] regardless of whether a given part of the nation lives within or outside the primary state of the entire nation" (emphasis added).[90] Both Globocnik and Rainer were "deeply shocked" when they learned on 11 March 1938 that the German army would invade Austria. Indeed, Globocnik even sought to forestall the invasion by telling Göring over the telephone at 5:00 P.M. that evening that Seyss-Inquart was chancellor and that SS and SA troops were being employed as auxiliary police—even though these events did not come to pass until after midnight, as Göring found out to his dismay when he spoke to Seyss-Inquart at 5:30 P.M.[91] Seyss-Inquart himself, after his appointment as chancellor, sought to reach Hitler in the early morning hours of 12 March and to convince him to rescind the invasion order.[92] Nevertheless, all efforts of the Austrian Nazis to delay or cancel the invasion were in vain.

Though in retrospect it was naive of the Austrian Nazis to have believed that they would have received treatment different from other "coordinated" provinces of the Third Reich, Hitler's intentions were by no means clear to contemporaries. Since the Führer was an Austrian, the Austrian Nazis thought that they enjoyed a special, personal relationship to him and that he would instinctively understand the unique nature of the Austrian character and

[89] E. Kaltenbrunner, "Memoir," pp. 35, 53; E. Kaltenbrunner, "Lebenslauf," p. 8, F-190, IfZ Munich.

[90] Globocnik Memo, May 1938, T-84/16/44251, NA.

[91] On Globocnik and Rainer shock, see testimony of Franz Hueber, Landgericht Salzburg, 11 June 1947, G 13, p. 21, IfZ Munich. See also telephone transcripts, Göring-Globocnik (5:00 P.M.), Göring-Seyss-Inquart (5:26 P.M.), 11 March 1938, 2949-PS, in Der Hochverratsprozess gegen Dr. Guido Schmidt vor dem Wiener Volksgericht (Vienna: Druck und Verlag der österreichischen Staatsdruckerei, 1947), p. 461; Black, "Austrian Nazis," pp. 193-195.

[92] Notice of Altenburg, 12 March 1938, DGFP, Series D, Vol. 1, no. 364, pp. 584-585; Gehl, Austria, pp. 193-194.

would know better than to subjugate Austria to "northern Germany." The dictator was well aware of such sentiments and exploited them to the full. In July 1936, after exhorting Rainer and Globocnik to adhere strictly to the 11 July treaty, he noted their surprise and then told them: "I am, after all, the loyal Eckard of Austria." In the case of the Upper Austrians, Hitler was even more effective. He had elaborate models of Linz as a Central European metropolis prepared and promised that Upper Austria would have a special role to play in the Third Reich.[93] Kaltenbrunner and others could believe, if they wished, that Hitler meant what he said, despite the disappointing reality of 1938-1945. They felt that "after the war," Hitler, a true son of Austria, would make good his promises.

The Austrian Nazi underground scene offered Kaltenbrunner an excellent training ground for acquiring skill in the kind of personal politics practiced in Hitler's Germany. Politics in the Third Reich were especially conducive to both factional rivalries and personal alliances contracted in a ceaseless pursuit of personal power within the guidelines imposed by the Nazi ideology. This was due in part to the unique concept of leadership embodied in the idea of the "Führer" and in part to Hitler's personal style of rule.

The very title "Führer" reflects the vaguely defined and in practice unlimited authority invested in the position. As chief of the state, Hitler was limited by its laws, but as Führer of the Movement, his person was identified with the progress of history itself, indeed, with the very essence of the German Volk. Political power and authority in the Nazi movement (and, eventually, in the Nazi state) were derived from the "will" of a man who believed himself, and was believed by his followers, to be "an agency of history destined to resurrect Germany's national greatness."[94]

If, in theory, Hitler's power was limitless, in practice the strength of his position lay in his role as the ultimate arbitrator, standing above a myriad of rival personalities and interest groups,[95] all of whom were loyal to him and endorsed his goals of national unity, military expansion, and racial purification, yet often differed on tactics as to how these goals were to be attained. Those enjoying the easiest access to the person of the Führer, to the embodiment of authority within the Nazi world, stood the best chance to increase not only their political influence but also the legitimacy of their policies. Since the Nazi movement lacked a strict institutionalized chain of

[93] Rainer Speech, 4005-PS, IMT xxxiv, p. 17; Holzinger Tape, pp. 5-6.
[94] Orlow, *Nazi Party, 1919-1933*, p. 301. See also Hans H. Gerth, "The Nazi Party: Its Leadership and Composition," in *Reader in Bureaucracy*, ed. Robert K. Merton et al. (Glencoe, Illinois: The Free Press, 1952), p. 103. For a discussion on the meaning of the "will of the Führer," see Hans Buchheim, "The SS—Instrument of Domination," in Krausnick, *SS State*, pp. 127-130; Arendt, *Totalitarianism*, p. 365.
[95] Orlow, *Nazi Party, 1919-1933*, p. 301; Arendt, *Totalitarianism*, p. 373.

command, the cultivation of personal contacts either with Hitler himself or with those in his inner circle assumed prime importance in the advancement of one's political ideas or personal career.

In Austria during the early 1930s, the struggle for power within and between agencies of the Nazi Party was exacerbated by two factors. First, Hitler was primarily concerned with preparing the German Party for the takeover of the German state and tended to neglect the Austrian movement, appointing nonentities to lead it as his representative. The practical effect of this policy was to encourage personal and regional rivalries.[96] Second, Hitler himself was not active in Austria, and was therefore "permanently unavailable" to settle administrative or personal disputes. Each Austrian Nazi leader could and did claim with equal justification that he alone was executing the "will" of the Führer. Unclear and often contradictory instructions sent from Munich by competing German Nazi factions further encouraged disunity among the Austrian leaders. Rivalries in the Reich (e.g., SA against SS) often spilled over the border, affecting the Austrian Nazi organization.[97]

In the fluid atmosphere created by the ban on the Austrian Nazi Party and the collapse of the 25 July 1934 putsch, Ernst Kaltenbrunner made his political career on the strength of his ability to make himself useful to virtually all political personalities who counted—both in Austria and Germany. After the failure of the July putsch, Hitler needed peace in Austria in order to pursue his plans for German rearmament; thus, Nazis in Germany and Austria were compelled to work toward an evolutionary Anschluss. Hitler permitted various personalities and factions to compete toward the same end: the establishment of fruitful contacts with the Schuschnigg regime. As the ultimate arbitrator, Hitler stood aloof from and above the often bitter competition, not only in a psychological sense, but also in a concrete physical sense; his public statements of noninterference in Austrian affairs formed a tactical support for his neutrality. Thus, each audience with him carried that much more weight and prestige. Moreover, as Hitler was often not available, influence had to be curried with his top minions: Göring, Himmler, Hess, and others. Access via personal contacts to the larger planets revolving around the unchanging sun of power became vital in having one's concept accepted in Berlin.[98]

[96] For numerous examples, see Carsten, *Fascist Movements*, pp. 144-163. On the role of regional affiliations and factionalism in the Austrian Nazi Party, see Luža, *Anschluss Era*, pp. 21-22.

[97] For examples of SS-SA rivalry, see Carsten, *Fascist Movements*, pp. 253-254.

[98] The relationship of European Communist leaders to Stalin and his advisers in the Comintern during the 1930s and 1940s suggests an interesting parallel and raises the question of whether such personalized command relationships are characteristic of totalitarian movements based in nontotalitarian states and drawing on the power and prestige of a "mother country."

Since, for reasons of foreign policy, Hitler not only needed peace in Austria, but also expected the Austrian Nazis to operate without overt aid or support from the Reich and to take the initiative in seeking a working agreement with Schuschnigg, contacts with independent nationalists and personalities in the Austrian government became all important. The more credit one had in these circles, the more quickly one could penetrate the government and, consequently, the more one's stock rose in Berlin. As one's status in Berlin depended on one's potential for wringing concessions from the regime by nonviolent means, the route to favor in Berlin lay ironically through Schuschnigg. On the other hand, since the Austrian Nazi movement was not strong or united enough to go "its own way," Austrian Nazi leaders, in order to appeal to Schuschnigg, had to have support in Berlin and to follow an evolutionary policy.

Kaltenbrunner, Rainer, and Globocnik were quick to grasp the fact that Schuschnigg would trust only "independent" nationalists such as Seyss-Inquart, Glaise-Horstenau, or Langoth; and, while retaining respective control over the SS and the Carinthian Nazi organization, they skillfully allowed these individuals—Seyss-Inquart in particular—to present a respectable front to the Austrian authorities. It was partly because of Kaltenbrunner that Himmler, Heydrich, Keppler, and—through Keppler and Mühlmann—Göring came to recognize Seyss-Inquart's value for the evolutionary course, a factor of great importance for the Kaltenbrunner-Rainer triumph over Leopold. For Leopold's popularity in the underground Nazi organization was ultimately useless against rivals, who, though they enjoyed far less popular support, maintained continuous contact with key personalities in Berlin and Vienna. With the collapse of the Leopold faction in February 1938, the Kaltenbrunner-Rainer group inherited the underground Nazi organization and could thus expect that, when the Nazis finally took over Austria, they would preside over its nazification. As one authority has noted, Kaltenbrunner "played his own game" in Austria with great success.[99]

Kaltenbrunner had come a long way in six years. When he took over the Linz SS in 1932, he was unknown outside of his home province. The putsch of 25 July 1934 gave him his chance, however. The SS alone remained under Reich German control; Kaltenbrunner was able to gain direct contact with Jost, Heydrich, and eventually Himmler via the SD. His friendship with Reinthaller brought him into contact with moderate nationalist leaders like Seyss-Inquart and Glaise-Horstenau as well as with the increasingly influential members of Klausner's staff in Carinthia. It further gained for him a measure of respectability in the Upper Austrian provincial government, which not only enabled him to carry on his illegal activities with relatively

[99] Browder, "Sipo and SD," pp. 224-225.

little harassment from the police, but also increased his value to the leadership of the Reich and to the moderate nationalist camp. Finally, he was able to enhance his status with Himmler by virtue of materials gleaned from "his" intelligence network in Vienna.

Kaltenbrunner's appointment as chief of the Austrian SS reflected Himmler's appreciation of the Austrian's personal contacts and intelligence activities, as well as his belief that Kaltenbrunner was a leader capable of keeping his followers on a tight rein. Kaltenbrunner's predecessor, Taus, did not exert enough authority over the Austrian SS; Kaltenbrunner, in addition to showing a "fanatical loyalty to Himmler,"[100] apparently got the job done.

As chief of the Austrian SS, Kaltenbrunner continued to strengthen his position through personal politics. He was involved in the illegal Hilfswerk in Upper Austria and thus controlled in part the funds clandestinely pouring into Austria from German Nazi Party coffers. His frequent trips to Germany made his face and name familiar in Berlin. Finally, he won the gratitude of the Carinthians and the moderate nationalists for pleading their case to the appropriate leaders in Germany. Through a myriad of intertwined personal and political relationships, Kaltenbrunner made a name for himself in the Nazi world. In assessing his service to the movement during the underground years, the Nazi Party leadership in Linz (Gau Oberdonau) determined that his "conduct during the illegal period [Verbotszeit] was outstanding [hervorragend] [and] worthy of his old [Nazi Party] number."[101]

If the emotional basis of Kaltenbrunner's ideological commitment to National Socialism was rooted in the borderland, "pioneer" psychology arising from the nationality conflict in the Habsburg Empire, his experience in the Austrian Nazi underground reinforced it in two distinct ways. First, unlike the Hugenberg nationalists in Germany, the conservative right in Austria was both strong and willing enough to crush the Nazi movement if it threatened the state; the Austrian Nazis could never have triumphed without the threat of German intervention. After 19 June 1933, it became a crime in Austria to belong to the Nazi Party or any of its formations. Thus, the Austrian Nazi, particularly if he was employed, truly risked his career by remaining active after this date. We have seen that Kaltenbrunner's right to practice law was revoked on account of his political activity. He was arrested several times and spent four months in an internment camp. Though such punishments were extraordinarily mild in comparison to those which Kaltenbrunner would mete out when his day arrived, they fed his hatred for the System.

[100] Interrogation of Seyss-Inquart, 25 July 1945, Seyss-Inquart File, ZS-300/IV, p. 5, IfZ Munich.
[101] *Personal-Fragebogen*, signed by Ernst Kaltenbrunner, 30 May 1938, RG-242/490/K02696, NA.

Second, the successful outcome of the five-year underground struggle strengthened the conviction that Hitler knew what he was doing and was always right. When the Austrian Nazis had wanted to fight in 1934-1935, Hitler had ordered them to keep the peace; when, on 11 March 1938, the Austrian Nazis feared international crisis and possible disaster for the Reich if the Germans invaded, Hitler ordered his troops to march and got away with it. The Führer's infallibility had been demonstrated by events. A strengthened faith in Hitler's success encouraged many Austrian Nazis to carry out the policies of his regime even when they conflicted with conscience or common sense.

Eight years after the Anschluss, Kaltenbrunner wrote that with the Anschluss "my political yearnings were fulfilled." Henceforth, he wanted only to "build up my profession, to prepare a calm, comfortable old age for my parents, and to put my family on its feet."[102] If Kaltenbrunner ever seriously thought that his political career was over, he was wrong. It had just begun.

[102] E. Kaltenbrunner, "Memoir," p. 49.

CHAPTER IV
From Vienna to Berlin

WHEN Kaltenbrunner entered the Austrian government as state secretary for security on 12 March 1938, he joined a moribund institution. Initially, Austria was to be ruled as a single unit under a Reich governor (*Reichsstatthalter*). On 15 March, Seyss-Inquart was appointed to this position and given authority over the former Austrian ministers and state secretaries. In the ensuing months, however, Hitler, fearing a revival of separatist sentiment, determined to obliterate the very concept of pre-1938 Austria. On 1 May 1939, an *Ostmark* law was promulgated, which, among other things, reorganized the Nazi Party districts in Austria in such a way as to encourage the independence of each from the others. The individual Gauleiter were simultaneously appointed chiefs of the provincial state administration with the result that they looked to Berlin for instructions rather than to the Austrian ministries. Seyss-Inquart's position was abolished; and on 11 January 1940, the former Austrian ministries melted away by decree.[1]

In the meantime, Himmler made certain that Kaltenbrunner was securely anchored in the SS and police organization of the Ostmark, as the provinces of the former Austrian state were now called. On 12 March 1938, he reorganized the hitherto illegal Austrian SS into the SS-Oberabschnitt Österreich;[2] nine days later, Kaltenbrunner was confirmed as its chief. Before the dissolution of the Austrian government in 1940, Himmler preserved Kaltenbrunner's position in the state apparatus by appointing him higher SS and police leader (*Höherer SS- und Polizeiführer*—HSSPF) for the Military District XVII (Vienna, Upper Austria, Lower Austria, and part of the Burgenland).[3] Kaltenbrunner now held positions simultaneously in the SS and in the state administration.

---

[1] For these administrative developments, see Luža, *Anschluss Era*, pp. 57-227; John A. Bernbaum, "Nazi Control in Austria: The Creation of the Ostmark, 1938-1940," doctoral dissertation, University of Maryland, 1972, pp. 64-82, 106-142, 194-199.

[2] The name of the SS-Oberabschnitt was later changed from Österreich to Donau. See order of Himmler, 24 June 1938, Aktenmappe SS, Ordner 304/6, p. 65, BDC.

[3] Order of Himmler, 12 March 1938, ibid., p. 41; "Personalverfügung Nr. 1," signed Schmitt [Chief of the SS Personnel Chancellery], 21 March 1938, SS-Sammelliste, vol. 43, pp. 140-144, BDC; RFSS Persönlicher Stab to Kaltenbrunner, 5 July 1939, E. Kaltenbrunner SS File, BDC; "Niederschrift über die von General Daluege abgehaltene Besprechung am 14.3.38, 22 Uhr, in der Herrengasse 7 in Wien," 16 March 1938, File HA-Orpo, R 19/401, pp. 16-18, BA.

It has been assumed that Kaltenbrunner's position as HSSPF merely provided him with a decorative role within the Nazi Reich, and that it in no way prepared or qualified him for his future career in the RSHA.[4] While the first is true, the latter is only partly valid; and to understand fully the reasons for Kaltenbrunner's rise, we must examine the purpose and responsibilities of the HSSPF, show how this office operated in practice, and then examine the nature and purpose of the RSHA.

The position of HSSPF was developed in 1937, as Himmler sought to coordinate his rapidly expanding SS-police empire and to give the many and varied political tasks of the SS a single focus on the regional level. In his person, the HSSPF represented an amalgamation of the SS, an organization of the Nazi Party, with the German police, a part of the state apparatus. This fusion of state and Party organizations was reflected at the center by Himmler's appointment as Reichsführer SS and Chief of German Police in the Reich Ministry of the Interior (*Reichsführer SS und Chef der deutschen Polizei im Reichsministerium des Innern*) on 17 June 1936. As chief of police, Himmler was legally tied to the German state apparatus and to the laws that defined police functions and procedures. As chief of the SS, however, he was the personification of what Hans Buchheim calls the "Führer executive," the implementor of the "supra-State Führer will," upon which no temporal considerations were binding. By combining the SS and police in his person, Himmler was able to draw the latter out of its traditional relationship to the state (without relinquishing funds provided by the state), and to tie its executive powers to the limitless will of the Führer.[5]

The HSSPF was to function on the regional level exactly as Himmler functioned at the center—that is, to represent in his person the fusion of SS and police. He supervised all SS and police forces in his assigned district. These included: the Security Police (*Sicherheitspolizei*—Sipo), which was composed of the Secret State Police (*Geheime Staatspolizei*—Gestapo) and the Criminal Police (*Kriminalpolizei*—Kripo); the Security Service (*Sicherheitsdienst*—SD); the Regular Police (*Ordnungspolizei*—Orpo); the General SS (*Allgemeine* SS); the Death's Head Units (*Totenkopfverbände*), which guarded the concentration camps; the Military SS (*Waffen* SS); and the local offices of the Reich Commissar for the Strengthening of German Nationhood (*Reichskommissar für die Festigung deutschen Volkstums*—RKFDV), which carried out racial and resettlement policy. While in peacetime the HSSPF exercised only a supervisory role over these agencies, which reported

---

[4] Hagen, *Geheime Front*, p. 82; Hagen, *Unternehmen Bernhard*, p. 94. Wendell Robert Houston concedes that Kaltenbrunner's power was more than nominal. See his "Kaltenbrunner," p. 76.

[5] On Himmler's position and the significance of the fusion of SS and police, see Buchheim, "SS," pp. 139-140, 157; Browder, "Sipo and SD," pp. 142-144.

directly to their central offices in Berlin, he took direct command of all SS and police forces in his district in the event of an emergency. Before the war, Himmler thought of such an emergency in terms of an attempted military coup against the Nazi regime. The war then conveniently created a state of "permanent emergency," during which the HSSPF exercised in theory continuous and direct command over all SS and police units assigned to him.[6]

In order to insure maximum freedom from state supervision, official relations between the HSSPF and the local authorities were deliberately ill-defined. The boundaries of the former's jurisdiction were aligned with those of the Wehrmacht military districts (*Wehrkreise*); and Himmler candidly admitted that "only in a few cases did the borders [of the military districts] coincide with those of the state administrative authorities." Since the HSSPF's area of competence often encompassed parts of two or more provincial units, to each of whose chiefs he was "personally and directly subordinated," state officials had little effective control over the HSSPF. As Hans Buchheim writes, "under these circumstances, the regional chiefs of the state administration were not in a position to carry on any type of supervision worthy of the name over the HSSPF or even to have an influence on any HSSPF's activity that went beyond the realm of pure routine."[7]

As Himmler's personal representative, the HSSPF had two functions besides that of emergency command. First, he represented the political interests of the SS and police. This involved participation in administrative power struggles with civilian, military, and Party authorities and supervision of special ideological tasks ordered by the Führer (e.g., the deportation and destruction of Jews, Gypsies, and other real or imagined enemies of Germany). In the Old Reich and Austria, the HSSPFs remained weak owing to the strong entrenchment of local Party and state authorities, but in the occupied territories during the war—particularly in Eastern Europe and the Soviet Union—where Nazi Party and German state had no established organization and where "ideological tasks" were carried out frequently and regularly, they exercised vast and often arbitrary power.[8]

Second, the HSSPF was "to guarantee and promote the unity of the entire

[6] On the formation of the HSSPF and emergency powers, see decree of Frick [Reich minister of the interior], 13 November 1937, T-175/123/2649407, NA. See also Buchheim, "Höheren," pp. 362, 369. On Himmler's concern about military putsch, see Neusüss-Hunkel, *SS*, pp. 48-51. On increased actual powers for the HSSPF during the war, see circular of Himmler, "Dienstanweisung für die Höheren SS- und Polizeiführer," 18 December 1939, T-175/123/2649421-2649423, NA.

[7] Buchheim, "Höheren," p. 364. On Himmler's candid admission, see decree of Himmler, 6 December 1939, T-175/123/2649416, NA.

[8] Buchheim, "The SS," pp. 220-227. For the official basis for the HSSPF's power in the Soviet Union, see decree of Himmler, 21 May 1941, NOKW-2079, NA.

SS and police organization"; he was to encourage on the regional level that gradual amalgamation of SS and police which was symbolized by Himmler's position at the top. In his speech to the SS-*Gruppenführer* at Poznań in October 1943, the Reichsführer SS made this point clear: "I see one overriding, concrete task for the higher SS and police leaders and it applies also to the heads of the [SS] main offices . . . it must and will be that even under Reichsführer SS no. 10, this SS order and all of its parts—General SS, Military SS, Regular Police, Security Police, our entire economic administration, our training, our ideological education, the whole question of racial stock—is one bloc, one body, one Order."[9] In the person of the HSSPF, the two pillars of the suprastate Führer executive—SS and police—would fuse into one. As Reinhard Heydrich, the chief of the RSHA, explained to Kurt Daluege, the chief of the Orpo Main Office:[10]

> The old police administration as well as the new offices of the higher SS and police leaders . . . exist side by side as instruments of leadership of the police, and together are too many. They thus must be fused into one. The temporarily still valid but insufficient powers of the higher SS and police leaders . . . in the territory of the Reich are too weak to resist the [state] administration, which raises ever greater demands for authority over the police. . . . Our entire organization of SS and police must therefore already be set up correctly and methodically as an organization for the time when, after the war, the administration and the state go about establishing a new order.

It would thus be inaccurate to describe the HSSPF as merely a glorified police chief. On the contrary, he was the regional commander of an elite *Staatsschutzkorps* (Corps for the Protection of the State),[11] which protected the Reich not only or even primarily because its members were policemen or bureaucrats doing their job, but because of innermost conviction, out of a consciousness of belonging to a military, racially pure elite, whose raison d'être was to defend the Reich from an endless array of enemies. As one Nazi police official put it, the new police would view the unity and well-being of the nation as "indivisible"; under the new order, "each attempt to assert or even to *adhere to* another political ideal would be eliminated . . . as a *symptom of illness [Krankheitserscheinung]* that endangers the healthy unity of the indivisible national organism" (emphasis in the original).[12] SD chief Reinhard Heydrich stated that the new police must carry the "positive" impulse of a "corps-like community," and that men merely trained in

[9] Quoted in Buchheim, "Höheren," p. 379.
[10] Heydrich to Daluege, 30 October 1941, T-175/123/2648602; see also Buchheim, "Höheren," p. 391.
[11] Browder, "Sipo and SD," pp. 178-179.
[12] Excerpts from Werner Best, "Die Geheime Staatspolizei," in *Deutsches Recht*, 15 April 1936, File RSHA, R 58/243, pp. 119-122, BA.

administration and criminology were not fully qualified National Socialist policemen: "For beyond this, an unconditional acceptance of the National Socialist idea belongs to the struggle against the enemies of the state."[13]

Given his Burschenschaft background and his experience in the politics of the Austrian Nazi underground, Kaltenbrunner fitted into the ideal of a fighting community sworn to protect the Reich. In Vienna, he "enjoyed" establishing the SS-Oberabschnitt Donau. He would have taken yet more pleasure in his new position, had it not been stripped of real executive power by the Security Police and the SD in Berlin. Though he later claimed that he had simply been less interested in police work,[14] his relative inaction in the police sector resulted from his unequivocal defeat in the power struggle that raged in Austria after the Nazi takeover.

Himmler himself was unsure of how to structure police power in Austria. On the one hand he was concerned that Kaltenbrunner's authority over all SS and police in Austria be upheld. On 14 March, two days after the German invasion, Orpo chief Kurt Daluege explained to his subordinates that the inspectors of the Orpo and the Security Police would fall under the authority of the HSSPF and that Kaltenbrunner's official appointment would precede that of the police inspectors. Three days earlier, however, Himmler had entrusted Heydrich with the execution of all political police measures and with the task of reorganizing the Austrian Security Police to fit Reich standards.[15] These contradictory orders signaled the commencement of the struggle for power.

It is not clear when Kaltenbrunner and Heydrich first crossed paths, but it is certain that they did not get along. Heydrich considered Kaltenbrunner a crude subaltern and delighted in making insulting jokes about the size of Kaltenbrunner's behind (he had heavy hips, whereas Heydrich was slender and very proud of his "Nordic" physique). Moreover, the Security Police chief suspected the Austrian Nazi leaders of planning to create an island of autonomy in Austria. Heydrich was so certain of this that he had prominent Austrian leaders, including Kaltenbrunner and Seyss-Inquart, shadowed by the SD in Vienna. He even planted a spy on Kaltenbrunner's personal staff.[16]

Heydrich was determined to limit Kaltenbrunner's influence in Austria.

[13] Excerpts from Reinhard Heydrich, "Die Bekämpfung der Staatsfeinde," in Deutsches Recht, 15 April 1936, ibid., pp. 123-125.

[14] On this and "enjoyment," see E. Kaltenbrunner, "Memoir," Nuremberg, July-August 1946, p. 50, Kaltenbrunner File.

[15] "Niederschrift über die von General Daluege abgehaltene Besprechung am 14.3.38, 22 Uhr, in der Herrengasse 7, Wien," 16 March 1938, File HA-Orpo, R 19/401, pp. 16-18, BA; order of Himmler, 11 March 1938, ibid., p. 10.

[16] Interview with Dr. Wilhelm Höttl, Bad Aussee, 14 and 15 April 1977, Höttl Tape, pp. 4, 11; affidavit of Wilhelm Höttl, 10 October 1945, 1746-PS, exhibit B, p. 17; interview with Elisabeth Kaltenbrunner, Linz, 25 March 1977; testimony of Seyss-Inquart, IMT xv, p. 635.

On the night of 12-13 March 1938, he sent two of his agents, SS-*Obersturmführer* Walter Schellenberg and SS-*Untersturmführer* Adolf Eichmann, to Vienna with lists of political enemies and prominent Jews scheduled for arrest. Schellenberg was able to seize Austrian documents and records pertaining to political and military intelligence in Austria during the Schuschnigg regime. Kaltenbrunner attempted to gain control of police policy toward the Jews in Austria during the summer of 1938, but without success; Heydrich and his representatives, Eichmann and Vienna Inspector of Security Police and SD Walter Stahlecker, established a Central Office for Jewish Emigration, which was independent of Kaltenbrunner's control.[17] Heydrich also made certain that men personally loyal to him ran the Security Police and the SD in Vienna. Franz Josef Huber, chief of the local Gestapo office, was Bavarian born and had worked closely with Heydrich in the Security Police since 1933; while Friedrich Polte, leader of the SD Main Sector (*Leitabschnitt*), was also a "typical creature of Heydrich."[18]

Heydrich formalized his control in a circular issued shortly after the Anschluss. It provided that the "main state police office [*Staatspolizeileitstelle*] and the state police offices [in the provinces] receive direct instructions from the chief of Security Police and the Secret State Police Office in Berlin which is subordinated to him. They report directly [to these authorities]." Kaltenbrunner was granted the right to issue instructions on all matters to the Gestapo in Vienna only if they did not conflict with orders emanating from Berlin: "In case of doubt, the decision of the *Reich central authority* [i.e., the Security Police Main Office] is to be sought" (emphasis added). Likewise, the SD office in Vienna was given full responsibility for collecting political intelligence. Its chief, Polte, reported directly to Berlin; Kaltenbrunner was merely informed from time to time.[19]

[17] Walter Schellenberg, *Secret Service*, p. 329; Browder, "Sipo and SD," p. 226; Adolf Eichmann, "Meine Memoiren," 9 May-16 June 1960, Eichmann Prosecution Documents (hereafter EPD), no. 1492, p. 70, IfZ Munich. On the triumph of Heydrich, Stahlecker, and Eichmann over Kaltenbrunner in the question of control over Jewish policy in Austria, see undated memorandum of SD office II 112 [Hagen], probably early September 1938, File RSHA, R 58/486, p. 23, BA. For the activities of the Central Office for Jewish Emigration, see Luža, *Anschluss Era*, pp. 224-225.

[18] Höttl Tape, p. 11. Höttl has exaggerated the extent of mistrust and hostile feeling between Kaltenbrunner and Huber; for Kaltenbrunner wrote Himmler in 1942 that he considered Huber particularly fit to run the Gestapo office in Vienna. Kaltenbrunner to Himmler, 23 December 1942, T-175/57/2572336-2572337, NA.

[19] Decree of Heydrich, 15 March 1938, File HA-Orpo, R 19/401, pp. 31-32, BA; telegram of Chief of Security Police [signed Best] to Gestapo, Kripo, and SD offices, 22 March 1938, File RSHA, R 58/801, BA. Heydrich's victory was consolidated by a Himmler circular of 18 March 1938, which adopted Heydrich's language on the issues of command authority and reporting channels. Circular of the Reichsführer SS and chief of German Police in the Reich Ministry of the Interior, "Organisation der Geh. Staatspolizei in Österreich," 18 March 1938, T-175/355/2865350, NA.

Heydrich thus removed the key functions of the Security Police and the SD—political arrests, intelligence collection, and Jewish "affairs"—from Kaltenbrunner's control. The Austrian SS leader took his defeat very badly. By early 1939, it was apparent that much "ill-feeling" existed between the two men. Heydrich, however, won even on this point; Himmler ordered Kaltenbrunner to initiate a reconciliation. The Austrian SS leader dutifully obeyed.[20]

The defeat left Kaltenbrunner extremely sensitive to efforts of other central SS and police offices to whittle away at his authority. Like Heydrich with the Security Police, SS-Obergruppenführer Kurt Daluege, chief of the Orpo Main Office, sought to retain all local Orpo personnel under his direct control. On the eve of the Anschluss, he issued a circular creating for Austria an inspector of the Orpo, who was "not subordinated to the [local] police administrator, but in the future receives instructions from the chief of the Orpo . . . in his field of competence."[21] Daluege's efforts to exercise such prerogatives in practice led to an open breach with Kaltenbrunner in the fall of 1938, when each leader claimed responsibility for security arrangements during the impending visit to Vienna of Hungarian chief of state Miklós Horthy. Himmler again intervened, advising Kaltenbrunner "to settle such matters in a suitable fashion and to iron out any remaining differences in an amiable manner." Kaltenbrunner duly made the approach, and Daluege, apparently urged by Himmler to yield, stated that "in the future, such difficulties will no longer arise, since the HSSPF will be the sole responsible authority in such cases throughout the Reich."[22]

This victory was hollow compared to the defeat in the affair of the Security Police. The intensity of Kaltenbrunner's anger reflected frustration at his failure to assert the power that he believed to be his by virtue of his appointment as HSSPF in Austria. His authority was even curtailed geographically in April 1939, when the SS-Oberabschnitt Donau was divided into two new Oberabschnitte. Kaltenbrunner remained in Vienna as chief of SS-Oberabschnitt Donau, which included Vienna, Upper and Lower Austria, and the northern part of the Burgenland; Salzburg, the Tyrol, Vorarlberg,

---

[20] Kaltenbrunner to Heydrich, 27 May 1939, E. Kaltenbrunner SS File, BDC; Kaltenbrunner to Himmler, 29 May 1939, ibid. Kaltenbrunner took his revenge on Heydrich's widow by refusing to release to her a file of family papers that had remained at the RSHA in a safe after Heydrich's death in 1942. See Lina Heydrich to Kaltenbrunner, 1 September 1943, T-175/R256/2747960, NA; Lina Heydrich to SS-Hauptsturmführer Eimers [RSHA], 1 October 1944, ibid., 2747961.

[21] Circular of Daluege, 11 March 1938, File HA-Orpo, R 19/401, pp. 7-9, BA.

[22] Himmler to Kaltenbrunner, 15 October 1938, E. Kaltenbrunner SS File, BDC; Himmler to Daluege, 15 October 1938, ibid.; Kaltenbrunner to Daluege, 5 November 1938, ibid.; Daluege to Kaltenbrunner, 14 November 1938, ibid.

Carinthia, Styria, and the southern part of the Burgenland were reorganized into the SS-Oberabschnitt Alpenland, with its seat in Salzburg.[23]

The exclusion of Kaltenbrunner from direct control over the Security Police in Austria by no means precluded his participation in the execution of "ideological" and other tasks carried out by the SS-Police apparatus. As HSSPF he used his power to curb the policy of "wild Aryanization" (i.e., random confiscation) of Jewish property, carried out by individual Austrian Nazi Party members. On 6 August 1938, he ordered local offices of the Party and its formations to gather all valuables (bank books, currency, jewelry, securities, art objects, etc.) previously confiscated from Jews by Party members in the first months after the Anschluss, to deposit them in a bank for later distribution, and to provide the office of the HSSPF with an exact list of the deposited items. Warning that further unauthorized actions of this sort would be prosecuted by the police, Kaltenbrunner legalized the thefts already committed by decreeing the stolen items to be "confiscated property of enemies of the state . . . in view of the special circumstances of the times."[24] He also sought to replace the wild looting during the *Kristallnacht* riots of November 1938 with a policy of orderly, systematic theft, ordering that Jewish-owned businesses be guarded by police patrols. On 17 November he informed the Viennese police president that all closed Jewish businesses had been taken over by the Reich and were therefore to be regarded as state property.[25]

If Kaltenbrunner disapproved of the random seizure of Jewish property, he had no qualms about the principle of confiscation itself. In the summer of 1939, the Wilhelm-Gustloff-Stiftung, a German firm, expressed interest in purchasing the Hirtenberg ammunition works in Vienna. These had been owned by a Jew named Fritz Mandl, who had fled Austria at the time of the Anschluss. The Wilhelm-Gustloff-Stiftung approached Seyss-Inquart in July 1939 with an offer to buy out Mandl. Seyss-Inquart passed the request on to Kaltenbrunner's office. The viewpoint there was that the sale, if made public, "would cause general indignation in the population of the Ostmark and would very much weaken the esteem of and trust in the National Socialist Party and the leadership of the state." Kaltenbrunner's office suggested instead that Mandl need not be paid at all, since he had lost his citizenship when he left Austria.[26]

[23] Circular of the Chief of the SS Main Office [Heissmeyer], 25 April 1939, File RuSHA, NS 2/78, pp. 68-69, BA.

[24] Order of Kaltenbrunner, 6 August 1938, T-580/62/Ordner 304, NA. In a circular issued four days later, the Gauleiter of *Gau Niederdonau* (Lower Austria) stated frankly that the Kaltenbrunner order "served to legalize confiscations already carried out." See Circular of Jury, 10 August 1938, ibid.

[25] Millesi [police president in Vienna] to Barth [Staff of the Reich Commissar for the Reunification of Austria with the German Reich], 21 November 1938, 2237-PS, NA.

[26] SD-Führer of SS-Oberabschnitt Donau to Seyss-Inquart, 12 July 1939, 3627-PS, NA.

Though Heydrich and Daluege directed the deportation of the Austrian Jews, Kaltenbrunner was kept closely informed in his capacity as HSSPF. In the spring of 1941, he was informed by the deputy Gauleiter of Vienna, Karl Scharizer, that according to a decision of Himmler himself, the Jews of Vienna would be deported to occupied Poland. Henceforth, one freight car carrying Viennese Jews would be attached to each train leaving Vienna for Kraków. By the end of 1942, 47,555 Austrian Jews had been deported to labor camps, ghettos, and extermination centers in Bohemia, Poland, White Russia, and Latvia. Kaltenbrunner was kept informed at every step.[27]

Since, as HSSPF, he was the nominal commander of the SS Death's Head Units guarding the notorious concentration camp Mauthausen and its adjacent labor camps on the outskirts of Linz, Kaltenbrunner was also consulted in the planning of economic projects involving camp labor. In December 1941, he participated in the discussion of a plan for the Hermann Göring Works to establish a timber industry at Mauthausen utilizing inmate labor. A few months later, he approved a plan to set up a brick works in Prambachkirchen, also using concentration-camp labor. The request for his approval indicates that, despite his later disclaimers at Nuremberg, Kaltenbrunner did have a say in the employment of concentration-camp labor and thus in the policies of the camp itself.[28]

While still involved in the unequal struggle over control of the Security Police, Kaltenbrunner was confronted with yet another battle for power. One contestant was Reich Governor Seyss-Inquart. In the summer of 1938, Seyss-Inquart drafted a plan for a Vienna-based Southeast Institute to collect economic and cultural data on Southeastern Europe and to promote cultural exchange between the Reich and the Balkan nations with the ultimate aim of creating out of the latter a unified economic and cultural bloc under German influence. Another of his projects was the plan to establish an Austrian cultural institute in Vienna: the *Ostmärkische Kunst- und Kulturstätten* (Ostmark Art and Cultural Monuments), which would be entrusted

[27] Lammers to Schirach, 3 December 1940, 1950-PS, IMT XXIX, p. 176; Reich governor in Vienna to Kaltenbrunner, Millesi, and Huber, 18 December 1940, ibid., p. 177; Scharizer to Kaltenbrunner, 20 March 1941, File 1456, DöW; dispatch signed Daluege, 24 October 1941, 3921-PS, IMT XXXIII, pp. 534-535. On the figure of deported Jews, see Luža, *Anschluss Era*, p. 225; Hilberg, *Destruction*, p. 299. Jonny Moser has estimated that a total of 65,459 Austrian Jews were murdered in Nazi concentration and extermination camps. See his *Die Judenverfolgung in Österreich, 1938-1945* (Vienna: Europa Verlag, 1966), pp. 51-52.

[28] Notice of Dr. Hohberg [SS Economic and Administrative Office], 12 December 1941, NID-12324, NA; text of contract between the German Reich, the Reich Gau Oberdonau (Upper Austria), the city of Linz, the Deutsche Erd- und Steinwerke G.m.b.H., the district of Grieskirchen, and the Construction Auxiliary Service of the German Labor Front, 9 February 1942, NO-4329, NA. For Kaltenbrunner's disclaimers, see testimony of Kaltenbrunner, IMT XI, pp. 269, 333.

with the administration of principal cultural institutions throughout Austria and would act independently of the Reich Ministry for Enlightenment and Propaganda.[29]

Such projects reflected Seyss-Inquart's expectation that Hitler would permit him to form an "Austrian ministry" that would gradually guide the Ostmark into a firm union with the German Reich. Austria, so Seyss-Inquart reasoned, must dissolve into the Greater German Reich in such a way that Austrians could feel themselves and their homeland to be an integral part of that Reich. Efforts must be made to encourage the survival of local peculiarities: "the possibility and encouragement of this individual life [Eigenlebens] would create a spiritual preparedness of the Ostmärker to enter the pan-German sphere of life without inhibitions." In short, Seyss-Inquart expected that Hitler, the Austrian, would allow an Austrian "ministry" to serve not only as a focal point for Austrians within the Third Reich, but also as a springboard to realize a goal which stemmed from the time of Prince Felix zu Schwarzenberg, that of an "Austrianization" of the Reich. Far from a Gleichschaltung, the ministry Seyss-Inquart envisioned would prepare not only Austria for union with the Reich, but also the Reich for union with Austria.[30]

Though Hitler appears to have encouraged Seyss-Inquart's illusions as late as March 1939, he ultimately mistrusted his fellow Austrians. Moreover, Seyss-Inquart faced a formidable enemy in Josef Bürckel, the Gauleiter of the Saarpfalz. Bürckel had won Hitler's admiration for his successful organization of the plebiscite that in 1935 brought the Saarland back to Germany; the dictator expected that his Gauleiter could turn the trick again. On 13 March 1938, Bürckel was appointed commissioner of the Austrian Nazi Party with full authority to regroup that organization and to see that the upcoming plebiscite, set for 10 April, would confirm with near unanimity the Anschluss of Austria to the Reich.[31] Significantly, Seyss-Inquart was appointed Reich governor two days after Bürckel had received his assignment.

Bürckel's power in Austria was confirmed by an impressive victory at the polls on 10 April (99.73% voted yes to the union). On 23 April 1938, Hitler appointed him Reich Commissar for the Reunification of Austria with the German Reich (Reichskommissar für die Wiedervereinigung Österreichs an das Deutsche Reich). In this capacity, Bürckel was responsible only to Hitler

[29] Luža, Anschluss Era, pp. 136-137, 139-140. For the structure of the Southeast Institute, see "Organisationsplan des Südostinstituts," April 1938, Nachlass Seyss-Inquart/23, BA.

[30] "Grundsätzliche Vorbemerkungen" [unsigned, but originating from Seyss-Inquart's office], n.d., T-454/75/1302-1307, NA. See also analysis of Rosar, Seyss-Inquart, pp. 299-340 and especially p. 327.

[31] Rosar, Seyss-Inquart, pp. 314, 327-328; Bernbaum, "Ostmark," p. 69.

and was authorized to give orders to all government and Party agencies in Austria.[32]

Like Hitler, Bürckel lacked sentiment for the "special Austrian character" and was suspicious of Austrian Nazis who championed it. His policy was basically that of Hitler: to liquidate the symbols and ideals of the old Austria that the Führer had always despised and to tie the geographical remnant closely to the Reich.[33]

The Ostmark Law of 1 May 1939 symbolized Bürckel's triumph and destroyed Seyss-Inquart's plans for an Austrian ministry. "Austria" disappeared as a political concept. In its place, seven Gaue were established, each rigidly centralized under the control of its Gauleiter, who was also appointed chief of the civilian administration. No links between the provinces were perpetuated or encouraged. Indeed, in 1942, even the name *Ostmark* disappeared; the Austrian Gaue were henceforth called the *Alpen- und Donaugaue*. After bitter protests to Bormann, Göring, and Himmler, Seyss-Inquart was forced to admit defeat.[34] On 1 May 1939, he was appointed Reich minister without portfolio; four months later, he left Vienna to serve in the administration of occupied Poland. He spent the balance of World War II as Reich Commissar for occupied Holland, where he earned himself a seat in the defendants' dock at Nuremberg.

During his last months in Vienna and later, from Kraków, Seyss-Inquart persisted in his efforts to weaken Bürckel's influence and sought in Kaltenbrunner a last bastion of "Austrian" interests. As early as July 1939, he had urged Himmler to "anchor" Kaltenbrunner's position as HSSPF within the state administration. He also sought support in the Ministry of the Interior for a special Austrian police office within that ministry;[35] but neither Himmler nor Minister of the Interior Wilhelm Frick was any more anxious than Bürckel to foster Austrian unity or autonomy. The request was ignored.

If Seyss-Inquart really expected Kaltenbrunner to stand up to Bürckel on

---

[32] Decree signed Hitler, Frick, and Lammers, 23 April 1938, *Reichsgesetzblatt*, I, 1938, p. 407, NG-3207, TWC XII, pp. 744-745. Most of the plebiscite vote was genuine. According to Luža, the election returns "appeared to represent less an outright endorsement of Nazism than an espousal of the all-German idea." Influential too was the general satisfaction at the destruction of the hated Saint-Germain settlement and a general sense of relief and emotional release after the five years of tension under Dollfuss and Schuschnigg. See Luža, *Anschluss Era*, pp. 70-76.

[33] Orlow, *Nazi Party, 1933-1945*, pp. 237-238.

[34] On the *Ostmark* law, see Bernbaum, "Ostmark," pp. 129-139; Luža, *Anschluss Era*, pp. 241-243. On bitter emnity between Bürckel and Seyss-Inquart, see Rosar, *Seyss-Inquart*, pp. 320-341 and especially the Seyss-Inquart correspondence with Bürckel, Göring, and Himmler in ibid., pp. 343-369.

[35] Seyss-Inquart to Himmler, 24 July 1939, Nachlass Seyss-Inquart/3, BA; Seyss-Inquart to Stuckart, 24 August 1939, ibid.

behalf of "Austrian" interests, he must have been disappointed. Although the Austrian SS leader sympathized with some of Seyss-Inquart's ideas and later lamented from his prison cell that they were not applied, he was not willing to arouse Bürckel's wrath on their account. When Bürckel began to intrigue against Seyss-Inquart's supporters, Kaltenbrunner did nothing to protect them. In January 1939, Bürckel forced the dismissal of Globocnik, who had been Gauleiter in Vienna since the plebiscite, and succeeded to the vacant post. Five months later, Mühlmann, a close friend of Seyss-Inquart, was removed from his position as state secretary for cultural affairs in Vienna. Finally, Neubacher, the mayor of Vienna and another close friend of Seyss-Inquart, was hounded out of office in the winter of 1939-1940.[36]

Rainer and Kaltenbrunner were the only members of the Seyss-Rainer coalition who made their peace with Bürckel. Kaltenbrunner was careful not to antagonize the vindictive Reich commissar and apparently won his respect. Whenever the Seyss-Neubacher-Mühlmann clique sought a minor concession from Bürckel, Kaltenbrunner would invite Bürckel to a *Heuriger*[37] and work it out over a few liters of wine. Rainer also took pains to stay on good terms with Bürckel.[38]

Apprehensive that his personal sympathy for Seyss-Inquart might jeopardize his relationship with Bürckel, Kaltenbrunner sought a reconciliation between the two rivals. When Seyss-Inquart arrived in Vienna on 18 December 1939 to address a reception for the SS in the office of the HSSPF, at which the Government General and German tasks in Southeastern Europe were to be the subjects of discussion, Kaltenbrunner invited Bürckel to attend. The Reich commissar curtly declined and then dashed off a note to Himmler, complaining that Seyss-Inquart was seeking to establish a "consulate of the Government General in Vienna," and was using the SS as a front to sabotage Bürckel's policy in Austria. Exasperated, Kaltenbrunner asked Himmler to mediate, expressing his concern "that my appreciation for the political sagacity and intellectual qualities of our SS comrade Seyss will conflict with my self-evident subordination to the concerns of the Gauleiter and Reich commissar." Himmler ordered Kaltenbrunner to explore possible avenues of reconciliation; eight months later, Kaltenbrunner replied that neither Bürckel nor Seyss-Inquart was interested.[39]

[36] These intrigues can be followed in Luža, *Anschluss Era*, pp. 111-113, 147-148, 265-268. On Kaltenbrunner's later lament, see E. Kaltenbrunner, "Memoir," pp. 35, 50, 52, 53.

[37] *Heurigen* are small taverns in Vienna, whose custom it is to dole out the new wine at the end of a vintage. Patrons generally bring their own food.

[38] Höttl Tape, pp. 8, 12; Rainer to Bürckel, 23 October 1939, T-84/13/10333-10334, NA.

[39] Seyss-Inquart to Wolff, 5 January 1939, T-175/33/2541131-2541132, NA; Bürckel to Himmler, 15 December 1939, ibid., 2541054-2541055; Kaltenbrunner to Himmler, 22 December 1939, ibid., 2541051-2541053; Brandt to Kaltenbrunner, 5 January 1940, ibid., 2541050; Kaltenbrunner to Himmler, 3 August 1940, ibid., 2541046-2541047.

Seyss-Inquart's protest against the Gleichschaltung of Austria found limited support among the Austrian populace. On the whole, the Austrian people remained enthusiastic and hopeful about the Anschluss throughout 1938. Bürckel's failure to control steep inflation and to alleviate the housing crisis in Vienna harmed him more than his lack of feeling for Austrian "uniqueness"; and the unfavorable reaction to his anti-Catholic measures initially reflected the population's attachment to the Church rather than to Austria. Moreover, Bürckel's rigidity in dealing with subordinates and his favoritism to his old comrades from the Saarpfalz eventually alienated much of the rank and file of the Austrian Nazi Party. Widespread opposition to the "Prussianization" of Austria and the evolution of a genuine Austrian identity did not develop until the German invasion of the USSR, however, long after both Bürckel and Seyss-Inquart had departed from the scene.[40]

By the summer of 1940, Kaltenbrunner's dilemma had resolved itself. Bürckel's task of liquidating the Austrian state was complete; in July, he returned to the Saarpfalz and was replaced in Vienna by former Hitler Youth leader Baldur von Schirach. Though Schirach (who was also a Reich German) was equally unpopular in Vienna, Kaltenbrunner took pains to establish and preserve a "harmonious" working relationship with him.[41] Though Kaltenbrunner might later moan in his cell in Nuremberg that the Reich had misunderstood and abused Vienna and Austria, in practice his commitment to Austria never overshadowed his willingness to obey the man in power.

When not participating in such intrigues, Kaltenbrunner worked on routine police administration, transmission of Security Police orders from Berlin to police units in Vienna, and supervision both of the indoctrination of new SS recruits and the amalgamation of the SS and police in the SS-Oberabschnitt Donau. His reports on the progress of these tasks were read "with delight" by Himmler, who assured him that he would make a good HSSPF. The Austrian SS leader also spent much of his time providing jobs for unemployed SS men, and keeping them out of trouble (e.g., restraining them from unauthorized participation in the arbitrary confiscation of Jewish property).[42]

Yet, just as when he had been a lawyer in Salzburg and Linz in the 1920s, Kaltenbrunner was bored by such mundane activities. In the same way as he had been unable then to adjust to a "normal" life in the Austrian Re-

[40] Luža, *Anschluss Era*, pp. 144-145, 264-265; Bernbaum, "Ostmark," pp. 149-157, 160-161, 173-175, 188-189.

[41] Herff [SS Personal-Hauptamt] to Wolff, 19 December 1942, T-175/59/2574392-2574393, NA.

[42] Himmler to Kaltenbrunner, 28 January 1941, E. Kaltenbrunner SS File, BDC; E. Kaltenbrunner, "Memoir," p. 50.

public after the excitement of the Burschenschaft, he could not adjust now to everyday life in Nazi Austria after the tension and intrigue of the underground years. His lack of control over the Security Police and SD apparatus only heightened his frustration and restlessness. He wrote later that "after the storm of enthusiasm [over the Anschluss in the spring of 1938] came the hard work, which I actually did not find very fulfilling, since it was directed centrally from Berlin." To one colleague, he even confided that he would prefer to be sent to the front.[43]

As HSSPF in Vienna and, later, as RSHA chief, Kaltenbrunner continued to indulge in the favorite nonpolitical pastimes of his fraternity days, wine and women. Otto Picha related that the Austrian SS leader was a habitual heavy drinker and sought every excuse to "celebrate." Wilhelm Höttl recalled that Kaltenbrunner "drowned his frustrations in alcohol." On one occasion, while intoxicated, he drove like a madman through the streets of Vienna until his companion, Police Vice-President SS-Oberführer Josef Fitzthum, managed to bring him to his senses. The Nazi Party *Ortsgruppenleiter* of Peuerbach (Upper Austria) testified under interrogation that Kaltenbrunner was known to have drunk more than his fill from time to time.[44]

Women provided Kaltenbrunner with another distraction. While in Vienna, he was often seen in public with the daughter of a Viennese coffeehouse owner. According to Höttl, the Austrian SS leader behaved as if he were the woman's "fully authorized spouse" and "was not ashamed to stage frightful scenes of jealousy whenever she spoke to another man." It was also rumored that Kaltenbrunner enjoyed the favors of two aristocratic Upper Austrian women. Later, as RSHA chief, Kaltenbrunner had an intimate relationship with Countess Gisela von Westarp, who in March 1945 bore him twins. Even while he carried on with Gisela, he saw other women. Wilhelm Höttl, who was himself far from prudish, remarked to this author that there was "something pathological" about Kaltenbrunner's insatiable appetite for variety.[45]

Beyond such conventional pastimes, Kaltenbrunner also dabbled in intelligence collection and in intrigues with tiny Nazi groups in neighboring Czechoslovakia and Switzerland. Although he later told the court at Nurem-

[43] E. Kaltenbrunner, "Memoir," p. 50; Kaltenbrunner to Pancke [chief of SS Race and Settlement Main Office], 19 June 1940, R. Kaltenbrunner RuS (Sippenamt) File, BDC.

[44] Interview with Otto Picha, Vienna, 26 January 1977; Höttl Tape, pp. 12, 13; interrogation of Alois Trappmaier by the Linz Gestapo, 12 November 1943, Landgericht Linz, KMS 56/44. The author is grateful to Peter Kammerstätter of Linz for making this document available.

[45] Höttl Tape, pp. 11-12, 26. Supporting evidence on rumors of Kaltenbrunner's amorous associations, see report of Linz Gestapo to the Prosecutor's Office at the Special Court in Linz, 8 February 1944, 2016/44-II2-, Landgericht Linz, KMS 56/44. On Gisela von Westarp's twins, see also Roman Catholic Rectory, Alt Aussee [signed Trunkel], to the author, 10 January 1977.

berg that, while he was HSSPF in Vienna, he had established a "rather large political intelligence service radiating from Austria to the Southeast," Wilhelm Höttl told this author that in fact Kaltenbrunner had no contacts in Southeast Europe outside Slovakia.[46] As he had done with the SD net in Vienna, Kaltenbrunner utilized an intelligence organization that had been established and operated by others to enhance his own reputation in Berlin as an expert in the field. These "others" belonged to the Vienna-based Southeast Europe Society (*Südosteuropa-Gesellschaft*—SOEG). Founded on 8 February 1940, the SOEG was an offshoot of the Reich Ministry of Economics aimed at streamlining and coordinating German policy in the Danube Basin. As its business manager wrote, a major task of the SOEG was "to cultivate, strengthen, and improve German contacts with the Southeast European lands."[47]

In the fall of 1940, August Heinrichsbauer, the executive director of the SOEG, approached Kaltenbrunner and intimated that he occasionally received confidential information on political and economic trends in the Balkans. He wished to know whether Kaltenbrunner was interested in receiving copies of these reports. Kaltenbrunner was so impressed with the sample report sent by Heinrichsbauer that he urged expeditious delivery of further reports so that events would not render them obsolete. If Kaltenbrunner can be believed, these reports from "his" intelligence service made an excellent impression on Himmler; he later claimed that the reports suggested to Himmler the idea of choosing him to replace Heydrich at the RSHA.[48] Generally written by businessmen and academics, the reports were of uneven quality, though Himmler and Heydrich, themselves more competent in intrigue than intelligence evaluation, may not have noticed this. Any intelligence reports written directly by Kaltenbrunner at this time have yet to be found, if indeed they ever existed.

Slovakia was one land where Kaltenbrunner did have his own contacts. His relations with the chief of the *Karpatendeutsche Partei* (KdP), Franz Karmasin, were close. Through Karmasin, Kaltenbrunner established contact with such right-wing Slovak politicians as Ferdinand Durčanský and Karol Sidor in 1937. After he was appointed state secretary for ethnic Ger-

[46] Höttl Tape, p. 13; testimony of Kaltenbrunner, IMT xi, p. 237.

[47] Heinrichsbauer to Ronneberger, 11 July 1940, File SOEG, R 63/63, BA. For the scheme of the SOEG organization, see "Gliederung des Südosteuropa-Gesellschaft," 11 November 1942, Aktenmappe SOEG, Ordner 364, pp. 211-219, BDC. For a history of the SOEG, see Dietrich Orlow, *The Nazis in the Balkans: A Case Study of Totalitarian Politics* (Pittsburgh: University of Pittsburgh Press, 1968); Luža, *Anschluss Era*, pp. 130-131.

[48] Heinrichsbauer to Kaltenbrunner, 10 October 1940, File SOEG, R 63/35, BA; Kaltenbrunner to Heinrichsbauer, 11 October 1940, ibid.; Kaltenbrunner to Heinrichsbauer, 29 October 1940, ibid. On Kaltenbrunner's claim, see testimony of Kaltenbrunner, IMT xi, p. 237; E. Kaltenbrunner, "Memoir," p. 50.

man affairs in Slovakia in the wake of the Munich Pact, Karmasin kept Kaltenbrunner informed on the activities of the newly autonomous Slovak government.[49]

During the months before the final dismemberment of Czechoslovakia in March 1939, the SD in Vienna received orders to foment unrest and to encourage separatist sentiment in Slovakia. Kaltenbrunner helped to direct such activities by means of his control over the ethnic German Volunteer SS (*Freiwillige Schutzstaffel*), which was comprised of units originally established as a paramilitary wing of the Karpatendeutsche Partei. Like the Austrian SS, the Volunteer SS had been organized directly under German SS standards and command. After the incorporation of the Sudetenland into the Reich in October 1938, the remaining Volunteer SS units were based at the universities in Prague and Brno; in Slovakia, they were chiefly active in Bratislava. Kaltenbrunner's influence over the Volunteer SS was promoted by Seyss-Inquart, who worked closely with the Austrian SS leader in Slovakia.[50]

Kaltenbrunner was concerned that the Volunteer SS units be properly uniformed and equipped. In February 1939, he wrote Reich Cabinet chief Hans Heinrich Lammers, requesting an advance of 50,000 RM for the Moravian SS. The Austrian SS leader complained that the Moravian units were ill-equipped and had no uniforms, and that their morale was poor. He argued that they could perform their duties effectively only if they appeared "impressive and unified to the outside." With the aid of Seyss-Inquart, Kaltenbrunner secured 60,000 RM for the Moravian SS.[51]

By late February, the SS-Oberabschnitt Donau had begun to smuggle weapons and explosives to Volunteer SS units in Moravia and Slovakia for the purpose of simulating Czech nationalist "attacks" on buildings and homes owned by ethnic Germans. During the final crisis in Czechoslovakia in mid-March 1939, Kaltenbrunner was involved in an attempt to strongarm Slovak Prime Minister Karol Sidor into proclaiming Slovak independence. When this effort failed, the Slovak-based Volunteer SS were instrumental in provoking "disturbances" that "encouraged" the Slovak declaration of independence on the night of 14 March 1939. On the next day, under Kaltenbrun-

---

[49] Jörg K. Hoensch, *Die Slowakei und Hitlers Ostpolitik: Hlinkas Slowakische Volkspartei zwischen Autonomie und Separation, 1938-1939* (Cologne-Graz: Böhlau Verlag, 1965), p. 59.

[50] On SD instructions to foment unrest in Slovakia, see ibid., p. 224; Schellenberg, *Secret Service*, p. 51; Hagen, *Geheime Front*, p. 174. On the Volunteer SS in Bohemia, Moravia, and Slovakia, see speech of Karl Hermann Frank, "Die Schutzstaffel am 15. März 1939," *Böhmen und Mähren: Blatt des Reichsprotektors*, Jahrgang 2 (1941), 2826-PS, IMT xxxi, pp. 195-198. On Kaltenbrunner's control, see Flor to Seyss-Inquart, 20 December 1938, Nachlass Seyss-Inquart/39, BA.

[51] Kaltenbrunner to Lammers, 23 February 1939, NG-1439, NA; Seyss-Inquart to Kaltenbrunner, 24 April 1939, Nachlass Seyss-Inquart/3, BA.

ner's orders, the Volunteer SS seized local police offices in Prague and Brno and prevented the Czech police from destroying their files. After the dissolution of the Czechoslovak state, Kaltenbrunner maintained close contacts with the ethnic German SS in Slovakia and with the quasi-fascist Slovak Hlinka Guard.[52]

If the coup in Slovakia could be considered, at least in part, a success for Kaltenbrunner, his flirtation with the aspirations of a tiny group of Swiss exiles in Vienna spotlighted his ignorance of political conditions in Switzerland. In January 1941, he was approached by a Swiss journalist named Franz Burri, and received an outline of Burri's ideas. Noting that the "Alemannic-Burgundian nation" had suffered an era of decline owing to English, French, and Masonic influence in Switzerland, Burri contended that a union of German-speaking Switzerland with the Reich would reverse this trend. Since, however, he was forced to realize that the vast majority of Swiss opposed such a solution and were thus "hostile to the Reich," he declared that simple annexation was not viable as an immediate goal and suggested that if the Swiss Nazis could come to power with the aid of German funds and political pressure, they could "reeducate" the Swiss people toward a positive acceptance of union with the Greater German Reich. Burri explained that he controlled a "fighting unit" of eighteen hundred men inside Switzerland, known as the Swiss Renewal Movement (*Schweizer Erneuerungsbewegung*—SEB), and a group of émigrés in Germany, the Union of Swiss in Greater Germany (*Bund der Schweizer in Grossdeutschland*—BSG); he requested that his people be accepted into the SS in order to strengthen his political clout—and that of the "true" National Socialists in Switzerland—against an array of tiresome rivals within and outside of Switzerland. He had approached Kaltenbrunner in the knowledge that the Austrian SS leader had "participated decisively in the struggle of the German Volk in Austria and for this reason had understanding for the struggle of the Alemannic race."[53]

Kaltenbrunner passed Burri's memorandum on to Himmler without checking up on the Swiss's story. In fact, Burri's following among the Swiss Nazis, who themselves were divided into several "fronts" and organizations,

---

[52] On explosives and weapons, see Hoensch, *Slowakei*, p. 224. On Volunteer SS seizure of police offices, see ibid., pp. 281-282; speech of Frank, "Schutzstaffel," 2826-PS, IMT xxxi, pp. 195-198. An officer from Kaltenbrunner's staff, SS-Hauptsturmführer Riegler, commanded the so-called *Einsatztruppe Sturmbann*, the elite battle corps of the Volunteer SS. See Berger to Himmler, 30 April 1943, T-175/75/2593667-2593668, NA. On Kaltenbrunner's contacts with ethnic German SS and Hlinka Guard in Slovakia, see Querner to Himmler, 1 April 1943, T-175/62/2578265, NA.

[53] Franz Burri, "Zur Lage in der Schweiz," 22 January 1941, p. 1, SS-HO/2293, BDC. See also Walter Wolf, *Fascismus in der Schweiz: Die Geschichte der Frontenbewegung in der deutschen Schweiz, 1930-1945* (Zurich: Flamberg Verlag, 1969), p. 100.

was virtually nonexistent; most of his rivals considered his Anschluss aims high treason. He had had no significant contact with underground Nazi organizations within Switzerland itself. Since 1938, he had lived in Vienna, where he joined with a former Swiss army major, Ernst Leonardt, who had fled to the Reich after his splinter group, the National Socialist Swiss Workers' Party, had been dissolved by the Swiss police. Leonardt controlled a tiny group of fanatics inside Switzerland, known as the Swiss Society of Friends for an Authoritarian Democracy (SGAD), whose activity consisted mainly of distributing Burri's hate pamphlets. This, then, was the "fighting unit" that Burri wanted accepted into the SS.

Meanwhile, in June 1940, Burri had founded the BSG, through which he hoped to mobilize the Swiss community in Germany for an eventual seizure of power in Switzerland. Within a month of its creation in Stuttgart, the BSG (which never numbered more than eighteen hundred persons) was torn apart by factional strife, while the SGAD was challenged in Swiss underground Nazi circles by the rival National Movement of Switzerland, which was not nearly as enthusiastic about Anschluss to Germany. SS-Sturmbannführer Klaus Hügel, chief of the SD office in Stuttgart, sought in vain to induce the BSG leaders to make peace, but the ambition of each to become a Swiss Hitler and the total lack of support, not only from within Switzerland itself, but also from the Swiss community living in Germany, prevented any meaningful negotiations.[54] Against this background, Burri brought his ideas to Kaltenbrunner.

Kaltenbrunner and Himmler may have found such mumbo jumbo about the Alemannic-Burgundian race appealing, but Heydrich, who presumably had been informed of the real situation by Hügel, warned that the Nazis inside Switzerland resented Burri's comfortable living conditions in Vienna and would reject any German recognition of the journalist's claim to leadership. Besides, Burri was a charlatan not equal in value to a single underground fighter. On Heydrich's recommendation, the matter was discreetly forgotten.[55]

Despite such a glaring case of incompetence, Kaltenbrunner's work in Slovakia and with the Southeast Europe Society in the Balkans helped to establish him in Himmler's mind as a man who knew intelligence work. That the Austrian SS leader was a rank amateur did not seem to disturb Himmler, for, after all, the Reichsführer SS himself was nothing more.

[54] On the various Swiss Nazi movements, see the somewhat polemical Wolf, *Faschismus*. For a good summary of German-Swiss and Latin-Swiss movements and their aims, see also Peter Gilg and Erich Gruner, "Nationale Erneuerungsbewegungen in der Schweiz, 1925-1940," *VfZ* 14 (January 1966), 1-25.

[55] Kaltenbrunner to Himmler, 25 January 1941, SS-HO/2293, BDC; Heydrich to Himmler, 5 April 1941, SS-HO/2297, BDC.

KALTENBRUNNER'S character and personality revealed little of themselves behind the official mask of his position and activities both in Vienna and later, as chief of the RSHA. Impressions of him left by contemporaries divide into two categories. Those who liked or admired him found him handsome, soft-spoken, jovial, a loving husband, a kind father, a reliable comrade, a just superior. Two Gauleiter of Vienna agreed on his striking physical appearance. One wrote that the 6'4" scar-faced SS leader was physically appealing to both women and men. The other declared that Kaltenbrunner "was a very handsome man, a man who greatly affected women . . . he was . . . really a very elegant man. In a dress uniform he looked quite fine." Kaltenbrunner's wife thought him splendid and dashing; one of his schoolteachers described him as a "dashing young man [*Feschak*]," a "handsome and pleasing sight." A comrade in the Austrian Nazi underground remembered Kaltenbrunner as "calm, modest, secure, and reliable." A subordinate in the RSHA testified that he was "irreproachable," devoid of cheap ambition and a lust for power. A friend, Hermann Neubacher, said under interrogation that the Austrian SS leader was "a typical, sturdy, kind-hearted Austrian."[56] Hansjörg Kaltenbrunner remembers his father in a most positive way: Kaltenbrunner "spoke with a soft voice," took pleasure in making jokes, was careful to pick up hitchhikers on the road from Vienna to Linz, put wounded Waffen SS soldiers up in his house, continually invited guests to his dinner table, in short was a kind and generous if often absent father.[57]

Kaltenbrunner had an enduring nostalgic attachment to his native Upper Austria. To subordinates in the RSHA he liked to express his dream of returning to the Upper Austrian Innviertel after the war to lead the simple life of a peasant. Though we should not take such musings too seriously (Hitler, for example, often talked of a retirement to Linz to pick up his "career" as an artist and architect),[58] Kaltenbrunner was willing to intercede for ideological opponents of the Nazi regime, provided that he did not consider them too dangerous and that they were Upper Austrians. In August 1944, Ernst Koref, formerly the acting chief of the Upper Austrian Social Democratic Workers' Party and also Kaltenbrunner's schoolteacher in the

---

[56] Letter of Alfred Frauenfeld to the author, 20 February 1977; interview with Leopold Tavs, Vienna, 21 January 1977, Tavs Tape, p. 5; interview with Elisabeth Kaltenbrunner, Linz, 25 March 1977; letter of Dr. Ernst Koref to the author, 9 December 1976; letter of Franz Peterseil to the author, 17 May 1977; affidavit of Rudolf Mildner, 29 March 1946, ZS-431, IfZ Munich; 1st Lt. George Winzer, CI Intermediate Interrogation Report, 29 January 1946, folder CI-IIR, no. 36, p. 36, NA (Hereafter cited as: Winzer Report).

[57] Dr. Hansjörg Kaltenbrunner, "Persönliche Eindrücke über meinen Vater von meiner Kindheit," Gramastetten, 11 June 1977, pp. 4, 6, 7, 12, and passim.

[58] Affidavit of Wilhelm Waneck, 15 April 1946, Kaltenbrunner-8, IMT XL, p. 341; affidavit of Wilhelm Höttl, 10 October 1945, 1746-PS, exhibit B, p. 19. On Hitler's musings, see, for example, Albert Speer, *Inside the Third Reich* (New York: Macmillan, 1970), pp. 297-298.

Realgymnasium in Linz, was arrested in the general roundup following the failure of the 20 July 1944 conspiracy and, on the orders of Gauleiter Eigruber, was to be sent to Dachau. When Franz Langoth, now mayor of Linz, heard of this, he appealed to Kaltenbrunner. Although he knew not only of Koref's political past but also of his partly Jewish ancestry, the Austrian SS leader intervened to achieve Koref's release. Other isolated cases exist. In 1939, Kaltenbrunner prevented the incarceration in Dachau of his old roommate at the Katzer boarding house in Linz, Wilhelm Pöschl, who had been an anti-Nazi Heimwehr member in the 1930s. In 1943, the Austrian SS leader interceded with the authorities of the Nazi People's Court (*Volksgerichtshof*) to prevent the pronunciation of a death sentence against a member of an Upper Austrian legitimist resistance group.[59] Such cases were exceptions, however; there are no reports of Kaltenbrunner's intercession in cases involving persons who were not Upper Austrians.

Kaltenbrunner's brother Werner remarked to this author that Ernst was, "inside, a soft man [*Ernst war innerlich ein weicher Mensch*]." Thirty years earlier, Heinrich Müller, the chief of the Gestapo office in the RSHA, referred to Kaltenbrunner as "the soft Austrian [*der weiche Österreicher*]." Another RSHA subordinate recalled that Kaltenbrunner "was not the energetic man whom we in his inner circle believed to see in him . . . he lacked the drive for execution. . . . He did not have the ultimate greatness." A counterintelligence report of the U.S. Army stated that Kaltenbrunner was a "procrastinator, forever dodging decisions."[60] Indeed, it might seem that Kaltenbrunner's sentimentality, softness, and indecisiveness made him remarkably unfit and unlikely to assume a leadership post in a system that prized ruthlessness, brutality, and decisiveness.

Yet, there are other, far less flattering or humane descriptions of the man. Otto Picha related that Kaltenbrunner had a "brutal face," and was both a "drunkard" and a "ruffian." Felix Kersten, Himmler's masseur, told Walter Schellenberg that he had "seldom had such a tough, callous ox to examine as this fellow Kaltenbrunner . . . he's coarse, hard-bitten, probably only capable of thinking when he's drunk." Swedish diplomat Count Folke Bernadotte, who met Kaltenbrunner in February 1945, remembered the latter's "cold and inquisitorial eyes." A member of the German military intelligence

---

[59] Dr. Ernst Koref to the author, 9 December 1976; Harry Slapnicka, *Oberösterreich—als es "Oberdonau" hiess, 1938–1945* (Linz: Oberösterreichisches Landesverlag, 1978), p. 59; Dr. Erich Thanner to the author, 12 April 1977.

[60] Interview with Dr. Werner Kaltenbrunner, Vöcklabruck, 25 March 1977. On Müller's remark, see Eberhard Zeller, *Geist der Freiheit: Der zwanzigste Juli 1944* (Munich: Hermann Rinn, 1952), p. 275. See also interrogation of Wilhelm Waneck, 9 January 1948, p. 6, ZS-1579, IfZ Munich; CG U.S. Third Army, Interrogation Report No. 10, 21 June 1945, p. 3, NA.

service (*Abwehr*) described Kaltenbrunner as a "large, uncouth creature formed like an Alpine lumberjack, with cheeks marred by scars." SS-Obergruppen-führer Karl Wolff, chief of the SS and police forces in Italy, referred to Kaltenbrunner as an "ice-cold guy"; an adjutant at Hitler's headquarters said that the Austrian SS leader had "remarkably broad shoulders and clawlike hands—whenever he shook hands with me, I worried."[61]

The most unappealing description of Kaltenbrunner was offered by Walter Schellenberg, the chief of the RSHA foreign intelligence office:[62]

> Kaltenbrunner was a giant in stature, heavy in his movements—a real lumber-jack. It was his square, heavy chin which expressed the character of the man. The thick neck, forming a straight line with the back of his head, increased the impression of rough-hewn coarseness. His small penetrating brown eyes were unpleasant; they looked at one fixedly, like the eyes of a viper seeking to petrify its prey. When one expected Kaltenbrunner to say something, his angular wooden face would remain inexpressive; then, after several seconds of oppressive silence, he would bang the table and begin to speak. I always had the feeling that I was looking at the hands of an old gorilla. They were much too small and the fingers were brown and discolored. . . . My first proper contact with him was in January 1943 and from the first moment he made me feel quite sick. He had very bad teeth and some of them were missing so that he spoke very indistinctly. . . . Himmler also found this extremely unpleasant and eventually ordered him to go to a dentist.

Even Kaltenbrunner's son remembered a second side to his father. One night, the boy, who should have been asleep but who had been sitting on the apartment staircase, overheard one of his father's telephone conversations. Kaltenbrunner "shouted and dealt rudely" with the speaker on the other end of the line. The boy rushed back to his room and "hid" in bed; his father seemed "a completely different man from the one I was used to."[63]

Where völkisch or ideological issues were involved, Kaltenbrunner showed neither softness nor indecisiveness. Though trained in law, he adopted the Nazi view of how the law ought to operate: that written ("Roman") law was invalid in judging the case of a faithful ideological soldier. We have seen in chapter 3 how Kaltenbrunner was willing to protect Königsberg SS men from

---

[61] Interview with Otto Picha, Vienna, 26 January 1977; on Kersten, see Schellenberg, *Secret Service*, p. 328. See also Count Folke Bernadotte, *The Curtain Falls: The Last Days of the Third Reich* (New York: Alfred A. Knopf, 1945), p. 25; Karl Heinz Abshagen, *Canaris, Patriot und Weltbürger* (Stuttgart: Union Deutsche Verlagsgesellschaft, 1950), pp. 354-355; Gerd Buchheit, *Der deutsche Geheimdienst: Geschichte der militärischen Abwehr* (Munich: Paul List Verlag, 1966), p. 417; interrogation of Karl Wolff, 16 December 1947, ZS-317/IV, pp. 36-46, IfZ Munich; Gerhard Boldt, *Hitler: The Last Ten Days* (New York: Berkeley Medallion, 1973), p. 70.

[62] Schellenberg, *Secret Service*, p. 328.

[63] H. Kaltenbrunner, "Persönliche Eindrücke," p. 6.

the legal consequences of their acts on the basis that these were "political" in nature. Another case is that of the former mayor of Linz, SS-Sturmbannführer Josef Wolkerstorfer. Wolkerstorfer had been arrested in April 1942 on suspicion of collusion in criminal negligence, whereby the food administration of the Hermann Göring Works in Linz had allowed a supply of 250,000 kilograms of potatoes to spoil. Worse still, he perjured himself during the preliminary investigation. Kaltenbrunner, who knew Wolkerstorfer from the underground years, sought to intercede with Himmler on the grounds that Wolkerstorfer possessed a Blood Order Medal awarded for time spent in prison under the Schuschnigg regime. When Himmler refused to act, Kaltenbrunner wrote directly to Roland Freisler, then state secretary in the Reich Ministry for Justice. Fearing that Wolkerstorfer would get a harsh sentence in accordance with Hitler's new hard line on economic corruption and negligence, he urged Freisler to dismiss the charges and, in a remarkable passage for an officer in the SS, extolled the virtues of an independent judiciary: "The administration of justice is a blessing when it is carefully thought out by an *independent judge* and when it emanates from the Volk [*volkstümlich bleibt*]" (emphasis in the original). Kaltenbrunner thought that Wolkerstorfer's record as a "tried and true follower of our Führer" should be considered before handing down an indictment. His request was rejected, though his fears on Wolkerstorfer's behalf proved to be unjustified. Wolkerstorfer was indicted, convicted, and fined 3,000 RM.[64]

Another example of Kaltenbrunner's political interpretation of the law is the case of Helmuth Pess, an air force officer stationed in Brussels. It appears that Pess had been having an affair with the wife of Belgian fascist leader Léon Degrelle. On 12 April 1943, Pess was found in an alley with a bullet in his heart. Shortly afterward, Degrelle phoned the Gestapo office in Brussels and reported that Pess had "wished to commit suicide." Kaltenbrunner, by that time chief of the RSHA, had little faith in the suicide story, but nevertheless decided not to pursue the matter on the grounds that "the moral right" stood with Degrelle. The investigation was shelved for "political reasons."[65]

Kaltenbrunner took Nazi symbolism and regalia equally seriously. His apartment in Vienna had a garden in which there stood a flagpole. On special occasions, Kaltenbrunner would run up the flag of the SS—two white runic figures on a solid black background. When Hansjörg Kaltenbrunner

[64] Kaltenbrunner to Freisler, 16 June 1942, SS-Sammelliste, vol. 69, pp. 146-151, BDC; Kaltenbrunner to Wolff, 17 April 1942, T-175/58/2573235-2573237, NA; Wolff to Kaltenbrunner, 4 May 1942, ibid., 2573234; Kaltenbrunner to Wolff, 13 June 1942, SS-Sammelliste, vol. 69, pp. 142-143, BDC; Kaltenbrunner to Hauptamt SS-Gericht, 14 August 1942, ibid., pp. 157-159.

[65] Kaltenbrunner to Himmler, 21 April 1943, T-175/126/2650991-2650992, NA.

entered primary school, he was permitted to take part in the ceremony. Kaltenbrunner was concerned that his son be familiar with Nazi symbols, for it was planned to send the boy to a NAPOLA, a special Nazi school for leadership training.[66]

Kaltenbrunner was thus a man with several faces. At home with his family, out with his comrades or lovers, even while interceding on behalf of political opponents, he could be soft-spoken, gentle, protective, and even sensitive. On the other hand, when challenged on his rigid ideological beliefs or thwarted in his drive for personal power, his "soft" disposition hardened into steely obstinacy, his gentleness into vindictive persecution, his protectiveness into a pose struck for attack, his sensitivity into a coarse vulgarity. His irresoluteness lay rooted in his personality; but, after all, his original acceptance of the Nazi creed was emotionally based on his unwillingness to view the world in any but the most black and white terms. The Nazi precept of absolute obedience rendered any kind of decision making superfluous. It saved him from the agony of existing in a pluralistic world in which values and principles were relative. The conflict within him was never resolved. The same eyes that Schellenberg could compare to those of a viper were viewed by Albert Speer—certainly no friend of Kaltenbrunner—as bearing a "curiously mild look."[67]

If, as a high-ranking SS leader, he hoped and was expected to erase that "soft," irresolute element in his personality, Kaltenbrunner found little opportunity in Vienna to test his "iron will" in the performance of the more "difficult" ideological tasks of the regime. By the spring of 1942, he languished in obscurity, political impotence, and boredom. Most of Austria's Jews had emigrated or had been deported by this time, most of their businesses had been closed or "Aryanized." Heydrich's minions ran the Security Police and the SD in Vienna, while the "Alpine and Danube" Gauleiter, appointed Reich defense commissars (*Reichsverteidigungskommissare*) at the outbreak of World War II, were encroaching on the powers of the state administration as well as on those areas of routine police work in which Heydrich had no interest. The growing power of Martin Bormann's Nazi Party Chancellery blocked the spread of local SS influence in the Austrian Nazi Party rank and file despite the unpopularity of Bürckel's successor, Schirach. Thus, by 1942, Kaltenbrunner's position had indeed become largely ceremonial. He continued to supervise the transfer of policemen into the SS, to approve training programs for new SS candidates, to serve as arbitrator for appeals of individual decisions handed down by the Vienna branch of

---

[66] H. Kaltenbrunner, "Persönliche Eindrücke," pp. 3, 19. On the NAPOLAs (*Nationalpolitische Erziehungsanstalten*), see H. W. Koch, *The Hitler Youth: Origins and Development, 1922-1945* (New York: Stein & Day, 1976), pp. 180-181.

[67] Albert Speer, *Spandau: The Secret Diaries* (New York: Pocket Books, 1977), p. 8.

the Main Office SS Tribunal (*Hauptamt SS-Gericht*); but without the idealism of the Burschenschaft or the political intrigue of the underground years, these routine activities brought him no personal fulfillment.[68] Though he was authorized to take command of all SS and police units in the SS-Oberabschnitt Donau in the event of an enemy invasion or a military coup, neither possibility seemed impending in the late spring of 1942. With few personal connections in Germany other than Himmler and with a determined opponent in Heydrich, Kaltenbrunner appeared to have reached a professional dead end. On 4 June 1942, however, RSHA chief Reinhard Heydrich succumbed to wounds received in an assassination attempt carried out by Czech agents who had parachuted into Bohemia from England.

With Heydrich's death, the top spot in the Reich Main Office for Security (RSHA) fell vacant. The RSHA had seven departments in 1942. *Amt* (Office) I, led by SS-Gruppenführer Bruno Streckenbach, was a personnel office, while Amt II handled administration, legal problems, and funding. Amt III, under the former *Einsatzgruppe* (task force group) commander SS-Gruppenführer Otto Ohlendorf, was the internal intelligence department (*SD-Inland*), which reported on conditions inside the Reich. Amt IV was the notorious Secret State Police (Gestapo), which was responsible for executive measures against "enemies" of the state and through which was organized the deportation of Jews, Gypsies, and other "undesirables" to their deaths in the East; its chief was SS-Gruppenführer Heinrich Müller. Amt V was the Criminal Police (Kripo), commanded by SS-Gruppenführer Artur Nebe. Amt VI was the foreign intelligence service (*SD-Ausland*) under SS-Brigadeführer Walter Schellenberg, while Amt VII under SS-Standartenführer Franz Six was devoted to "ideological and scientific research."[69]

The unification of the Nazi Party intelligence service, the SD, with the executive wing of the Security Police (Gestapo and Kripo) in the RSHA had created an instrument of great power for Himmler and Heydrich. As an "ideological" intelligence organization, the SD insured that the police executive would eventually become fully nazified. Since the RSHA was chiefly engaged in defining and pursuing "enemies" of the regime, it developed a tremendous significance in that it carried out policies of racial extermination and political oppression in the Third Reich and throughout occupied Europe. In a circular written shortly after Heydrich's death, Himmler empha-

[68] E. Kaltenbrunner, "Memoir," p. 50.

[69] For literature on the SD, the Gestapo, and the RSHA, see Buchheim, "SS," pp. 143-187; Neusüss-Hunkel, SS, passim.; Browder, "Sipo and SD," passim.; Höhne, SS, pp. 182-292; Reitlinger, SS, pp. 72-146; Shlomo Aronson, *The Beginnings of the Gestapo System: The Bavarian Model in 1933* (Jerusalem: Israel Universities Press, 1969). On offices of the RSHA, see RSHA memorandum, 1 March 1941, 185-L, NA.

sized the importance of the RSHA for the SS and the Nazi regime as a whole:[70]

> Of the SS main offices, the Reich Main Office for Security alone has the possibility, through its predominately political work, of having constant and direct contact with every phase of political development. I therefore order that all SS main offices direct all politically significant procedures to the Reich Main Office for Security for purposes of a uniform decision before these procedures are laid before me or directed to agencies outside the SS.

So crucial was the RSHA to the SS and Police empire that Himmler himself took over the office for the first eight months after Heydrich's death. Though he appointed Streckenbach as his deputy, he received the reports of his department chiefs directly.[71] By early December 1942, however, the Reichsführer had determined to replace Heydrich with Kaltenbrunner; and on 10 December he received Hitler's approval.[72] A few days later, Himmler summoned Kaltenbrunner and asked him to take over the RSHA. Later, Kaltenbrunner claimed that he had declined the appointment on the grounds that he did not agree with the centralized police structure that the RSHA represented; and that Himmler had then retorted that Kaltenbrunner would have no responsibility for the Gestapo and the Kripo, but would merely run the SD, and work toward a unification of political and military intelligence operations in the Third Reich. According to Kaltenbrunner's story, Himmler angrily dismissed the Austrian SS leader when the latter reiterated his aversion to the centralized police authority in the RSHA. In January 1943, however, Himmler summoned Kaltenbrunner again and ordered him to take over the RSHA.[73]

What actually transpired at these meetings is unknown, but documentary evidence renders Kaltenbrunner's testimony suspect. Since Himmler had informed Oswald Pohl, the chief of the SS Economic and Administrative Main Office (*Wirtschafts- und Verwaltungshauptamt*—WVHA), as early as 19 December 1942 that Kaltenbrunner would take over the RSHA, it is likely that the Austrian SS leader had accepted Himmler's first offer in De-

---

[70] Circular of Himmler to the SS Main Office chiefs, 25 June 1942, Aktenmappe RSHA, Ordner 457, pp. 64-65, BDC.

[71] Walter Schellenberg, *Memoiren* (Cologne: Verlag für Politik und Wirtschaft, 1959), p. 259. On the appointment of Streckenbach and Himmler's direct rule, see decree of Himmler, 11 July 1942, Streckenbach SS File, BDC; affidavit of Otto Ohlendorf, 5 November 1945, 2644-PS, NA.

[72] "Aktennotiz über die kurze Besprechung beim Führer am Donnerstag, dem 10. Dezember 1942 in der Wolfsschanze, 1830 Uhr," signed Himmler, 12 December 1942, E. Kaltenbrunner SS File, BDC.

[73] Testimony of Kaltenbrunner, IMT XI, pp. 238-240.

1. (*Above*) Franz Ritter von Epp, Bavarian Nazi leader and later Reich governor of Bavaria (center, with bouquet) visiting Linz in 1932. Standing in front, Upper Austrian Gauleiter Andreas Bolek (in shorts, right of Epp) and Landesleiter Alfred Proksch (with cap and medals). In back (second from right), Linz SS leader Kaltenbrunner (Oberösterreichisches Landesarchiv, Linz).

2. (*Left*) Himmler (front) and Kaltenbrunner salute the grave of a National Socialist killed in the 25 July 1934 putsch, March 1938 (Österreichisches Institut für Zeitgeschichte, Vienna).

3. (*Left*) Gauleiter Odilo Globocnik (saluting) at unveiling of memorial to putschists of 25 July 1934 in front of the Reich Governor's Office in Vienna, July 1938 (Österreichisches Institut für Zeitgeschichte, Vienna).

4. (*Below*) Members of the Austrian Provincial Government arriving in Berlin for a session of the Reichstag, March 1938. From left: Hans Fischböck, Kaltenbrunner, unidentified, Arthur Seyss-Inquart, unidentified, Edmund von Glaise-Horstenau, Hugo Jury, Friedrich Rainer, unidentified, Hubert Klausner (partially obscured), Josef Bürckel, unidentified, Rudolf Neumayer (Österreichisches Institut für Zeitgeschichte, Vienna).

5. Himmler (front center) swearing in the Austrian Federal Police on the Heldenplatz, Vienna, 15 March 1938. On platform: chief of the HA-Orpo, Kurt Daluege (right); chief of the Security Police, Reinhard Heydrich (left). Behind platform: chief of Himmler's Personal Staff, Karl Wolff (left of Heydrich); Kaltenbrunner and Vienna Police Vice-President Josef Fitzthum (between Himmler and Daluege) (Österreichisches Institut für Zeitgeschichte, Vienna).

6. Himmler at the July festival of the Old Party Guard in Vienna, 1938. To his left, along the table: son and widow of 25 July putschist Franz Holzweber, Vienna Police Vice-President Josef Fitzthum, Vienna Gauleiter Odilo Globocnik, Vienna Mayor Hermann Neubacher, Reich Governor Arthur Seyss-Inquart (Österreichisches Institut für Zeitgeschichte, Vienna).

7. Inspection of the Austrian police formations, 27 March 1938. Left to right: unidentified, chief of Himmler's Personal Staff Karl Wolff, Vienna Police President Otto Steinhäusl, chief of Security Police Reinhard Heydrich, chief of SS-Oberabschnitt Donau Ernst Kaltenbrunner, Reich Commissar for the Reunification of Austria with the German Reich Josef Bürckel (in raincoat), Vienna Police Vice-President Josef Fitzthum, Reichsführer SS Heinrich Himmler, chief of the HA-Orpo Kurt Daluege (Österreichisches Institut für Zeitgeschichte, Vienna).

8. At the Hotel Pöstlingberg, Linz, looking out over the Hermann Göring Works. Center, Upper Austrian Gauleiter August Eigruber (talking to Hitler); extreme right, Kaltenbrunner (photo given to the author by Dr. Hansjörg Kaltenbrunner).

cember. On 30 January 1943, Hitler made the appointment official.[74] Ernst Kaltenbrunner suddenly found himself catapulted into the mainstream of Nazi politics.

Why was Kaltenbrunner chosen? Contemporaries and historians have found the choice puzzling. Wilhelm Höttl wrote that Kaltenbrunner possessed "neither the police experience nor the personal relations which were necessary to reach a high post in the Third Reich." Himmler, Höttl explained, had been frightened by Heydrich's increasing personal power and had wanted as chief of the RSHA a man on whose loyalty he could always count. Rudolf Mildner, a Gestapo official, has also advanced this theory. One historian has called Kaltenbrunner's appointment "indefensible"; two others concur that Kaltenbrunner was a "second-rater selected by Himmler . . . solely to insure that there should not be another Heydrich."[75]

Yet this surely was not the reason for Kaltenbrunner's appointment. Himmler's alleged fear and mistrust of Heydrich has never been convincingly proven, and his sense of loss at Heydrich's death appears to have been genuine. Moreover, if Himmler had merely wanted a stand-in for Heydrich, he could have done quite well with Streckenbach, who was a fair if unimaginative administrator. One reason for bringing Kaltenbrunner to Berlin was his reputation as an intelligence expert, built up during his years as an underground SS leader and as HSSPF in Vienna. Apparently, there was some dissatisfaction in Berlin with the management of the SD-Ausland; Himmler may have been ordered to find a competent assistant in this field.[76] Kaltenbrunner told interrogators at Nuremberg that Himmler, who "had no political sense at all," wanted a man with experience in foreign intelligence:[77]

Had Himmler possessed an instinct for politics, I would never have been called to Berlin, for he would have kept the entire office in his hands. Thus, a great deficiency arose in the intelligence service and in the political assessment of the situation, because after Heydrich, Himmler had done nothing in the political sector. In addition, Canaris [chief of military intelligence] was already suspected of being a traitor, and so it was necessary to have a new chief of intelligence. Under the new chief, the political and military [intelligence services] would fuse into one. . . . That was the actual purpose of my appointment.

[74] Himmler to the chiefs of the RSHA and WVHA, 19 December 1942, T-175/59/2574390, NA; decree of Hitler, 30 January 1943, E. Kaltenbrunner SS File, BDC.

[75] Höhne, SS, p. 624; Houston, "Kaltenbrunner," p. 84; Reitlinger, SS, p. 237; Hagen, Geheime Front, p. 82; Höttl Tape, p. 15; affidavit of Rudolf Mildner, 29 March 1946, Kaltenbrunner-1, IMT xi, pp. 225-227.

[76] Schellenberg, Secret Service, p. 327.

[77] Interrogation of Kaltenbrunner, 16 September 1946, p. 20, ZS-673, IfZ Munich.

Kaltenbrunner's view was seconded by the chief of the Balkan group in the SD-Ausland (*Gruppe* VI E), Wilhelm Waneck, who claimed that Himmler was willing to take responsibility for the Security Police if Kaltenbrunner would concentrate on the reorganization of the SD, for he (Himmler) "believed that he could rely on Kaltenbrunner's political instinct in questions of foreign policy."[78] Although Kaltenbrunner's actual competence in the intelligence field might be questioned, Himmler, who had received from him Austrian Foreign Office documents and reports on Southeastern Europe, thought highly of Kaltenbrunner's work. Whether the "political instinct" that Kaltenbrunner possessed and Himmler lacked referred to plans to send out peace feelers to the Western Allies (see chapter 7) or to undermine the domestic position of the German military intelligence agency (see chapter 6) remains unclear.

A second and more important reason for Kaltenbrunner's appointment was Himmler's feeling that the Austrian SS leader would remain loyal to him and the National Socialist ideology without showing weakness in other matters. Kaltenbrunner had had close relations with Himmler since 1936; while he was HSSPF, he was reputed to have been utterly loyal to the Reichsführer. Under interrogation at Nuremberg, Kaltenbrunner's friend Hermann Neubacher testified that Himmler perceived in Kaltenbrunner a "loyal and fair coworker."[79] Himmler demonstrated his confidence in Kaltenbrunner's loyalty and commitment by consulting him along with other "deserving higher SS and police leaders" on general questions that the Reichsführer deemed vital—such as the solution of internal disputes in the SS—and by bringing him to Hitler's headquarters to discuss policy on SD reporting.[80] By choosing Kaltenbrunner, Himmler, in addition to having a man whom he considered a top intelligence expert, stood to gain a loyal comrade who might be Heydrich's equal both in operating the RSHA and in championing the ideological aims of the SS.

Third, there is evidence that both Hitler and Nazi Party Chancellery chief Martin Bormann pressed for Kaltenbrunner's appointment. Hitler may have had doubts about Himmler's loyalty and hoped that Kaltenbrunner's presence would keep the Reichsführer in line. Although Upper Austrian *Landser* sentiment was unimportant to him, the Führer may have perceived its importance for Kaltenbrunner and therefore felt that he could depend on the Austrian SS leader. Walter Schellenberg wrote later that Himmler's mas-

---

[78] Affidavit of Waneck, 15 April 1946, Kaltenbrunner-8, IMT XL, p. 335.

[79] Winzer Report, p. 6; affidavit of Waneck, 15 April 1946, Kaltenbrunner-8, IMT XL, p. 342.

[80] Himmler to Jüttner, 5 March 1942, T-175/122/2647660-2647663, NA; *Heeresadjutant bei Hitler 1938-1943: Aufzeichnungen des Major Engel,* ed. Hildegard von Kotze (Stuttgart: Deutsche Verlags-Anstalt, 1974), p. 119.

seur, Felix Kersten, had remarked that Kaltenbrunner had been Hitler's choice. Schellenberg added that "Hitler seemed convinced that this tough cookie [Kaltenbrunner] possessed all the necessary qualifications for such a post, of which unconditional obedience, personal loyalty, and the fact that [Kaltenbrunner] . . . was a fellow Austrian were signficant." Finally, Kaltenbrunner himself told interrogators that Hitler had tried to bring him to Berlin— unfortunately for the historian, the interrogator cut off Kaltenbrunner's efforts to explain this. Moreover, Bormann may have backed Kaltenbrunner in the hope that the Austrian SS leader would support Bormann's own aim to get himself appointed secretary to the Führer (this Bormann achieved in April 1943). At any rate, Bormann was kept closely informed of the appointment process.[81]

Finally, the choice of an HSSPF to fill Heydrich's shoes was not illogical. If the HSSPF's task was in part to amalgamate the SS with the police at the local level, the Reich Main Office for Security was an attempt to fuse the ideological idealism of the SD onto the bureaucratic apparatus of the Security Police at the center. With the creation of the RSHA on 27 September 1939, Himmler and Heydrich expected that eventually the ideological zeal of the SD would phase out the "bureaucratic/civil-servant mentality" of the professional policemen and create a corps of ideological soldiers who were committed to the protection of Führer, Volk, and Movement, and who would be prepared in pursuit of this aim to carry out orders, however barbaric or cruel.[82]

To run this key apparatus, Himmler needed a man who possessed Heydrich's fanaticism and who was capable of furthering the interests of the RSHA against other agencies of the Reich. He did not need a policeman or an administrator, of whom he had plenty in the Gestapo, the Kripo, and the administrative departments of the RSHA. He needed a fighter, who could hold his own in the incessant struggles that wracked the internal politics of the Reich; and he needed an ideological soldier, who would shrink from no task that the Führer might order. Finally, he needed an ideological administrator, who, through personnel policy and training programs, would work toward that desired fusion of the SS mentality onto the executive power of the police.

Kaltenbrunner had already shown his flair for personal politics and in-

[81] On Hitler's mistrust of Himmler, see Tavs Tape, pp. 4-5; Winzer Report, p. 6. On possible Hitler sponsorship of Kaltenbrunner, see Schellenberg, *Memoiren*, p. 296; Schellenberg, *Secret Service*, p. 328; interrogation of Kaltenbrunner, 8 October 1945, NCA, Supplement B, pp. 1305-1306. On Borman being informed, see Himmler to Bormann, 20 January 1943, T-175/59/2574389, NA (a copy of this letter dated 21 January 1943 is in T-175/62/2578271, NA); Browder, "Sipo and SD," pp. 377-378.

[82] Browder, "Sipo and SD," pp. 177-186.

trigue in the Austrian Nazi underground; as HSSPF, he had had no qualms about deportations of the Jews or concentration-camp incarceration for other "enemies." Moreover, he had supervised the amalgamation of the SS and the police on the local level. Why should he not continue to do so in Berlin? In April 1943, the new RSHA chief issued a circular ordering that "political training" and "alignment of Security Police personnel with the SD was to continue despite the ever-increasing workload in the offices under the RSHA." As Himmler explained in a decree of 24 February 1943, he wanted not only "solid soldiers" but also troops that were "in ever-higher measure convinced and devout carriers of our Weltanschauung."[83] Thus, a local HSSPF was a more logical choice to run the RSHA than an RSHA department chief or even another main office chief, whose immersion in Berlin intrigues would jeopardize cooperation toward the ultimate goal. Chief of the RSHA was a political position, not a job for a mere policeman.

Even before Heydrich's death, Himmler had been seeking to draw Kaltenbrunner out of the Austrian quagmire. As early as 1940, the Reichsführer had offered to "lend" Kaltenbrunner to the German Foreign Office for duty as ambassador to Switzerland. In 1942, when the possibility of replacing the military government in Belgium with a civilian commissariat was under consideration, Himmler suggested Kaltenbrunner as a candidate. The proposed Reich commissar would have enjoyed direct contact with Hitler and was to have been "a strong personality, who could secure the solution of . . . völkisch-political, economic, and social problems."[84]

Having chosen him to take over the RSHA, Himmler clearly wanted Kaltenbrunner to utilize the power that Heydrich had held. On 6 January 1943, he advised the Austrian SS leader to "reestablish the contacts that Heydrich had held in his hands." In April, the Reichsführer even considered a merger of the RSHA and the Orpo Main Office into a Reich Security Ministry under Kaltenbrunner's leadership. He dropped this plan only when his appointment as minister of the interior in August 1943 made it superfluous.[85]

In a sense, then, the RSHA and Kaltenbrunner found one another in the months after Heydrich's death. Frustrated by his lack of power and bored by the lack of excitement in Vienna, Kaltenbrunner sought a more active po-

[83] Circular of Kaltenbrunner, "Weltanschauliche Erziehung," 27 April 1943, T-175/429/2958942-2958944, NA; decree of Himmler, 24 February 1943, ibid., 2958945-2958946.

[84] Stuckart to Lammers, 9 October 1942, File Reichskanzlei, R 43 II/678a, pp. 51-53, BA; memorandum of Lammers, 28 October 1942, ibid., p. 61; Konrad Kwiet, *Reichskommissariat Niederlände: Versuch und Scheitern nationalsozialistischer Neuordnung* (Stuttgart: Deutsche Verlags-Anstalt, 1968), pp. 61-68. On Switzerland, see interrogation of Baron Gustave Steengracht von Moyland, 20 March 1947, ZS-1546, pp. 24-36, IfZ Munich.

[85] Himmler to Kaltenbrunner, 6 January 1943, E. Kaltenbrunner SS File, BDC; Brandt [Persönlicher Stab des Reichsführer SS] to Becker [HA-Orpo], 29 March 1943, T-175/128/2653865, NA; Browder, "Sipo and SD," p. 378.

litical role in the SS-police system. Conversely, Himmler needed a loyal and capable man to operate the most important office of the SS.

Kaltenbrunner's reaction to his new job was mixed. On the one hand its promise of power, excitement, and intrigue, blending with a sense of ideological commitment to the regime, appealed to him; on the other hand he was nervous about being suddenly thrust into the mainstream of Nazi politics in Berlin, where he had little experience and few contacts. A comrade wrote that Kaltenbrunner "seemed both delighted and terrified by his new tasks." Kaltenbrunner's contact in the Southeast Europe Society, Heinrichsbauer, noted after a visit with the new RSHA chief in Berlin that Kaltenbrunner was "homesick for the times in Vienna." Another comrade, Otto Skorzeny, remarked that Kaltenbrunner, "even with all the external splendor, did not feel quite at home there [in the RSHA]."[86] Surprisingly, the RSHA chiefs initially accepted the newcomer. Walter Schellenberg, later so hostile to Kaltenbrunner, expressed his satisfaction at the choice when he announced the appointment to his subordinates in the SD-Ausland on 14 December 1942; two months later, he told his men that the appointment would "put an end to the terrible interregnum" which had followed Heydrich's death.[87]

Three days after Kaltenbrunner took over the RSHA, the remnants of the German Sixth Army surrendered to the Russians at Stalingrad. By a combination of fantasy and brute force, the Nazis had extended their world to its physical limits. Henceforth, the Grand Alliance would gouge holes in that world until, hollowed out by defeat in the field and flaming death from the skies, it collapsed in a heap of ruins. At the very moment of his political triumph, Kaltenbrunner had either to continue to accept the foundations of the Nazi dream as reality or to draw the consequences from the collapse of that dream. The nature and manifestations of his choice form the subject of the following chapters.

[86] Becker [Befehlshaber der Ordnungspolizei, Kraków] to Querner [HSSPF, Hamburg], 29 December 1942, Becker SS File, BDC; August Heinrichsbauer, "Bericht über meine Berliner Aufenthalt in der Zeit vom 3. Mai–8. Mai 1943," 12 May 1943, File SOEG, R 63/206, p. 60, BA; Otto Skorzeny, *Geheimkommando Skorzeny* (Hamburg: Hansa Verlag Josef Toth, 1950), pp. 85-86.

[87] "Gruppenleiterbesprechung am 14. Dezember bei VI/V," signed Schüddekopf [SD-Ausland], December 1942, T-175/458/2975422-2975423, NA; "Protokoll über die Gruppenleiter- und Referentenbesprechung des Amt VI," 10 February 1943, File RSHA, R 58/1280, BA.

CHAPTER V

Implementing Nazi War Policy, 1943-1945

WHILE ON trial at Nuremberg, Kaltenbrunner claimed that he had come to Berlin solely to reorganize the political intelligence service of the Nazi Party (i.e., the SD), that his position as RSHA chief was ceremonial with respect to the Security Police, that Gestapo chief Müller and Kripo chief Nebe reported directly to Himmler after he took office and, finally, that "the special assignments which had been given to Heydrich, such as the assignment with regard to the final solution of the Jewish problem, were not only unknown to me at the time, but were not taken over by me."[1] The purpose of this chapter will be first to test this claim against the evidence: that is, to determine the exact nature of Kaltenbrunner's authority, functions, and activities as chief of the RSHA and to examine the way in which he exercised that authority and performed those functions, particularly with regard to such special "ideological" tasks as racial and resettlement policies and the extermination of the Jews. Second, we will examine whether and in what way Kaltenbrunner's activities reflected his continuing ideological commitment to the Nazi regime.

Kaltenbrunner's claim that he had no responsibility for the Security Police is not supported by any outside evidence and was contradicted by the testimony of other RSHA officials. A former Kripo officer testified that all important documents directed to agencies outside the RSHA were read and signed by Kaltenbrunner. A Gestapo official recalled that individual orders for executions by Security Police personnel came from Himmler through Kaltenbrunner and Müller and were passed on to the concentration-camp commanders. Another Gestapo official testified that Kaltenbrunner was unmistakably king of his castle: "To my knowledge, no department head or other official authorized to sign reports had the authority to make a decision on any principal matters or affairs of special political significance without the agreement of the chief of Security Police, not even during the latter's temporary absences."[2] Walter Schellenberg, the chief of the foreign intelli-

---

[1] Testimony of Kaltenbrunner, IMT XI, p. 241. See also E. Kaltenbrunner, "Memoir," Nuremberg, July-August 1946, pp. 53-54, Kaltenbrunner File.

[2] Affidavit of Kurt Lindow, 3 August 1945, 50-L, IMT XXXVII, pp. 462-463; affidavit of Rudolf Mildner, 29 March 1946, ZS-431, IfZ Munich and IMT XI, pp. 225-226, 254; affidavit of Wilhelm Bonatz, 21 September 1945, 2196-PS, NA.

gence department of the RSHA, reported that "in his official relations with all of us who were his department chiefs, he [Kaltenbrunner] made it explicitly clear that he was the chief of the office, who exercised full executive power and determined all matters of policy. He permitted us to issue instructions within the organization in our own name . . . in accordance with guidelines set by him, but all important matters had to be submitted to him whether we or he signed them."[3] Finally, Otto Ohlendorf, the chief of the internal intelligence service and far less hostile to Kaltenbrunner than Schellenberg, testified that the Austrian SS leader was determined to be the boss in the RSHA; even when department chiefs received direct orders from Himmler, Kaltenbrunner had to be informed. Ohlendorf concluded that "in the Party and the state Kaltenbrunner was acknowledged as Heydrich's successor."[4]

Contemporary documents also reveal Kaltenbrunner's direct responsibility for the Security Police. He appointed and dismissed commanders of the Einsatzgruppen of the Security Police and the SD, the mobile killing units charged with the extermination of undesirable political and racial elements in the occupied territories, and received regular reports on the activities of these units, which "substantially facilitated" his decisions on "the most practical deployment of Security Police forces at any given time." He also dealt directly with the Reich justice authorities on police matters. In September 1943, the Reich minister for justice, Otto Thierack, complained to Kaltenbrunner that Himmler had unilaterally extended the length of time for police arrest from two to three weeks, and that this measure was not anchored in Reich law. Kaltenbrunner responded blandly that in wartime it was necessary to provide the police "with room to maneuver that exceeds narrow legal bounds." That Kaltenbrunner was well informed of Security Police executions is indicated by two Himmler decrees of November 1944, stipulating that all requests for executions of Reich Germans and foreigners residing in the Reich be sent through Kaltenbrunner for Himmler's approval. In the case of non-Germans outside the Reich, Kaltenbrunner himself was authorized to approve executions.[5] Thus, virtually all available evidence pertaining to Kaltenbrunner's sphere of authority in the RSHA indicates that its new chief effectively exercised the right of command in all aspects of the office.

---

[3] Affidavit of Walter Schellenberg, 17 November 1945, 2939-PS, IMT xxxi, pp. 323-326.

[4] Affidavit of Otto Ohlendorf, 5 November 1945, 2621-PS, NA.

[5] Telegram signed Kaltenbrunner to SS Personnel Main Office, Hauptamt Orpo, and various civilian and police authorities in White Russia, the Ukraine, and Prague, 28 August 1943, H. Böhme SS File, BDC; Kaltenbrunner to Himmler, 2 November 1944, E. Ehrlinger SS File, BDC; note of Thierack, 29 September 1943, NG-345, NA; decree of Himmler, 1 November 1944, File RSHA, R 58/243, pp. 310-311, BA; decree of Himmler, 4 November 1944, ibid., p. 312.

During World War II, the Security Police carried out two types of policy made by the Nazi leadership. First, short-range measures were developed in response to specific situations arising from the war itself. Here might be included Nazi policy on prisoners of war, Allied commandos, and partisan warfare, which may be categorized as tactical war policy. Though brutal and often illegal according to international standards, implementation of such measures does not necessarily indicate a lasting commitment to the National Socialist ideology, for such policies lacked a permanent place in the basic Nazi creed of expansion and purification. Kaltenbrunner's involvement in them reflects on his role as chief of the Security Police, but cannot serve as conclusive evidence of ideological commitment to the Nazi idea.

Other policies in which Kaltenbrunner was involved clearly reflected long-range goals derived from basic tenets of Hitler's ideology. Hardly mere reactions to specific wartime situations, they were planned and implemented behind the smokescreen of "national emergency" that the war so conveniently provided. Included here are racial and resettlement policy, treatment of foreign labor imported from Eastern Europe and the Soviet Union, concentration camps, persecution of the churches and extermination of entire ethnic groups such as Jews and Gypsies. In such areas lay the core of the Nazi revolution. These might come under the general heading of ideological war policy. Ideological orders fell under the vaguely defined but potentially unlimited "will of the Führer." Active participation in their execution represented something beyond mere legal commitment to the German state; it symbolized a "specific ideological assent"[6] to the aims and means of the Nazi movement. By carrying out ideological orders, Kaltenbrunner displayed his enduring commitment to Adolf Hitler and the National Socialist creed.

In the Third Reich, tactical war policy was aimed at the elimination of elements presenting an immediate, if not always significant, danger or nuisance to the German war effort. Escaped prisoners of war, enemy commandos, and partisans were a worrisome inconvenience. They tied up military and police forces needed elsewhere. Nazi thinking on this problem was simple: it was more convenient to eliminate than to contain such irritations.

Kaltenbrunner defined his attitude toward partisans and those who helped or supported them in a circular issued on 16 June 1944, in which he stated that the execution of hostages was "still the most effective means against 'terrorism.' "[7] If this type of retribution did not sufficiently discourage partisan activity or sabotage, "more suitable means" should be employed to induce the population at large to play a positive role in the struggle against

---

[6] Hans Buchheim, "Command and Compliance," in Krausnick, SS State, p. 365.

[7] Excerpts of circular in note of Wagner [chief of department Inland II Geheim in the German Foreign Office], 11 August 1944, NG-2990, NA.

partisans. These included cutting off food supplies, gas and electric services, telephone contact, and mail delivery.

In March 1944, the RSHA issued the notorious "Bullet Decree." Signed by Gestapo chief Heinrich Müller, it ordered that escaped prisoners of war— officers and noncommissioned officers (except for Anglo-Americans)—be handed over to the Security Police and the SD upon recapture, regardless of the circumstances of escape. They were then to be shackled and sent to the concentration camp Mauthausen, where, under an operation called *Aktion Kugel*, they would be shot. According to one of the Mauthausen executioners, Kaltenbrunner sent verbal and written orders in December 1944 to camp commandant Franz Ziereis, announcing the impending shipment of thirteen hundred escaped prisoners of war and foreign laborers to Mauthausen for execution under Aktion Kugel.[8]

Another example of Nazi tactical war policy was the instruction on the treatment of Anglo-American fliers who had been forced to bail out over Germany. In the summer of 1943, Himmler issued a statement declaring that it was "not the task of the police to interfere in disputes between members of the German Volk and English and American terror fliers who have bailed out." In other words, the German police were to encourage or remain indifferent to efforts by the local population to murder Allied fliers who had been shot down over Germany. Apparently, however, neither local policemen nor the population at large comprehended the "significance" of this order, for the latter only rarely sought revenge, and, in these isolated cases, policemen intervened to protect the fliers. In April 1944, Kaltenbrunner felt compelled to issue a decree, which not only reiterated Himmler's original order, but also provided that German citizens, who in "especially crass cases" out of "evil intention" or "misplaced sympathy" helped or protected Anglo-American fliers, be packed off to a concentration camp. Under the new regulation, any fliers who offered resistance or who wore civilian clothes under their uniforms were to be shot on sight.[9]

This blank check for lynch law disturbed the High Command of the Armed Forces (*Oberkommando der Wehrmacht*—OKW), for the German military leaders feared Allied reprisals against German prisoners of war. Even Himmler became concerned about possible repercussions. In early June 1944, he

[8] On "Bullet Decree," see decree of chief of Security Police and SD [signed Müller.], 4 March 1944, 1650-PS, IMT xxvii, pp. 425-428. On meaning of *Aktion Kugel*, see affidavits of Lt. Col. Giuvante de Saint Gast and Lt. Jean Veith [prisoners in Mauthausen], 13 May 1945, 2285-PS, IMT xxx, pp. 141-143. On shipment of prisoners of war and foreign laborers, see affidavit of Josef Niedermayer, 7 March 1946, 3844-PS, IMT xxxiii, pp. 211-212.

[9] Decree of Himmler, 10 August 1943, T-175/22/2526979, NA; circular of Kaltenbrunner to commanders of Security Police and SD, RSHA groups IV A and IV B (Gestapo) and department chiefs I, II, III, VI (SD and administrative departments of the RSHA), 5 April 1944, 3855-PS, IMT xxxiii, pp. 243-246.

convened with Foreign Minister Joachim Ribbentrop and *Luftwaffe* chief Hermann Göring to iron out a joint policy on the treatment of captured Allied fliers. Himmler sent Kaltenbrunner on 6 June to the deputy chief of the Wehrmacht Operations Staff, General Walter Warlimont, to inform him of the result. It had been decided that only those fliers who were found guilty of "strafing attacks that are directly aimed at the civilians and their property" should be turned over to the population for lynching. Still uneasy, Warlimont suggested that all fliers captured by the Wehrmacht be confined at the Luftwaffe prisoner-of-war camp at Oberursel until their "guilt" or "innocence" had been established. If guilty, they would then be handed over to the SD for "special treatment [*Sonderbehandlung*]." Kaltenbrunner thought this a splendid idea.[10]

Another area where the Nazis responded to a specific wartime situation was in their policy toward enemy commandos. Informed of British commando instructions providing that prisoners be shackled and, in special cases, killed, Hitler, in a fit of rage, issued the commando decree of 18 October 1942, which stipulated that enemy commandos be denied status as prisoners of war. If seized by Wehrmacht personnel, they were to be liquidated whether or not they wore uniforms or tried to surrender. Any commandos captured by civilian authorities were to be delivered to the SD for execution.[11]

The commando policy remained a point of conflict between the RSHA and the OKW until the end of the war. Not that either side took issue with the policy itself—the quarrel arose over where the responsibility for the executions lay. Instead of killing captured commandos immediately as required by the Hitler decree, Wehrmacht officers generally handed them over to the SD for execution. In June 1944, the RSHA demanded that the Wehrmacht counterespionage people do their job. Four months later, however, the OKW Operations Staff informed the RSHA that four Allied agents had been captured in uniform and were then handed over to the SD. Experts in the RSHA retorted that the four should have been "shot while trying to escape" as provided by the Führer decree. In January 1945, Kaltenbrunner himself intervened, stating that the SD would liquidate spies and civilian saboteurs only, since these were not covered by the Geneva Convention stipulations on prisoners of war. Commandos in uniform, protected by international law, had to be eliminated in "battle" so that no further questions need be asked.[12]

[10] Notation of deputy chief of Wehrmacht Operations Staff [Warlimont], 6 June 1944, 735-PS, IMT xxvi, pp. 276-279.

[11] Decree of Hitler, 18 October 1942, 498-PS, ibid., pp. 100-101. On Hitler's rage, see Bradley F. Smith, *Reaching Judgment at Nuremberg* (New York: Basic Books, 1977), p. 245.

[12] Chief of Security Police and SD [signature illegible] to OKW, Wehrmacht Operations Staff, 17 June 1944, 1276-PS, IMT xxvii, pp. 91-93; OKW, Wehrmacht Operations Staff to chief of Security Police and SD, 28 October 1944, 546-PS, NA; Chief of Security Police and SD to OKW Operations Staff, 8 November 1944, 547-PS, NA; Kaltenbrunner to Polleck [OKW Operations Staff], 23 January 1945, 535-PS, IMT xxvi, pp. 138-140.

This intervention was more an example of Kaltenbrunner's cynicism regarding international rules of war than of his direct guilt in the commando affair.

Kaltenbrunner also inherited from Heydrich full or partial responsibility for ideological war policies: race and resettlement, concentration camps, policy toward the churches, and the "Final Solution" of the Jewish question. Here he initiated few new policies and was content to supervise or formally define the role of the RSHA in each area. His personal intervention in these affairs belies his protestations of innocence at Nuremberg.

The involvement of the SS in race and resettlement plans derived from a Hitler decree of 7 October 1939 appointing Himmler Reich Commissar for the Strengthening of German Nationhood (RKFDV).[13] In this capacity, Himmler was entrusted with three tasks: (1) repatriation of persons of German race resident abroad insofar as they were considered "suitable for permanent citizenship in the Reich"; (2) elimination of the "harmful influence" of "alien parts of the population" that constituted "a danger to the Reich and the German community"; and (3) creation of new German colonies in the East by resettling German citizens and ethnic Germans. Each of these tasks fell to a different SS main office: (1) the Race and Settlement Main Office (*Rasse- und Siedlungshauptamt*—RuSHA) handled the "racial examination" of candidates for German citizenship; (2) the RSHA was responsible for the removal of "harmful influences"; and (3) the local offices of the RKFDV managed the actual details of resettlement. Through this process of examination, selection, and resettlement, Himmler's racial idealists planned to alter the ethnic composition of Eastern Europe and European Russia in such a way as to enable German settlers, living in small communities, to enjoy the status and power of a master race from the Rhine to the Urals.

In 1941, Himmler had determined that the RSHA would be responsible for all situations involving the presence of "alien blood" within Germany and the occupied territories. It was charged with the task of isolating foreign nationals within the Reich and exercised the right to evaluate individuals who fit RuSHA racial requirements as to their political and ideological reliability. In occupied Poland, which served as a testing ground for the realization of Himmler's racial fantasies, the RSHA chief—first Heydrich and later Kaltenbrunner—was entrusted with the deportation of Poles, Jews, and others not of German blood from regions designated for German settlement.[14]

After Kaltenbrunner came to power, RSHA officials sought to muscle in

---

[13] This decree is published in Koehl, *RKFDV*, pp. 247-249.

[14] On RSHA competence, see decree of Himmler, 28 November 1941, NO-4237, published in Koehl, *RKFDV*, pp. 251-253. On evaluation of RuSHA candidates by the RSHA, see affidavit of Otto Hofmann, 4 August 1945, L-49, IMT xxxvii, pp. 460-461. On Nazi policy in Poland, see also Martin Broszat, *Nationalsozialistische Polenpolitik, 1939-1945* (Frankfurt-Hamburg: Fischer Bucherei, 1965).

on RuSHA territory by demanding the right to reject on grounds of political unreliability any candidates declared racially suitable by RuSHA examiners. In August 1943, experts from each office held a conference at which RSHA representatives demanded the last word on determination of "germanizeability" (*Eindeutschungsfähigkeit*). The officials of the RuSHA insisted that racial criteria were more important for the purpose of "saving" German blood than any suspicions of political unreliability. On 20 August, Kaltenbrunner and RuSHA chief Richard Hildebrandt reached an agreement that in content signified a victory for the RSHA. Henceforth, the RSHA would determine the political reliability of potential "germanizeables," and, if the results were positive, the candidate would be sent over to the RuSHA for a racial examination.[15]

In practice, RSHA evaluations became severely backlogged owing both to understaffing and to German military reversals. Already in March 1943, Kaltenbrunner had to concede that Himmler's order to repatriate 35,000 to 40,000 ethnic Germans from Halberstadt in the Ukraine could not be carried out in view of the fact that thousands of ethnic Germans in Slovenia, Poland, and Alsace-Lorraine were still awaiting evaluation by the RSHA's Immigration Center (*Einwanderungszentrale*—EWZ).[16]

Kaltenbrunner also made policy defining the status and rights of East Europeans (Poles, Serbs, Balts, and Soviets) within the Reich and the German sphere of power. As the Wehrmacht swept eastward through Poland and the Soviet Union, millions of Polish and Soviet citizens fell under the jurisdiction of the Security Police. As the fighting wore on, Germany's labor supply dwindled rapidly. Several thousand Poles and Soviets were put to work in factories and on farms throughout Germany, Austria, Bohemia, Moravia, and the Government General.[17] The RSHA was responsible for disciplining these foreign laborers. On 30 June 1943, Kaltenbrunner issued a circular establishing regulations for punishing crimes committed by Poles and Russians in Germany proper. All criminal proceedings were to be handled by the Gestapo and the Kripo; the Reich Ministry for Justice and the German courts would be excluded, except in those cases where "for reasons of general political morale a court verdict seems desirable and where it is

---

[15] "Aktenvermerk über die am 18.8.43 stattgefundene Besprechung zwischen den Vertretern des Reichssicherheitshauptamtes und des Rasse- und Siedlungshauptamt-SS," signed Schultz [chief of the Race Office of the RuSHA], 19 August 1943, NO-1763, NA; notice of chief of RuSHA, 20 August 1943, NO-1761, NA; Koehl, *RKFDV*, p. 165.

[16] Kaltenbrunner to Himmler, 6 March 1943, SS-HO/2277, BDC.

[17] The Government General (*Generalgouvernement*) was that part of Poland not annexed directly by Germany or the Soviet Union in 1939. It was ruled by a German Governor General, Hans Frank, who had his seat in Kraków. Though not annexed directly to provinces of the Reich as were Danzig, West Prussia, Silesia, and Białystok, the Government General was legally part of the Reich and was intended to be an area for future German settlement.

arranged beforehand that the court would impose the death sentence." Kaltenbrunner suggested that the Security Police handle the prosecutions on the following principle: "one must consider . . . that the Pole or Soviet Russian represents by virtue of his very existence a danger for the German racial order [*Volksordnung*] and that it is therefore not so important to find a suitable punishment for the crime committed . . . as to prevent him from presenting any further danger to the German racial order."[18] From the wording of this decree, it can be easily inferred that "criminals" were to be killed or shipped to a concentration camp.

The Security Police also determined policy toward foreign laborers who became pregnant. In accordance with a Kaltenbrunner decree of 27 July 1943, the pregnant workers were not sent home, or admitted to German hospitals (unless to serve as testing material for German medical and nursing programs). They gave birth in the infirmary of the labor camp in which they were housed and were sent back to work almost immediately afterward. Special day-care centers "of the simplest sort" (often barns and garden sheds) were established within the labor camps; they had notoriously poor facilities and many of the infants died in them. In the event that the father proved to be German or "Germanic" (i.e., Scandinavian, Dutch, etc.), SS race experts would examine both child and mother as to their suitability for germanization. Should the examination prove positive, an agonizing choice faced the mother: she could either keep the child, exposing it to the fully inadequate care of the day-care centers; or she could relinquish it to the custody of the National Socialist Public Welfare Organization (NS-*Volkswohlfahrt*), which would deposit the child in a home for "foreign children of suitable race." The principle involved was to "prevent the loss of German blood to alien racial bodies [*Volkskörper*]."[19]

Another concern of the Security Police was the problem of sexual relations between Germans and foreign laborers, referred to as *Rassenschande* ("besmirching of the race"). In February 1944, Kaltenbrunner issued a decree that defined sexual intercourse between Germans and Poles, Lithuanians, Russians, or Serbs as a crime subject to prosecution by the Security Police. If the male was non-German, he would be subject to immediate arrest. A German male could be prosecuted only if he had utilized his official position to force intercourse. Female members of non-German nationalities could expect to be interned in a concentration camp. The usual fate of non-German males was indicated by a report of twenty-five cases of illegal sexual inter-

[18] Circular of Kaltenbrunner, 30 June 1943, records of the Stapoleitstelle Frankfurt, pp. 43-44, IfZ Munich.

[19] Decree of the Reichsführer SS and chief of German Police [signed Kaltenbrunner], 27 July 1943, T-175/428/2957108-2957115, NA.

course in Württemberg-Baden: all twenty-five men were hanged. In these cases, authorization for executions had to be obtained from the RSHA.[20]

Though evolved in wartime, such policies had little to do with military necessity or even convenience, nor were they a response to specific wartime needs or objectives. Like the völkisch nationalists of the nineteenth century, the Nazis viewed the East European peoples—especially the Slavs—as morally, socially, intellectually, and physically inferior. Fearing as well that the Slavs were reproducing more rapidly than the Germans, the Nazis planned to decrease gradually the numbers of the Slavs through extermination, deportation, slave labor, and inadequate supplies of food and medicine. From the Nazi point of view, hanging a Pole for having cohabited with a German woman, or shooting a Russian for having stolen a loaf of bread, was neither illogical nor cruel; it insured not only that the Pole or Russian would not make any further trouble, but also that he would not reproduce more Poles or Russians. Provisions on criminality, abortions, and racial selection represented initial guidelines for the treatment of "inferior" races and foreshadowed the grim future that Slavs and other East Europeans could expect under Nazi rule.

That Kaltenbrunner, like his predecessor Heydrich, intended to prevent the Reich legal authorities from bringing even a modicum of standard criminal justice into the administration of occupied Soviet territory is apparent from a letter he sent to SS Main Office chief Gottlob Berger in the autumn of 1943. Berger, who also served as Himmler's liaison man in Alfred Rosenberg's Reich Ministry for the Occupied Eastern Territories, had sent Kaltenbrunner protests of the German courts in Kaunas, Lithuania, against arbitrary executions by the Security Police of foreign nationals charged with crimes that fell under the jurisdiction of the German courts. Kaltenbrunner replied that the complaints of the prosecutor's office in Kaunas did not concern him; that Hitler had given the police the task of securing the occupied Eastern territories; that the police therefore must "take action with police [i.e., executive] measures against those elements which endanger police security [in the region]"; and that "one of the police measures which will be ordered individually according to the seriousness of the case is special treatment [i.e., execution]."[21]

Kaltenbrunner was born and grew up in regions where the German population lived side by side with Czechs and Slovenes. Given his exposure to

---

[20] Decree of the Reichsführer SS and chief of German Police [signed Kaltenbrunner], 10 February 1944, NO-1365, NA; affidavit of Otto Hofmann [HSSPF in Württemberg-Baden from 1943 to 1945], June 9, 1947, NO-4699, NA. On RSHA authorization for executions, see decree of Kaltenbrunner, 4 May 1943. NO-1532, NA.

[21] Berger to Hauptabteilungsleiter II, Reich Ministry for the Occupied Eastern Territories, 19 November 1943, NO-2719, NA.

pan-German ideas both in the home and among his peers, he must have shared the hatred, contempt, and fear of the Slavs so common among Germans living on the Eastern borderlands. He was unmoved by the harsh and callous measures pertaining to foreign laborers in the Reich or by the anguish of Slavic mothers of "racially suitable children"; his signature appeared on the decress ordering such measures. This, then, is but one more aspect of his willingness to serve the ideological aims of the Third Reich.

As under Heydrich, the Security Police under Kaltenbrunner assigned individuals to concentration camps, though it was never responsible for the administration of the camps themselves. From 1934, when the concentration-camp system was unified, until 1940, the camps were subordinated to the Inspectorate of the Concentration Camps, whose chiefs were SS-Obergruppenführer Theodor Eicke (1934-1939) and SS-Gruppenführer Richard Glücks (1939-1945). On 3 March 1942, the Inspectorate was incorporated into the newly created SS Economic and Administrative Main Office (WVHA) under SS-Gruppenführer Oswald Pohl. Pohl's WVHA also handled the finances and general administration of the entire SS and supervised SS business interests and building concerns. Under Pohl's influence, the concentration camps, whose original purpose had been detention, increasingly served as vast pools of slave labor tapped by both SS-owned industries and private German firms.[22]

Kaltenbrunner was well aware of what went on inside the concentration camps. Between the summer of 1942 and the summer of 1943, he visited Mauthausen (near Linz) at least three times. According to one prisoner, he accompanied Himmler on an inspection of the camp in the summer of 1942. A former SS guard testified that the Austrian SS leader witnessed an execution by gas in Mauthausen during a visit in the autumn of 1942. Three inmates placed Kaltenbrunner in Mauthausen during the summer of 1943. According to one, the RSHA chief had on this occasion witnessed three types of execution: hanging, gassing, and shooting. The executions had been prepared for his benefit.[23]

Although the RSHA did not administer the camps themselves, it authorized individual and mass arrests, determined the length of incarceration, and gave orders for executions. Moreover, the RSHA was also responsible for transport to the camps of those to be incarcerated (or, in the case of the five

[22] Martin Broszat, "The Concentration Camps, 1933-1945," in Krausnick, SS State, pp. 484-494. See also Höhne, SS, pp. 440-443.

[23] Deposition of Karl Reif, 29 May 1946, 4032-PS, IMT xxxiv, pp. 92-93; affidavit of Alois Höllriegel, 7 November 1945, 2753-PS, IMT xxxi, p. 93; interrogation of Johann Kanduth, 30 November 1945, 3846-PS, IMT xxxiii, pp. 241-242; interrogation of Albert Tiefenbacher, 7 December 1945, 3845-PS, ibid., p. 226; affidavit of Hans Marsalek, 8 April 1946, 3870-PS, ibid., p. 285.

death camps in Poland, exterminated). Officials of the camps and Gestapo officers testified that the RSHA performed such functions under Kaltenbrunner. Rudolf Höss, the camp commandant at Auschwitz from 1940 to 1943, related that, though in matters of internal administration he reported to Glücks and Pohl, orders for individual and collective incarcerations, punishments, and executions came from the RSHA. Höss added that most of these orders were signed by Gestapo chief Müller as Kaltenbrunner's deputy—only rarely did the signatures of Kaltenbrunner or Himmler appear. Several of these points have been confirmed by others. Two Gestapo officials reported that all internment orders had to be approved by Heydrich and, later Kaltenbrunner. Finally, Hermann Pister, the commandant of Buchenwald from 1943 to 1945, stated that all inmates in that camp had been sent there by the RSHA and that orders for protective arrest (*Schutzhaft*) uniformly carried Kaltenbrunner's signature.[24]

Numerous protective-arrest orders signed by Kaltenbrunner survived the war and were used as evidence against him in Nuremberg. Paula Traxel, a Reich German, was sent to Ravensbrück because she had had sexual relations with a Pole and because she generally did not show the "necessary reserve toward members of alien races." As late as March 1945, Kaltenbrunner packed people off to concentration camps for such offenses as: "continued shirking and activity causing annoyance"; "perpetuation of forbidden intimate relations with a . . . French prisoner of war despite previous warning by the state police"; and "anti-German" or "defeatist" remarks.[25]

Differences between the RSHA and the WVHA, to which the camp commandants were responsible, were ironed out at periodic conferences or through correspondence. Whenever Pohl attended these conferences, Kaltenbrunner was also present—otherwise Müller represented the RSHA.[26]

Like Pohl, Kaltenbrunner was anxious to steer the concentration camps clear of any judicial review. Since 1942, the Main Office SS-Tribunal (Hauptamt SS-Gericht) had tried in vain to investigate alleged crime in the camps. In 1943, after months of frustration, the SS and Police Court XXII in Kassel filed charges of corruption and unauthorized murder against Karl

---

[24] Affidavit of Höss, 5 April 1946, 3868-PS, IMT XXXIII, pp. 275-279; testimony of Höss, IMT XI, pp. 405-406, 408, 414; affidavit of Rudolf Mildner, 1 August 1945, L-35, NCA VII, pp. 780-781; testimony of Gustav Nosske, Case IX, Einsatzgruppen Trial, transcripts pp. 3478, 3486-3493, 3544-3557, 3676-3679, Eichmann Document 674, EPD, IfZ Munich; affidavit of Hermann Pister, 1 August 1945, L-38, IMT XXXVII, p. 46.

[25] RSHA [signed Kaltenbrunner] to Stapostelle Saarbrücken, 18 June 1943, 2582-PS, IMT XXX, p. 608; telegrams of the commander of the Security Police in Prague [signed Kaltenbrunner] to the State Police in Darmstadt, 12 March 1945, 2239-PS, ibid., pp. 28, 30-31, 33-34, 38.

[26] Affidavit of Mildner, 1 August 1945, L-35, NCA VII, pp. 780-781; affidavit of Höss, 5 April 1946, 3868-PS, IMT XXXIII, pp. 275-279.

Koch, the erstwhile commandant of Buchenwald, on the basis of an extensive investigation conducted by SS-Sturmbannführer Konrad Morgen. Koch was executed; and Morgen was authorized to investigate cases in other camps. He soon uncovered a net of corruption involving the administrations of Maidanek, Oranienburg, S'Hertogenbosch, Flossenbürg, Dachau, and Auschwitz. Determined to wipe out corruption within the camps, Himmler ordered the establishment of a Provisional SS and Police Court for Special Purposes under Morgen's leadership. While working on cases in Maidanek and Auschwitz, however, Morgen learned to his dismay that thousands of persons were being liquidated daily and began to doubt whether, under the circumstances, the investigation of a few murders had any meaning. In the naïve hope that Himmler would subject the camps to clearly defined legal regulations, Morgen and his collaborators planned to convince the Reichsführer that the brutality of camp life (and death) encouraged the corruption and unauthorized violence which he so deplored.

Frightened by the example of Koch, the camp commandants fought back. Here they could count on support from Pohl and Kaltenbrunner. In June 1944, the two main office chiefs requested that the Morgen investigations be shelved on the grounds that they incited disorder in the camps. Pohl initially had to push for Kaltenbrunner's support, for the RSHA chief had wished to remain neutral. But when Morgen's investigators began to look into allegations of torture in Gestapo prisons, Kaltenbrunner rushed to Pohl's aid. Himmler gave in and ordered Morgen to restrict his investigations to the Koch case at Buchenwald.[27]

The concentration camps were no passing phenomenon of the Nazi regime. Initially justified under the Emergency Decree for the Protection of Volk and State issued after the Reichstag fire on 28 February 1933, their continued existence in the 1930s and their sudden expansion during World War II indicated that, as long as the "emergency" continued to exist, as long as "enemies" against whom the German nation needed protection still lived, they would continue to serve a function. Since the Nazis viewed history in terms of racial conflict, it is clear that the "state of emergency" would exist perpetually as the struggle for survival waxed and waned. The camps, too, would continue to exist as "centers of forced labor, biological and medical experiments, and the physical extermination of Jewish and other unwanted life."[28]

[27] Kurt Mittelstaedt, "Die Unrechtsbekaempfung in Konzentrationslagern und aehnlichen Einrichtungen," Oberursel, 1945, F 65, pp. 1-2, 8-10, 12-14, IfZ Munich; affidavit of Konrad Morgen, 28 December 1945, F 65, IfZ Munich; Hans Buchheim, "The SS—Instrument of Domination," in Krausnick, SS State, pp. 248-254; Höhne, SS, pp. 437-438; Hilberg, Destruction, pp. 578-579.

[28] Broszat, "Camps," p. 400.

On the stand at Nuremberg, Kaltenbrunner bitterly denied having had any relations with Pohl and the WVHA beyond the discussion of RSHA finances. He maintained that he had never set foot in Mauthausen, that he learned only in March 1944 that Auschwitz-Birkenau was an extermination camp, and that he protested to Hitler and Himmler as soon as he learned of the extermination process.[29] These claims were simply not true. Beyond his repeated denials, Kaltenbrunner could provide no evidence to support his story. He clearly had assumed the supervisory and liaison role with respect to the camps that was incumbent upon him as chief of the RSHA. Whatever, therefore, he may have thought privately, he officially treated the camps as a vital factor in the survival of the Third Reich.

Kaltenbrunner's policy toward the Christian churches is of interest and importance because in this area he was considered a moderate in contrast to Heydrich. Wilhelm Höttl has written that Kaltenbrunner, though "certainly far from living or acknowledging himself as a Christian," could not fathom how Heydrich "could harbor such a deadly hatred of the [Catholic] Church." Werner Kaltenbrunner remembered that Ernst was the only Kaltenbrunner brother not to leave the Catholic Church; Kaltenbrunner's SS personnel file confirms this. Both Höttl and Kaltenbrunner's first biographer, Wendell Robert Houston, maintained that Kaltenbrunner reverted to his Catholic faith while a prisoner at Nuremberg.[30]

We have already seen in chapter 1 that Kaltenbrunner claimed to have lost his Catholic faith while still a child in Raab. Years later, in Nuremberg, he wrote that he did believe in God, but perceived His divine presence as rooted in nature, operating independently of any institution created by man. From his cell, he exhorted his children to seek God in nature and advised them that one need not perceive any man-made signs of His existence: "You will find it easier to say that it must have been God who originated life. It could only have been one [God], you only have to look at the miracle of a flower or at the variety of living things, each of which has its peculiarities and its details. That could not have been created by many, only by a Master."[31]

This concept of an impersonal higher being as the source of natural phenomena was by no means peculiar to Kaltenbrunner. On one occasion, Himmler remarked to his masseur and confidant, Felix Kersten, "Surely common sense must tell you that some higher being—whether you call it God or Providence or anything else you like—is behind nature and the

[29] Testimony of Kaltenbrunner, IMT xi, pp. 263, 269, 270, 274-275, 318, 321-326.

[30] Hagen, *Geheime Front*, p. 35; testimony of Otto Ohlendorf, IMT iv, p. 335; interview with Dr. Werner Kaltenbrunner, Vöcklabruck, 25 March 1977; E. Kaltenbrunner SS File, BDC; Houston, "Kaltenbrunner," p. 182.

[31] E. Kaltenbrunner, "Memoir," p. 15.

marvelous order which exists in the world of men and animals and plants."[32] In fact, Himmler frowned on atheists and did not want them in his SS.

Kaltenbrunner claimed to be tolerant of private belief in God or religious practice as such, but he abhorred men who "dressed up God beyond recognition," and who, in their "blindness, lust for power, and ambition stand outside of and against the Volk." Life on earth should be determined by man alone. Kaltenbrunner objected to churches and religions because they placed the well-being of the individual soul and preparations for the afterlife above and beyond the tenets of National Socialism, above and beyond the "political faith" demanded by the movement of its followers.[33] That the Christian faith with its emphasis on the individual soul would by its very nature clash with the Nazi concept of race was not clear to Kaltenbrunner, for he continued to proclaim tolerance for the role of religion in the private sphere, provided that it did not override secular responsibilities to the racial community.

If Kaltenbrunner was unaware of this inherent contradiction, Hitler and Himmler were not, though they recognized that open struggle against the churches might weaken popular support for the regime. Hitler himself favored a truce for the duration of the war as long as churchmen stayed out of politics. Himmler, too, was not anxious for an open test of strength. As early as 1935, he had decreed that he would not "tolerate that the opinions and convictions of other members of the race which are sacred to them be ridiculed or slandered by SS members." He warned his SS not to participate in any defacement of church property or holy symbols and threatened those who disobeyed with expulsion from the SS. Two years later, the Reichsführer announced that "such attacks and insults describing Christ as a Jew are unworthy of us [the SS] and are certainly untrue from a historical viewpoint." During the war, Heydrich, though a fanatical enemy of the churches, ordered the Gestapo to avoid anticlerical actions, citing Hitler's concern about their effects.[34] Even such a pathological enemy of Christianity as Martin Bormann, the chief of the Nazi Party Chancellery, warned Party officials not to provoke unrest among the population by attacking the churches. Sharing Bormann's concern, Himmler sent orders to Kaltenbrunner demanding

[32] Quoted in John M. Steiner, *Power Politics and Social Change in National Socialist Germany: A Process of Escalation into Mass Destruction* (The Hague–Paris: Mouton Publishers, 1976), p. 113.

[33] E. Kaltenbrunner, "Memoir," pp. 16-17. On "political faith," see Hans Buchheim, *Glaubenskrise im Dritten Reich: Drei Kapitel nationalsozialistischer Religionspolitik* (Stuttgart: Deutsche Verlags-Anstalt, 1953), pp. 17-24, 203.

[34] Circular of Himmler 20 September 1935, Aktenmappe SS und Kirche, Ordner 245, pp. 287-288, BDC; circular of Himmler, 28 June 1937, ibid.; on Heydrich, see Peterson, *Hitler's Power*, p. 215.

that SS propaganda inciting individuals to leave the churches be squashed.[35] One can thus conclude that "moderation" toward the churches was not at variance with the policies of the top leadership of the Nazi regime—at least for the duration of the war.

Despite this, the RSHA had followed a hard-line, if unrealistic, anticlerical policy until Heydrich's death. Within the Gestapo, Heydrich established a small action group for clerical matters under SS-Sturmbannführer Albert Hartl, a defrocked priest with a healthy aversion to the Catholic Church. In September 1941, Hartl addressed a conference of Gestapo experts in Aachen on church policy. He stressed the need to extend the Gestapo's intelligence network in clerical circles, since large-scale actions against churches and monasteries had been forbidden. This intelligence was to be documented and stored in preparation for future "decisive measures." One of Hartl's pet schemes was to infiltrate the Catholic Church by sending young, reliable Nazis into the priesthood and thus gradually nazifying the clergy.[36]

When Kaltenbrunner took over the RSHA, he dismantled the Hartl apparatus because he thought that Hartl's plan to infiltrate the Catholic clergy was ridiculous, not because he had any moral qualms about its intent. In his heart, Kaltenbrunner rejected churchmen who tried to influence the secular affairs of their parishes; nor did he harbor any reservations about persecuting clerics who dared to criticize the Nazi regime. While he was HSSPF in Vienna, Kaltenbrunner had recommended that a subordinate be awarded the SS dagger in recognition of his "daring and uncompromising attitude toward political Catholicism," which was manifested in his successful efforts to withdraw state subsides and tax credits from parochial schools in Vienna and Lower Austria. As chief of the RSHA, Kaltenbrunner did not hesitate to persecute Catholic theologians who preached "defeatism." On 25 March 1944, the RSHA issued a ban on the sermons of Dominican Father Johann Vetter on the grounds that they were "intended to have a defeatist effect." Nine days earlier, Johann Götz, a Stuttgart priest, had been forbidden to preach "on account of [his] behavior [which was] injurious to the state." On 29 December 1944, a similar ban was applied to Josef Krucker of Ulm/Donau because "his sermons invariably contain remarks harmful to the state, which are intended to upset law and order."[37]

[35] Circular of Bormann, 26 April 1943, T-175/66/2581860-2581861, NA; Himmler to Bormann, 24 April 1943, ibid., 2581862.
[36] "Vermerk über die Arbeitstagung der Kirchenberater bei den Staatspolizei(leit)stellen," 8 October 1941, 1815-PS, IMT XXVIII, pp. 446-448. On Hartl's plan, see interview with Dr. Wilhelm Höttl, Bad Aussee, 14 and 15 April 1977, hereafter Höttl Tape, p. 18.
[37] Kaltenbrunner to Wolff, 7 October 1938, T-175/33/2541171, NA; order of Stapoleitstelle Stuttgart, 25 March and 6 April 1944, T-175/486/9346785, 9346786, NA; order of Stapoleitstelle Stuttgart [signed Mussgay], 12 January 1945, ibid., 9346788.

Leniency toward the Catholic or Protestant Churches on Kaltenbrunner's part cannot, therefore, be attributed to a slackening ideological commitment, for Hitler himself had ordered that the churches be left in peace for the duration of the war. Moreover, it is more than likely that Hitler, Himmler, and Bormann were planning a final reckoning with organized religion, in particular with the Catholic Church.[38] In October 1942, Himmler told Felix Kersten of his postwar plans:[39]

> Everywhere you find at decisive moments the intervention of two great world powers: the Catholic Church and the Jews. Both strive for world domination; they are at heart bitterly hostile to one another, but they are united in the struggle against Germandom. We have eliminated one of these powers, at least in Germany; we will settle accounts with the other after the great war. Today, unfortunately, our hands are tied; we must restrain our true feelings in favor of diplomatic prudence, but the times will change. Then we will defrock the priests, then no God and no Virgin Mary will help them. I would like most of all to clean up here in Rome among the race of priests and settle accounts with the Holy Father.

As Arthur Greiser, the Gauleiter of the Wartheland (seat Poznań), explained, the aim was "to reduce the [Christian] churches to the status of private clubs and then to destroy their moral and ethical influence."[40]

The most heinous and barbaric of Nazi policies was the Final Solution, the war of annihilation against the Jews of Europe. When Kaltenbrunner came to Berlin in February 1943, the gas chambers in the death camps had been in operation for some eight months; deportations had been going on for more than a year. The new RSHA chief inherited from Heydrich a smoothly functioning apparatus operated by an experienced action commando, the infamous Gestapo Department IV B 4, commanded by SS-Sturmbannführer Adolf Eichmann.[41] It was thus unnecessary for Kaltenbrunner to play a direct role in carrying out the Final Solution. He needed only to make certain that the apparatus continued to function smoothly.

[38] J. S. Conway, *The Nazi Persecution of the Churches, 1933-1945* (New York: Basic Books, 1968), pp. 232, 284-285.

[39] Felix Kersten, *Totenkopf und Treue: Heinrich Himmler ohne Uniform* (Hamburg: Robert Mölich Verlag, n.d.), p. 196.

[40] Orlow, *Nazi Party, 1933-1945*, pp. 290-291.

[41] The most exhaustive work on the extermination of the European Jews remains Hilberg's *Destruction*. On the Eichmann commando, see ibid., pp. 262-263. Other basic works are: Gerald Reitlinger, *The Final Solution: The Attempt to Exterminate the Jews of Europe, 1939-1945*, 2nd ed. (London: Vallentine, Mitchell, 1968); Lucy S. Dawidowicz, *The War Against the Jews, 1933-1945* (New York: Bantam, 1976). For an example of how RSHA IV B 4 handled the technical details of the deportations, see memorandum of Günther [RSHA IV B 4 a], "Richtlinien zur technischen Durchführung der Evakuierung von Juden nach dem Osten (KL Auschwitz)," 20 February 1943, T-175/657/18-24, NA.

Kaltenbrunner sought to convince the tribunal at Nuremberg that he had learned only in March 1944 of the murder of the Jews in Auschwitz and that he had then protested to both Himmler and Hitler, drawing their attention to "my personal attitude and my completely different conception which I had brought over from Austria and to my humanitarian qualms."[42] The evidence that has survived renders such disclaimers ludicrous. As early as 22 February 1943, Himmler's adjutant sent Kaltenbrunner foreign press clippings on the "accelerated annihilation of the Jews in occupied Europe."[43] One month earlier, on 18 January, Himmler had ordered the Reich inspector for statistics, Richard Korrherr, to compile a statistical report on the progress of the "Final Solution of the European Jewish Question" to date. The Reichsführer informed Korrherr that he would have access to relevant records from the files of the RSHA, and ordered the incoming RSHA chief to discontinue the statistical reports being compiled in his office and to cooperate with Korrherr. Based on statistical data provided by the RSHA, the infamous top secret Korrherr report, entitled "The Final Solution of the European Jewish Question," was read by Himmler on 27 March 1943. The RSHA may not have been pleased at Korrherr's involvement in this sensitive issue; for, when a report was compiled for Hitler, Himmler ordered Korrherr to provide a shortened version of his report for inclusion into a larger RSHA memorandum.[44] These reports could not have escaped the attention of the chief of the RSHA.

Kaltenbrunner's personal knowledge of and involvement in the annihilation of the European Jews remained constant and consistent. In April 1943, he discussed "Jewish affairs" and negotiations with Glücks, the inspector of the concentration camps, with Himmler on the telephone. One month later, he spoke to Himmler about "evacuation of the Jews," a phrase that, in Nazi parlance, meant deportation to a death camp. In late May, Himmler informed the governor general in Poland, Hans Frank, that he would send Kaltenbrunner, SS-Obergruppenführer Friedrich Wilhelm Krüger (the HSSPF in the Government General), and SS-Obergruppenführer Otto Winkelmann, a high-ranking official in the HA-Orpo, to represent the interests of the SS and police at a security conference called by Frank for 31 May. One

[42] Testimony of Kaltenbrunner, IMT xi, p. 275.

[43] Brandt [Persönlicher Stab, Reichsführer SS] to chief of Security Police and SD, 22 February 1943, T-175/68/2584398, NA.

[44] Himmler to Inspekteur für Statistik, 18 January 1943, ibid., 2584401; Himmler to the chief of the Reichssicherheitshauptamt, 18 January 1943, ibid., 2584399; Inspekteur für Statistik, "Die Endlösung der europäischen Judenfrage," n.d. [initialed by Himmler on 27 March 1943], T-175/103/2625029-2625045, NA; Korrherr to Himmler, 19 April 1943, with appended report, ibid., 2625016-2625023. Korrherr's first report estimated that four million Jews out of a total population of ten million European Jews had emigrated or died; his second report increased that estimate to four and one-half million.

SS policy aim that Himmler was determined to have represented by Kaltenbrunner, Krüger, and Winkelmann was that "the evacuation [deportation] of the last 250,000 Jews in [the Government General], which for some weeks will undoubtedly excite unrest, must be completed as quickly as possible despite all difficulties." Six weeks after the conference, Himmler wrote Kaltenbrunner a letter suggesting that the RSHA play up "ritual murder" propaganda in the Eastern European press in order to "facilitate the extraction [Herausnahme] of the Jews" from Hungary, Romania, and Bulgaria, whose leaders had refused to deport their Jewish citizens.[45]

Under interrogation in the Nuremberg prison, Kaltenbrunner aired a few thoughts on the role of the Jews when asked what he knew of the notorious Einsatzgruppen reports. In a discourse on "Eastern Jewry," he remarked that "unlike [the situation] in cultured European lands, the Jew in the East was not merely a member of the professions: high finance, literature, journalism, medicine, and law; rather he exclusively was the intellectual, the sole ruler of all business, therefore that very class which possessed enough intellect to provide the enemy [i.e., Nazi Germany's enemies] with the essential personnel to carry out his plans." Kaltenbrunner claimed that in Slovakia there was "no cobbler, no tavernkeeper, no tailor, no baker, no business at all that was not 100 percent Jewish. . . . An American would not believe this, but it is so." The Jews in Russia, Kaltenbrunner continued, had formed the backbone of the partisan movement: "All partisan activity, every resistance movement, every form of espionage had the Jew as its organizer, as the principal mainstay of the Bolshevik idea; he was the decisive element in every hostile action." Thus one should not be surprised, Kaltenbrunner told his interrogator, that an Einsatzkommando killed large numbers of Jews while fighting Soviet partisans: "If, therefore, it is said in the reports of the Einsatzgruppe . . . that, let us say, of 11,000 enemy dead, 500 or 600 of them were Jews, that was to be expected [so ist das etwas ganz Normales gewesen]; it corresponded to local conditions and did not constitute a will to annihi-

---

[45] Handwritten log of Himmler's telephone conversations, 16 September 1941-17 August 1943, F 37/2, 2133/58, IfZ Munich; telegram of Himmler to Frank, 26 May 1943, T-175/128/ 2654162, NA; Himmler to Kaltenbrunner, 19 May 1943, ibid., 2654164. Under pressure from German civilian and military authorities in the Government General, Krüger explained to Kaltenbrunner at the conference that Himmler's order to replace Jewish skilled workers in the armaments industries with Poles in order to complete the liquidation of all Jews in the Government General could not be implemented without serious repercussions on the German war effort. Kaltenbrunner was asked "to illustrate this situation to the Reichsführer SS and to request him to abstain from the removal of this Jewish labor force." See record of the conference, "Sicherheitslage im Generalgouvernement," 31 May 1943, p. 15, Diensttagebuch des Generalgouverneurs, Vol. xxxii, 2233-PS, NA. On ritual murder propaganda, see Himmler to Kaltenbrunner, 19 May 1943, in Reichsführer! Briefe an und von Himmler, ed. Helmut Heiber (Munich: Deutscher Taschenbuch Verlag, 1970), p. 267.

late."[46] It is clear that, in the East, Kaltenbrunner saw the Jew as the major enemy.

The details of the Final Solution—concentration, deportation, and extermination—were arranged by Eichmann's office with the Reich Ministry for Transportation and the camp commandants of the five extermination centers in Poland (Auschwitz-Birkenau, Bełżec, Chełmno, Sobibór, and Treblinka). Eichmann's experts used the services of both indigenous policemen in the occupied territories and local Jewish leaders themselves, who registered indigenous Jews and selected them for transport. Arrangements with the Reich Ministry for Transportation were handled by Franz Novak, one of Eichmann's assistants. Once the deportees arrived at the extermination camps, they became the responsibility of the camp commandant and his staff. Eichmann reported to his immediate superior, Gestapo chief Müller; the death camp officials were responsible to the Inspectorate of the Concentration Camps—*Amtsgruppe* D in the SS Economic and Administrative Main Office in the case of Auschwitz, and to the SS and police leader in Lublin (Odilo Globocnik) in the cases of Bełżec, Treblinka, Sobibór, and Chełmno. The genocide apparatus was operating with chilling efficiency months before Kaltenbrunner came to Berlin, and he was content to supervise the process, intervening only when necessary.

Within days of his appointment, Kaltenbrunner eagerly sought to demonstrate his willingness and ability to aid in the "difficult" but "necessary" task of evacuating Jews to the East. In February 1943, he wrote Himmler, explaining that 5,000 Jews under sixty years of age had just been shipped from the Theresienstadt (Terezín) Ghetto in Bohemia to Auschwitz-Birkenau. Himmler and Heydrich had originally established the Theresienstadt Ghetto as a "model settlement" in which elderly Jews, prominent German and European Jews, and disabled or decorated Jewish veterans of World War I could live out their days in peace. Should foreign governments or international organizations (e.g., the Red Cross) inquire about the fate of a prominent Jew or request clarification of rumors that the Jews were being killed in the East, the German Foreign Office could point to the "secure, peaceful life" in Theresienstadt. The ghetto also provided Himmler with a convenient explanation for those Germans who pondered why an octogenarian or an armless war veteran should be resettled and put to work in the East.

Kaltenbrunner had little use for such subtleties. He calculated that there were some 46,735 Jews in Theresienstadt, of whom 25,375 were unable to work owing to age, illness, or disability. He suggested that Himmler authorize him to "loosen up" the large group of Jews over sixty years of age and infirm in order to free 4,800 Jews capable of work, but presently engaged in caring for the aged and the ill. The RSHA chief then asked for permission

---

[46] Interrogation of Kaltenbrunner, 19 September 1946, pp. 16-17, ZS-673, IfZ Munich.

to remove 5,000 additional Jews to Auschwitz and promised that only those Jews who had "no special . . . contacts at their disposal and who do not have war decorations" would be deported. Himmler, however, wished to preserve Theresienstadt's good reputation and rejected Kaltenbrunner's suggestion.[47]

Kaltenbrunner was kept closely informed of impending legislation depriving Jews of legal rights. In the late summer and autumn of 1942, the Reich minister of justice, the Reich minister of the interior, and the chief of the Nazi Party Chancellery debated whether new regulations concerning the status of Jews remaining in the Reich were necessary. On 25 September, a draft decree was drawn up. According to its provisions, Jews were deprived of reprieve or appeal against administrative or judicial decisions, pronounced incapable of swearing an oath [eidunfähig], and divested of their property by the Reich upon their death.[48] In early 1943, while the gas chambers operated at maximum efficiency, the Reich authorities decided that this decree was superfluous. Kaltenbrunner, however, urged that the decree be promulgated for these reasons: (1) it would cover those Jews who had not yet been deported because they were married to Germans; (2) it would legalize and simplify the confiscation of Jewish property by the Reich; and (3) it would anchor in the law the notion that "the prosecution of criminal proceedings against the Jews passes from the Ministry for Justice to the police." Though the minister of the interior thought the law to be unnecessary "in view of the development of the Jewish question," Kaltenbrunner got his way: on 21 April 1943, a new decree was drafted, providing that "criminal proceedings against Jews will be handled by the police" and that "with the death of a Jew, his property falls to the Reich."[49]

The RSHA chief also endeavored to provide an administrative framework for the deportation and extermination of non-German Jews in the Reich. On 5 March 1943, he issued a decree subjecting all Jews in the Reich who possessed citizenship papers from Poland, Luxemburg, Slovakia, Croatia,

[47] Kaltenbrunner to Himmler, February 1943, T-175/22/2527354-2527356, NA; Brandt to Kaltenbrunner, 16 February 1943, ibid., 2527353. See also Hilberg, *Destruction*, p. 284.

[48] Draft decree, "Verordnung über Rechtsbeschränkung der Juden," 25 September 1942, NG-151, NA. For correspondence on these measures, see Reich Ministry for Justice to Reich Ministry of the Interior, Reichsführer SS and chief of German Police, Reich Ministry for Propaganda and Enlightenment, the Foreign Office, the chief of the Party Chancellery, and the Reich Protector for Bohemia and Moravia, 3 August 1942, ibid.; Reich Ministry for Justice to Reich Ministry for Propaganda and Enlightenment, 13 August 1942, ibid.; chief of the Party Chancellery to Reich Ministry of the Interior, 21 August 1942, ibid.; Reich Ministry for Nutrition and Agriculture to Reich Ministry of the Interior, 20 August 1942, ibid.

[49] Kaltenbrunner to Frick, 8 March 1943, NG-151, NA; note from the Reich minister of the interior, 3 April 1943, ibid; notice for Frick, 21 April 1943, ibid. The decree was issued on 25 April. See Uwe Dietrich Adam, *Judenpolitik im Dritten Reich* (Düsseldorf: Droste Verlag, 1972), p. 352.

Romania, Bulgaria, Greece, Holland, Belgium, France, the Baltic States, and Norway to the police law of 1 September 1941 requiring designation by the yellow star and restrictions on virtually all public activities.[50] At the same time, these Jews were "from now on to be included in the deportation measures." On the same day, Kaltenbrunner issued another decree providing that all non-German Jews from the Reich who had been deported to the Government General or to the Soviet Union and who possessed the above-mentioned citizenship papers "were to be included in the general measures already taken or to be taken against the Jews in those regions." Such measures entailed extermination.[51]

Throughout occupied Europe, Kaltenbrunner supported the deportation teams in their efforts to round up and ship the European Jews to the death camps. When Eichmann's experts discovered in early 1943 that the Italian occupation authorities were not surrendering Greek Jews who had fled Saloniki for the Italian zone, the RSHA requested that the Foreign Office dissuade the Italians from offering them asylum or citizenship. In May 1943, after the destruction of the Warsaw Ghetto, Commander of the Security Police and SD in Warsaw SS-Standartenführer Ludwig Hahn made arrangements to deport the survivors to Sobibór and Treblinka on Kaltenbrunner's orders.[52] In July 1943, the RSHA chief passed on to SS-Standartenführer

[50] After a protest from the Romanian government, the German Foreign Office noted that Jews with Romanian citizenship would be excluded from the general measures outlined in this decree. See Thadden to branch office of the Foreign Office in Kaunas, 15 July 1943, NG-2652-G, NA. The Bulgarian government apparently did not make a similar protest.

[51] Two decrees of Kaltenbrunner, 5 March 1943, NG-2652-G, NG-2652-A, NA. These decrees did not cover Jews in the Reich who were citizens of either Germany's more sensitive allies (Italy, Finland, Hungary, Romania, Denmark) or the European neutrals (Switzerland, Spain, Portugal, Sweden, Turkey). The Reich government had requested that these nations recall their Jewish citizens, but by July 1943 the RSHA had become impatient. On 5 July the Foreign Office was instructed to inform the respective governments that their Jewish citizens would be issued exit visas only until 31 July, after which date the "remaining Jews in the German sphere of power would be put on an equal par with the Jews of German citizenship." After this deadline had passed, Müller ordered the internment of the Jews involved; the men were sent to Buchenwald and the women and children to Ravensbrück until such time as they could be "resettled." See Eichmann to Thadden, 5 July 1943, NG-2652-F, NA; Wagner to Ribbentrop, 12 July 1943, NG-2652-F; decree of Müller, 23 September 1943, NG-2652-H. British, United States, and Argentine Jews were exempted from the deportations.

[52] On Greek Jews, see Bergmann to the Foreign Office, 15 February 1943, NG-4957, NA; Reitlinger, *Final Solution*, p. 404. On Warsaw Jews, see affidavit of Jürgen Stroop [SS and police leader in Warsaw], 24 February 1946, 3841-PS, IMT XXXIII, pp. 201-202; affidavit of Karl Kaleske, 24 February 1946, 3840-PS, ibid., pp. 199-200. Kaleske was Stroop's adjutant. Kaltenbrunner apparently intervened to select three hundred Jews of non-Polish nationality captured in Warsaw for the purpose of a future exchange with the Western Allies; but these Jews appear to have been gassed at Treblinka in July 1943. See Reitlinger, *Final Solution*, p. 276n.

Rudolf Mildner, the commander of the Security Police and the SD in Copenhagen, Himmler's order to round up the Danish Jews despite the protest of the Reich plenipotentiary in Copenhagen, SS-Obergruppenführer Werner Best, that the action would jeopardize the satisfactory working relationship between the Danish administration and the German authorities. Warned of the impending deportation action at the end of September by a contact from Best's office, the Danish authorities secreted 7,000 Danish Jews to Sweden and safety by ship. Afterward, Kaltenbrunner steadfastly refused to release some 90 Danish half-Jews who, along with 350 full Jews, represented the meager booty of the Eichmann commando.[53] Nevertheless, the Reich remained reluctant to deport the Danish Jews to the death camps for reasons of foreign policy. These Jews were held in Theresienstadt until the end of the war.

Wherever the Eichmann team ran into difficulties, Kaltenbrunner jumped into the breach. In August 1943, after the mysterious death of King Boris, RSHA agents demanded that the Foreign Office "exert stronger pressure on the Bulgarian government in the Jewish question in order to solve this problem as soon as possible through . . . evacuation to the Eastern territories." Although they had been willing to deport some 12,000 Jews from the territories that they had occupied as a result of the defeat of Yugoslavia and Greece (Thrace, Macedonia, and Pirot), the Bulgarian leaders, lacking strong anti-Semitic sentiment, sensitive to overwhelming popular opposition to the deportations, and perceptive of Allied warnings and German military defeats, were reluctant to take measures against the approximately 50,000 Jews living in Old Bulgaria. The Foreign Office had to inform an impatient Kaltenbrunner that it appeared "hopeless" and "politically dangerous" to pressure the Bulgarians further at this time.[54] In February 1944, the RSHA chief discovered that the tiny Amsterdam community of Sephardic Jews (numbering 370) had not been included in the deportations from Holland. Experts in the office of the Reich commissar for the occupied territories of the Netherlands explained that the Sephardim were not "genuine" Jews. Kaltenbrunner saw no reason to make such a distinction, since the Sephardim were certainly Jews "seen from the viewpoint of race." He even cited the "Jewish view" in which it was "explicitly established that the Sephardim were Jews from Spain and Portugal" and ordered SS-Brigadeführer Erich Naumann,

---

[53] Affidavit of Eberhard von Thadden, 16 April 1948, Eichmann document 816, EPD, IfZ Munich; affidavit of Wagner, 13 May 1948, Eichmann document 817, ibid.; statement of Mildner, 22 June 1945, 2375-PS, NA; interrogation of Mildner, IMT xi, p. 255.

[54] Wagner to Kaltenbrunner, 31 August 1943, NG-3302, NA. An excellent monograph on the Bulgarian Jews during World War II is Frederick B. Chary, *The Bulgarian Jews and the Final Solution, 1940-1944* (Pittsburgh: University of Pittsburgh Press, 1972).

the commander of the Security Police and the SD in The Hague, to deport the Sephardic Jews "immediately." For unclear reasons, this order was never carried out; the Sephardic Jews of Amsterdam survived the war.[55]

Kaltenbrunner's most spectacular and consistent intervention to accelerate the extermination of the European Jews took place in Hungary. Under the leadership of Admiral Miklós Horthy, Hungary had joined the Axis in 1941; before 1944, the Germans had stationed no troops there and generally avoided direct interference in the country's internal affairs. Policy toward the Jews under Horthy's rule was equivocal.[56] Though the regime was prepared to restrict the economic and political life of the Hungarian Jews within a clearly defined legal framework, it rejected the German policy of annihilation. Thus, Hungary became a haven of relative peace and security not only for its own Jews but also for refugees from Poland and Slovakia.

As the tide of war turned against the Germans and Russian troops appeared in the eastern foothills of the Carpathians, Horthy's prime minister, Miklós Kállay, discreetly sought opportunities to disentangle his homeland from the crumbling Axis. Despite intense German pressure, he publicly refused to permit the deportation of any Hungarian Jews. On the evening. 18 March 1944, the Germans, aware of Kállay's intention to desert the Axis, invited Horthy to Schloss Klessheim, where he was kept on ice while German troops occupied Hungary. Horthy was induced to appoint a German-ophile government under the former Hungarian minister to Berlin, General Döme Sztójay; and, since the admiral had also agreed in principle to permit the shipment of Hungarian Jews to Germany for "labor purposes," thus providing the Germans with a legal cover to deport them to Auschwitz, the Eichmann commando arrived in Budapest shortly after the invasion to make the necessary arrangements.[57]

[55] Kaltenbrunner to Naumann, 3 February 1944, Eichmann document 614, EPD, IfZ Munich.

[56] Raul Hilberg has estimated that 750,000 Jews were living in Hungary in March 1944 (see *Destruction*, p. 309). According to the census of 1941, 725,007 Jews plus 100,000 non-Jews considered as Jews (i.e., baptized Jews, etc.) lived in Hungary. See Rudolph L. Braham, *The Politics of Genocide: The Holocaust in Hungary* (New York: Columbia University Press, 1981), II, p. 1144. A surviving leader of the Jewish Rescue Committee in Budapest estimated that the influx of refugees from Poland and Slovakia had swelled the number of Jews in Hungary to 900,000 in 1944. Andreas Biss, *Der Stopp der Endlösung: Kampf gegen Himmler und Eichmann in Budapest* (Stuttgart: Seewald Verlag, 1966), p. 24. The German Foreign Office had come to the same estimate in 1944. See memorandum of Wagner to the Reich foreign minister, 27 October 1944, NG-5573, NA.

[57] On German pressure to deport Jews, see memorandum of Luther [Foreign Office], 6 October 1942, no. 70 in Randolph L. Braham, *The Destruction of Hungarian Jewry: A Documentary Account* (New York: World Federation of Hungarian Jews, 1963), I, pp. 135-142. On Kállay's resistance, see note of Jagow, 13 November 1942, no. 84, ibid., pp. 170-171; note of Sztójay to German Foreign Office, 2 December 1942, no. 86, ibid., pp. 175-182. On the

Kaltenbrunner was on the train that carried Horthy back to Budapest from Klessheim. On 22 March he met with Sztójay and persuaded him to cooperate in the "speediest solution" to the Jewish problem. Sztójay dutifully promised that the Hungarians would not obstruct the deportations, and, on Kaltenbrunner's request, took two avowed anti-Semites, László Baky and László Endre, into the Ministry of the Interior as state secretaries in charge of the Jewish question.[58] Kaltenbrunner remained in Budapest for a few days conferring with the Hungarian authorities on the deportations and on the structure of the German police administration in occupied Hungary. That he had specific instructions from Himmler regarding the deportations is also indicated by the fact that Foreign Minister Joachim Ribbentrop, though kept uninformed, guessed the purpose of Kaltenbrunner's visit and asked Foreign Office Special Plenipotentiary in Budapest SS-Standartenführer Edmund Veesenmayer to spy on the RSHA chief. After completing his mission, Kaltenbrunner returned to Berlin, leaving the details to the Eichmann commando, which sent him regular reports on further negotiations with the Hungarians. The RSHA also made arrangements to provide railroad cars and timetables for the deportations, which commenced in mid-May 1944; by 30 June, 381,600 Jews had been shipped to Auschwitz, where some 240,000 were gassed.[59]

---

significance of Horthy's verbal concessions at Klessheim, see Randolph L. Braham, "The Rightists, Horthy and the Germans: Factors Underlying the Destruction of Hungarian Jewry," in *Jews and Non-Jews in Eastern Europe, 1918-1945*, ed. George Mosse and Bela Vago (New York-Toronto: John Wiley & Sons, 1974), pp. 143, 147-151. For details on German plans for the occupation of Hungary, see Mario D. Fenyo, *Hitler, Horthy, and Hungary: German-Hungarian Relations, 1941-1944* (New Haven: Yale University Press, 1972), pp. 158-177.

[58] László Baky, a top official in the Hungarian gendarmerie, had been proposed as a useful tool for German policy in a pro-German Hungarian regime in a policy memorandum drafted by Wilhelm Höttl and presented by Kaltenbrunner to Hitler via Ambassador Walther Hewel, Ribbentrop's liaison man at Hitler's headquarters, on 11 March 1944. This was eight days before the German occupation of Hungary. See chief of Security Police and SD to Hewel, 11 March 1944, D-679, NA. See also Braham, *Genocide*, I, pp. 368, 400. Kaltenbrunner had supported Reich Special Plenipotentiary in Hungary Edmund Veesenmayer's suggestion for a decisive intervention from Himmler or Göring to divorce Kállay from his pro-Allied advisers as early as February 1944. See memorandum of the Germanische Leitstelle [SS Main Office, Amtsgruppe D] to chief of SS Main Office, 3 February 1944, E. Spaarmann SS File, BDC.

[59] These figures are from Reitlinger, *Final Solution*, pp. 460, 466. SS-Obergruppenführer Otto Winkelmann, the HSSPF in Hungary, told Plenipotentiary Veesenmayer on 15 June 1944 that 326,009 Jews had been deported from Hungary up to that date. Horst Wagner, the chief of the German Foreign Office's Gruppe Inland II Geheim, reported in October 1944 that 437,402 Jews had been deported from Hungary by 10 July 1944. See Veesenmayer to Ritter [date illegible, mid-June 1944], NG-5667, NA; memorandum of Wagner to the Reich foreign minister, 27 October 1944, NG-5573, NA. Randolph Braham states that a grand total of 564,507 Hungarian Jews were deported by train or marched on foot from Hungary between March and December 1944. See *Genocide*, II, p. 1144. On Kaltenbrunner's negotiations in Hungary, see

Kaltenbrunner's powers of intervention in the deportations from Hungary are apparent in a 30 June 1944 letter to SS-Brigadeführer Hanns Blaschke, the mayor of Vienna. Blaschke had requested that he be supplied with a trainload of Hungarian Jews, whom he wished to put to work in Vienna's factories and on the fortifications works outside the city. On 30 June 1944, Kaltenbrunner informed Blaschke that he had diverted four trainloads of Jews bound for Auschwitz to the labor camp Strasshof near Vienna. The RSHA chief explained that only 30 percent of the 12,000 Jews involved were capable of work. Women, children, the aged and disabled were to be "kept ready for a special action for which one day they would be removed."[60] In Nazi terminology, "special action" meant extermination.

Even as Soviet troops approached Budapest, Kaltenbrunner insisted on the deportation of the Hungarian Jews. On 15 October 1944, the SS had engineered a coup d'état, toppling the Horthy regime and replacing it with a government controlled by the fascist Arrow Cross movement. Though Horthy had halted the deportations by decree in July and August 1944 (the second decree moved a disgusted Eichmann to request recall to Berlin) and though Arrow Cross leader and now Hungarian Prime Minister Ferenc Szálasi was, on account of foreign protests, reluctant to transport any more Jews to Germany, Arrow Cross Minister of the Interior Gábor Vajna was still willing to cooperate with the Germans. On 17 October, Kaltenbrunner sent Eichmann back to Budapest with the suggestion that 50,000 Jews be deported immediately and that the remainder of the Budapest Jews be concentrated in designated places on the periphery of the city. Since transit by train had become difficult because of Allied bombings and the advance of Soviet troops, and since Auschwitz itself was threatened by the Soviet onslaught, Eichmann suggested that the Hungarian Jews be marched on foot over 120 miles to the Strasshof detention camp near Vienna. Kaltenbrunner gave the necessary orders, and the marches began on 20 October. Lacking food, clothing, and adequate footwear, about 35,000 Jews were marched off from Budapest to Strasshof and elsewhere in Austria in rain, sleet, and snow. Several thousand

---

Wilhelm Höttl, "Die Entziehung des jüdischen Vermögens in Ungarn in der Zeit vom 19. März 1944 bis zur Besetzung Ungarns durch die Rote Armee," 25 July 1972, p. 4, ZS-429/II, IfZ Munich; statement by the council president of the People's Court in Budapest on the testimony of Döme Sztójay, 4-22 April 1946, 3869-PS, NA; interrogation of Veesenmayer, 28 April 1947, ZS-1554/I, pp. 59-64, IfZ Munich; testimony of Veesenmayer, Darmstadt, 23 May 1961, 24 AR 334/61, Eichmann Interrogation Book, 2904/62, IfZ Munich; Höttl Tape, p. 19; Braham, *Destruction*, I, pp. xvi-xvii. On Ribbentrop's suspicions and Eichmann's reports to Kaltenbrunner, see Ritter to Veesenmayer, 31 March 1944, NG-5564, NA; affidavit of Dieter Wisliceny, 29 November 1945, NCA VIII, p. 615; Thadden to Veesenmayer, 28 April 1944, Braham, *Destruction*, I, p. 351.

[60] Kaltenbrunner to Blaschke, 30 June 1944, 3803-PS, IMT XXXIII, pp. 167-169; Braham, *Genocide*, II, p. 650.

collapsed or were shot on the way.[61] That Kaltenbrunner was personally responsible for this cruel and brutal process is indicated by his indignant note to Horst Wagner, chief of department Inland II in the Foreign Office, in which he complained that an emissary of the Swiss legation had distributed special passes among the members of one of the marching columns. They had simply vanished when the Hungarian police accepted them as being under the protection of the Swiss government. Protests from the Vatican and the Swedish legation induced Szálasi to halt the marches on 21 November, but these orders did not deter bands of Arrow Cross men from slaughtering hundreds of Jews remaining in Budapest and dumping their bodies into the Danube. The fall of Budapest to Soviet troops on 13 February 1945 put an end to these massacres.[62]

Kaltenbrunner's role in the Final Solution was that of a supervisor, who intervened only when the deportation apparatus was slowed or hindered in some way. His one initiative, the suggestion that 5,000 Theresienstadt Jews be shipped to Auschwitz, was rejected by Himmler; after this, he restricted himself to negotiations with outside authorities on specific aspects of the deportations. Yet, he retained full control of the apparatus. As one of Eichmann's colleagues later testified, "all measures taken in the field of Jewish affairs were submitted to Kaltenbrunner for basic decisions; first Heydrich, and later Kaltenbrunner."[63] If Kaltenbrunner remained relatively passive in terms of the destruction process, this is not an indication of disagreement with aims or means, but rather a sign of how efficiently the annihilation apparatus worked.

[61] On footmarches and Kaltenbrunner's orders, see Veesenmayer to the Foreign Office, 18 October 1944, NG-5570, NA; interrogation of Eichmann, April 1960, pp. 77-78, Eichmann Document 1423, EPD, IfZ Munich; Braham, *Genocide*, II, pp. 833-843; Fenyo, *Horthy*, pp. 191-192, 215. On Eichmann's disgust in August, see Veesenmayer to the Foreign Office, 24 August 1944, no. 213, Braham, *Destruction*, II, p. 480. On the roundup of Jews in Budapest and the beginning of the footmarches, see two cables of Veesenmayer to the Foreign Office, 20 October 1944, NG-5570, NA; Veesenmayer to the Foreign Office, 26 October 1944, ibid. Veesenmayer reported on 13 November that around 27,000 Jews had left Budapest on foot for the Reich. See Veesenmayer to the Foreign Office, 13 November 1944, ibid. Biss (*Endlösung*, pp. 228-229) estimates that some 35,000 to 40,000 Jews were marched to Austria. Reitlinger (*Final Solution*, p. 484) places the figure between 30,000 and 40,000 ; while Braham (*Destruction*, I, p. xxvi) reports that 20,000 civilians and 15,000 members of Jewish labor battalions from all over Hungary were marched to the Austrian border. Dieter Wisliceny (affidavit, NCA VIII, p. 616) testified at Nuremberg that 30,000 Jews were marched to Austria in November and December 1944.

[62] On Kaltenbrunner's indignation, see Kaltenbrunner to Wagner, 11 November 1944, no. 393, Braham, *Destruction*, II, p. 810. On halt to footmarches, see Hilberg, *Destruction*, p. 553.

[63] Testimony of Dieter Wisliceny, 14 November 1945, p. 14, Eichmann document 856, EPD, IfZ Munich.

Kaltenbrunner's low-keyed supervisory role in the process of genocide stood in sharp contrast to the ruthless zeal with which he conducted his other most important wartime assignment, the direction of the commission that investigated the attempt on Hitler's life on 20 July 1944.[64] This attempt and its consequences should not be viewed merely as a temporary reaction to a specific wartime event, for the conspiracy offered the Nazi leadership an opportunity to settle accounts with the German army establishment. Underlying the savage persecution of those connected with the German resistance was a deep-seated mistrust and contempt for the traditional German officer corps with its castelike mentality and for the conservative civil servants inherited from the Wilhelmine and Weimar eras. The near vacuum of power left by the decimation of the non-Nazi military establishment after 20 July 1944 was filled by Himmler's SS and Bormann's Nazi Party Chancellery.[65] In the long run, the Nazi regime intended to erase those elites traditionally loyal to a social class or a legal state authority and to replace them with one ideologically committed to Führer and Nazi movement; the days of the "nonpolitical" soldier or civil servant were nearly over. In this sense, the persecution of the 20 July conspirators represents a glimpse of the future in store for the traditional pillars of the German state within the Third Reich.

The attempt to assassinate Hitler on 20 July 1944 caught the RSHA completely by surprise. Kaltenbrunner and Müller had been closely monitoring the Beck-Goerdeler group and the "Kreisau Circle" centered around Helmuth Graf von Moltke. Moltke had been arrested in January 1944 and, on 17 July 1944, the RSHA issued a warrant for Goerdeler's arrest. Yet, despite sketchy knowledge of a link from Beck to Colonel Claus Schenk Graf von Stauffenberg, chief of staff of the Reserve Army and the man who planted the bomb at Hitler's headquarters in Rastenburg, Kaltenbrunner's police seem to have been unaware of the Stauffenberg plot.[66]

At 1:15 P.M. on 20 July 1944, thirty minutes after Stauffenberg's bomb had exploded at Rastenburg, Kaltenbrunner was summoned to Hitler's headquarters. When he left Berlin, he was still uncertain as to what had actually happened. At 8:00 P.M. that evening, he returned to the capital with Himm-

---

[64] The most complete history of the German resistance and the most detailed account of the events of 20 July is Peter Hoffmann, *The History of the German Resistance, 1933-1945* (Cambridge: MIT Press, 1977).

[65] After becoming minister of the interior in August 1943, Himmler was appointed commander in chief of the Reserve Army in July 1944. In October, he was put in charge of all affairs dealing with prisoners of war; in December, he took command of Army Group Upper Rhine in southwest Germany. Bormann's power was anchored in the local Gau organizations, whose leaders, as Reich defense commissars, became ranking civilian authorities as enemy troops approached their Gaue.

[66] Höhne, *SS*, pp. 599-600; Hedwig Meier, "Die SS und der 20. Juli 1944," *VfZ*, 14 (July 1966), 299-303.

ler, who placed him in charge of investigating the assassination attempt. Kaltenbrunner's first act was to dispatch a commando of Security Police under SS-Standartenführer Walter Huppenkothen, the chief of the Gestapo counterintelligence department (RSHA IV E), to the offices of the Reserve Army in the Bendlerstrasse with orders to arrest Stauffenberg and his fellow conspirators. To his dismay, Huppenkothen found that General Friedrich Fromm, the commander in chief of the Reserve Army, had already had Stauffenberg and three others shot for treason. Anxious to conceal his own flirtation with the conspirators, Fromm was preparing another group for execution, when Kaltenbrunner arrived and ordered that no one else be shot. The RSHA chief wanted live witnesses.[67]

Yet, the full significance of Kaltenbrunner's actions on 20 July 1944 remains unclear. Stauffenberg and his comrades were executed shortly after midnight. Kaltenbrunner did not speak to Fromm until 1:00 A.M. on 21 July. Why then, was there a four-hour gap between Kaltenbrunner's arrival in Berlin and his meeting with Fromm on the Bendlerstrasse? In part, the SS leadership was still shocked by the assassination attempt and ignorant of the identities of the direct perpetrators. On the other hand, one authority has suggested that the SS kept a low profile in light of the fact that units of the army itself, under command of the loyalist Major Otto Ernst Remer, were engaged in crushing the putsch. The SS leadership did not wish to become involved in a conflict with Wehrmacht units. Another author has suggested that Himmler was waiting to see whether the conspirators would succeed and, if they did, to offer them his services. Most interesting with respect to Kaltenbrunner is the account of Albert Speer, the Reich minister of armaments. Around 11:00 P.M., Speer was informed that several conspirators had been arrested in the Bendlerstrasse and that Fromm was preparing to execute them after a summary court-martial. An hour later, Speer arrived at the Bendlerstrasse with the intention of persuading Fromm to delay the executions. At the corner of the Bendlerstrasse and the Tiergartenstrasse he was stopped by Kaltenbrunner and SS-Obersturmbannführer Otto Skorzeny, who had been concealed in the shadows. Kaltenbrunner motioned Speer over and told him that he (Kaltenbrunner) did not intend to interfere in the affairs of the Wehrmacht, that no SS would participate in the suppression of the putsch or in the punishment of the perpetrators, and that he had forbidden RSHA personnel to enter the Bendlerstrasse.[68] An hour after this, Kaltenbrunner halted the summary executions.

[67] Walter Huppenkothen, "Der 20. Juli 1944," ZS-249/1, pp. 152-154, IfZ Munich; Hoffmann, *Resistance*, pp. 510-511.

[68] Speer to Thierack [Reich minister of justice], 3 March 1945, T-84/150/1518879-1518884, NA; Speer, *Inside*, p. 387. On SS reaction to the putsch and its possible motives, see Hoffmann, *Resistance*, pp. 510-511; Meier, "SS," pp. 299-316.

Lack of evidence in this mysterious case renders possible only speculative conclusions. If Himmler indeed planned to join a successful coup, it is plausible that he ordered Kaltenbrunner to lie low until the outcome was certain. There is no evidence, however, that Kaltenbrunner also toyed with the idea of associating himself with a successful putsch; and he certainly was in a position to know that the revolt had failed by the time he met Speer in the shadows on the corner of the Bendlerstrasse. It is more probable that, given the smoldering animosity between Wehrmacht and SS, Kaltenbrunner wished to restrain the SS and allow Wehrmacht loyalists to wipe out any remaining pockets of resistance. An earlier intervention might have brought about an alliance between loyalist and rebel troops on the basis of a common hatred of the SS.

Kaltenbrunner's loyalty to the regime and his attitude toward those who conspired against it were clearly defined in the days, weeks, and months that followed the unsuccessful putsch. As SS investigators began to uncover the complicated network of the anti-Hitler conspiracy, it became necessary to form a "Special Commission 20 July 1944" (Sonderkommission 20. Juli 1944) under the leadership of Müller, the Gestapo chief. Directly under Kaltenbrunner's command, the Special Commission operated independently of the Gestapo and the Kripo, and was exclusively concerned with arrests, interrogations, and investigations pertaining to the conspiracy.[69]

Over the following weeks and months, the Special Commission traced links of the conspiracy to an ever wider circle of military officers, civilian administrators, and underground opponents of the regime. Throughout the summer and autumn of 1944, Kaltenbrunner sent daily reports summarizing the information gleaned from the interrogations to Martin Bormann in the Party Chancellery.[70] Though strict orders were issued that the putsch be portrayed officially as the work of a "relatively small clique of officers," Kaltenbrunner and his policemen passed on a far more accurate picture to Hitler and Bormann. The RSHA chief knew that not all of the conspirators had acted out of "base motives." Although support for the conspiracy was generally derived from "the open opposition of the old reactionaries and former trade-union officials and the defeatism of certain office generals" as well as from "a distorted idea of loyalty and comradeship among otherwise

[69] Walter Huppenkothen, "Personale Zusammensetzung und Aufgabenverteilung der Sonderkommission 20. Juli 1944," ZS-249/1, pp. 80-81, IfZ Munich. See also Schellenberg, *Secret Service*, p. 351; John Wheeler-Bennett, *The Nemesis of Power: The German Army in Politics, 1918-1945* (New York: St. Martin's Press, 1954), p. 675.

[70] These reports survived the war and were published in part. See Karl Heinrich Peter, ed., *Spiegelbild einer Verschwörung: Die Kaltenbrunner-Berichte an Bormann und Hitler über das Attentat vom 20. Juli 1944. Geheime Dokumente aus dem ehemaligen Reichssicherheitshauptamt* (Stuttgart: Seewald Verlag, 1961).

decent soldiers," Kaltenbrunner was disconcerted to learn that several of those arrested had been convinced Nazis up to and even after 1933. Many of the statements he passed on to Bormann reflected a sense of disillusionment among former Nazis and pro-Nazis.

Kaltenbrunner's reports emphasized the conspirators' criticism of the abuse of Nazi promises rather than direct criticism of the Nazi ideology itself. SA-Obergruppenführer Wolf Heinrich Graf von Helldorf, the police president of Berlin and an enthusiastic Nazi in the 1930s, told his interrogators that his "personal view is today as always, that I accept National Socialism as it was conceived and professed by us in the years of struggle [*Kampfjahre*]"; but that he could "no longer approve of that which is represented to me today as the realization of National Socialism." Stauffenberg's brother, Berchtold Graf von Stauffenberg, stated under interrogation that "in the internal political sector we had *accepted the basic ideas of National Socialism for the most part*: the idea of *leadership, experienced and responsible leadership*, linked to a sound hierarchical order and the Volksgemeinschaft, the principle of the '*commonweal before self-interest*,' the struggle against corruption, the emphasis on *ruralism*, the struggle against the spirit of the large cities, the *concept of race* and the will for a new *order determined by the Germans* seemed to us to be sound and full of promise" (emphasis in the original).[71]

Nor was the idea of race rejected out of hand by all of the conspirators. Stauffenberg's uncle, Nikolaus Graf Üxküll-Gyllenband, stated that the conspirators had planned to "retain the concept of race, insofar as that was possible." Johannes Popitz, Prussian minister of finance in the 1930s, explained that "in the Jewish question I, as a competent expert on the conditions during the time of the System, was absolutely of the opinion that the Jews must disappear from economic and political life. As to the method, I have repeatedly recommended a somewhat more gradual process, especially in consideration of foreign policy." Berchtold Graf von Stauffenberg told his interrogators that he "and his brother accepted the basic National Socialist concept of race in itself, but had considered it *exaggerated* and *excessive*" (emphasis in the original).[72] Though much of this testimony was deliberately slanted to increase chances of survival, its appeal to ruralism, antiurbanism, and race seems to have won Kaltenbrunner's grudging respect.

[71] Kaltenbrunner to Bormann, 30 August 1944, ibid., p. 325; Kaltenbrunner to Bormann, 16 October 1944, ibid., pp. 447-448. On strict orders concerning public portrayal of the putsch, see circular of Bormann to Reichsleiter and Gauleiter, 24 July 1944, reproduced in Ludwig Jedlicka, *Der 20. Juli 1944 in Österreich*, 2nd ed. (Vienna-Munich: Verlag Herold, 1966), p. 71; circular of the chief of Security Police [signed Ehrlinger], 17 August 1944, T-175/232/2721185-2721186, NA.

[72] All quotes in Kaltenbrunner to Bormann, 16 October 1944, Peter, *Spiegelbild*, pp. 449-450.

Disillusionment on the part of the conspirators with corruption and sel-fishness among the Nazi leaders cropped up consistently in the Kaltenbrun-ner reports. One prisoner declared that "corruption in our previously so pure people is pursued on such a scale as never before by high and highest dig-nitaries of the Nazi regime. While outside our soldiers fight, bleed and fall, men like Göring, Goebbels, Ley, and company lead a life of luxury, fill their cellars and lofts, demand that the people hold out and, with their retinue, dodge in a cowardly fashion the sacrifice which is being made." Helldorf told his interrogators that "it was inherent in my position that from all parts of Germany I was presented with more or less justified grievances from individuals who felt that they had been treated unjustly. From this abundance of incidents I was compelled to conclude that very often not *objective principles* but rather *personal* prejudice was decisive in making judgments" (emphasis in the original). Another prisoner stated that "to a large degree I was seriously affected by the behavior of individual leading personalities of whose actions and antics I, as a result of my position, was compelled to take note. In this case I am thinking especially of the Reich Marshal [Göring], who in his personal behavior and life style in no way responds to the requirements of the war." In October 1944, Kaltenbrunner's interrogators postulated that many of those interrogated had "drawn the con-clusion that the maxim that the commonweal comes before self-interest had been betrayed by leading personalities of National Socialism itself, and that, in fact, the opposite was true. Selfish creatures in high and highest positions had made use of the war to enrich themselves shamelessly at the cost of their own and foreign peoples. This has made a mockery of the noble principle that the commonweal comes before self-interest."[73]

Though the Kaltenbrunner reports were garnished with diatribes and po-lemics against the conspirators—to assure Hitler and Bormann of the loyalty of the RSHA—it is nevertheless likely that Kaltenbrunner hoped to induce Hitler to remedy some of the conditions which the conspirators so deplored. Pictures of Ribbentrop's incompetence, Göring's opulence, and Ley's drunk-enness may have been geared to suggest that such people be removed in favor of more "honest" Nazis like Bormann and perhaps himself. In a letter to Bormann in August 1944, Kaltenbrunner hinted at such intentions. He noted that a key reason for disillusionment among former adherents of Hitler was reflected "in the criticism of the lifestyle of leading personalities of the Reich and the allegation of a growing corruption against which the Party undertakes so little that one must reckon that it receives official toleration." While disclaiming any sympathy for the conspirators' political views, Kalten-

---

[73] Kaltenbrunner to Bormann, 30 August 1944, appendix 2, ibid., pp. 327-328; Kaltenbrun-ner to Bormann, 16 October 1944, ibid., pp. 453, 454, 455.

brunner considered their arguments "important enough to be especially emphasized since similar criticism has spread among the population itself." While the claims of the conspirators were admittedly "exaggerated," Kaltenbrunner "feared" that many Germans "would have fallen for the demagogically proposed demands to eliminate corruption and favoritism regardless of person or position, to act ruthlessly . . . , to enforce modest and simple life styles and the like, because the population is often sensitive on these points, even if [it has] a completely positive basic attitude."[74]

Another indication of Kaltenbrunner's aims was his determination to give Hitler a complete and accurate report on the motives behind the conspiracy. He was reported to have instructed the members of the Special Commission that:[75]

> Hitler must be given an unrelentingly clear picture of the causes which led to the assassination attempt. This cannot be done by simple establishment of findings for the prosecution, but only by culling out the actual motives. There are so many men of outstanding professional and personal qualities involved in the conspiracy that Hitler, through this knowledge, will hopefully experience the shock which is necessary to induce him to [make] the essential changes.

Kaltenbrunner did not hesitate to inform Bormann of his opinion that the authentic sources of the conspiracy would not be revealed in the transcripts of the hearings before the People's Court (*Volksgerichtshof*) and its president, Roland Freisler. A report of 20 August 1944 describing the reaction of the population to the proceedings of the People's Court pointed out that:[76]

> certain drawbacks are derived from the fact that the conduct of the trials had obviously prevented a frank display in the confessions of all the defendants of their *true motives*. Despite all its detail, the official press report leaves many questions open. Doubtless one is concerned here with a group of men who were in a position to survey Germany's military and political responsibilities, and of whom one could scarcely accept that they planned and carried out such a detestable crime for no reason and without any deliberation. (emphasis in the original)

[74] Kaltenbrunner to Bormann, 30 August 1944, ibid, pp. 325-326. On general motive for passing on uncomplimentary pictures of activities of some Nazi leaders, see Davidson, *Trial*, pp. 324-325.

[75] Gerhard Ritter, *Carl Goerdeler und die deutsche Widerstandsbewegung* (Stuttgart: Deutsche Verlags-Anstalt, 1954), pp. 415-416. Ritter cites a report on the 20 July investigation by an SS man named Georg Kiesel: "Kiesel Bericht," *Nordwestdeutsche Hefte*, 1947, pt. 2, pp. 5-34. The authenticity of parts of this report has been contested. See Zeller, *Geist der Freiheit*, p. 299.

[76] "Stimmungsmässige Auswirkung der Verhandlung vor dem Volksgerichtshof gegen die Attentäter des 20.7.44," appendix 1 to Kaltenbrunner to Bormann, 20 August 1944, Peter, *Spiegelbild*, p. 276.

Kaltenbrunner was also revolted by Freisler's style, regardless of his own lack of concern for legal forms when dealing with "enemies." After listening to Freisler's howling invectives during the trial and sentencing of former Field Marshal Erwin von Witzleben, the RSHA chief reportedly returned to the Gestapo office in the Prinz-Albrecht-Strasse muttering under his breath, "this Freisler is a swine."[77]

Despite his interest in the motives of the conspirators, Kaltenbrunner clearly viewed them—especially the military men—as enemies of National Socialism and hence of Reich and Volk. Especially suspect were those military officers who referred to themselves as "nonpolitcal." On 20 August 1944, he sent a scathing report to Bormann, defining the real loyalties of these "nonpolitical soldiers." He thought the topic important enough to circulate an enlarged version of the report to all higher SS and police leaders, commanders and inspectors of the Security Police and the SD, and local Gestapo, Kripo, and SD offices.[78]

The report stated bluntly that those declaring themselves "nonpolitical" were in fact implacable enemies of the Nazi regime. They exhibited a *"complete lack of understanding for National Socialism as a Weltanschauung encompassing life in its entirety"* and did not realize that the "National Socialist movement has shown itself to be a revolution in the true sense of the word" (emphasis in the original). Kaltenbrunner carped that such "nonpolitical" officers had sworn an oath to Hitler just as they had sworn an oath on the constitution of the Weimar Republic, and that they would have "no reservations about swearing a new oath if the regime changes and the Wehrmacht as a whole swings to its support." The oath to Hitler meant no more to them than the oath to Ebert; the officers remained aloof from Party and Movement, acting "according to their own laws." The nonpolitical officers were condemned as reactionaries: "The apparent nonpolitical attitude of the 'Soldiers Only [*Nur-Soldaten*]' reveals itself *on closer examination to be rigid adherence to the world concept and ideas of the nineteenth century and the time before the outbreak of the First World War*." Their innate hostility to National Socialism lay in their perception that it sought to transform that world: *"For all these allegedly nonpolitical officers, National Socialism became as unpleasant as Communism at that moment when it required of them an ideological decision against an age which they preserved behind the walls of the Wehrmacht throughout the Republic"* (emphasis in the original).[79]

[77] Hagen, *Unternehmen Bernhard*, p. 96. For a biography of Freisler, see Gerd Buchheit, *Richter in roter Robe: Freisler, Präsident des Volksgerichtshofes* (Munich: Paul List Verlag, 1968).

[78] Kaltenbrunner to Bormann, 20 August 1944, Peter, *Spiegelbild*, pp. 271-276; "Der unpolitische Offizier—der 'Nur-Soldat,' " October 1944, appendix to circular of Kaltenbrunner, 24 October 1944, T-175/281/2774922-2774939, NA.

[79] "Nur-Soldat," ibid., 2774926, 2774927. See also 2774931, 2774932, 2774935, 2774936.

Kaltenbrunner warned that even those officers not involved in the plot placed loyalty to their caste above loyalty to the Führer and that their viewpoint continued to "corrupt" young officers rising through the ranks.

This report indicates a deep ideological commitment to National Socialism and its condemnation of the nineteenth century. For the RSHA chief, the Nazis were making an internal and external revolution both against nineteenth century individualism and against those bodies of society that resisted the ideological commitment required in the völkisch era. Years before, Hitler had told a follower that "he who interprets National Socialism merely as a political movement knows scarcely anything about it. It is even more than a religion, it is the will to create mankind anew."[80] The National Socialists proposed to sweep aside all traditional inequalities—birth, status, wealth, inheritance, class, education—and to impose in their place a single standard of inequality: that of race. Under the leadership of the Führer, all persons of "Germanic-Aryan" origin were to be equal to one another and equally superior to members of other races. Though in practice the traditional inequalities reappeared, or, better said, never disappeared, the aim was to eliminate them, by physical annihilation if necessary. In this radical right-wing revolt against the values of the century ushered in by the French Revolution of 1789, Kaltenbrunner found his ideological nest. In the Nazi world, there was no place for those who did not make the "ideological decision" required of each and every *Volksgenosse* (member of the race), or for those who doubted the authenticity of the Nazi racial myth. However much Kaltenbrunner may have respected the motives of some of the conspirators, he condemned their refusal to accept that they were an aristocracy by race rather than by class. However disgusted he might have been at Freisler's mode of dispensing justice, he still regarded the conspirators and the nineteenth-century world that they represented as near extinct yet still dangerous dinosaurs of an age gone by, whose influence had to be combatted and ultimately eliminated. In this sense, the retribution exacted by the Nazis after 20 July 1944 was no mere revenge for the assassination attempt, but indicative of ultimate intentions to make a complete, final, and radical break with the traditions and symbols of the nineteenth century.

Summarizing Kaltenbrunner's role in the Security Police, we might pose two questions. The first—what credence can be given to his story that he had no jurisdiction over or knowledge of Security Police, concentration camps, and killing centers, that he played no significant role in the executive apparatus of the SS and police system—has already been answered. Though Kaltenbrunner never wavered in his denial of responsibility, the evidence—both that which was presented at his trial and that which has come to light

[80] Hermann Rauschning, *Gespräche mit Hitler* (Vienna: Europa Verlag, 1973), p. 232.

since—goes overwhelmingly against him. Virtually all of his subordinates who were questioned testified that he was Heydrich's successor in name and in fact. Even those witnesses (Mildner and Höttl) who testified on Kaltenbrunner's behalf were forced to retreat on this issue under cross-examination by the prosecution.[81] Kaltenbrunner's name was inextricably linked both to Nazi tactical war policies such as the execution of Allied commandos and the murder of recaptured prisoners of war, and to long-term Nazi projects such as racial and resettlement policies, concentration camps, and genocide. Measures pertaining to Slavs and foreign labor within the Reich that were implemented under Kaltenbrunner's name reveal a profound contempt for and brutal callousness toward the peoples of Eastern Europe, offering a chilling preview of what these peoples could have expected from a victorious Nazi regime; the horrors of the deportations and the death camps speak for themselves. Faced with incriminating documents at Nuremberg, Kaltenbrunner blandly denied having signed or seen any of them.[82] He stubbornly maintained that others had signed his name and thus transferred the responsibility that was theirs onto his account. Yet his name appears so frequently on so many documents that in order to give his story any credence, we would be obliged to consider him an incompetent fool to have allowed his name to be used so often in connection with policies with which he allegedly disagreed. Kaltenbrunner may have been a fanatic, even a frustrated fanatic, but he was no fool; and there is no reliable evidence, written or verbal, to support his version of the events.

We can say that Kaltenbrunner rarely needed to exert his own direct influence in matters of Nazi ideological war policy. Here the role of the Security Police had been defined under Himmler and Heydrich; the destruction process had operated at maximum efficiency well before Heydrich's death. As the example of the Hungarian Jews indicates, however, Kaltenbrunner was prepared to break down potential local obstacles standing in the way of the Eichmann commando. Other policies, such as the measures concerning foreign laborers, were initiated during Kaltenbrunner's period; and there is no evidence that he ever protested against them or prevented their implementation. In short, Kaltenbrunner carried out the tasks assigned to him both as chief of the Security Police and of the SD.

The second question, why Kaltenbrunner involved himself in Nazi criminality, is more difficult to answer, for little evidence of his private opinions on such policies survives. We must, therefore, analyze both his actions and the commitment expected of him as an SS leader in order to construct an admittedly somewhat speculative answer as to his motivation.

[81] IMT XI, pp. 225-231, 253-260.
[82] See especially testimony of Kaltenbrunner, ibid., p. 346.

It has been concluded that Kaltenbrunner was nothing more than a crude killer without a conscience. Eugene Davidson has written that Kaltenbrunner's "first instinct was to kill," that he was "at bottom . . . a cold and ruthless killer who gladly did without any legal forms if the renunciation meant fewer Jews or Slavs." On the basis of a Rorschach test taken in the prison at Nuremberg, Florence Miale and Michael Selzer concluded that Kaltenbrunner was "a creature adapted to the bottom [of the ocean, i.e., primitive]. His perceptions are distorted by a suspiciousness that is quite paranoid. He is quite unable to experience or respond to feelings of gentleness or sensitivity. . . . In certain situations he recognizes but cannot feel emotions. . . . Such emotion as he has becomes distorted in the service of his manipulative opportunism." The prison psychiatrist left an equally unflattering description, characterizing Kaltenbrunner as "a great, hulking, tough-looking murderer who is at heart a shivering coward," as "a typical bully, tough and arrogant when in power, a cheap craven in defeat." Wendell Robert Houston's thesis that Kaltenbrunner (1) was corrupted by the possession of power; (2) was a "dominant-submissive personality" and thus compelled to obey Hitler's orders; and (3) lacked the moral courage to jeopardize his political and social position in the Third Reich by refusal to comply with the extermination policies of the regime, is more sophisticated analysis, but (in this author's opinion) places too little emphasis on Kaltenbrunner's active and positive commitment to carry out Nazi war policy. Kaltenbrunner is compared to Eichmann and is characterized by Hannah Arendt's controversial adjective: "banal."[83]

Since we cannot be certain of Kaltenbrunner's thoughts, we must try to gauge what his attitude might have been, given the nature of the SS-Police apparatus of which he was a part and his active role in that apparatus. This does not exclude the possibility that he had doubts or even moral qualms about the radical methods which the Nazis used to achieve their ends; indeed, occasional doubts probably existed.[84] Nevertheless, his willingness to accept a position in a vital part of the security apparatus with full knowledge of its tasks indicates the presence of what Hans Buchheim labels "ideological assent." Buchheim has argued that anyone entering the SS before the outbreak of the war "was committing himself publicly to the regime and placing

[83] Davidson, *Trial*, pp. 321, 327; Miale and Selzer, *Mind*, p. 125; Kelley, 22 *Cells*, pp. 133-134; Houston "Kaltenbrunner," pp. 152-155, 187-189. See also Arendt, *Eichmann*, pp. 287-288, for a rebuttal to those who interpreted her definition of "banal" to mean ordinary or commonplace.

[84] Even so notorious a mass murderer as Odilo Globocnik, who managed the extermination of the Polish Jews, was reported to have exclaimed to a friend while in a drunken stupor that "my heart's no longer in it, but I am so deeply involved in such things that I have no alternative but to ride to victory with Hitler or go under." See Höhne, *SS*, p. 440.

himself expressly at its service." The very foundation of membership in the SS was personal loyalty to Hitler and Himmler and willingness to carry out whatever they ordered. In joining the SS, let alone accepting a leading position in the security apparatus, Kaltenbrunner had to be aware that he would be expected to carry out the ideological orders of the regime regardless of their legality and that this obedience was intrinsic to the very meaning of his membership; after all, the SS motto was, "Loyalty is my honor." As Führer, Hitler gave orders that transcended both the law and the conception of the German state as it had existed before 1933; he expected his followers to obey, *not* on the basis of loyalty to that state, but solely on the basis of personal loyalty to himself as the personification of the will of the German Volk. In executing this will, SS leaders confirmed their positive commitment to the regime in whose service they had voluntarily and unconditionally placed themselves by joining its praetorian guard.[85]

What this commitment might entail was apparent as early as 30 June 1934. When Röhm and the SA hierarchy as well as several political foes of the regime were murdered by SS squads in a crass violation of the laws of the German state, it must have been clear to all those SS men who remained in or joined the SS thereafter that they, too, would be expected to carry out similar tasks if the Führer to whom they swore obedience thought them necessary or desirable. In a speech to the SS-Gruppenführer at Poznań on 4 October 1943, Himmler stressed the relationship of the Röhm purge to the mass murder of the Jews:[86]

> In all frankness I would also like to bring a very grave matter [i.e., the "evacuation" of the Jews] to your attention. Among ourselves, we can for once speak of it quite openly, yet we will never discuss this publicly. Just as we did not hesitate on 30 June 1934 to perform our duty as required and to stand our comrades who had gone astray against the wall and to shoot them, so we have never spoken about it and we will never speak about it. . . . We were all horrified, but each one of us understood completely that he would do it the next time if such orders were issued and if it were necessary.

Kaltenbrunner also described the nature of this ideological commitment to obey in spite of inner doubt. At Nuremberg, he told his interrogator that "the political soldier will, if he is of firm character, follow each order exactly, but will experience resistance in doing so. He will make his decisions based on subjective, indeed political thought."[87] For Kaltenbrunner, the

---

[85] Buchheim, "Command," pp. 313, 365. On ideological assent, see ibid., pp. 327, 358-359, 389, 390.

[86] Speech of Himmler to SS-Gruppenführer at Poznań, 4 October 1943, 1919-PS, IMT XXIX, p. 145.

[87] Interrogation of Kaltenbrunner, 12 September 1946, p. 8, ZS-673, IfZ Munich.

ideological soldier must be prepared to obey orders of a political nature on the basis of his political thinking, regardless of his moral or personal objections.

If ideological commitment in the Third Reich meant positive willingness to place oneself at the Führer's disposal for the execution of *any* orders he might issue, SS men were nevertheless not expected to be mere automatons. Hitler himself stressed that he wished to work with men who fused personal ambition and initiative with a basic ideological assent to the National Socialist idea. In other words, he wanted men who would do *more* than their duty; it was expected that the implementors of a Führer order would "recognize the intent of the order given and to act accordingly."[88] A chilling depiction of this mentality was presented to the International Military Tribunal at Nuremberg by Otto Ohlendorf, former chief of the SD-Inland in the RSHA and commander of the Einsatzgruppe D in southern Russia. When asked whether the illegality of orders to kill Jews and Soviet commissars was deliberately obscured in transmission to the Einsatzgruppe personnel in order to facilitate their ability to carry them out, Ohlendorf replied: "I do not understand the question; since the order was issued by superior authorities, the question of legality could not arise in the minds of these individuals, for they had sworn obedience to the people who had issued the orders." In a similar vein, Rudolf Höss, the commandant of Auschwitz, recalled that when Himmler gave him the order to implement the Final Solution, Höss "had nothing to say; I could only say *Jawohl!*"[89]

The SS-Police system developed in response to the need of the Nazi leadership to have at its disposal an apparatus through which ideological orders could be carried out regardless of legal or moral inhibitions. As early as 1935, Hitler had declared that "where the normal bureaucracy of the state should prove to be unfit to solve a problem, the German nation will charge its more vital organization with the assertion of its existential necessities." The fusion of a bureaucratic apparatus such as the German police with the "ideological fanaticism" and "charismatic legitimation of authority" that characterized the SS created what Frederic S. Burin has labeled an "ideological bureaucracy."[90] For the men who operated the apparatus, duty toward the state was replaced by loyalty to the National Socialist movement as the very essence of Germany's historic destiny. Thus, Kaltenbrunner's statement that he came to Berlin in 1943, "bound by nothing other than the law

---

[88] Arendt, *Totalitarianism*, p. 399.

[89] Testimony of Otto Ohlendorf, IMT iv, p. 354; Gilbert, *Nuremberg Diary*, p. 230.

[90] Frederic S. Burin, "Bureaucracy and National Socialism: Reconsideration of Weberian Theory," in Robert K. Merton et al., *Reader in Bureaucracy* (Glencoe, Illinois: The Free Press, 1952), p. 39. For Hitler quote, see Steiner, *Power Politics*, p. 142.

and the soldier's duty to obey,"[91] is inaccurate insofar as the law and the German *state* were concerned, for his oath as an SS man bound him only to Hitler's person—it was an oath to the Nazi regime, not the German state. That he remained in the SS and accepted a high position in the ideological executive indicates, not passive obedience of orders, but rather active commitment to the National Socialist ideology.

After the war, many Nazis justified their participation in crimes by pointing out the consequences of refusal to obey orders: arrest, concentration camp, or death. However, such consequences did not, in fact, threaten the SS leader. Hans Buchheim has listed three different responses available to any SS man who found an order incompatible with his moral standpoint or his honor: (1) a plea of incapability; (2) presentation of insuperable tactical obstacles to execution; and (3) silent evasion of the order. If Kaltenbrunner really felt that the policies of the Security Police were morally reprehensible, he could have told Himmler that he was simply incapable of doing the job, or have allowed Himmler to draw this conclusion by simply not doing the job; he would not thereby have risked life and limb. What he did risk was the possibility of making himself unacceptable to the social environment provided by membership in the elite formation of the National Socialist movement; that is, he risked the possibility, indeed the probability, that he would be considered to be of "weak character," unfit for membership in the SS.[92] He was clearly not willing to take this risk. By accepting the post of chief of Security Police and SD with relatively complete knowledge of its purpose and functions, and by remaining at that post long after he knew of and participated in *all* of its activities, Kaltenbrunner symbolized his ideological commitment to Adolf Hitler and the National Socialist movement.

Kaltenbrunner implemented the war policy of the Nazi regime because he was one of those in the movement who "accept . . . [the] political party program, [the] . . . formulation of ideologies and policies, and are able to identify emotionally with the underlying values and norms, and, finally, are intellectually, professionally, and technically in a position to administer and execute them in a relatively organized manner." He could justify the harshest brutality and intolerance toward others in the same way available to every SS leader: a belief that "such actions were in accordance with what members of the SS understood to be the eternal and immutable laws of the universe and nature which had their origin in God or Providence."[93] Those to be exterminated, sterilized, or sent to concentration camps were "enemies" of the Volk as defined in the Party dogma. The Reich, that mystical symbol of

[91] E. Kaltenbrunner, "Memoir," p. 1.
[92] Buchheim, "Command," pp. 373-382, 386-387.
[93] Steiner, *Power Politics*, p. 28, 113.

the German nation, was in danger; only the most ruthless measures would save it from going under. Like others, Kaltenbrunner was convinced that the execution of ideological measures required for the survival of the regime must transcend any and all traditional and legal restraints on application of force to annihilate enemies of the Nazi movement. In response to SS Main Office chief Gottlob Berger, who had brought to his attention complaints on the part of the German judicial authorities in Kaunas about arbitrary executions carried out by the Security Police in Lithuania, Kaltenbrunner wrote:[94]

> It is obvious that measures ordered by the police in the execution of their security responsibilities will overlap with [the responsibilities] of the judicial authorities as long as the judicial authorities consider themselves solely authorized to punish criminal acts committed by the indigenous population. Such overlapping can only be avoided if the justice authorities base their claims of jurisdiction on the actual political situation and not on doctrinare [i.e., legal or statutory] considerations, since the security tasks of the police do not permit the development of any basic alteration of the present application of police means of coercion.

For Kaltenbrunner, the "enemies" or "elements" against whom the Reich and its conquests had to be secured were much the same as they had been twenty years earlier in Graz: socialists, communists, Catholics, capitalists, plutocrats, Slavs, Germans who refused to acknowledge the validity of the Nazi movement and its precepts, and—last, but most dangerous—the Jews. The massacre of the Jews was specifically presented to the perpetrators as a moral act. In October 1943, Himmler told his Gruppenführer that "we had the moral right, we had the duty toward our race to kill this race which wanted to kill us."[95] Nazi folklore had so dehumanized the image of the Jew that directors and implementors of the Final Solution could convince themselves that they were not at all murderers, but rather soldiers in a desperate struggle against an insidiously evil and morally depraved enemy, or expeditors of a just death sentence on a race of inveterate criminals.[96] That Kaltenbrunner thought in such terms was revealed during an interrogation: though usually careful to say nothing about the Jews except that he did not know what was happening to them, Kaltenbrunner slipped and declared that the death of many Jews was not incomprehensible, since the "partisans" in Po-

[94] Excerpt of letter from Kaltenbrunner to Berger [SS-Hauptamt], in Berger to Hauptabteilungsleiter II (Justice), Reich Ministry for the Occupied Eastern Territories, 19 November 1943, NO-2719, NA.

[95] Speech of Himmler to SS-Gruppenführer at Poznań, 4 October 1943, 1919-PS, IMT XXIX, p. 146.

[96] Erich Goldhagen, "Weltanschauung und Endlösung: Zum Antisemitismus der nationalsozialistischen Führungsschicht," VfZ, 24 (October 1976), 400.

land, White Russia, and the Ukraine were largely organized by Jews.[97] Given his faith in Hitler, his conviction that the Jews were an implacable foe, his gnawing fear that Germany might lose the war, and the social and political pressure to take the harshest measures against all "enemies," Kaltenbrunner would have had to possess great moral courage to evade orders with respect to the Final Solution or, for that matter, any ideological orders emanating from the Nazi leadership. He would have had not only to relinquish his power and position, but also to sacrifice the unified totality of the Nazi myth, the comfortable mentality that lent simple, palatable meaning to a complicated, confusing world. He would have had to test the validity of the Nazi dream world against empirical data found in the real world,[98] to relinquish the conscience-saving faith that the "harsh measures" against "enemies" were part of an admittedly grisly, but necessary task. This he clearly could not and—more important—did not want to do.

Most of the SS and policemen who operated the extermination apparatus knew exactly what they were doing and yet did not have a criminal self-image. Mentally and emotionally, they separated obvious criminal actions from their idealistic mission to reform society or to protect it against enemies. As George Browder has written, "Many acutely felt and some even contritely confessed their criminal actions," but "their sanity required them to deny responsibility for their deeds and for the objectionable missions of the Sipo [Security Police] and the SD."[99] The executors of Nazi ideological war policy were not, then, unaware of its basic illegality and immorality. Without recognizing this basic consciousness of right and wrong, it would be difficult to explain why, while thousands of innocent people were being murdered every day, Kaltenbrunner could write to the state secretary in the Reich Ministry for Justice to plead for a fair and just sentence for a member of the Volk in the following words: "The pronouncement of justice in criminal cases is a blessing when it is considered by an independent judge and remains national [volkstümlich]." It would be equally difficult to fathom the sincerity of Kaltenbrunner's deputy in Minsk, Commander of Security Police and SD Eduard Strauch, who expressed righteous anger when he told a conference of German occupation authorities in White Russia:

> I can conclude with the assurance that we are doing all we can here to assist the *Gauleiter* and [to do] our duty for our nation and [our] Führer. It is true that we must carry out harsh and unpleasant tasks sometimes, but it offends me when some people believe that they can look down their noses at us. We do not understand that, gentlemen. We can carry out this occupation [i.e., security

---

[97] Interrogation of Kaltenbrunner, 19 September 1946, pp. 14-15, ZS-673, IfZ Munich.
[98] Arendt, *Totalitarianism*, p. 385.
[99] Browder, "Sipo and SD," p. 425.

police service] only because we are convinced that someone must carry out these tasks. I can say with pride that my men, regardless of how evil these tasks are, behave in a correct and decent manner, and can look anyone in the eye and [return] home to be fathers to their families. They are proud to have been active for their Führer out of conviction and loyalty.

Finally, it would also be difficult to understand how Kaltenbrunner could seriously be shocked by Freisler's antics in the courtroom, or to grasp the full significance of Rudolf Höss's final statement that the commandant of the Auschwitz extermination center "had a heart and . . . was not evil."[100]

It would be simplistic and perhaps inaccurate to write off such statements as mere hypocritical drivel, although the attempt to preserve a respectable image may play a role here. Nevertheless, it is not unreasonable to assume that Kaltenbrunner was at times uncertain as to the justice of exterminating Jews, enslaving Slavs, or plundering the economic and cultural resources of Europe. He may even have entertained the thought that, under normal circumstances, such operations were wrong and inhumane; but, like others, he could and did rationalize his involvement in such affairs with the presumption "that fulfillment of an historical (or political) necessity produced an exceptional situation calling for the suspension of all recognized and normally respected standards." In the words of Hans Buchheim, his consciousness of wrongdoing was "in partial suspense."[101] He successfully stifled any pangs of conscience that might have interfered with his commitment to the National Socialist creed. Closing his eyes to doubt, he fell into the psychologically less painful track of faith and obedience. In SS terminology, he remained "hard."

[100] Kaltenbrunner to Freisler, 16 June 1942, SS-Sammelliste, vol. 69, pp. 146-151, BDC; speech of Strauch, 10 April 1943, "Protokoll über die Tagung der Gebietskommissare, Hauptabteilungsleiter und Abteilungsleiter des Generalkommissars in Minsk vom 8. April bis 10. April 1943," 16 July 1943, R 93/20, pp. 137-146, BA; Rudolf Höss, *Kommandant in Auschwitz: Autobiographische Aufzeichnungen*, ed. Martin Broszat (Munich: Deutscher Taschenbuch Verlag, 1981), p. 156.
[101] Buchheim, "Command," p. 362.

CHAPTER VI

Struggle with the Rival Chieftains, 1943-1945

HIMMLER did not call Kaltenbrunner to Berlin solely to supervise the implementation of Nazi war policy. The Austrian SS leader was also expected to represent, defend and, if possible, further the interests of the RSHA vis-à-vis its rivals in the context of the internal struggle that characterized Nazi politics.

The nature and style of Hitler's rule encouraged bureaucratic infighting and personality politics. By proclaiming himself Führer and linking his own person to the abstract "destiny" of the German Volk, Hitler not only removed all institutional limitations on his authority, but also personalized the very source and justification for all legitimate authority in the Third Reich. The absence of clearly defined institutional channels of command also personalized the transmission of "legitimate" authority from the top to the lower echelons, for political power was no longer linked to institutions or agencies of the German state or German society, but rather to personal connections with the Führer and his entourage or to ideological affinity with their aims.

As a result of the noninstitutional, personalized command relationships, there developed in Nazi Germany "no carefully thought-out apparatus, ordered to the utmost detail, but rather a confusion of privileges and political contacts, competences and plenipotentiaries, which finally became a fight of all against all."[1] Such conditions produced two consequences: a considerable degree of adminstrative chaos and spectacular opportunities for career building.

To preserve or expand his interests in the struggle for power, each Nazi chieftain needed one or more able assistants, "directly loyal to him, who constantly guarded the domain from encroachment by others and expanded it when possible."[2] Although the RSHA could depend on Hitler's unequivocal support for the ideological tasks carried out by the Security Police, the position of the SD among the myriad of intelligence services in the Third

---

[1] Buchheim, *SS und Polizei*, pp. 16-17.

[2] Christopher R. Browning, "Unterstaatssekretaer Martin Luther and the Ribbentrop Foreign Office," *Journal of Contemporary History*, 12 (April 1977), 313.

Reich was by no means so clearly defined.[3] Himmler, who viewed control over intelligence collection and distribution as a source of power in the struggle with his rivals, needed an active, able, and trustworthy man to fight for the power and prestige of the SD. In Kaltenbrunner, he found a loyal collaborator, a skilled intriguer, and an enthusiast for spy games—in short, a man who would effectively defend SD interests. In this chapter, I will analyze three conflicts carried on by Kaltenbrunner on behalf of Himmler and the SD (with the Foreign Office, the Abwehr, and the Nazi Party Chancellery), with the intent of judging the success of Kaltenbrunner's career-building efforts through his participation in Nazi personal politics.

When he arrived at his new post in Berlin, Kaltenbrunner was greeted warmly by the personnel of RSHA Amt VI, the SD-Ausland; his passion for secret service work was well known and it was logical to assume that he would promote the interests of the SD-Ausland. The latter had evolved from the Abwehr (counterespionage) department of the SD Main Office, which was established after Himmler became chief of police in 1936. It had been an amateur affair, run directly by SD chief Reinhard Heydrich and managed by his deputy, SS-Oberführer Heinz Jost. Reporting was careless, sources unreliable, and incompetence endemic. Though aware of these deficiencies, Heydrich was much too occupied with the internal struggle for police power to devote much time to matters of foreign intelligence. The outbreak of the war, however, provided some impetus for reform in the SD Abwehr office, which on 27 September 1939 was incorporated into the RSHA as Amt VI, the SD-Ausland. Disgusted with Jost's lack of energy, Heydrich sacked him on 22 June 1941 and appointed as acting SD-Ausland chief a favorite protégé, SS-Sturmbannführer Walter Schellenberg. Born in 1910 in Saarbrücken and permitted to finish his legal studies by generous grants that the Nazi state offered him in exchange for his allegiance, Schellenberg was a young, ambitious police official, who had hitherto managed the counterespionage department of the Gestapo (RSHA Amt IV E) and had been instrumental in planning the formation of the RSHA.

Schellenberg improved the caliber of intelligence reporting significantly enough to install himself as Heydrich's and, after his death, Himmler's special adviser on foreign affairs. Ultimately, he hoped to unify political and

---

[3] Intelligence organizations outside the RSHA included: the Information Division of the German Foreign Office; the *Amt Auslands/Abwehr* attached to the High Command of the Armed Forces; the Investigation Office (*Forschungsamt*) of Reich Marshal Hermann Göring's Luftwaffe; the organizations Foreign Armies West (*Fremde Heere West*) and Foreign Armies East (*Fremde Heere Ost*), which were attached to the High Command of the Army (*Oberkommando des Heeres*—OKH); the intelligence service of the German navy; the Nazi *Auslandsorganisation*, tied to the Nazi Party Chancellery; and the intelligence department of the Ministry for Propaganda and Enlightenment. See David Kahn, *Hitler's Spies: German Military Intelligence in World War II* (New York: Macmillan, 1978), pp. 42-63.

military intelligence services in Germany in a superintelligence organ, romantically modeled on the British Secret Service. He also planned to detach the SD-Ausland from the RSHA and place it—and thus himself—directly under the command of the Reich leadership. Such plans were utopian, however, for the caliber of SD-Ausland work did not rise as quickly as this amateur spymaster had expected. In February 1943, Schellenberg still felt the need to berate his subordinates for a "lack of commitment," manifesting itself in chronic lateness, petty internal squabbles, and gullibility with respect to unscrupulous agents in the field.[4]

Despite an initial cordiality, Schellenberg soon found himself at odds with the new RSHA chief. In the first place, Kaltenbrunner's appointment was an obstacle to the realization of Schellenberg's own ambitions; and in the second, he was put off both by Kaltenbrunner's slavish devotion to the National Socialist ideology and by his drinking habits. Kaltenbrunner, on the other hand, was aware of Schellenberg's plans to detach the SD-Ausland from the RSHA. Moreover, he distrusted Schellenberg as a politically unreliable careerist and resented his close contact with Himmler. The upshot of this personal animosity was that Schellenberg maintained and exploited his direct contact with Himmler, while Kaltenbrunner mobilized a group of Austrians in RSHA Amt VI (SS-Sturmbannführer Wilhelm Waneck, chief of RSHA Amt VI E—Balkans; SS-Sturmbannführer Wilhelm Höttl, chief of the Italian and Hungarian desks in RSHA VI E; and SS-Sturmbannführer Otto Skorzeny, chief of the sabotage and special missions department of the SD-Ausland, RSHA VI S) to check Schellenberg's influence.[5]

Regardless of personal feelings and ambitions, however, Kaltenbrunner and Schellenberg agreed on policy for the SD-Ausland: to further its interests at the expense of other intelligence agencies, with the ultimate aim of creating a superintelligence agency under SD control. One Gestapo official recalled that though relations between Kaltenbrunner and Schellenberg were strained, the two men cooperated closely on this issue, for Kaltenbrunner "sponsored Amt VI and respected Schellenberg's wishes."[6]

From the beginning of his regime, Kaltenbrunner emphasized that the foreign intelligence service of the Reichsführer SS merited special concern. On 9 April 1943, one of his deputies issued a circular requiring all specialists

[4] "Protokoll über die Gruppenleiter- und Referentenbesprechung des Amt VI," 10 February 1943, File RSHA, R 58/1280, BA. On Schellenberg's ambitions, see Schellenberg, *Memoiren*, pp. 138-139, 140, 183.

[5] On animosity between Schellenberg and Kaltenbrunner, see Schellenberg, *Secret Service*, pp. 329-330; interrogation of Otto Ohlendorf, 20 November 1946, p. 36, ZS-278/II, IfZ Munich; interrogation of Kaltenbrunner, 19 September 1946, pp. 7, 9-10, ZS-673, ibid. On Austrian "group," see interrogation of Schellenberg, 4 December 1946, pp. 3, 6, ZS-291/II, ibid.; interrogation of Ohlendorf, 2 December 1946, p. 7, ibid.

[6] Affidavit of Kurt Lindow, 22 January 1948, NG-4509, NA.

to attach to their intelligence reports annexes, which explained how the reports were put together and outlined obstacles to accurate reporting presented by enemy tactics and obstruction by rival agencies. In this way, the "chief" could be given a "clear picture of the actual position of the political intelligence service [i.e., the SD] in the Reich."[7]

Results furnished by these reports and his own personal observations indicated to Kaltenbrunner that the SD-Ausland was too small and too lacking in trained personnel to compete with the Anglo-American and Soviet secret services. In his opinion, many SD agents gave away more information than they gleaned due to incompetence or treachery. Another key problem was the lack of adequate strongpoints abroad that could be operated under cover of the German diplomatic and military missions. For reasons of personal prestige, so Kaltenbrunner later claimed, the Foreign Office under Joachim Ribbentrop, and the Amt Ausland/Abwehr of Admiral Wilhelm Canaris sabotaged SD efforts to streamline the system of intelligence collection and distribution, and contributed to the general failure of the Reich in this field.[8]

The key issues causing tension between the SD and the Foreign Office were the RSHA's policy of installing its agents in the German missions abroad and Ribbentrop's concern that the SD would suggest foreign policy to the Nazi leadership without consulting him. At the outbreak of World War II, each contestant had sought Hitler's support for its interests; the result was a setback for the SD. Perhaps still basking in his euphoria over the Nazi-Soviet pact concluded just ten days earlier of which Ribbentrop had been the architect, Hitler issued a decree on 3 September 1939, proclaiming the Foreign Office superior to all Nazi Party organizations (which included the SD, despite its informal and ultimately decisive relationship to the Security Police) in the field of foreign policy. This decision brought Heydrich to the negotiating table, and, on 26 October 1939, a compromise was reached. Ribbentrop agreed not only to acknowledge the right of the SD to gather political intelligence abroad and to permit the assignment of SD representatives to the German legations, but also granted the SD the privilege of reporting directly and secretly to the RSHA. In addition, the RSHA would have a free hand in carrying out "illegal tasks," about which diplomatic niceties required the legation staffs to be ignorant. In return, the Foreign Minister insisted that all intelligence pertaining to German foreign policy and domestic political, social, and economic trends in the host countries had to be examined, evaluated, and approved in the *Abteilung II Deutsch-*

---

[7] Circular of Gruppenleiter D, Amt VI, RSHA, 9 April 1943, T-175/458/2975509-2975510, NA.

[8] Interrogation of Kaltenbrunner, 16 September 1946, pp. 22-23, ZS-673, IfZ Munich.

land (Department II Germany), which housed the Information Division of the Foreign Office.[9]

If Ribbentrop had hoped to limit the expansion and independence of the SD by means of this agreement, he was soon disillusioned. Based on the pact of 26 October 1939, Himmler and Heydrich installed "police attachés" at several German diplomatic posts in nations either neutral toward, or allied with, Germany. These police attachés, to whom SD agents in the field were responsible, began to operate as early as the fall of 1939, but Ribbentrop, who aimed at bringing them fully under the control of the legations, insisted on defining their functions in a formal agreement with Himmler. Under a new compromise, drawn up and signed on 8 August 1941, the official task of the police attaché was to report on the police system in the host country. He was further required to report to and take orders from the legation chief and was strictly forbidden to interfere in the internal politics of the host country.

Though the agreement appeared to confirm the Hitler order of 3 September 1939, Himmler and Heydrich inserted a gaping loophole into the system. Not only did the police attaché have the duty to report directly to them in matters of extreme importance, but also—as explained in the service regulations issued on 28 August 1941—his responsibility to the Reichsführer SS was "unaffected [*unbeschädigt*]" by his formal subordination to the German legation chief. Heydrich's determination not to yield on this point was clear in his note to SS-Obergruppenführer Karl Wolff, Himmler's liaison officer at Führer headquarters, written a few days before the Himmler-Ribbentrop agreement. If the foreign minister "stubbornly" refused to give the police attachés a free hand in gathering intelligence, Himmler must press Hitler to declare all territory under Reich influence to be an "internal sphere of interest." This would exclude the Foreign Office from any interference with SD intelligence reporting. To emphasize further the importance of the police attachés, Himmler ordered in August 1942 the establishment of a

---

[9] Decree of Hitler, 3 September 1939, T-175/199/2739650, NA; Browder, "Sipo and SD," pp. 337-340. A copy of the 26 October 1939 agreement has not been uncovered, but a memorandum by Rudolf Likus, an official of the *Abteilung II Deutschland*, refers to it in detail. See "Aufzeichnung über den Einsatz des SD in Ausland," 8 August 1940, published in Hildegard von Kotze, "Hitlers Sicherheitsdienst im Ausland," *Politische Meinung*, 8 (July-August 1963), 78-80. On *Abteilung II Deutschland*, see Browning, "Martin Luther," pp. 320-326; Paul Seabury, *The Wilhelmstrasse: A Study of German Diplomats under the Nazi Regime* (Berkeley–Los Angeles: University of California Press, 1954), pp. 107-108. That Himmler and Heydrich may have had Hitler's tacit support in wringing these concessions from Ribbentrop is implied in Heydrich's blunt statement to Ernst von Weizsäcker, the state secretary in the Foreign Office, that "it does not correspond to the concept of the Führer that this decree of 3 September 1939 should also apply to the SS and police." See Heydrich to Weizsäcker, 20 June 1941, T-175/199/2739639, NA.

Police-Attaché Group directly subordinate to the RSHA chief. The office would have the purpose of administrating and delivering SS orders to police attachés in Sofia, Copenhagen, Athens, Rome, Tokyo, Zagreb, Lisbon, Bucharest, Bratislava, and Madrid.[10]

Not all SD leaders were content merely to limit Ribbentrop's influence; some were prepared to topple him from power. Convinced by the summer of 1942 that a separate peace with the Western Allies was imperative for the survival of the Reich and that he possessed the diplomatic finesse to bring about such a settlement, Schellenberg began the slow process of persuading Himmler that the possibilities of negotiation should be explored. Since Ribbentrop was totally unacceptable to the Western Allies as a negotiating partner, the SD-Ausland chief explained, he had to be sacked as a prelude to any action. In December 1942, with Himmler's tacit and hesitant support, Schellenberg contacted the chief of Abteilung II Deutschland in the Foreign Office, Martin Luther, whose subordinates also hoped to remove Ribbentrop and initiate peace feelers to the Western Allies. Responding to Schellenberg's promise of SS support, Luther's men compiled a thick file on Ribbentrop's personal behavior (the tone of which questioned the foreign minister's sanity) and passed it on to Himmler. The Reichsführer SS, however, got cold feet and, encouraged by his liaison officer at Hitler's headquarters, Karl Wolff, turned the file over to Ribbentrop himself, who brought it to Hitler as proof of Luther's personal insubordination. Himmler remained silent, Schellenberg was frustrated, and Luther was confined in a concentration camp.[11] Not surprisingly, relations between Ribbentrop and the RSHA were less than cordial when Kaltenbrunner arrived in Berlin at the end of January 1943.

Kaltenbrunner later described Ribbentrop as "intolerant," "extremely ambitious," and "conceited." He remarked that he had sincerely tried to cooperate with the Foreign Office by sending SD reports directly to it, but that Ribbentrop had refused to pass on to Hitler any material that had not been compiled and analyzed by the legation chiefs or the Information Division of the Foreign Office.[12] Whether Kaltenbrunner actually tried to cooperate with Ribbentrop cannot be proven, but it is certain that the RSHA chief soon

---

[10] Heydrich to Wolff, 5 August 1941, T-175/281/2774548-2774550, NA; order of Himmler, 12 August 1942, T-120/706/330501-330502, NA; circular of the chief of the Security Police and the SD [signed Ploetz], 23 October 1942, File RSHA, R 58/240, BA. See also text of agreement signed by Himmler and Ribbentrop, 8 August 1941, T-175/123/2649331-2649333, NA; "Dienstanweisung für die einigen deutschen Botschaften und Gesandtschaften zugeteilten Polizei-Attachés," signed Himmler and Ribbentrop, 28 August 1941, File RSHA, R 58/243, pp. 286-288, BA; Schellenberg, *Memoiren*, pp. 208-209.

[11] Browning, "Martin Luther," pp. 338-339. For Schellenberg's typically self-serving version of the incident, see Schellenberg, *Secret Service*, pp. 298-299, 307, 308, 320-325.

[12] Interrogation of Kaltenbrunner, 21 September 1945, *NCA*, Supplement B, pp. 1295-1296.

joined his colleagues in the SD in their efforts to restrict or eliminate the influence of the man whom Hitler had once called a second Bismarck.

After Luther's fall, Ribbentrop cleaned house in the Foreign Office. He dissolved Abteilung II Deutschland and reorganized it as *Gruppe Inland II Geheim* (Group Internal Affairs II Secret) under SS-Standartenführer Horst Wagner, who had joined the Foreign Office on Ribbentrop's appointment in 1938. Department Inland II A, under SS-Sturmbannführer Eberhard von Thadden, supervised cooperation with the RSHA in the deportation of the Jews from Germany's allies and satellites. Inland II B, under an official named Geiger, served as a general liaison office to the RSHA, handling in particular questions concerning the police attachés. As Wagner explained after the war, the purpose of Inland II was twofold: (1) to receive requests and complaints of foreign authorities and to pass them on to internal authorities within the Reich; and (2) to pass on to foreign governments orders and information from agencies of the Ministry of the Interior, the police, the SD, and other agencies of the Reichsführer SS that handled questions of race.[13] As for the Information Division, Ribbentrop placed it directly under the new state secretary, Baron Gustav Steengracht von Moyland.

Despite the tension created by the Luther affair, officials of the Foreign Office and the RSHA attempted to maintain cordial relations and to work out suitable compromises. On 7 November 1943, Kaltenbrunner met with Wagner and Steengracht to discuss outstanding problems. Steengracht complained that SS and police leaders assigned to Germany's satellites (Slovakia, Croatia, Vichy France, and Salò Italy) simply ignored directives of the German mission chiefs. After some haggling, Kaltenbrunner conceded that henceforth HSSPFs and SS and police leaders (SSPFs) would receive instructions "in the political sector" from the German embassy or legation staff, but would continue to take orders "on police matters" from the Reichsführer SS. As such police matters were often "political" in nature, the RSHA chief was in fact making no real concession, but Steengracht, lacking the leverage to support the Foreign Office's interests, accepted this meager peace offering. The state secretary then brought up the sensitive question of the SD reports, insisting that they go to Hitler only after prior examination by Ribbentrop's staff. Kaltenbrunner accepted this as a general principle, but reserved the right to report directly to Hitler in "exceptional cases." As the definition of what constituted an "exceptional case" remained unclear, the Foreign Office again gained no tangible advantage. Kaltenbrunner then went over to the offensive, commenting on the incompetence of the Foreign Of-

---

[13] Interrogation of Wagner, 19 June 1947, ZS-1574, pp. 61-68, IfZ Munich; interrogation of Thadden, 5 December 1947, ZS-359/t, pp. 1-8, ibid.; organization chart of Gruppe Inland II Geheim, included in Wagner to Bohle [chief of the Nazi Auslandsorganisation], 5 July 1944, NG-3007, NA.

fice's Information Division and predicting that difficulties would result from the present tendency of the Foreign Office and the SD "to work at cross-purposes." Finally, he declared that he would be "especially thankful" if Ribbentrop would permit the assignment of SD men in the diplomatic posts in Bern, Budapest, Barcelona, and the Vatican.[14] Steengracht politely resisted this thrust; the meeting ended on cordial terms with nothing solved. Nevertheless, the two major issues dividing the Foreign Office and the SD were clearly spelled out: the relationship of SD personnel abroad to the German legations, and the question of the proper channels for intelligence reporting.

The "Cicero" affair serves as an illustration of the egotistical intensity with which Kaltenbrunner and Ribbentrop guarded their respective prerogatives over the transmission of foreign intelligence to Hitler's headquarters. "Cicero" was an Albanian national named Elyesa Bazna, who took advantage of his job as valet for the British ambassador to Turkey to photograph top secret embassy documents and sell them to the Germans. Established in late October 1943, the contact with Cicero was handled by SS-Obersturmbannführer L. C. Moyzisch, the police attaché at the German embassy in Ankara. In the spirit of the agreement of 8 August 1941, Moyzisch consulted the German ambassador to Turkey, Franz von Papen, showing him several samples of the Cicero material, which among other items, outlined British policy in Turkey, Allied plans for the military defeat and occupation of Germany, Allied intentions to try the top Nazi leaders as war criminals, and differences between the Western Allies and their Soviet partners. Ribbentrop, intent on keeping the material from Kaltenbrunner, ordered Moyzisch in early November 1943 to bring the documents to Berlin. Moyzisch, however (though he plays this down in his postwar account), kept Kaltenbrunner informed as well (as was his duty, since Kaltenbrunner was his superior); and, while Moyzisch's plane was refueling in Sofia, Kaltenbrunner's agents intercepted him and brought him directly to the RSHA in Berlin. After hearing Moyzisch's report, Kaltenbrunner declared that Ribbentrop, out of "sheer pigheadedness," would stick to the theory that Cicero was a British agent and that the documents had been deliberately steered into Moyzisch's hands. The experts in the RSHA, however, were convinced that the Cicero documents were genuine and did not want them "rotting" in Ribbentrop's desk. Henceforth, Moyzisch was not to receive funds from the Foreign Office; all instructions and funds for Cicero were to come from the RSHA (in fact, Cicero was paid in forged pound notes manufactured by the SD-Ausland using artists interned in the concentration camp Oranienburg). After leaving Kaltenbrunner's office, Moyzisch reported to Ribbentrop, who not only re-

[14] Memorandum of Steengracht, 7 November 1943, NG-5036, NA.

fused to pass the Cicero material on to Hitler until he was satisfied that it was genuine, but also forbade Moyzisch to forward any more reports to the RSHA. Moyzisch, however, quite logically continued to report to both Kaltenbrunner and Ribbentrop.[15] The irony of this senseless squabble lay in the fact that neither Kaltenbrunner nor Ribbentrop dared to forward the priceless material to Hitler and thus gain credit for the intelligence coup because each feared that Hitler's wrath, which might be aroused by the revelation that the Allies were so confident of victory, would be directed toward himself by the other.

Foreign Office officials tried in vain to assert what Ribbentrop felt to be his authority in matters of foreign policy and political intelligence. When relations between the Reich plenipotentiary in Denmark, SS-Obergruppenführer Werner Best (who reported to Ribbentrop) and the HSSPF in Copenhagen, SS-Obergruppenführer Günther Pancke, grew strained in September 1944 after Pancke had ordered independent police actions, Steengracht demanded that the SS leadership issue a written order establishing Pancke's formal subordination to Best. Kaltenbrunner retorted that this was fine with him as long as Best "did not assume any powers of command over the police executive organs." In January 1944, Kaltenbrunner installed SS-Hauptsturmführer Gustav Richter as police attaché at the German legation in Bucharest with specific orders to send all correspondence directly to the RSHA without informing the German minister to Romania, SA-Obergruppenführer Manfred von Killinger. One month later, as the SD prepared to devour the military intelligence service of the *Oberkommando der Wehrmacht* (OKW), the Abwehr, Ribbentrop insisted that he be consulted on all issues pertaining to the reorganization of the Abwehr and that all reports concerning military intelligence be submitted to him for examination. To this Himmler was prepared to agree; but he gave the SD an escape clause to the effect that under "special conditions" reports would go directly from the RSHA *Amt Mil* (Military Department established in June 1944) to Hitler's headquarters. Finally, when Kaltenbrunner traveled to Hungary in March 1944 to negotiate with Hungarian leaders concerning the deportation of the Hungarian Jews, Ribbentrop ordered his representative in Budapest, Reich Plenipotentiary and SS-Brigadeführer Edmund Veesenmayer, to spy on the RSHA chief, discover his mission, and prevent his SD from "meddling with the tasks and powers assigned to you [Veesenmayer]." The foreign minister

---

[15] The details of the Cicero adventure can be pieced together from the accounts of the most immediate participants. See Elyesa Bazna, *I Was Cicero* (London: André Deutsch, 1962); L. C. Moyzisch, *Operation Cicero* (New York: Coward-McCann, 1950); Papen, *Memoirs*, pp. 509-519; Schellenberg, *Secret Service*, pp. 331-339. On Moyzisch, Kaltenbrunner, and Ribbentrop, see Moyzisch, *Cicero*, pp. 84, 94-97; Seabury, *Wilhelmstrasse*, pp. 130-131. On Moyzisch reporting, see Ribbentrop to Papen, 17 June 1944, NG-4852, NA.

was especially concerned that Veesenmayer alone handle arrangements for the "settlement" of the Jewish question.[16]

Like Schellenberg, Kaltenbrunner was not averse to toppling Ribbentrop should the opportunity arise. The diaries and diplomatic papers of Count Galeazzo Ciano, Mussolini's son-in-law and the Italian foreign minister from 1936 to 1943, appeared to offer just such an opportunity. After the overthrow of Mussolini in July 1943, Ciano requested and was granted asylum in Germany. After Italy's surrender to the Allies on 8 September 1943 and the establishment of Mussolini's neo-Fascist regime at Salò, however, Ciano, whose role in the overthrow of Mussolini during the Fascist Grand Council meeting of 25 July 1943 was clear to the new rulers in Salò, grew uneasy and expressed a desire to emigrate to Spain. When Hitler refused to allow Ciano to leave German-controlled territory, Ciano contacted SS-Sturmbannführer Wilhelm Höttl, chief of the Italian desk in the SD-Ausland, and offered to leave his private diaries with the SD if he and his family were deposited safely in Spain. During the course of these conversations, Ciano hinted broadly that if the contents of the diaries were revealed, Ribbentrop would be so compromised as to make his continued service impossible. Höttl reported the offer to Kaltenbrunner, whom he knew to have "scarcely a greater personal-political wish than to see Ribbentrop ousted from his post." Interested, Kaltenbrunner ordered Höttl to make arrangements for the Cianos' journey. At this point, however, Edda Mussolini Ciano, against the advice of her husband and Höttl, insisted on obtaining Hitler's blessing for the journey. When he learned what was afoot, the Führer ordered Himmler and Kaltenbrunner to cancel the Cianos' travel plans. Ribbentrop, who guessed that Ciano's diaries might compromise him, and Goebbels, who despised Ciano as a traitor to Mussolini, were instrumental in persuading the dictator to prevent Ciano's flight.

The affair was not yet over, however. On October 1943, Mussolini requested Ciano's return to Italy. When the count arrived in Verona on 19 October, he was promptly arrested and placed under the jurisdiction of a special court created to investigate and try the "traitors" of 25 July; by Christmas, it was clear that he would be convicted and executed. On 28 December 1943, a friend of Ciano's contacted SS-Brigadeführer Wilhelm Harster, the commander of the Security Police and the SD in Verona, and explained to him that if Ciano were executed, Edda would send the diaries to the United States for publication. If the SS would rescue Ciano, however, the diaries

---

[16] On Denmark, see memorandum of Steengracht, 4 September 1944, NG-4756, NA. On Killinger, see decree of Kaltenbrunner, 7 January 1944, NO-966, NA. On the Abwehr, see Ribbentrop to Himmler, 27 March 1944, NG-3509, NA; unsigned, undated memorandum of an agreement between Himmler and the Foreign Office [possibly June 1944], NG-4852, NA. On Veesenmayer, see Ritter to Veesenmayer, 31 March 1944, NG-5564, NA.

would be placed at Himmler's disposal. Harster reported to Kaltenbrunner, who in turn secured Himmler's support for "Operation Conte," a plan to kidnap Ciano and transport him to Switzerland. Hitler would be informed after the fact; it was hoped that the diaries would sweeten the bitter pill of disobedience.

On 2 January 1944, Kaltenbrunner, Harster, and Höttl met with Ciano's contact and made final arrangements for "Conte." Ciano was to reveal the hiding place of his diplomatic papers in Rome so that the SD could secure them. Then SD agents would kidnap Ciano from his cell in Verona and transport him and his family to Switzerland. Once safe on Swiss soil, Ciano would turn his diaries over to the SD. On 5 January, Harster received Ciano's diplomatic papers. The "springing" of Ciano was scheduled for 7 January, the day before his trial, but at the last moment Himmler and Kaltenbrunner lost their nerve and sought Hitler's approval for "Conte." The dictator flew into a rage at this contemplated disobedience and threatened the severest punishment if "Conte" were attempted. On 8 January, Edda Ciano fled to Switzerland, carrying Ciano's war-years diaries; three days later, the count was executed in Verona.[17] Willing enough to intrigue against Ribbentrop but unable or unwilling to disturb the bond of loyalty that tied him to Hitler, Kaltenbrunner had no intention of disobeying a direct Führer order. He shelved his plans to remove Ribbentrop.

Bickering between the RSHA and the Foreign Office continued virtually unabated until the last months of the war; the approach of military disaster seemed only to abet the struggle for power. In August 1944, Himmler ordered Kaltenbrunner to organize underground communications networks in those areas soon to be occupied by Soviet troops. These were to be manned by pro-Nazi elements, who would carry out partisan operations behind the Soviet lines. In accordance with these plans, the police attaché at the German legation in Finland, SS-Sturmbannführer Alarich Bross, had established two underground radio centers just before the Finns broke off relations with the Germans on 12 September 1944. Kaltenbrunner hoped to install Bross at the German legation in Stockholm, from where the Finnish "partisan movement" could be organized and directed, but Ribbentrop made

[17] This account is taken from Hagen, *Geheime Front* pp. 433-448; and Howard McGaw Smyth, *Secrets of the Fascist Era: How Uncle Sam Obtained Some of the Top-Level Documents of Mussolini's Period* (Carbondale-Edwardsville: Southern Illinois University Press, 1975), pp. 25-40. On Kaltenbrunner's "personal-political wish," see Hagen, *Geheime Front*, p. 445. On Goebbels's feelings about Ciano, see *The Goebbels Diaries, 1942-1943*, ed. Louis P. Lochner (New York: Doubleday, 1948), pp. 479-480. On Edda Ciano's wish to confer with Hitler, see Schnitzler [Personal Staff, Reichsführer SS, Adjutancy Munich] to Kaltenbrunner, 20 September 1943, T-580/72/Ordner 338, NA.

clear his wish that his own legation secretary, a reputed expert on Finland named Metzger, handle the operation.

In the meantime, Bross had made contact with what he believed to be a sharply anti-Soviet, fascist-oriented Finnish organization, known as the League of Veterans of the Front and led by a man named Janssen. SD agents offered to send Janssen radio equipment and weapons via U-boat; they planned at the same time to pick up several escaped German prisoners of war who had found shelter with Janssen.

In late November 1944, however, Metzger intervened independently on behalf of the escaped prisoners of war, of whom he had learned from an SD courier. Without informing Bross or Kaltenbrunner, the legation secretary sent an agent to Finland with food provisions for the prisoners of war. Janssen, who took Metzger's agent for an agent of the SD, was dismayed to receive neither radio equipment nor weapons. Nevertheless, he informed Metzger's man that his group was not connected to any Finnish underground movement and that he was cooperating with the SD on his own initiative.

Puzzled by the failure of the "SD agent" to bring the promised radio equipment and weapons, Janssen radioed Bross to ask what had happened. Bross in turn carped to Kaltenbrunner that Metzger was trying to muscle in on his operation. Enraged, Kaltenbrunner sent a sharply worded letter to Steengracht, accusing the Foreign Office of endangering the entire intelligence network in Finland. Metzger's acts, Kaltenbrunner blustered, constituted a "clear infringement of the principle of the 'unified German secret service' ordered by the Führer." Metzger drafted a defense of his actions, but Foreign Office officials thought it too polemical to send. Steengracht's reply to Kaltenbrunner was most diplomatic: the state secretary expressed his regret for the misunderstanding and offered to introduce Metzger—"whose expert knowledge of Finland might interest you"—to the RSHA chief.[18] This squabble over contacts with a completely insignificant underground organization was typical not only of the extent to which the tasks of various agencies in the Third Reich overlapped, but also of the intense jealousy with which fields of competence were guarded.

Even as the last year of the Nazi Reich dawned, as Soviet troops poured into East Prussia, Pomerania, and Silesia, and Allied units approached the Rhine, the RSHA and the Foreign Office continued to bicker. In mid-January 1945, the German minister to the puppet government of Msgr. Jozef Tiso in Slovakia, SA-Obergruppenführer Hans Ludin, reported that his po-

---

[18] Kaltenbrunner to Steengracht, 8 December 1944, T-120/354/267150-267153, NA; memorandum of Metzger, 14 December 1944, ibid., 267154-267157; memorandum to Steengracht, 20 December 1944, ibid., 267165; Steengracht to Kaltenbrunner, 24 December 1944, ibid., 267167-267169.

lice attaché and the commander of the Security Police and the SD in Bratislava were quarreling over the responsibility for reorganizing the Slovak police, and requested Foreign Office support for the attaché, with whom Ludin "stood well." Kaltenbrunner, however, sent the chief of the police attaché office in the RSHA, SS-Standartenführer Karl Zindel, to Bratislava, where Zindel bluntly told Ludin that, though the wishes of the police attaché would be respected, the commander of the Security Police was "responsible [*federführend*]" in the question of Slovak police reorganization.[19]

The wartime rivalry between the SD and the Foreign Office was not generated by differences in ideological outlook or policy, but rather by considerations of personal power and prestige. Neither Kaltenbrunner nor Ribbentrop questioned the legitimacy of Hitler's power or policies; neither wished to disobey the Führer, even when minor disobedience (i.e., on nonideological matters such as the Ciano affair) offered the opportunity of removing his rival. The rivalry boiled down to a struggle for personal power in which the RSHA proved stronger by installing its agents at the German diplomatic posts and maintaining direct and secret lines of communication with them. This success was inevitable, for as Nazi policy grew more radical and as more and more nations were drawn into the war against Germany, the execution of foreign policy by diplomatic methods (which had never appealed to Hitler) became progressively more illusory. It is logical to assume that Ribbentrop dimly realized this; hence his efforts to delineate the boundaries of his competence by means of a specific agreement with Himmler and the RSHA. His own experience of intriguing against the Foreign Office in the 1930s should have reminded him that formal agreements in the Third Reich were meaningless if one of the parties could repeatedly refer to "special conditions" or direct contacts with a Führer whose "will" invalidated any agreement, including those made by himself. After the war, Ribbentrop glumly admitted that agreements reached between Kaltenbrunner and himself "no longer had any effect [*wirkte sich nicht mehr aus*]"; and added that Hitler's "method of working" generally invalidated formal agreements on competence.[20] The final irony, however, is that, save for the personal gratification of neutralizing an opponent, Kaltenbrunner's victory over Ribbentrop was Pyrrhic; Hitler rarely read, let alone acted on, intelligence reports, especially when they brought grim tidings. The SD reports that Kaltenbrunner so successfully protected from the scrutiny of the Foreign Office were most often laid to rest in the file drawers of Himmler or Martin Bormann.

---

[19] Ludin to the Foreign Office, 13 January 1945 and report of Legationsrat Bobrik, 22 January 1945, NG-3487, NA.

[20] Joachim von Ribbentrop, *Zwischen London und Moskau: Erinnerungen und letzte Aufzeichnungen*, ed. Annelies von Ribbentrop (Leoni am Starnberger See: Druffel Verlag, 1954), pp. 130-131.

Another rival in matters of foreign intelligence was the military intelligence apparatus of the High Command of the Armed Forces (OKW), the *Amt Ausland/Abwehr*, or merely the Abwehr, as it was commonly known.[21] Chief of the Abwehr since 2 January 1935 was Admiral Wilhelm Canaris. Born in 1887 near Dortmund, Canaris had been a naval officer during World War I and a veteran of radical right-wing politics in the early 1920s. Though he remained a political conservative, locked into the social and political outlook of the Wilhelmine officer class, he sympathized with the Nazi aims of restoring Germany's greatness and "purifying" German national life. Canaris was also fascinated by certain personalities of the Nazi regime—Himmler and Heydrich in particular. With these political rivals he was both careful and eager to remain on good terms. As a result of these factors and a chronic fatalistic pessimism, Canaris was never able to follow the example of several of his colleagues and subordinates who committed themselves to genuine opposition against the Nazi regime.[22]

Counterespionage and foreign intelligence were the key issues on which the Abwehr-SD struggles turned. During the Weimar Republic, both of these areas had been the sole prerogative of the military intelligence apparatus. In the first years of the Nazi regime, the Gestapo began to encroach on the counterespionage functions of the Abwehr, while the SD aimed to break the military's monopoly on foreign intelligence collection. In an effort to quell the growing tension, Canaris and Heydrich delineated the rival spheres of competence by means of formal agreements. The agreement of 17 January 1935, concluded two weeks after Canaris took office, reserved for the Abwehr the sole responsibility for the collection of military and political intelligence abroad, and for counterespionage within the Reich as it pertained to the Reichswehr and to industries producing for military consumption. The Gestapo was responsible for all executive matters of arrest and

---

[21] As of 1941, the Abwehr consisted of five departments. First was the *Amtsgruppe Ausland* under Kapitän zur See Leopold Bürkner; it served as a liaison office between the OKW and the Foreign Office and supervised military, naval and air attachés assigned to German diplomatic posts. *Abwehr Abteilung* Z, under Major General Hans Oster, handled personnel and administrative matters. Abwehr I, under Lieutenant Colonel Hans Piekenbrock, was responsible for the collection of military and political intelligence abroad; Abwehr II, led by Lieutenant Colonel Erwin Lahousen, handled sabotage operations abroad; and Abwehr, III, under Lieutenant Colonel Egbert von Bentivegni, carried on counterespionage within the Reich. See Buchheit, *Geheimdienst*, pp. 106-112.

[22] On Canaris, see the laudatory biographies: Buchheit (former Abwehr member), *Geheimdienst*; Abshagen (former Abwehr member), *Canaris*; Roger Manvell and Heinrich Fraenkel, *The Canaris Conspiracy* (New York: Pinnacle, 1972); Paul Leverkuehn (former Abwehr member), *German Military Intelligence* (London: Weidenfeld & Nicolson, 1954); Ian Colvin, *Chief of Intelligence* (London: Gollancz, 1951); André Brissaud, *Canaris* (New York: Grosset & Dunlap, 1973). See also the critical biography by Heinz Höhne, *Canaris: Patriot im Zwielicht* (Munich: Wilhelm Goldmann Verlag, 1978).

interrogation of persons suspected of espionage within the Reich. Finally, the SD, as yet excluded from the field of foreign intelligence, was responsible for political intelligence of a general nature inside Germany. The agreement of 21 December 1936, known as the "Ten Commandments" owing to its ten points, addressed the still disputed field of counterespionage. To the Abwehr fell the responsibility for reconnaissance of *military* espionage carried out by the enemy, while the Gestapo had the authority to investigate and prosecute all cases of espionage and treason. Both sides were pledged to assist one another in every way.[23] Such agreements scarcely papered over the actual and bitter struggle for power; their vague formulation encouraged further encroachment by the Gestapo and the SD on Abwehr areas of responsibility.

As the importance of counterespionage and foreign intelligence increased with the outbreak of World War II, the conflict between Abwehr and Gestapo-SD (incorporated into the RSHA in 1939) grew more acrimonious. Gestapo officials refused to cooperate with the Abwehr on counterespionage and treason cases, while the SD, whose police attachés were installed at the German diplomatic posts during the winter of 1939-40, openly disregarded the provisions of the January 1935 agreement that had called for an Abwehr monopoly on the collection and evaluation of foreign intelligence. As the war progressed, Heydrich and his department chiefs, Müller and Schellenberg, began to bear down hard on the Canaris organization. Compounding the ever present jurisdictional and personal rivalries was the conviction of Heydrich and his assistants that: (1) in 1940, someone in the Abwehr organization had betrayed to the endangered nations the dates of the German invasions of Northern and Western Europe; (2) Canaris himself had provided the British navy with documentation on German U-boat construction between 1922 and 1935; and (3) with Canaris's tacit approval, Abwehr agents had sought in the winter of 1939-40, with the mediation of the Vatican, to contact the governments of the Western Allies and to sound out their attitude toward a possible peace offer from a post-Hitler German government.[24]

---

[23] On 17 January 1935 agreement, see circular of Jost to all State and Political Police Offices in the Länder [containing excerpts from the agreement], 2 April 1936, T-175/403/2926114-2926116, NA; Walter Huppenkothen [chief of RSHA IV E (counterespionage) from 1941 to 1945], "Canaris und Abwehr," p. 7, Aktenmappe Sonderakt Canaris, BDC; Höhne, *Canaris*, p. 177. On the "Ten Commandments," see "Grundsätze für die Zusammenarbeit zwischen der Geheimen Staatspolizei und den Abwehrstellen der Wehrmacht vom 21.12.36," published in Buchheit, *Geheimdienst*, pp. 455-457. See also Höhne, *Canaris*, p. 203.

[24] Major General Hans Oster, the chief of the Abwehr Abteilung Z and an unequivocal enemy of the Nazi regime, had indeed warned the governments of Denmark, Norway, Holland, Belgium, France, and England of impending German attacks in Northern and Western Europe. Attempts to sound out the British on possible negotiations with a post-Hitler Germany were carried on with the aid of the Vatican by the Munich lawyer Josef Müller, who was on

By early 1942, RSHA pressure had brought Canaris to the negotiating table, and on 1 March a new agreement was reached. This pact confirmed Gestapo responsibility for investigations and arrests in cases of espionage and treason and excluded the Abwehr from participation in cases involving enemy *political* espionage within the Reich. The RSHA also extended its authority to cover counterespionage operations in all German-occupied territories, including those directly behind the front, where the Gestapo and the SD claimed the right to "instruct" military commanders on the "political situation" in their respective zones of occupation. In addition, collection of political intelligence abroad, previously the sole prerogative of the Abwehr, was transferred to the competence of the SD-Ausland; thus, all political intelligence reporting was henceforth "exclusively the task of the Security Police and the SD." In short, the pact stripped the Abwehr of jurisdiction over reporting on political developments within and outside the Reich, drastically reducing its basis for internal political power. Drawn up at Wannsee, the agreement was signed and announced at a conference for Gestapo, Kripo, SD, and Abwehr personnel at the Hradčany Palace in Prague.[25]

Though Heydrich's death—just three weeks after the Hradčany conference—eliminated a most determined enemy of the Abwehr, it did not afford Canaris much relief. Despite the RSHA's relentless pressure on the Abwehr, Heydrich and Canaris had maintained a certain level of mutual respect and even admiration. Perhaps it was based on a common link to the German navy (Heydrich had been a naval officer in the late 1920s and had known Canaris at that time) or the once close relationship between the violin player Heydrich and the music lover Erika Canaris (Canaris's wife). Indeed, the passing of the RSHA chief was no blessing for the Abwehr, for in their determination to devour the Canaris organization, Schellenberg and Müller were unencumbered by such personal sentiment. In the months following his chief's death, Schellenberg urged his subordinates in the SD-Ausland to "continually increase our influence in the ministries and to try to outstrip the predominant position of the Abwehr." Though Himmler, for unknown reasons, continued to protect Canaris by suppressing the information in Schellenberg's thickening file on the Abwehr, it became apparent that a

---

the staff of the Abwehr office in Munich. These efforts yielded no result. Though Müller's activity enjoyed Canaris's passive support, Oster's actions were known to, but deplored by, the Abwehr chief. Canaris's alleged betrayal of German U-boat information to the British navy appears to have been a figment of Schellenberg's (and perhaps also Heydrich's) imagination. On the activities of Müller and Oster, see Höhne, *Canaris*, pp. 371-403. See also Schellenberg, *Memoiren*, pp. 327-330.

[25] Agreement signed by Heydrich and Canaris, "Aufgabengebiete des SD, der militärischen Abwehr und der G[eheimen] F[eld-] P[olizei]," 1 March 1942, NOKW-3228, NA. See also Höhne, *Canaris*, p. 449. On the Hradčany conference, see Schellenberg, *Memoiren*, p. 255; Buchheit, *Geheimdienst*, pp. 189-190; Huppenkothen, "Canaris und Abwehr," p. 9.

serious mistake on Canaris's part might result in the collapse of his organization.[26]

Kaltenbrunner's arrival in Berlin in January 1943 gave new impetus to the RSHA's campaign against the Abwehr. Like Heydrich and Schellenberg, Kaltenbrunner suspected Canaris of committing, or at least tolerating, treason in the Abwehr; he was also convinced that, owing to Canaris's failings as a leader, the Abwehr organization was riddled with incompetence and corruption, a not unwarranted charge.[27] Moreover, unlike Heydrich or Schellenberg, the new RSHA chief was driven by an intense personal contempt and loathing for both the Abwehr and Canaris himself. This passion supplemented his burning ambition to command a unified secret intelligence service. During an interrogation at Nuremberg, Kaltenbrunner expressed this extreme hatred and disgust:[28]

> The [Abwehr personnel] were personally corrupt, as venal as possible, money-hungry; they were sordid [schmutzig]: indeed, more than 80% of the Canaris people were sexually perverse. These are things which an intelligence service can never endure. From such soil treason would and did blossom. . . . He [Canaris] only utilized such persons who received from him enormous sums of money and were so arranged by him that a masochist, a sadist, and an active and passive homosexual were always together.

Kaltenbrunner did not hesitate to reveal his hostility to Canaris. When he met the Abwehr chief for the first time at the Hotel "Regina" in Munich on 22 February 1943, he rebuffed Canaris's friendly greetings and launched into a tirade against the chief of the Abwehr office in Vienna, Colonel Rudolf Graf von Marogna-Redwitz, accusing him of sympathizing with the conservative opposition to Hitler in Austria and of maintaining unnecessarily close contact with the "Anglophile" Hungarian secret service. Canaris's reaction to the scar-faced Austrian was hardly less negative. After the meeting, he reportedly exclaimed, "Have you seen the hands of that fellow? Murderer's paws!"[29]

[26] On relationship of Heydrich and Erika Canaris, see Höhne, *Canaris*, p. 450. On Schellenberg urging subordinates, see "Protokoll über die Gruppenleiter- und Referentenbesprechung des Amt VI," 19 September 1942, File RSHA, R 58/1280, BA. Höhne has speculated that Himmler, in addition to his conviction that the SD apparatus was not sufficiently experienced to take over the tasks of the Abwehr, was realistic enough to understand that if the war were to go badly, Canaris might be a useful ally with whom one could pursue peace negotiations with the Western Allies. See Höhne, *Canaris*, p. 486. In the German edition of his memoirs, Schellenberg speculated that Canaris knew of his efforts to persuade Himmler to seek a political solution to the war, and that Himmler feared that Canaris might talk if arrested. See Schellenberg, *Memoiren*, p. 332.

[27] For examples, see Höhne, *Canaris*, pp. 467-471.

[28] Interrogation of Kaltenbrunner, 16 September 1946, pp. 24, 25, ZS-673, IfZ Munich.

[29] Abshagen, *Canaris*, p. 356.

It was Kaltenbrunner's good fortune that, just as he was getting adjusted to the atmosphere in Berlin, the Abwehr was shaken to its foundations by a scandal from which it never recovered. At the end of August 1942, Major Wilhelm Schmidhuber, a Bavarian businessman attached to the Abwehr office in Munich, was arrested by German customs officials for a currency violation. After seeking and being denied Canaris's protection, Schmidhuber hinted to his interrogators that he had knowledge of the Abwehr efforts to contact the British through the Vatican in the winter of 1939-40. Schmidhuber's interrogators called in the Gestapo; SS-Untersturmführer Franz Xaver Sonderegger was assigned to investigate the case. By February 1943, Schmidhuber's testimony had led Sonderegger to Hans von Dohnanyi, a legal expert in the Abwehr Abteilung Z and the right-hand man of its chief, Major General Hans Oster, who was the heart and soul of the anti-Hitler group in the Abwehr. It had been through Dohnanyi that Josef Müller had been recruited for his attempt to contact the British with the mediation of the Vatican. Sonderegger's report concluded with the suspicion that Canaris himself was behind the entire operation.

To the surprise and frustration of Kaltenbrunner, Müller, Schellenberg, and Sonderegger, Himmler refused to take the material to Hitler and instead passed it on to the military justice authorities. On 5 April 1943, Dohnanyi was arrested and Oster was relieved of his command. As spring wore on, it appeared that the Schmidhuber thread might unravel the entire organization of the Abwehr. Only in July 1943, thanks less to the fatalistic Canaris than to some of his more energetic subordinates, could OKW chief Wilhelm Keitel be persuaded to order the overzealous investigating judge, Manfred Roeder, to quietly cancel further proceedings in the affair.[30]

The Abwehr was only temporarily saved, however, for Canaris's own suspicious role in the wake of the Italian surrender to the Allies in September 1943 gave the RSHA a chance to knock another pillar out of its fragile foundation. Five days after Mussolini's fall and arrest, the Abwehr chief had a private talk in Venice with the chief of Italian military intelligence, General Cesare Amé. Amé revealed to Canaris the intentions of Mussolini's successor, Field Marshal Pietro Badoglio, to arrange a separate peace with the Allies. Hoping that Badoglio's example might inspire a military *fronde* against Hitler, Canaris sought to prevent the German leadership from taking adequate precautions against Badoglio by assuring the OKW that Italy had no intentions to desert the Axis. Schellenberg, however, who had begun to receive alarming reports from his own agents in Italy, submitted to Himmler with Kaltenbrunner's support a report depicting Canaris's treachery. Much

[30] Höhne, *Canaris*, pp. 474-504, contains the most informative account of the Schmidhuber affair and its consequences. See also Buchheit, *Geheimdienst*, pp. 418-420; Abshagen, *Canaris*, pp. 356-359; Manvell and Fraenkel, *Conspiracy*, pp. 170-192; Brissaud, *Canaris*, pp. 299-300.

to the dismay of the two intriguers, Himmler permitted Canaris to persuade him that favorable reports had been deliberately forwarded to OKW chief Keitel because Keitel did not relish handing unpleasant news on to Hitler. Again, Himmler refused to move against Canaris.

Kaltenbrunner and Schellenberg did not have to wait much longer, however, for, in the first weeks of 1944, a series of incidents enabled them to close in for the kill. On 12 January, Gestapo officials, after three months of patient observation, arrested the entire membership of a resistance group around Hannah Solf, the widow of a former German diplomat; Major Otto Kiep, an officer of the Abwehr Amtsgruppe Ausland, was among those arrested. Ten days later, the successful Allied landing at Anzio caught the German commanders in Italy by surprise because they had put their faith in erroneous Abwehr reports that an Allied landing on the Italian coast behind the German front was highly unlikely. On 27 January, an Abwehr agent in Istanbul, Kurt Vermehren, and his wife deserted to the British, who in turn milked the affair for all possible publicity. On 7 February 1944, Kaltenbrunner added to the Führer's rage over the incident by reporting that Vermehren had been working for the British Secret Intelligence Service. On 11 February, just three days after Hitler had forbidden the Abwehr to carry out any acts of sabotage on Spanish soil or in Spanish waters as a result of Ribbentrop's complaints that Abwehr activities in Spain had harmed German foreign policy to the advantage of the Allies, the Führer—with the Vermehren scandal fresh in his mind—received a report that Abwehr agents had planted a bomb on a British ship carrying oranges from Spain.[31]

The decision to destroy the Abwehr was made in a fashion typical of Hitler's impulsiveness. Upon hearing of the Abwehr bomb attack, the dictator flew into a hysterical rage, spewing out invective at both Canaris and the Abwehr. As he paused to catch his breath, SS-Brigadeführer Hermann Fegelein, Himmler's liaison man at the Führer's headquarters, casually remarked that the "whole business [ganzer Kram]" should be entrusted to the Reichsführer SS. Hitler stopped his temper tantrum, summoned Himmler, and authorized him to create a unified intelligence service based on a fusion of Abwehr and SD.[32]

On 12 February, Himmler passed on the good news to Kaltenbrunner, Müller, Schellenberg, and the chief of the Gestapo counterespionage de-

---

[31] On the Amé incident, see Höhne, *Canaris*, pp. 506-509. On Kiep and Solf circle, see Buchheit, *Geheimdienst*, p. 428; Abshagen, *Canaris*, pp. 365-366; Höhne, *Canaris*, pp. 511-513. On Anzio landings, see Höhne, *Canaris*, p. 514. On Kaltenbrunner and Vermehren, see chief of Security Police and SD, "Deutsche Verratsquelle in der Türkei," 7 February 1944, cited in ibid., pp. 521-522. On Abwehr bomb attack in Spanish waters, see Höhne, *Canaris*, pp. 521, 527.

[32] Huppenkothen, "Canaris und Abwehr," p. 11; Höhne, *Canaris*, pp. 526-527.

partment (RSHA IV E), SS-Standartenführer Walter Huppenkothen. Schellenberg proposed that the SD-Ausland incorporate the Abwehr in its entirety. Himmler was uncertain: he feared that the RSHA would only be able to absorb the foreign intelligence and sabotage departments of the Abwehr. Kaltenbrunner sided with Schellenberg, but proposed that the Abwehr be taken as a whole into the general framework of the RSHA rather than into the specific framework of the SD-Ausland. Himmler agreed, and Kaltenbrunner drafted a decree for Hitler's signature. On the next day, 13 February 1944, the RSHA chief appeared at Führer headquarters to place the draft decree before OKW chief Keitel and Keitel's chief of staff, General Alfred Jodl. Armed with the approval of the OKW, Kaltenbrunner then presented the decree to Hitler. Backdated to 12 February, it symbolized one of his greatest triumphs. It read:

> I order that:
> 1. a unified German secret intelligence service be created.
> 2. With the leadership of this German intelligence service I commission the Reichsführer SS.
> 3. Insofar as the military intelligence and counterespionage service is affected by the foregoing, the Reichsführer SS and the chief of the OKW take the appropriate measures in mutual agreement.
>
> signed: Adolf Hitler

Kaltenbrunner later told Huppenkothen that when he handed Hitler the decree to sign, the Führer had asked him facetiously whether he was now satisfied. The RSHA chief had triumphantly replied that he now lacked only the Information Division of the Foreign Office.[33]

Himmler authorized Kaltenbrunner to negotiate with the OKW on the fate of the Abwehr. Within a few weeks of Canaris's dismissal on 12 February 1944, Keitel sent a draft proposal to the RSHA chief. The Keitel draft provided that all espionage and sabotage functions of the Abwehr (Abwehr I and Abwehr II) be subordinated to the Reichsführer SS. From Abwehr III (counterespionage) Himmler would take responsibility for: (1) protection of armaments industries; (2) military counterespionage abroad and in the occupied territories; and (3) all units of the Secret Field Police (Geheime Feldpolizei) not directly concerned with military police tasks in the Wehrmacht. Left to the OKW were espionage and counterespionage departments of Abwehr III that pertained directly to the safety of the troops themselves, and

---

[33] Huppenkothen, "Canaris und Abwehr," p. 12; Höhne, Canaris, p. 528. On preparation of draft decree for Hitler's signature, see Huppenkothen, "Canaris und Abwehr," pp. 11-12; Höhne, Canaris, p. 528; interrogation of Kaltenbrunner, 19 September 1946, pp. 9-10, ZS-673, IfZ Munich. For the text of the decree, see decree of Hitler, 12 February 1944, T-78/497/6485650, NA.

control over the military police. All Abwehr staff personnel transferring to the RSHA would be discharged from the army; all members of the new military Amt in the RSHA would fall under SS and police disciplinary procedures. The new military Amt would be financed in public by the OKW, in secret by the RSHA. Finally, Oster's personnel office, Abteilung Z, would be dissolved.[34]

Though the terms of this draft proposal were vehemently opposed in the headquarters of the Army High Command (*Oberkommando des Heeres*— OKH), Keitel and his Abwehr negotiators were in fact trying to salvage what they could from the wreckage of the Abwehr. Their point was that Abwehr I and Abwehr II would not be directly incorporated into the RSHA, but would rather be attached to it as single "military Amt" under the chief of Abwehr I, Colonel Georg Hansen. In this way, Keitel and Abwehr III chief Bentivegni would be assured that the OKW could at least maintain its influence and "spirit" in the military intelligence office.[35]

When Kaltenbrunner returned to Berlin from Budapest, where he had been strong-arming Hungarian officials with respect to the Jewish question, he studied Keitel's draft, threw it aside, and demanded that the Abwehr be split up and completely incorporated into the corresponding departments of the Gestapo and the SD-Ausland. Keitel complained to Himmler that this was "irresponsible," arguing that a united military intelligence office, staffed with military personnel, placed under military regulations, and requiring special military training not available to members of the SD was necessary to serve the war needs of the Wehrmacht. The OKW chief also insisted that the Amt Mil, as the new office would be called, be removed from Kaltenbrunner's control as far as appointments and transfers were concerned in that Kaltenbrunner be required to negotiate via Himmler with the appropriate military authorities. In a note to Kaltenbrunner, Keitel even advised that the RSHA chief be given an appointment in the OKW to legitimize his authority over Amt Mil![36]

Kaltenbrunner was not inclined to tie his hands in any way with respect to the OKW. The final agreement between Himmler and Keitel reflected a compromise between the competing interests; but the RSHA held the distinct advantage. This pact provided for the temporary existence of an Amt Mil, consisting of the former Abwehr departments I and II, but foresaw the eventual fusion of Amt Mil with RSHA Amt VI, the SD-Ausland. Abwehr

[34] Draft of agreement between the chief of the OKW and the Reichsführer SS, n.d. (probably March 1944), T-78/497/6485671-6485674, NA.

[35] Höhne, *Canaris*, pp. 531-532. On OKH opposition, see draft of letter of the chief of Army General Staff to Keitel, April 1944, T-78/497/6485660, NA.

[36] Keitel to Himmler, 11 April 1944, T-78/497/6485663-6485665, NA; chief OKW to chief of Security Police and SD, n.d., ibid., 6485676.

III would be carved up as outlined in the Keitel draft. On 23 May 1944, Kaltenbrunner issued a decree which as of 1 June provided that: (1) those sections of Abwehr III transferred to the competence of the Reichsführer SS be incorporated into the Gestapo; (2) the Abwehr departments I and II temporarily form a "military Amt of the chief of the Security Police and the SD"; (3) the former Abwehr department Z be divided between Amt I (Personnel) and Amt II (Administration) of the RSHA; and (4) the eventual fusion of Amt Mil and RSHA Amt VI be prepared by the chief of the latter (i.e., Schellenberg). Finally, on 30 June 1944, Gestapo chief Müller issued a decree announcing the incorporation of Abwehr III Wi (counterespionage in major war industries) into the Gestapo.[37] Though Keitel was to have his Amt Mil, it was clear from the outset that the RSHA would control it and that its very existence would be temporary.

The collapse of the Abwehr was a great coup for Kaltenbrunner, Müller, and Schellenberg. At one stroke, their chief rival in the areas of foreign intelligence and counterespionage was neutralized. Canaris was dismissed and sent off on vacation. Colonel Georg Hansen, who took over Amt Mil in June 1944, was expected to adhere to Kaltenbrunner's wishes; indeed, it is possible that the RSHA chief saw in Hansen a bulwark against Schellenberg's ambitions.[38] In an action symbolizing the victory of the RSHA, the SD-Ausland took control of all Abwehr offices abroad on 1 June 1944.

Canaris's fall from power did not halt Kaltenbrunner's efforts to eliminate him. Arrested after 20 July 1944, Canaris was subjected to rigorous interrogation by the Gestapo for eight months. The discovery of the Oster-Dohnanyi files in a safe in the former Abwehr headquarters in Zossen in September 1944 enabled Kaltenbrunner to report triumphantly to Bormann that plans to topple Hitler had been made as early as the Blomberg-Fritsch crisis of February 1938 and that Canaris had been involved in these plans through Oster. Depicting Canaris's role in the Vatican negotiations, Kaltenbrunner added:[39]

[37] Agreement signed Chief OKW [Keitel] and Reichsführer SS [Himmler] 14 May 1944, ibid., 6485651-6485654; decree of Kaltenbrunner, 23 May 1944, ibid., 6485655-6485658; decree of chief of Security Police and SD [signed Müller], 30 June 1944, Gestapo-19, IMT XLII, pp. 295-298. For a chart showing the creation of Amt Mil in the RSHA, see Organization Plan for the Incorporation of the Abwehr into the RSHA, n.d. (after June 1944), T-175/232/2720825, NA.

[38] In fact, Hansen, along with another RSHA department chief, Kripo chief Artur Nebe, had contacts with the conservative wing of the anti-Hitler resistance. Both were executed after 20 July 1944. Hans Bernd Gisevius, Wo ist Nebe? Erinnerungen an Hitlers Reichskriminaldirektor (Zurich: Droemer, 1966).

[39] Kaltenbrunner to Bormann, 29 November 1944, in Peter, Spiegelbild, pp. 509-510. See also Kaltenbrunner to Bormann, 2 October 1944, ibid., pp. 430-431.

The interrogations . . . have clearly revealed the irreparable role which the opposition groups, in particular the activity of the Amt Ausland/Abwehr under its chief, Canaris, had for German policy. The *flow of oppositional elements abroad* who made no secret of their hostile attitudes and who kept foreign circles thoroughly informed about the existing opposition groups in Germany, have *again and again nourished . . . the hope of the enemy for an internal collapse of Germany and have thereby strengthened the hopes of the enemy for a rapid victory without a decisive final struggle again and again at great damage to the Reich.* (emphasis in the original).

On orders from Hitler, Kaltenbrunner and Huppenkothen continued the investigations of Canaris, Oster, and Dohnanyi until April 1945. On 4 April, RSHA agents discovered Canaris's secret diaries and presented them to Hitler as proof of the Abwehr chief's guilt. Canaris, Oster, and Dohnanyi were sentenced to death by an SS court-martial. On 8 April 1945, Dohnanyi was hanged at Sachsenhausen; Canaris and Oster were executed at Flossenbürg the next day.[40]

The RSHA-Abwehr struggle was generously nourished by personal and political ambitions and represented an effort on the part of each side to be the principal intelligence organ of the Third Reich. Conservative, antidemocratic, and initially willing to serve Hitler as he was, Canaris was no Nazi; but command of the Abwehr had meant the revival of a career that appeared to be finished under the Weimar regime. For Schellenberg and Müller, each in his own fashion cynically contemptuous of National Socialist ideology, personal ambition played the leading role in motivating their efforts to gain control of the Abwehr. Kaltenbrunner, too, was lured by the romantic prospect of becoming the chief spymaster of the Third Reich and was aware of the potential power inherent in such a position; he viewed his victory over Canaris as a personal triumph. Unlike Schellenberg and Müller, however, he was further driven by an almost pathological hatred for Canaris and the Abwehr,[41] a hatred arising not only from personal ambition and jealousy but also from ideological outlook; for Canaris, despite his fascination and flirtation with the Nazis, was the epitome of that which Kaltenbrunner most despised: the "nonpolitical soldier," devoted not to Hitler and the National Socialists, but to the standards, symbols, and outlook of the

[40] Interrogation of Huppenkothen, 24 April 1948, ZS-249/1, p. 97, IfZ Munich; Höhne, *Canaris*, pp. 563-569.

[41] On Kaltenbrunner's hatred of Canaris and sense of personal triumph at the latter's dismissal, see E. Kaltenbrunner, "Memoir," Nuremberg, July-August 1946, p. 41, Kaltenbrunner File. Carl Haensel, counsel for the SS organization at the Nuremberg Trial, spoke to Kaltenbrunner at length about Canaris and commented cryptically: "Kaltenbrunner hated and persecuted Canaris, whom he secretly admired and from whom he could never break away; this hate-love for Canaris tied him to Himmler for better or for worse." Carl Haensel, *Das Gericht vertagt sich* (Hamburg: Claasen Verlag, 1950), p. 152.

Wilhelmine military elite. Thus, though fought out and concluded in the context of Nazi personal politics, the struggle between the RSHA and the Abwehr was given an ideological tinge by Kaltenbrunner's political view of what Canaris and the Abwehr symbolized.

In the Nazi Party bureaucracy and its chief, Reichsleiter Martin Bormann, Kaltenbrunner's RSHA faced a considerably more adept and dangerous opponent than either Ribbentrop's Foreign Office or Canaris's Abwehr. Bormann possessed an extraordinary talent for intrigue and manipulation. Since his appointment in July 1933 as chief of staff in the office of Deputy Führer Rudolf Hess, Bormann had been at the Führer's side and had understood perfectly how Hitler ruled. Born in Halberstadt in 1900, he had served in the artillery during the last years of World War I and, after the war, had helped to manage the estate of Hermann von Treuenfels, a right-wing landowner in Mecklenburg. There he fell in with the Rossbach Freikorps and was involved in the brutal *feme* murder of a comrade suspected of being a communist infiltrator. After serving a year in prison, Bormann joined the Nazi Party and organized a financial-aid office in the SA for those rowdies who were injured in the street battles of the 1920s and early 1930s. In July 1933, Hess brought him into the Deputy Führer's office. After Hess's flight to England in May 1941, Hitler abolished the position of Deputy Führer and created a Party Chancellery to handle staff and personnel problems in the Nazi Party; Bormann unobtrusively became its chief. Although on paper his new position gave him potential control over the Party apparatus and many of its affiliated organizations, Bormann understood that the real source of his power lay in his institutionally undefined role as administrator of Hitler's private affairs, translator of Hitler's late-night ramblings into decrees and regulations, and doorman to the Führer's antechamber. Recognized and praised by the dictator for his fanatical personal loyalty and his inexhaustible energy for administration, Bormann gradually gained control of access to Hitler, thus enabling him to determine who was to see Hitler, how often, and for how long.[42]

The struggle between the RSHA and the Party Chancellery, which, like the conflicts with the Foreign Office and the Abwehr, was fueled by the personal ambitions of the chiefs and punctuated by temporary truces, was waged on two levels: over reports drawn up by the internal intelligence organization of the SS, the SD-Inland (RSHA Amt III); and over administrative control of the Reich as it fell under the threat of foreign invasion.

To depict the background of the conflict between Bormann and the RSHA

---

[42] On Bormann's life, see Josef Wulf, *Martin Bormann—Hitlers Schatten* (Gütersloh: Siegbert Mohn Verlag, 1962); Jochen von Lang, *Der Sekretär: Martin Bormann, der Mann, der Hitler beherrschte* (Stuttgart: Deutsche Verlags-Anstalt, 1977). On his role in the Nazi Party, see Orlow, *Nazi Party, 1933-1945.*

over intelligence reports, it would be helpful to outline the evolution of the SD within Germany. The Security Service of the Reichsführer SS (*Sicherheitsdienst des RFSS*) had been created by Himmler in the spring of 1931 in response to Hitler's need for a reliable intelligence service to provide accurate information on political opponents within and outside of the Nazi Party. Under Heydrich, who took over the SS intelligence service (then known as the Ic Service) in October 1931, the SD developed three main functions: to supply the Nazi Party with political intelligence on specific opponents in German society and politics; to provide intelligence for assisting the SS in its responsibility for the protection of the Führer and other Nazi leaders; and to gather "ideological intelligence" on the "invisible" enemies of the Nazi Weltanschauung, the "wire pullers" behind the more obvious opponents of the Nazis (i.e., Jews, Freemasons, Liberals, etc.). By mid-1934, the SD had outclassed its rivals; for on 9 June, Deputy Führer Rudolf Hess decreed it the sole intelligence service of the National Socialist Party.[43]

In the years following the Nazi seizure of power, the Gestapo gradually assumed the political intelligence functions of the SD. This was inevitable, for, given Hitler's conquest of the German state and his identification of it with the German Volk, opponents of Hitler and the Nazis by definition became opponents of the state and hence fell under the jurisdiction of the state police. As a result, SD leaders placed greater emphasis on the collection of "ideological intelligence," seeing as their task the discovery and surveillance of "all forces, events, and facts that are of importance to the rule of the National Socialist idea and movement." While the Gestapo pursued political enemies of the regime—the "obvious" enemies—the SD took as its goal the definition and exposure of the "hidden" enemies of the regime and the links between these and the obvious enemies. As the continued existence of hidden enemies required the permanent presence of an ideological watchdog to monitor their machinations, the SD manufactured a permanent raison d'être.[44]

Though the SD, as a Party organization, was theoretically responsible to the office of the Deputy Führer, it remained in fact independent of Party control by virtue of Himmler's direct access to Hitler. In June 1936, a liaison officer of the SD was attached to the staff of each Gauleiter. The SD network, however, remained outside the Gauleiter's control; as late as December 1938, Hess reminded the Gauleiter that although they could assign tasks

[43] Decree of Hess, 9 June 1934, Aktenmappe RSHA, Ordner 457, pp. 101-105, BDC. On the early history of the SD, see Browder, "Sipo and SD," pp. 31-32; testimony of Hoeppner, IMT xx, pp. 187-188; Höhne, SS, pp. 191-193.

[44] Werner Best, *Die deutsche Polizei* (Darmstadt: L. C. Wittich, 1940), p. 38; Browder, "Sipo and SD," pp. 183-186.

to the SD liaison officers, the SD alone was responsible for intelligence collection.[45]

This issue developed into one of considerable concern for the Party leaders as they discovered that SD agents were spying on them and their operations. With his decree of 1 July 1937, Heydrich had enlarged the field of SD research to include "spheres of life" within the Reich. According to this decree, the SD was to compile regular reports on general political developments, racial and folk lore, education, art and communications, and developments in the Party and the state. After the outbreak of World War II, the SD-Inland, now incorporated into the RSHA, saw its major task in "observing the effects of . . . measures carried out by leading authorities of the Reich . . . and in determining how the circles affected reacted to them." It became essential to discover "what the moods and attitude of . . . various classes of society were during the course of the war."[46]

Given the nature of their tasks and the manner in which they viewed them, the leaders of the SD-Inland became convinced that they were the elite of the elite, the "purest" National Socialists, committed to inform the leadership of the Reich of conditions in the Reich with the most relentless accuracy, objectivity, and honesty, regardless of persons or institutions involved. In pursuit of such idealistic aims, SD agents began to probe into Party affairs, exposing frequent cases of corruption and mismanagement at the local level. The circulation of such intelligence naturally incited considerable hostility toward the SD on the part of the Party leadership and even awakened the mistrust of Himmler himself.[47]

In the months before Kaltenbrunner's arrival in Berlin, the Gauleiter began to retaliate to the often embarrassing exposure of their political and administrative ineffectiveness. Albert Forster, the Gauleiter of Danzig–West Prussia, complained to Bormann about SD snooping and encouraged his subordinates to uncover and expose the identities of local SD agents. An SD report depicting the negative reaction of Düsseldorf's population to the Party's role in the celebrations of the nineteenth anniversary of the Munich Beer Hall Putsch provoked a bitter complaint from Gauleiter Friedrich Karl Florian that the SD was interfering in Party affairs. In January 1943, Gau-

[45] Order of Taubert [chief of staff of Security Main Office (the SD before its incorporation into the RSHA)], 22 June 1936, T-175/240/2730223-2730224, NA; decree of Hess, 14 December 1938, 3385-PS, IMT xxxii, pp. 250-251.

[46] Testimony of Otto Ohlendorf, IMT iv, p. 353. See also Browder, "Sipo and SD," p. 196; Höhne, SS, pp. 264-268. On "spheres of life," see decree of Heydrich, "Gemeinsame Anordnung für den Sicherheitsdienst des Reichsführers-SS und die geheime Staatspolizei," 1 July 1937, File RSHA, R 58/239, BA.

[47] Interrogation of Otto Ohlendorf, 29 May 1947, ZS-278/iv, pp. 13-18, IfZ Munich.

leiter Karl Weinrich of Hessen-Nassau-Nord wrote to Bormann, comparing the SD to the Soviet secret police.[48]

Given this tension, which appears to have peaked in November 1942–January 1943, Bormann's letter to Himmler on 7 December, reminding Himmler that during Heydrich's time problems between the SD and the Party were quickly settled, encourages speculation that the Party Chancellery chief may have contributed to the decision to replace Heydrich. In this context, it is interesting to note that Himmler submitted Kaltenbrunner's name to Hitler for approval on 10 December 1942.[49] If, however, Bormann expected Kaltenbrunner to be more cooperative on the issue of SD reports, he was, at least initially, to be disappointed.

Of all his department chiefs in the RSHA—with the possible exception of Kripo chief Artur Nebe—Kaltenbrunner appears to have most respected the chief of the SD-Inland and the principal source of SD difficulties with the Gauleiter, SS-Gruppenführer Otto Ohlendorf. Born in 1907, Ohlendorf had joined the Nazi Party at the age of eighteen and the SS two years later; in 1934, he joined the SD. Ohlendorf swore by that part of the Nazi ideology which extolled the virtues of the small independent entrepreneur and took equally seriously the Nazi promise of a racial community cleansed of impurities and unethical business practices. A dour, humorless fanatic, he was determined that the SD-Inland, which he took over after the establishment of the RSHA in 1939, serve as the conscience of the Nazi leadership, attacking big business, championing the interests of the middle class against the centralizing efforts of the state and the collectivist leanings of the German Labor Front (*Deutsche Arbeitsfront*—DAF), and, above all, detecting and exposing corruption and megalomania in the Nazi Party.[50]

---

[48] On Forster, see Bormann to Forster, 27 November 1942, T-175/59/2574892-2574893, NA. On Florian, see Florian to Bormann, 30 November 1942, ibid., 2574435-2574437; Bormann to Himmler, 7 December 1942, ibid., 2574433-2574434; Himmler to Bormann, 18 March 1943, ibid., 2574420-2574421. On Weinrich, see Weinrich to Bormann, 22 January 1943, ibid., 2574429-2574430.

[49] See chapter 4 text at n. 72, above. On Bormann's remainder, see Bormann to Himmler, 7 December 1942, T-175/59/2574433-2574434, NA.

[50] On Ohlendorf's ideology, see Ohlendorf to D'Alquen [editor of *Das Schwarze Korps*, the SS newspaper], 14 August 1942, T-175/31/2539059-2539062, NA. Ohlendorf's loudmouthed puritanism repeatedly embarrassed Himmler and Heydrich, who had to patch up the rifts between the SS and the Nazi Party that were provoked by the SD reports. In an attempt to sober his troublesome subordinate, Heydrich assigned Ohlendorf to command the notorious Einsatzgruppe D, a mobile killing unit operating in Southern Russia with explicit instructions to liquidate all "potential enemies" of the Reich left behind the lines of the invading German troops. With the same fanaticism that inspired him at the SD office, Ohlendorf and his men managed in six months to slaughter 90,000 Jews and thousands of other enemies (Gypsies, Soviet commissars, isolated Red Army soldiers, and anyone else who seemed "dangerous"). Upon his return to the RSHA in 1942, after Heydrich's death, Ohlendorf continued to annoy

In a memorandum composed for the short-lived Dönitz regime in the days after Hitler's suicide, Ohlendorf put on paper his concept of the function of an intelligence service in Nazi Germany. He postulated that, in a state organized on the Führer principle and thus lacking facilities for public criticism of regime policies, the leadership required for wise government an internal intelligence service which, by virtue of an "independent position," could present its "interpretation regardless of persons at hand and without rigid attachment to doctrines." Ideally, the SD was "an objective representative of a healthy public opinion [*Volksmeinung*]," an escape valve for "unreleased tensions." Ohlendorf valued an agency "which in place of public criticism is supposed to place the leadership in a position to become familiar with and to take into consideration opinion present, or arising, in the Volk."[51] Writing after Hitler's death and in the face of the disintegration of the Nazi state, Ohlendorf apparently thought it prudent to play down the wartime SD commitment to ideological purism.

Of all his colleagues, Kaltenbrunner rated Ohlendorf "by far the most decent." Ohlendorf was "an exceptionally correct and truth-loving person," who "never sweet-talked a superior or the chief of another agency, but rather presented his own carefully worked out opinion like a man." Though on his part, Ohlendorf thought Kaltenbrunner somewhat "coarse," he remembered his difficult relationship with Heydrich and made efforts to be pleasant. He appears to have convinced Kaltenbrunner of the necessity for the Nazi leadership to receive an accurate picture of the moods of the population and the failings of individual leaders. In words similar to Ohlendorf's, Kaltenbrunner told an interrogator at Nuremberg that it had been the "most important task" of the SD "to replace [public] criticism, to portray in a photographically exact manner and most objectively the existing picture of all spheres of life in the Reich."[52] His mode of reporting on the 20 July conspiracy was in line with this view.

Himmler and to enrage Party officials with his "objective" reporting on the antics of the Party leaders. As late as September 1943, he complained to Himmler's masseur, Felix Kersten, that the Reichsführer SS was not lending the "objective" reporting function of the SD sufficient support. See Kersten, *Totenkopf*, pp. 247-263.

[51] Memorandum of Ohlendorf, May 1945, T-77/864/5611192, 5611196, 5611200, NA.

[52] Interrogation of Kaltenbrunner, 19 September 1946, p. 22, ZS-673, IfZ Munich. Though Kaltenbrunner probably slanted his statement for the benefit of the interrogator, his concept so approximated Ohlendorf's—even to the wording—that one may assume, since the two men could not converse while prisoners at Nuremberg, that Kaltenbrunner and Ohlendorf had discussed the latter's ideas at length before May 1945. On Kaltenbrunner's opinion of Ohlendorf, see interrogation of Kaltenbrunner, 19 September 1946, 14-15, 22, ZS-673, IfZ Munich. On Ohlendorf's opinion of Kaltenbrunner, see interview with Dr. Wilhelm Höttl, Bad Aussee, 14 and 15 April 1977, Höttl Tape, p. 16. On Kaltenbrunner's support for Ohlendorf's concept, see testimony of Ohlendorf, IMT IV, p. 335.

Less than three months after Kaltenbrunner's arrival in Berlin, Bormann maneuvered himself into a position from which he could successfully resist the influence of Himmler's SS-Police system. On 12 April 1943, he was appointed secretary of the Führer (*Sekretär des Führers*). As chief of the Party Chancellery, Bormann had possessed official authority only in those affairs which directly affected the interests and institutions of the Nazi Party bureaucracy; as secretary of the Führer, he had the right to meddle in any and all affairs that concerned the Führer, and above all, to officially control access to the dictator.[53] Bormann's new position confirmed in writing his ever more successful efforts to isolate Hitler from the outside world and hence to become the sole medium for the expression of the Führer's will. The very choice of title—"Sekretär"—reflected not only Bormann's primitive concept of power, but also his expertise in manipulating the Hitlerian style of personal, charismatic authority to his own maximum advantage. While the vagueness of his field of competence permitted his interference in virtually every affair of Party, state, Wehrmacht, and SS (for these were, after all, concerns of the Führer), his position as secretary fortified him against every possible assault on his personal power. For, though a deputy can be accused of misinterpreting the words of his chief, a secretary merely carries out the will of his boss. Bormann could thus deflect attacks on himself by branding them as attacks on the Führer, whose will he (Bormann) was merely carrying out without question or interpretation. His access to and influence over the dictator represented a serious obstacle to those who sought to prevent him from interfering in their affairs.

Kaltenbrunner told his interrogators at Nuremberg that Bormann had been an "exceptionally ambitious, power-hungry man, who aimed not so much at realizing the Party program and the National Socialist idea, but rather at using the Party as an instrument to make himself indispensable to the Führer."[54] The new RSHA chief was not long in office before he experienced the animosity that existed between the SD-Inland and the Nazi Party bureaucracy. In early April 1943, the SD office in Danzig reported that, on the orders of the deputy Gauleiter of Danzig–West Prussia, various district and local Party offices (Kreis- und Ortsgruppenleitungen) were striving to uncover the SD intelligence net within their organizations. Kreisleiter Wilhelm Kampe (Danzig), for example, had exposed and denounced all of his coworkers who had been SD agents and had forbidden the remainder of his staff to cooperate in any way with the SD, explaining that one could "not

---

[53] "Aufgabengebiet des Sekretär des Führers," n.d. (probably May 1943), enclosed in Kaltenbrunner to Brandt, 26 July 1943, T-175/38/2547871, NA. See also Bormann to Himmler, 1 May 1943, ibid., 2547874; Orlow, *Nazi Party, 1933-1945*, p. 422; Lang, *Sekretär*, pp. 245-246.

[54] Interrogation of Kaltenbrunner, 24 September 1946, p. 1, ZS-673, IfZ Munich.

obey the Gauleiter and on the other hand be obligated to *Herr Himmler*" (emphasis in the original). The SD was clearly worried that Kampe's actions might be imitated elsewhere, for "in many cases block leaders and cell leaders of the NSDAP [Nazi Party] are active as agents. Should the order of Kreisleiter Kampe become generally valid, the work of the SD would suffer severely."[55]

Despite such obstacles, Kaltenbrunner took note of Bormann's rising star and sought to keep relations cordial, an effort that Bormann reciprocated because he saw in the SS an ally in a major assault on the remaining powers of the state bureaucracy. On 24 August 1943, the chief of the Party Chancellery issued a circular to the Gauleiter, forbidding them to establish private intelligence services that would compete with the SD and urging a wide exchange of information between the Party Chancellery and the RSHA. If a Gauleiter required certain intelligence essential for the administration of his Gau, he was to use the SD apparatus. In the spring of 1944, at a conference of Gau staff office leaders (*Gaustabsamtsleiter*), whom Bormann had installed in the Gauleitungen in November 1943 to spy on the often independent-minded Gauleiter, Kaltenbrunner pleaded for closer cooperation between Party and SD and urged Party officials to provide skilled comrades for the extension of the SD intelligence net.[56]

Such efforts did not succeed in easing the tension between the Party and the SD. In April 1944, Bormann complained to Himmler that the SD was usurping the right to judge the political reliability of new personnel entering the state administration, over which Himmler, appointed Reich minister of the interior in August 1943, now had decisive control. Bormann conceded that he was willing to use SD reports to discover what types of general problems were present in various areas of German society, but declared that he was not prepared to tolerate SD efforts to influence in the name of the Party the appointment, dismissal, or promotion of civil service personnel. He added that he had now forbidden all high Party functionaries to take part in any activity as honorary (i.e., nonsalaried) SD agents; in June 1944, he extended the ban to all Party personnel.[57]

In June 1944, Bormann also turned his sights on the "Reports from the Reich," the daily SD situation reports that had for so long irritated the Gau-

[55] "Bericht über die Einwirkung der NSDAP und der SA in dem Nachrichtennetz des SD im Reichsgau Danzig-Westpreussen," n.d. (according to internal evidence, in the first days of April 1943), T-175/117/2642434-2642437, NA.

[56] On Bormann's intentions, see Orlow, *Nazi Party, 1933-1945*, p. 431. On his instructions to the Gauleiter, see circular of Bormann, 24 August 1943, T-175/281/2774832-2774834, NA. On conference of Gau staff office leaders, see interrogation of Bertus Gerdes, 20 November 1945, 3462-PS, IMT XXXII, pp. 295-300.

[57] Bormann to Himmler, 27 April 1944, T-175/53/2567276-2567279, NA. See also Lang, *Sekretär*, pp. 295-296.

leiter and himself. Accusing the SD of reporting only on the opinions of "negative circles" among the population and branding its reports as the "mouthpiece of defeatism," he not only forbade his Party officials to maintain contact with the SD, but also induced Reichsleiter Robert Ley, chief of the German Labor Front, to follow suit. Finally, he declared that he would no longer read any "Reports from the Reich." Himmler, who as early as 1943 had been so annoyed with the tension caused by the reports that he had threatened Kaltenbrunner with the dissolution of the SD-Inland, did not protest; and the last regular SD reports reached the Party Chancellery in July 1944.[58]

Nevertheless, the SD continued to circulate reports to various Reich authorities until the end of the war; and these angered Party officials who learned of their contents. In late October 1944, Ohlendorf issued a strict warning to his subordinates that they refrain from criticizing the behavior of individual Party members and confine their reports to matters of a "general nature." Indeed, as late as April 1945, Bormann carped to Kaltenbrunner about the tendency of the reports to overgeneralize, lashing out in particular at SD criticism of the failure of the Gauleiter to evacuate the populations of their Gaue before the arrival of Anglo-American or Soviet troops.[59]

Of yet more concern to Kaltenbrunner were the efforts of the Party to usurp the duties of the state administration as Allied and Soviet troops approached the borders of the Reich. The Party had gained a solid foothold in the state administration through a Hitler decree of 1 September 1939, which provided that each military district (Wehrkreis) of the Reich be assigned a Reich defense commissar (Reichsverteidigungskommissar), who in time of emergency assumed control of the entire civilian administration in his district, except for the Reich postal service, the Reich railroads, and the regional administration of finance. On the suggestions of Hess and Bormann, Hitler appointed a Gauleiter as Reich defense commissar in each of the thirteen military districts of the old Reich. Though formally under the supervision of the Reich minister of the interior, the Reich defense commissars were in fact able to whittle away at the prerogatives of the local state authorities as the "emergency situation" created by the war became ever more permanent.[60]

---

[58] Heinz Boberach, ed., *Meldungen aus dem Reich: Auswahl aus den geheimen Lageberichten des Sicherheitsdienstes der SS, 1939-1944* (Munich: Deutscher Taschenbuch Verlag, 1968), p. 29. See also Höhne, *SS*, pp. 483-484. On Himmler's threat to Kaltenbrunner, see Kersten, *Totenkopf*, p. 255.

[59] Speech of Ohlendorf to SD-Abschnittführer, 31 October 1944, T-175/267/2762295-2762311, especially 2762297, 2762298, 2762302, NA; Bormann to Kaltenbrunner, 4 April 1945, T-81/5/13048-13051, NA.

[60] Peter Hüttenberger, *Die Gauleiter: Studie zum Wandel des Machtgefüges in der NSDAP* (Stuttgart: Deutsche Verlags-Anstalt, 1969), p. 153 and n. 52.

A Bormann circular of 31 May 1944 indicated clearly the aim of the Party Chancellery to secure for the Gauleiter and the Reich defense commissars a maximum of administrative control at the district level. In the event of an Anglo-American invasion (which was expected daily), the Gauleiter were to mobilize all possible manpower resources in the districts and precincts and to place them at the disposal of local Wehrmacht and police commanders. In a formal sense, these forces would fall under the command of the Wehrmacht for the purposes of covering them under the Geneva Convention stipulations on prisoners of war in the event of capture by the Allies, but actual control of them would remain with the Nazi Party. The Gauleiter were also to supervise and control the deployment of female units engaged in civil defense service and the military training programs for civilians. Moreover, the Party would have sole responsibility for the evacuation of the German population and all Party archives from areas directly threatened by enemy invasion. Finally, in the hope of usurping duties that were the responsibility of the SS and police, Bormann ordered all Kreisleiter to take the initiative in crushing any unrest among or uprising by foreign laborers in the Reich.[61]

Bormann's thrust was directed against the remaining powers of the German state administration. When Himmler took over the internal administration of the state by virtue of his appointment as minister of the interior on 20 August 1943, he became Bormann's chief target, despite the fact that relations between the two men remained personally cordial. Unlike Himmler, however, who was more interested in penetrating the military sphere, which his appointment as commander of the Reserve Army after the 20 July revolt had opened to him, Kaltenbrunner was well informed of Bormann's machinations and sought to warn his chief. In a letter of 26 August 1944, he noted that, in the emergency created by the deteriorating military situation, local Party leaders were usurping control of the state administration on the grounds that their responsibilities for the guidance of the population during the crisis required that they have access to levers of political and administrative control. Kaltenbrunner added that individual Kreisleiter were forming administrative staffs, creating their own executive organs, and claiming the right to issue instructions to existing executive authorities—including the police. Apparently these activities were encouraged by the Party Chancellery. Noting that open infighting between agencies of the Party, the SS, and the Wehrmacht would sap the strength of the leaders and exhaust the patience of the population, the RSHA chief suggested that Himmler, as minister of the interior, influence the Reich defense commissars in such a direction as to protect officials of the state administration from Party

[61] Circular of Bormann, 31 May 1944, 1163-PS, NA.

encroachments.[62] How ironic it was that a leader of the SS, which had contributed more than any other Nazi organization to undermining the foundations of the German state, took it upon himself to defend the state against Party encroachment!

Himmler approved of Kaltenbrunner's suggestions and sent them on to his state secretary in the ministry of the interior, SS-Gruppenführer Wilhelm Stuckart;[63] but no practical measures resulted, for Himmler was about to realize one of his oldest fantasies: that of taking a military command at the front. On 10 December 1944, Hitler appointed him commander of Army Group Upper Rhine in Southwest Germany; in January–March 1945, he commanded Army Group Vistula on the Eastern Front. It has been suggested that these appointments were the result of a shrewd move on Bormann's part both to isolate Hitler further from Himmler's influence and to insure that Himmler's inevitable failures on the front would tarnish his reputation in Hitler's eyes.[64]

Bickering between the Nazi Party and the RSHA continued until the collapse of the Reich itself. Neither side was able to score a decisive victory; and, as communications in Germany began to break down in the early spring of 1945, each lost effective control over its local offices. Bormann continued to guard Hitler's door until the very end, while Kaltenbrunner removed himself from Bormann's reach by transferring his headquarters to Austria in late March 1945.

The struggle between the RSHA and the Nazi Party differed from the rivalries with the Foreign Office and the Abwehr in two ways, both of which were crucial to the result of that struggle: stalemate and even RSHA recession. First, in attacking the Foreign Office and the Abwehr, the RSHA was an "ideological apparatus" pitted against traditional Weimar and even Wilhelmine institutions with clearly defined tasks and jurisdictions. Heydrich and Kaltenbrunner could persistently chip away at these jurisdictions by referring to "special circumstances" called forth either by the wartime emergency or, better still, by the "historic requirements of the German Volk." Against Bormann and the Party, however, Himmler and Kaltenbrunner found that this game could be played by both sides. Nevertheless, it seems unlikely

---

[62] Kaltenbrunner to Himmler, 26 August 1944, NG-2656, NA. See also *Documents on Nazism, 1919-1945*, ed. Jeremy Noakes and Geoffrey Pridham (New York: Viking, 1975), pp. 672-673; Lang, *Sekretär*, p. 295.

[63] Brandt to Stuckart, n.d., NG-2656, NA.

[64] Höhne, *SS*, pp. 622-629; Lang, *Sekretär*, p. 300; Jacques Delarue, *The Gestapo: A History of Horror* (New York: Dell, 1965), p. 379; Roger Manvell and Heinrich Fraenkel, *Himmler* (New York: Paperback Library, 1968), p. 216. Evidence that Bormann was encouraging Himmler's military ambitions can be found in a letter to his wife, dated 31 October 1944. Bormann mentions his request that "Uncle Heinrich" inspect bombing damage in the Ruhr. *The Bormann Letters*, ed. H. R. Trevor-Roper (London: Weidenfeld & Nicolson, 1954), p. 146.

that the Nazi Party bureaucracy could have halted the encroachment of the SS on state and Party affairs so effectively had it not been for the unique position of Martin Bormann. While Himmler in 1943–44, like Göring before him, began to collect more titles and jurisdictions than he was capable of effectively exploiting, Bormann remained content with two. The secretary of the Führer controlled personal access to Hitler, without which a Nazi leader could not legitimize his policies and without which he was exposed to the intrigues of his enemies who might obtain such access. On the other hand, the chief of the Party Chancellery exercised control over what also might be labeled an ideological apparatus—i.e., the Party bureaucracy— which equaled or exceeded that of the SS in numbers and local influence if not always in education and technical ability. Most important, however, the Nazi Party equaled the SS in the lack of traditional and legal restraints on its activities.

Placed in the center of the political power struggle by his appointment as chief of the RSHA, it was only natural for an ambitious man like Kaltenbrunner to attempt to enhance his personal authority and prestige by seeking what his powerful predecessor, Heydrich, had only dreamed of: direct access to Adolf Hitler himself, the source of legitimate authority in Germany.[65] Since Hitler based and delegated his authority on the principle of personal loyalty and confidence, he who sought political power had to be able— directly or indirectly—to confirm his personal loyalty to the dictator's satisfaction through personal contact and to present policy and tactical suggestions as evidence of that personal loyalty. To a certain degree, Kaltenbrunner attained this special relationship in the last two years of the Nazi regime.

When Kaltenbrunner first met Hitler face to face is unknown. The first recorded meeting took place on 15 March 1942, when Kaltenbrunner, then HSSPF in Vienna, accompanied Himmler on a visit to the Reich Chancellery to hear the Führer express his displeasure at the pessimistic tone of the "Reports from the Reich." As he had done with Heydrich, however, Himmler took pains to prevent his new RSHA chief from speaking with Hitler privately.[66]

Once settled in his new office, Kaltenbrunner sought ways to circumvent Himmler, perhaps less out of disloyalty than out of an effort to gain Hitler's approval for harsher measures against the Abwehr, whose weaknesses Himmler was reluctant to exploit. A key advantage in this quest was Kaltenbrunner's childlike devotion for the Nazi dictator. According to Wilhelm Höttl, Kal-

---

[65] After September 1941, Heydrich gained direct access to Hitler by virtue of his appointment as acting Reich protector for Bohemia and Moravia; but on matters of the Security Police and the SD, he was still compelled to approach Hitler through Himmler.

[66] Höttl Tape, p. 15. On Kaltenbrunner's meeting with Hitler, see Kotze, *Heeresadjutant*, p. 119.

tenbrunner "remained a slave to Hitler until the last moment" and "believed in him in spite of all reservations that he had [about the outcome of the war]." Such blind devotion overriding the dictates of common sense was congenial to the dictator, who, according to the speculation of one of Kaltenbrunner's rivals in the Austrian Nazi underground, was fully cognizant of that absolute loyalty and came to trust the RSHA chief even more than his "loyal Heinrich [Himmler]."[67]

Kaltenbrunner had been in Berlin for eight months when an event occurred which willy-nilly brought him to Hitler's attention. On 12 September 1943, Benito Mussolini, the fallen Italian dictator, had been snatched from the hands of the Badoglio government and spirited to Germany by a special commando under SS-Sturmbannführer Otto Skorzeny. Throughout August, Skorzeny and his agents, supervised by Schellenberg and Kaltenbrunner, had been searching for the Fascist leader, who had been carefully hidden by agents of the Badoglio government. The news of Mussolini's rescue from his mountain prison at the Campo Imperatori Hotel in Grand-Sasso Massino, after a bloodless assault via glider by Skorzeny and his men, was joyfully received not only by Hitler but also by large sections of the German population.[68] Overnight, Skorzeny was transformed into a legendary folk-hero.

Kaltenbrunner and Skorzeny had been close friends since the summer of 1927, at which time they had met in Linz. Then an engineering student at the university in Vienna, Skorzeny had come to Linz to help run the streetcars during the transit strike called by the Social Democrats in the wake of the crisis of 15 July.[69] Like Kaltenbrunner, Skorzeny had belonged to a Burschenschaft. An SS man since 1934, he had joined the Military SS (SS-Verfügungstruppe; after 1940, Waffen SS) at the outbreak of World War II; and in June 1943, Kaltenbrunner brought his old friend into the sabotage department of the SD-Ausland (RSHA Amt VI S).

Shortly after the arrest and disappearance of Mussolini on 25 July 1943, Himmler asked Kaltenbrunner for suggestions as to how to rescue the Italian dictator. The RSHA chief proposed to set up a special commando unit under Skorzeny. Himmler retorted that Skorzeny did not have the necessary experience, but Kaltenbrunner insisted and, after some argument, got his way. Later, the RSHA chief was able to exploit Skorzeny's well-publicized success. He greeted Skorzeny and Mussolini in Munich on 13 September, took personal responsibility for Il Duce's flight to Führer headquarters, and usurped the honor of personally presenting Mussolini to Hitler. Before lunch on the

[67] Interview with Leopold Tavs, Vienna, 21 January 1977, Tavs Tape, pp. 4-5. On Kaltenbrunner as slave to Hitler, see Hagen Unternehmen Bernhard, p. 96; Höttl Tape, p. 24.

[68] Goebbels, Diaries, pp. 449-453; SD Bericht zu Inlandsfragen, 13 September 1943, in Boberach, Meldungen, p. 352.

[69] Interview with Elisabeth Kaltenbrunner, Linz, 25 March 1977.

fourteenth, Kaltenbrunner and Skorzeny were closeted privately with the Führer, who wanted to hear all the details of the mission.[70]

Kaltenbrunner also endeavored to insure that his intelligence and political reports reached Hitler directly; and here he found two willing collaborators from within the Führer's inner circle. The first of these was SS-Brigadeführer and Ambassador for Special Purposes Walter Hewel, Ribbentrop's liaison man at Hitler's headquarters. Born in 1904 in Cologne, Hewel had marched with Hitler in the Munich putsch of 1923 and had shared six months with the dictator in Landsberg prison. As Ribbentrop's representative, Hewel saw Hitler daily and enjoyed the Führer's confidence. Kaltenbrunner had met Hewel during the running RSHA–Foreign Office struggle and apparently induced him to forward copies of SD reports with personal cover notes to Hitler. Hewel's support was won with the argument that both Ribbentrop and Himmler often refused to pass on important SD reports to Hitler and that Hewel must play this vital role for the Reich. Hewel's incapacitation in an automobile accident in the spring of 1944 forced Kaltenbrunner to cultivate a new contact: this was Himmler's liaison man at Hitler's headquarters, SS-Gruppenführer Hermann Fegelein. Formerly the chief of Amt VI (*Reit- und Fahrwesen*) of the SS Operations Main Office (*SS-Führungshauptamt— SSFHA*), Fegelein lacked both Hewel's intelligence and close personal contact with the Führer, but nevertheless had a few trumps of his own: his wife, Grete, was the sister of Hitler's mistress, Eva Braun, and he was one of Martin Bormann's favorite drinking companions.[71] By skillfully playing on Fegelein's vanity, Kaltenbrunner reopened the contact with Hitler broken by Hewel's accident.

Most important, however, was Kaltenbrunner's alliance with Martin Bormann. It is characteristic of the nature of personality politics in Nazi Germany that while as chiefs of the Party Chancellery and the RSHA they squabbled over SD reports and administrative jurisdictions at the local level, Bormann and Kaltenbrunner concluded an informal, personal alliance, which each party used to weaken Himmler's influence. When Bormann and Kaltenbrunner began to perceive possible allies in one another is unknown. If

[70] On Himmler-Kaltenbrunner discussion, see letter of Alfred Eduard Frauenfeld to the author, 19 December 1976. Frauenfeld maintained that Kaltenbrunner told him this story. On Kaltenbrunner, Skorzeny and Hitler, see Brandt to Baumert, 14 September 1943, T-175/117/ 2642388-2642389, NA. On Kaltenbrunner and Mussolini, see Skorzeny, *Geheimkommando*, pp. 157-159. Skorzeny romanticized about a "midnight tea" on the night of 14-15 September, at which only Hitler, Mussolini, Kaltenbrunner, and he were present. See ibid., p. 160.

[71] On Hewel, see Interrogation Report No. 15, U.S. Third Army Intelligence Center, "The SD and the RSHA," composed and dictated by Wilhelm Höttl, 9 July 1945, p. 46, 1746-PS, NA. See also Höttl Tape, p. 15; Capt. Inf. Harry F. Lennon, "Intermediate Interrogation Report," Headquarters, U.S. Twelfth Army Group Interrogation Center, 28 June 1945, folder CIR 4/3, IIR, Modern Military Records Branch, NA. On Fegelein, see Reitlinger, *SS*, p. 240.

Bormann had supported Kaltenbrunner's appointment as RSHA chief and if Kaltenbrunner had then backed Bormann's bid for the office of secretary of the Führer, a basis for collaboration had existed since the spring of 1943. As early as July 1943, the RSHA chief was sending Bormann carbon copies of intelligence reports directed to Himmler and dealing with internal Polish affairs. On 14 September 1943, the day on which Mussolini was brought to Hitler's headquarters at Rastenburg, Kaltenbrunner spent the entire afternoon and early evening closeted with the Party Chancellery chief. Morever, Kaltenbrunner's reports on the investigation of the 20 July conspiracy—running from 21 July to 15 December 1944—were sent directly to Bormann, not to Himmler; these apparently induced Bormann to arrange for Kaltenbrunner to speak to Hitler without Himmler being present (except for Himmler, Kaltenbrunner was the highest ranking SS leader to enjoy this privilege on a regular basis).[72] Albert Speer noted that by January 1945, the RSHA chief had begun to appear regularly at Hitler's situation conferences. One of Hitler's adjutants remembered how Bormann "slowly and discreetly" edged Kaltenbrunner into Hitler's sealed-off world with the result that the RSHA chief could take orders directly from Hitler without the obligation to inform Himmler. Finally, it is interesting to note that in February 1945, Kaltenbrunner conferred privately with Bormann at least four times in twenty-four days.[73]

Schellenberg has claimed that Kaltenbrunner's close relations with Bormann and access to Hitler caused Himmler to fear his second RSHA chief more than his first. At Nuremberg, Schellenberg declared that "toward the end [of the war] Himmler lived under constant pressure from Kaltenbrunner."[74] Whether Himmler really feared Kaltenbrunner is debatable. Himmler, who was interested in negotiating a separate peace with the Western Allies during the last months of the war, was probably uneasy about the extent of Kaltenbrunner's knowledge of his efforts in this direction. But it is just as likely that Schellenberg, who not only despised Kaltenbrunner as a personal rival but also sought to make his own relationship to Himmler appear as

---

[72] On intelligence reports to Bormann, see Kaltenbrunner to Himmler, 5 July 1943, T-175/33/2542158-2542162, NA. On Kaltenbrunner-Bormann conference on 14 September 1943, see Brandt to Baumert, 14 September 1943, T-175/117/2642388-2642389, NA. On 20 July reports, see Peter, *Spiegelbild*, passim. On Kaltenbrunner's visits with Hitler, see record of Hitler's daily schedule and appointments kept by his valet, SS-Hauptsturmführer Heinz Linge, 14 October 1944–28 February 1945, T-84/22, folder EAP 105/19a (no frames), NA.

[73] Speer, *Inside*, pp. 423-424; Boldt, *Last Ten Days*, pp. 71-72; Martin Bormann's appointment calendar, entries for 6, 11, and 15 February and 1 March 1945, in Lew Besymenski, *Die letzten Notizen von Martin Bormann: Ein Dokument und sein Verfasser* (Stuttgart: Deutsche Verlags-Anstalt, 1974), pp. 106, 107, 108, 147. On Bormann-Kaltenbrunner alliance, see Höhne, *SS*, p. 625; Delarue, *Gestapo*, p. 379; Reitlinger, *SS*, p. 240.

[74] Interrogation of Schellenberg, 13 November 1945, p. 17, NG-4718, NA.

"clean" as possible in view of his own impending trial, exaggerated or even invented the animosity between Kaltenbrunner and Himmler. Wilhelm Höttl told this author that he had "never heard of a serious deterioration of the relationship" between Kaltenbrunner and Himmler.[75] Moreover, though Kaltenbrunner despised Schellenberg and resented his influence with Himmler, there is no conclusive evidence that his alliance with Bormann served the purpose of establishing the basis for an attack on Himmler's personal position. Nevertheless, the alliance enabled him to ignore Himmler when he saw fit and to obstruct those plans of the Reichsführer with which he did not agree.

This was certainly ironic, for Himmler had chosen Kaltenbrunner to replace Heydrich in the expectation that the Austrian SS leader would not only represent SS-police interests against political and personal rivals but would also remain absolutely loyal. Himmler may even have hoped that the RSHA department heads would exploit their informal right to confer directly with him to discourage any undesired ambition on Kaltenbrunner's part. Perhaps the Reichsführer recalled how ineffective Kaltenbrunner had been in the struggle with Heydrich over the police in Austria; he would have done better to recall the talent for intrigue developed by the scar-faced Austrian in the atmosphere of the Austrian Nazi underground movement. For despite the frustration of 1938-1943, Kaltenbrunner was fully qualified and prepared to engage himself successfully in the internecine warfare so characteristic of the Third Reich. He was clever enough to win successes for Himmler while at the same time establishing an independent position of power. Using Himmler's vaguely defined and hence considerable political power, the RSHA chief neutralized Ribbentrop's position in the evaluation of foreign intelligence, destroyed the hitherto dominant position of the Wehrmacht in the field of political and military intelligence, and fiercely contested the growing power of the Nazi Party bureaucracy. When the Reichsführer proved unwilling or unable to meet Bormann's challenge, Kaltenbrunner drew the logical conclusion and forged a working alliance with the guardian of the Führer's will. Though dismayed by the independence of subordinates like Schellenberg, who continued to report directly to Himmler, the RSHA chief followed Schellenberg's example and opened a direct route to Hitler that effectively protected his personal position against intrigues on the part of his rival. Indeed, one might count Kaltenbrunner among the five most powerful men around Hitler in the last six months of the regime, in company with Bormann, Goebbels, Himmler, and Speer. For a provincial personality with no appreciable contact with Hitler before 1943, this was an impressive accomplishment. More remarkable still is the fact that of these five individuals,

---

[75] Höttl Tape, p. 20.

Kaltenbrunner alone wielded his power without the aid of an institutional-ized direct link to the Führer.[76] His promotion to SS-Obergruppenführer in June 1943 and the award of the Knight's Cross of the War Merit Cross with Swords on 9 December 1944[77] were merely symbolic of a very real power.

This power ultimately had little to do with Kaltenbrunner's technical competence as an intelligence expert, on which reputation, as he claimed at Nuremberg, he had been called to Berlin.[78] Indeed, Kaltenbrunner's ex-pertise as an intelligence chief remains a moot point. At Nuremberg, the former chief of the OKW Operations Staff, Alfred Jodl, commented that Kaltenbrunner's reporting on Southeast Europe "summed up our whole mil-itary situation with a frankness, soberness, and seriousness that had not at all been noticeable in Canaris's reports."[79] Moreover, the "Reports from the Reich" and the Kaltenbrunner reports on the 20 July 1944 conspiracy were, despite their bias, remarkably lucid and accurate. SD-Ausland agents were fairly well informed on the situation in Hungary and thus enabled first Ger-man troops (19 March 1944) and later SS commandos (15 October 1944) to forestall Horthy's efforts to extricate his nation from the war. On the other hand, the SD was caught by surprise in the wake of the coups in Italy (1943) and Romania (1944). Finally, Amt Mil was woefully misinformed as to the date and the place of the Normandy invasion.[80]

Yet, intelligence collection and reporting was really a secondary function of Kaltenbrunner's position. His main function was that of Himmler's "sub-vassal,"[81] sworn to actively represent the interests and expand the jurisdic-tions of the RSHA in the internal struggle for political power, and to imple-ment the ideological aims of the Nazi regime. Internal power struggles turned on questions of jurisdiction and personality rather than on issues of ideology or even technical competence. None of Kaltenbrunner's rivals (except for Canaris) ever seriously contested either the legitimacy of Hitler's claim to absolute power or the basic tenets of the National Socialist creed: expansion and purification. None (again except for Canaris) had much professional or

[76] Bormann, Goebbels, Himmler, and Speer reported directly to Hitler in their respective capacities as secretary of the Führer and chief of the Party Chancellery, Gauleiter of Berlin and Reich minister for propaganda and enlightenment, Reichsführer SS and Reich minister of the interior, and Reich minister for armaments and war production. Institutionally, Kaltenbrunner was responsible to Hitler only through Himmler. It is also interesting to note that whereas Kaltenbrunner lacked any regular contact with Hitler before 1943, Goebbels had been in Hit-ler's entourage since 1926, and Bormann, Himmler, and Speer had had frequent contact with the dictator since 1933.

[77] E. Kaltenbrunner SS File, BDC.

[78] E. Kaltenbrunner, "Memoir," p. 53.

[79] Testimony of Jodl, IMT xv, p. 428.

[80] Bullock, *Hitler*, pp. 667-668.

[81] Browning, "Martin Luther," p. 313.

technical training for his position. Ribbentrop and Kaltenbrunner fought over nothing more than the right to hand Hitler intelligence reports, which Hitler rarely read. The struggle with Canaris and the Abwehr, which did, to a limited degree, involve ideological conflict between totalitarianism and military elitism (and accordingly resulted in the decisive triumph of the former),[82] nevertheless turned on the issue of personal control over military intelligence, with Kaltenbrunner striving to gain it and Canaris seeking to prevent him from doing so. It is also important to note that Canaris was not dismissed on account of his ideological unreliability. The quarrel with Bormann was based on Bormann's dislike of SD reports that did not reflect the viewpoint he wished to present to Hitler, and on the Party's efforts to challenge Wehrmacht and SS-Police claims of responsibility for the defense of the Reich.

It has in fact been suggested that historians not overemphasize the effect of these personal rivalries on the implementation of Nazi ideological war policy. In his study of the SS Death's Head Division of the Waffen SS, Charles Sydnor has stated that the SS and the Waffen SS "functioned extremely well despite internal tensions and rivalries," and that this would not have been possible "without a formidable degree of institutional solidity—the presence of shared assumptions and beliefs, commonly accepted norms, and the unquestioned general values that enable large numbers of people, despite individual ambitions, dislikes, and disagreements, to work together in common purpose toward definite goals."[83] This widespread National Socialist consensus enabled Hitler to find approval and active support for his policies of persecution of the Jews, massive rearmament, resettlement of population groups, and territorial expansion from a governing apparatus that "consisted mainly of men willing and even eager to go far enough along these routes for Hitler to commit them willingly or unwillingly to the rest of the way."[84] The efficient implementation of the Final Solution, to which various rival civilian, military, Party, and SS agencies contributed, is only one example of the immunity of Nazi ideological policy to the effects of personal and institutional rivalries. Kaltenbrunner's cooperation with Schellenberg against the Abwehr is convincing evidence that in the Third Reich common aims even in a nonideological area could and did promote cooperation between bitter personal rivals.

---

[82] It should be noted here that outside of the pessimistically fatalist Canaris and the active resistance group around Oster and Dohnanyi, the Abwehr was not immune to nazification and that among the rank and file, jurisdiction rather than ideology was the major source of friction.

[83] Charles W. Sydnor, Jr., *Soldiers of Destruction: The SS Death's Head Division, 1933-1945* (Princeton, New Jersey: Princeton University Press, 1977), p. 346.

[84] Gerhard L. Weinberg, *The Foreign Policy of Hitler's Germany: Starting World War II, 1937-1939* (Chicago: University of Chicago Press, 1980), p. 664.

Personal ambition often outshadowed institutional loyalties in the fraternal squabble prevalent among the agencies of the Third Reich. Martin Luther could betray his boss, Ribbentrop, to an arch-rival, the SS, in the hope of preserving his personal position; Kaltenbrunner could conclude an alliance with his rival Bormann behind the back of his superior and previous bene-factor, Himmler. Indeed, Hitler had once told a follower that "men who are not ambitious should keep out of my way. I can only rely on the man who so links his own advancement with the general idea that neither one can be separated from the other."[85]

Whether or not it was the result of his conscious intent, Hitler's system embodied this ideal: the personal rivalries so endemic to the Third Reich reflected the striving for personal power molded onto a basic ideological and emotional assent to the Hitlerian framework of expansion and purification to such an extent that each reinforced the other.

Kaltenbrunner was successful in this world because he understood and exploited its rules. Power in the Nazi regime was legitimized neither through tradition nor by means of a rational-legal structural framework, but rested upon what Max Weber has defined as "charismatic authority."[86] Charis-matically legitimated authority derived from three elements in the Nazi movement: (1) the "existence of a person who is regarded by his followers as an individual of extraordinary powers or qualities"; (2) "the notion of a uto-pian ideal in the form of a Weltanschauung whose realization becomes the mission of the charismatic leader"; and (3) the "nonbureaucratic organiza-tion of the charismatically legitimated political order."[87] Early in his political career, Hitler had been able to convince his followers of his "connection with (including possession by and embodiment of) some very central feature of man's existence and the cosmos in which he lives."[88]

The fluid structure of Nazi ruling patterns enabled Hitler, whether con-sciously or not, to preserve an unassailable position above all personal and jurisdictional disputes by claiming to have a mystical connection to human destiny. Under this Nazi brand of "clientelism," group organization was based on the personal preferences of *the* leader or a subleader; a fixed bu-reaucratic or hierarchical order was incompatible with the dictator's claim to absolute authority. Hitler delegated power in a highly personal fashion; his followers were unencumbered by bureaucratic norms. The authority of a subleader rested neither on the powers inherent in his position nor on any

---

[85] Rauschning, *Gespräche*, p. 256.

[86] Max Weber, *The Theory of Social and Economic Organization* (New York: Oxford, 1947), p. 328.

[87] Nyomarkay, *Charisma*, pp. 9-10.

[88] Edward Shils, "Charisma, Order and Status," *American Sociological Review*, 30 (April 1965), 201.

previous qualifications that he might have for a given task, but solely on the extent to which he possessed Hitler's confidence.[89] Official agreements, like that which assigned the evaluation of foreign intelligence to the Foreign Office in 1939, were repeatedly and legitimately ignored by men like Himmler, Heydrich, and Kaltenbrunner, who through their personal and political ties to Hitler could claim to be executing the Führer's true will.

Kaltenbrunner was at home in such a system. From his experience in the faction-ridden Austrian Nazi underground, he was well aware of the importance of access to the dictator and how it invalidated traditional and bureaucratic command relationships in the Austrian Nazi Party. As HSSPF in Vienna, he had seen his personal and political ambitions frustrated by men like Heydrich and Bürckel, who enjoyed Hitler's personal confidence in regulating Austrian political and police affairs. Finally, he had been swept into power on the strength of Himmler's personal confidence, which in turn proved to be solid support for the RSHA chief's forays into jurisdictional spheres claimed by others. Once in power, Kaltenbrunner drew on Himmler's personal status with Hitler to advance the interests of the SD and to blunt or repulse efforts of outsiders to control or neutralize it. At the same time, he shrewdly perceived Himmler's inability or unwillingness to assert his interests against Bormann and the Party bureaucracy, and turned to Bormann as a medium to forge a line of direct personal contact to Hitler himself. In this way, he could not only promote pet policies of which Himmler did not fully approve, but also secure his own personal position against possible Schellenberg-Himmler intrigues. Kaltenbrunner's willingness to carry out Nazi policies on the basis of his assent to Hitler's claim to absolute power (ideological commitment) and his ability to realize his own and his superior's personal goals while executing those policies (acumen in personal politics) were the key factors in his rapid and spectacular accumulation of power.

Such assets were only useful, indeed meaningful, within the Reich that Hitler and the National Socialists claimed to be the destiny of the German Volk; and that Reich existed only by virtue of the faith of its believers. Yet the reports of Kaltenbrunner's SD agents and his own basic common sense must have given him cause for serious concern about the future. For the faithful, Hitler's firm commitment to final victory ruled out thoughts of defeat, but Kaltenbrunner found it difficult to deny the existence of Anglo-American and Soviet troops massed on the borders of the old Reich in the fall of 1944. For the past eighteen months he had enjoyed the power offered by a system based on ideological commitment and personal politics; in his attempts to save that system he would experience its limitations.

[89] Nyomarkay, *Charisma*, pp. 4-5, 22, 30-33, 37-38; Gerth, "Nazi Party" p. 102. For the term "clientelism" I am indebted to Dr. Joseph Rothschild of Columbia University.

CHAPTER VII

Ideology, Politics, and the Search for Peace

KALTENBRUNNER'S impressive achievements in supervising the activities of the Security Police, in advancing the interests of the RSHA, and in increasing his own personal power and prestige stood in marked contrast to the declining fortunes of the Reich that he served. Scarcely had he moved into his new office in the Prinz-Albrecht-Strasse when the last remnants of the German Sixth Army surrendered to the Soviets in the ruins of Stalingrad, a disaster followed in turn by the surrender of the German Army in North Africa on 7 May 1943 and the Allied landings on Sicily and the Italian mainland in July and September. In the summer of 1944, the Western Allies successfully invaded France, while the Soviets annihilated the German Army Group Center in their Byelorussian offensive of late June. As 1944 drew to a close, the Russians were sweeping past the landed estates of East Prussia and the coal mines of Silesia, while the Anglo-Americans were driving the Germans out of France and the Low Countries.

One might expect that such an unbroken string of military disasters would have induced even a fanatical leadership to consider an alternative solution to a war that could no longer be won, but Hitler entertained no such thoughts. On 1 January 1945, as Soviet troops raced for the Oder River, just 100 kilometers from Berlin, he told the German people over the radio that "staunchly and unshakably we shall do our duty in the new year, in the unwavering faith that the hour will come in which [the balance of] victory will finally tip toward that [power] which is most worthy of it; the Greater German Reich!"[1] Hitler tied the essence of National Socialism to faith in final victory, without which the German people had—and deserved—no future. Since the dictator would not listen to reports predicting or even hinting at anything less than victory, the loyal, but somewhat realistic National Socialist was torn between his emotional and psychological need to keep the faith and a desire to insure his own personal survival. And although the presence of Martin Bormann and a militant Nazi Party apparatus reminded the fainthearted that to "desert" the Führer at this desperate hour could cost

---

[1] Radio Speech of Hitler, 1 January 1945, in Max Domarus, *Hitler: Reden und Proklamationen, 1932-1945*, vol. II, pt. 2 (Munich: Süddeutscher Verlag, 1965), p. 2185.

them their lives and those of their families,[2] the well-publicized intentions of the Allies to try the Nazi leaders for war crimes moved some SS leaders to contemplate an alternate solution to the war, either through flight or negotiation with the enemy.

Kaltenbrunner also faced this dilemma. As chief of the Reich foreign intelligence service, he was in a position to know about Allied military superiority and postwar plans for a defeated Germany. He also realized that his command of the Security Police might have serious consequences in a world no longer dominated by the Hitler myth. As a devout Hitler follower, however, whose faith had already brought him substantial spiritual and material rewards, his political philosophy was intimately bound to that myth. At moments when his common sense outweighed his ideological fanaticism, only one alternative remained open to him: to stave off military defeat through political means, while at the same time preserving in Germany the Nazi system to which he owed not merely his career, but also his sense of political, cultural, and ideological identity. His efforts in this direction were doomed to failure.

Obsessed with secrecy, for fear Hitler would learn of his tentative moves, Kaltenbrunner committed little, if anything, to paper. As a result, much of the story is pieced together from the postwar testimony or memoirs of participants, whose motives were self-serving and whose accounts were colored by the pressures of the times. Despite these cautions, the task of reconstructing Kaltenbrunner's role in the abortive SS peace negotiations of 1944-45 has historical value in that it illustrates the limitations which ideological commitment and personal politics placed on those in the Third Reich who, in their more realistic moments, foresaw the collapse of the world in which they had lived for almost a generation.

It is impossible to know if and when Kaltenbrunner began to have doubts about the military outcome of the war; equally uncertain is the date when he first considered negotiation with the enemy. Kaltenbrunner himself testified that from the date of his appointment he had entertained no illusions as to the outcome of the war and immediately began to seek a political solution. This story is corroborated in part by two fellow Austrian Nazis, speaking after the war. Kaltenbrunner's friend Hermann Neubacher told the Nuremberg Tribunal that the RSHA chief had frequently spoken of a "so-called 'talk with the enemy,' " and that he had been "convinced that we could not come out of this war without the use of some large-scale diplomacy." Wilhelm Höttl wrote in 1950 that Kaltenbrunner had had no illusions about Germany's military situation and had hoped to use his position

[2] On resolve and loyalty of the Party Chancellery and the Gauleiter, see Orlow, *Nazi Party, 1933-1945*, pp. 478-481.

as SD chief to influence the diplomacy of the Reich toward a negotiated peace. When questioned by this author twenty-seven years later, however, Höttl reversed his opinion, explaining that Kaltenbrunner received regular reports on armaments production from Karl-Otto Saur, Albert Speer's deputy in the Reich Ministry for Armaments and War Production, and in fact believed until the spring of 1945 that victory was possible.[3] Such contradictory statements can be explained in part by Höttl's reputation for inconsistency, but might also reflect a conflict between ideological commitment and common sense in Kaltenbrunner's own thinking. At any rate, there are no reliable documents to prove that Kaltenbrunner approached Allied or neutral personalities before February 1945.

As chief of the SD, Kaltenbrunner was aware of efforts by Schellenberg's agents to contact their opposite numbers in the Office of Strategic Services (OSS) and the British Secret Intelligence Service (SIS). During the summer of 1942, Schellenberg became convinced not only that Germany could not win the war on both fronts, but also that the Grand Alliance was brittle and could be broken up by a skillful diplomatic initiative. Though realistic enough to accept Hitler's removal as the sine qua non for any initiative, he developed the fanciful idea that Himmler could be made acceptable to the Western Allies. In August 1942, he visited the Reichsführer at Himmler's headquarters in Zhitomir and suggested that the salvation of the Reich depended upon reaching a compromise peace with the Western Allies. Himmler huffed and puffed, sputtering something about treason and madness. Yet, while too cautious to make any commitments, he was sober enough—when removed from direct contact with Hitler's magnetic personality—to consider Schellenberg's proposals.[4] Heartened by this cautious passivity, Schellenberg ordered his agents to feel out the Allied position through secret-service contacts.

Schellenberg's hopes were not dampened by the Anglo-American declaration on unconditional surrender at Casablanca on 24 January 1943; for, less than a month later, the SD was able to report a nibble on its fishing lines. Since November 1942, Allen Dulles, ostensibly an assistant to the American ambassador to Switzerland, but in reality an agent of the OSS, had been gathering material on opposition groups within Germany from his base in Bern. In the course of his research, he had come into contact with Prinz Max-Egon Hohenlohe-Langenburg, a freelance SD agent who knew of Schellenberg's intentions. Hohenlohe, who had predicted military disaster from the outbreak of the war, was delighted when Dulles arranged to see

---

[3] Testimony of Kaltenbrunner, IMT xi, pp. 300-301; testimony of Neubacher, ibid., p. 425; affidavit of Wilhelm Höttl, 30 March 1946, Kaltenbrunner-2, ibid., p. 231; Hagen, *Geheime Front*, p. 83; interview with Dr. Wilhelm Höttl, Bad Aussee, 14 and 15 April 1977, Höttl Tape, pp. 21-22.

[4] Schellenberg, *Secret Service*, pp. 297-299, 304-312.

him in February 1943. He was deeply impressed by the OSS man, who intimated that "the German state must remain as a key to order and reconstruction [in postwar Europe]; partition or detachment of Austria was out of the question." The prince was thrilled to hear Dulles speak of pushing Poland to the East and retaining Romania and Hungary for the establishment of a "*cordon sanitaire* against Bolshevism and pan-Slavism"; he even recorded that the American had displayed "anti-Semitic tendencies."

In April, Hohenlohe spoke to Dulles again. His second report was no less encouraging than his first. Dulles bemoaned the fact that Nazi policy in Europe was grist to the mill of hardliners in England and the United States and declared that Germany had to find a "constructive solution"—i.e., remove Hitler—or else the Allied governments would develop a "fixed concept" of the postwar order. Finally, the American reportedly expressed his concern that Nazi Germany might turn its back on the West and conclude a separate peace with the Soviet Union.[5]

Schellenberg's assistants hastened to add their opinions on the promising developments. In late April, the chief of the England/United States desk in the SD-Ausland prepared a memorandum which concluded that the Americans, insecure about the alliance with the USSR and under pressure from voters of East European origin to prevent Soviet expansion into Europe, were receptive to peace feelers. The British, on their part, were uneasy about the possibility of either a Soviet-dominated continent or a permanent American presence in Europe. In order to preserve the balance of power on the continent, they were likely to promote a German-Soviet peace while both powers were still equal in strength and then to make peace in the West before American influence on the continent became a real factor. The report hinted throughout that unless a political solution were found, Germany would lose the war.[6]

Other "favorable" indications were passed on. An allegedly intercepted telegram of the American minister to Switzerland to the State Department mentioned a conversation between the minister and Hohenlohe in which the American expressed his concern that certain German circles would look

---

[5] It is interesting that this meeting allegedly took place in April 1943, for, just at this time, the Swedish press printed rumors of direct talks between German and Soviet dignitaries near Stockholm. See Alexander Fischer, *Sowjetische Deutschlandpolitik im Zweiten Weltkrieg, 1941-1945* (Stuttgart: Deutsche Verlags-Anstalt, 1975), p. 42. On Hohenlohe-Dulles meetings, see "Unterredung Pauls–Mr. Bull [Hohenlohe-Dulles]," February 1943 [possibly written by Otto-Ernst Schüddekopf, chief of RSHA VI D 7 (England/United States)], T-175/458/2975024-2975030, NA; "Aufzeichnung über Ausprachen mit Mr. Bull [Dulles] und Mr. Roberts," RSHA VI, n.d., ibid., 2975007-2975015. On Hohenlohe's contacts with Schellenberg and the SD, see Höhne, *SS*, pp. 586-588.

[6] Otto-Ernst Schüddekopf, "Die aussenpolitischen Tendenzen in England im April 1943," April 1943, T-175/458/2974995-2975005, NA.

to the Soviet Union for a compromise peace and Hohenlohe explained that Himmler's organization was "the best apparatus available for the preservation of internal order and resistance to communism." On 30 April 1943, an SD report on the Swiss contacts of former German Chancellor Josef Wirth alleged that Dulles had expressed concern about Soviet expansion into Central Europe to Wirth's agent and had even offered to pass on any German peace initiatives via direct channels to President Roosevelt himself.[7]

How far Schellenberg and Kaltenbrunner were taken in by Dulles's act (or how many of these reports were invented by Schellenberg's staff to encourage their chief and convince his superiors) is uncertain; but such a performance doubtlessly supported preconceived notions about the fragile nature of the Grand Alliance. That Kaltenbrunner saw at least one of these reports is confirmed by his handwritten comments on the section which described Dulles's concern about a German-Soviet rapprochement. Recognizing that the Führer would never permit negotiations on the basis of a post-Hitler Germany, the RSHA chief suggested using the Soviet bugaboo to frighten the Americans into concessions: "Since we cannot go to the Führer with such prospects . . . a . . . [illegible] propaganda action against Roosevelt [can] be started with the threat of a German-Soviet [illegible] . . . 28.4. [43]."[8] While such comments do not indicate serious consideration of peace negotiations, they do document Kaltenbrunner's awareness of what he took to be American willingness to bargain. Moreover, the reports probably strengthened Schellenberg's arguments for Himmler's benefit as well as his own conviction that the anti-Hitler coalition could be dissolved through diplomacy.[9]

While SD agents were talking to Dulles in Switzerland, Kaltenbrunner was taking other steps to pave the way for negotiations with the West—or so he would have us believe. He later claimed that in March 1943 he sent a personal request to Hitler advocating a positive policy statement on relations with the Catholic Church and increased contacts with the Vatican as preliminary gestures for establishing contact with the Allies. These efforts came to naught, however, for Bormann and Himmler convinced the Führer to ig-

[7] "Aktenvermerk" of the United States Ambassador in Bern [Harrison] to Burns [State Department], 7 April 1943 (copy of translation), file RSHA, R 58/441, pp. 40-41, BA, and also in T-175/458/2975043-2975044, NA; report of Ahrends [RSHA VI B (Western Europe, West Africa)] to RSHA VI D, 30 April 1943, File RSHA, R 58/441, pp. 28-33, BA, and T-175/458/2975031-2975036, NA.

[8] "Aufzeichnung über Aussprachen mit Mr. Bull und Mr. Roberts," RSHA VI, n.d., T-175/458/2975014, NA.

[9] Given the illusory flavor which hindsight lent to such machinations, it is understandable that Schellenberg does not refer to these reports in his memoirs. Whether or not he took them seriously is difficult to ascertain; but their contents fit his prescription for a compromise peace in the West.

nore Kaltenbrunner's suggestions. This story is confirmed only by Höttl, who claims to have himself been the driving force behind Kaltenbrunner's initiatives.[10]

Reliable evidence of such activities has not been found, and the story has serious weaknesses. First, it is unlikely that at this time Kaltenbrunner could have suggested anything to Hitler without Bormann or Himmler present, and it is equally unlikely that either would have agreed beforehand to his alleged proposals. Second, Kaltenbrunner unhesitatingly ordered the incarceration of Catholic priests for preaching what he later claimed to believe: that the war was lost. It is possible that the RSHA chief discussed such proposals with Höttl, or even Himmler; on the other hand, there is no irrefutable evidence available to prove that this whole story was not simply a fairytale, invented for the benefit of the Nuremberg Tribunal.

More credible if only because its fantastic nature is characteristic of the fictitious world in which many National Socialists operated was a series of arrangements known as Operation Herzog. In the spring of 1943, at the suggestion of Wilhelm Höttl, who increasingly assumed the same advisory role toward Kaltenbrunner that Schellenberg had toward Himmler, Kaltenbrunner ordered three SS-Obersturmbannführer assigned to the Balkan department of the SD-Ausland (Wilhelm Waneck, Werner Göttsch, and Höttl himself) to take up discreet contact with non-Nazi and anti-Nazi groups in Austria. Höttl, who views himself as the spiritual father of Herzog, believed that in a loosely organized group of "people who could be taken seriously [*ernst zu nehmende Leute*]," i.e., industrialists, businessmen, professionals, and so on, who were willing to use their foreign contacts, a preliminary apparatus for the initiation of peace feelers to the Western Allies could be constructed. If Greater Germany could not be saved, Höttl was content to angle for a settlement based on pre-Anschluss Austria, whereby he thought in terms of a postwar coalition regime of conservatives and crypto-Nazis with anticommunism as its major theme. Non-Nazi groups in Austria would be approached by moderate Nazis of the pre-1938 period: men like Hermann Neubacher, special plenipotentiary of the Foreign Office in the Southeast; SS-Oberführer Kajetan Mühlmann, Göring's "special plenipotentiary for securing valuable works of art in the Occupied Territories"; and Edmund Glaise-Horstenau, German military plenipotentiary in Croatia. The former two had worked closely with the Social Democrats in the Anschluss movement of the 1920s, while Glaise-Horstenau had connections with Catholic and legitimist circles. In retrospect it is difficult to imagine how such persons, tainted as they were with German policy in occupied Europe, could have

[10] Testimony of Kaltenbrunner, IMT XI, pp. 287-288; interrogation of Kaltenbrunner, 19 September 1946, pp. 11-12, ZS-673, IfZ Munich; affidavit of Wilhelm Höttl, 30 March 1946, p. 3, ZS-429/1, IfZ Munich, and IMT XI, pp. 228-231.

won credibility as negotiators; but they appear to have convinced themselves that as Austrians (and thus more civilized Nazis) they could form a viable bridge to the Western Allies based on a common fear of the Soviet Union.[11]

With Kaltenbrunner's permission, Höttl also contacted several low-level Catholic personalities in his native Vienna, many of whom had been enthusiastic Nazis in 1938 but who had since grown disillusioned. Apparently some of these persons had contact with actual opponents of Hitler and sought to provide Höttl with intelligence on anti-Hitler activities within Austria. Höttl was unable to establish any actual contacts with anti-Nazi groups in Vienna until January 1945.[12]

Occasionally, such fanciful lines of thought fathered odd schemes. In late 1943, Göttsch and Waneck came into contact (perhaps by searching a concentration camp) with a Viennese physician named Karl Doppler, who was a high officer of an Austrian Masonic lodge. Doppler aroused Kaltenbrunner's interest because he claimed not only to be a member of the same lodge as American President Franklin D. Roosevelt, but also to have been for a time the Roosevelt family physician and to have once treated Eleanor Roosevelt for a severe illness. Given the tenets of the Nazi myth world, where Freemasonry was a tightly organized international force, it appears to have made perfect sense to Kaltenbrunner and Waneck that the SD smuggle Doppler to Washington via U-boat, where he could personally conduct peace negotiations with his Masonic brother, Franklin Roosevelt.[13]

Höttl also tried his hand at direct contacts with American secret-service agents and claimed to have had some success in Lisbon in 1944. When he suggested to Kaltenbrunner that the Americans be approached with proposals for a separate peace with an independent Austria, however, the RSHA chief flatly forbade him to maintain any contacts with the enemy.[14]

While Kaltenbrunner alternately considered and forbade Höttl's schemes for peace in the West, others in the SS hierarchy turned East. In late September 1944, after a visit to the Western Front, SS Main Office chief Gottlob Berger wrote Himmler, urging an approach to the Soviet Union. Berger reasoned that if the Russians could be induced to sign an armistice stabilizing the front along a line including Warsaw and the eastern foothills of the Carpathians, the Germans could push the Western Front back to the Somme and hold out there indefinitely. In addition, he predicted, Roosevelt and

[11] Höttl Tape, p. 21; letter of Dr. Wilhelm Höttl to the author, 15 June 1977; statement of Höttl, 6 October 1945, 1899-PS, NA.

[12] Statement of Höttl, 6 October 1945, 1899-PS, NA; letter of Höttl to the author, 8 November 1979.

[13] Statement of Höttl, 6 October 1945, 1899-PS, NA; Höttl Tape, p. 21; interrogation of Kaltenbrunner, 19 September 1946, pp. 10-11, ZS-673, IfZ Munich; Lennon Report, p. 4.

[14] Statement of Höttl, 6 October 1945, 1899-PS, NA.

9. SS-Brigadeführer Ernst Kaltenbrunner, 1939 (Bundesarchiv, Koblenz).

10. Inside hall of Gestapo Headquarters (later RSHA), Berlin, Prinz-Albrecht-Strasse 8, 1934 (Bundesarchiv, Koblenz).

11. Kaltenbrunner (center, arms folded) listens to proceedings against a 20 July conspirator before Freisler's People's Court, 1944 (Bundesarchiv, Koblenz).

12. Hitler (left), Himmler (center), and Bormann (right) at a Reichstag session, 1939 (RG-242/HLB-2776-24, National Archives).

13. (*Left*) Chief of the SD-Ausland Walter Schellenberg (front) and Otto Skorzeny, the rescuer of Mussolini, 1943 (Bundesarchiv, Koblenz).

14. (*Below*) Kaltenbrunner in Nuremberg after his second brain hemorrhage, 1946 (RG-238/NTA-88, National Archives).

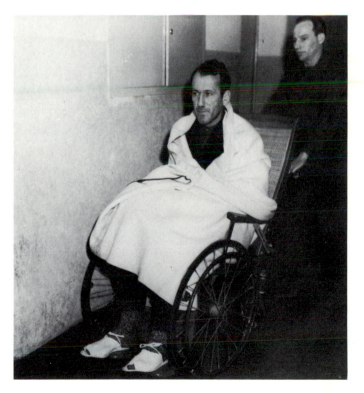

15. Former SD men as witnesses in Nuremberg, 1946. Left to right: Alfred Naujocks, Viktor Lischka, Wilhelm Höttl, Walter Schellenberg (RG-238/NT-443, National Archives).

16. Keitel (left), Kaltenbrunner (center), and Ribbentrop (right) compare notes on the defendants' dock at Nuremberg, 1946 (RG-238/NTA-27, National Archives).

Churchill could not survive such a diplomatic coup. Nor was Kaltenbrunner completely unreceptive to possibilities for armistice in the East. On 1 April 1944, he informed Propaganda Minister Josef Goebbels that, according to intelligence gleaned from recent Soviet prisoners of war and deserters, Soviet army propaganda was depicting the major Soviet war aim as a restoration of the borders of 1941, followed by a separate peace with Germany.[15]

In fact, the Soviet government had explored the possibility of such an arrangement periodically after the fall of 1942. Motivated in part by Stalin's mistrust of Western intentions and exacerbated by the long delay in the establishment of the Second Front, the Soviet initiatives appear indeed to have aimed at restoring the Soviet-German border of 1941.[16] Most Nazi leaders showed little interest in these feelers; to abandon the crude concept of Lebensraum and to revise the image of the Slavic-Asiatic *Untermensch* was far too painful and difficult for their ideologically inflexible Weltanschauung.

Despite the prevailing attitudes, the vague reports of Soviet feelers aroused Kaltenbrunner's interest. On 19 June 1943, he learned from SS-Standartenführer Peter Kleist, the chief of the central office for Eastern Europe in the Ribbentrop Special Bureau, that the Soviets were suspicious of an Anglo-American landing in the Balkans and were weary of fighting for Anglo-American interests. Kleist had been contacted in Stockholm by a businessman of Baltic-German descent named Edgar Clauss, who had reported that A. M. Alexandrov, chief of the European Division in the Soviet Commissariat for Foreign Affairs, would be in Stockholm on 7 July and urgently wished to talk to a German representative. Kleist urged Kaltenbrunner to follow up the Alexandrov contact in view of the military situation. Kaltenbrunner seemed interested, but expressed concern over an Abwehr report which maintained that both Clauss and Alexandrov were Jews. Hitler, who had been approached in the Alexandrov affair by Ribbentrop (to whom Kleist also reported), had flown into such a rage upon receiving this report that no one dared to pursue the matter. Kaltenbrunner therefore declined to make any initiatives of his own, but insisted that Kleist refrain from keeping Ribbentrop informed of future developments. The RSHA chief wanted a head start on the foreign minister should Hitler change his mind.[17]

[15] Berger to Himmler, 26 September 1944, in Heiber, *Reichsführer!* p. 366; Kaltenbrunner to Goebbels, 1 April 1944, Occ E (RA)—2, Berlin Collection, YIVO Institute for Jewish Research, New York City.

[16] Vojtech Mastny, "Stalin and the Prospects of a Separate Peace in World War II," *American Historical Review*, 77 (December 1972), 1365-1388; Fischer, *Deutschlandpolitik*, pp. 38-45.

[17] Peter Kleist, *Zwischen Hitler und Stalin, 1939-1945* (Bonn: Athenäum, 1950), pp. 244-250. See also the expanded version of Kleist's memoirs, *Die europäische Tragödie* (Göttingen: Verlag K. W. Schütz, 1971), pp. 185-189, 190-192. Vojtech Mastny has uncovered other

After a second Soviet feeler to Kleist was buried by Ribbentrop's disapproval in September 1943, Kleist was determined to steer all future initiatives into the offices of the SD. On 3 August 1944, he appeared in Schellenberg's office, reported that he had been contacted again, and urged that the SD pressure Ribbentrop into action. Convinced that Kleist's story was genuine, Schellenberg informed Kaltenbrunner; and, while the RSHA chief studied Kleist's report, Kleist himself was contacted again in Stockholm by Clauss, who informed him that a Soviet General Gilbich, a participant in the Finno-Soviet armistice negotiations, wished to talk to him. According to Clauss, the Soviets were concerned about the rapid Allied advance through France and feared Anglo-American landings in Denmark, Greece, and Bulgaria, where the Germans might be tempted not to resist. Kleist hurried back to Berlin to inform Ribbentrop and Kaltenbrunner and to press for authorization to meet Gilbich. Each rival stalled for time, partly out of fear that the other would denounce him to Hitler and partly out of suspicion concerning the authenticity of the feeler. When Kleist finally returned to Stockholm on September 16—still without authorization—the Finns had signed an armistice and Gilbich had returned to the Soviet Union. While trying to reconstruct the broken threads through Clauss, who had reported a flicker of Soviet interest in early October, Kleist was recalled to Berlin by Ribbentrop. Expressing his disappointment to Schellenberg and Kaltenbrunner, Kleist lamented that the opportunity for negotiations with the Soviets was now irretrievably lost.[18]

Whether or not the Soviet feelers in the late summer of 1944 were genuine remains a mystery; important for our purposes is the fact that Kleist and Kaltenbrunner considered them so. Moreover, Kaltenbrunner's treatment of the affair was consistent with his behavior during later peace initiatives. That he was genuinely interested in negotiating with the Soviets is unlikely; he probably hoped merely to use the threat of a German-Soviet rapprochement to frighten the Allies. Whatever his motives, however, he found his hands tied both by his loyalty to Hitler, who was unenthusiastic about peace feelers of any kind, and his fear of denunciation by his old rival, Ribbentrop. Thus, he could make no initiative, and looked on as the Nazi catastrophe un-

---

indications of Soviet feelers to the Germans at this time in Stockholm and suggests that Stalin's disappointment at the Roosevelt-Churchill announcement of 4 June 1943, which postponed the opening of the Second Front until 1944, may have motivated these efforts. See Mastny, "Stalin," pp. 1377-1379.

[18] Memorandum for the chief of the Security Police and the SD, signed Schellenberg, 4 August 1944, File RSHA, R 58/1225, BA; unsigned notice from Amt VI RSHA, 4 August 1944, ibid.; notice of Kleist for the foreign minister, 7 September 1944, ibid.; Kaltenbrunner to Himmler, 9 October 1944, ibid.; Kleist to Schellenberg, 10 October 1944, ibid. On September 1943 feeler, see Kleist, Tragödie, pp. 198-204; Mastny, "Stalin," p. 1383.

folded. This pattern would be repeated during the haphazard and confused efforts to contact the Western Allies in 1944-1945.

Personal rivalry played a key role in Kaltenbrunner's attitude toward the efforts of Himmler and SS-Obersturmbannführer Kurt Becher, the representative of the SS Operations Main Office in occupied Hungary, to negotiate with representatives of the Jewish Joint Distribution Committee in Switzerland during the summer and fall of 1944. In June, through Becher, Himmler had first attempted to exchange Hungarian Jews with the governments of the Western Allies for trucks and war supplies to be used on the Eastern Front. When in July it became apparent that the Allies were not interested in this kind of business relationship, Himmler's agents explored the possibility of selling the Hungarian Jews to international Jewish organizations for hard currency, which would then be used to buy materiel from neutral countries. Thus, in a grotesque irony, Himmler had convinced himself that the key to the Reich's salvation lay with the people which for three years he had been annihilating as its greatest enemy, the Jews. Victims of their own propaganda, Himmler and Becher indulged themselves in the illusion that once a good business relationship had been established between the SS and World Jewry, the latter would exercise its legendary influence to induce the Allies to open peace negotiations. Jewish leaders in Budapest and Jewish negotiators in Switzerland were aware of this mentality and exploited it to the full. Himmler showed his "good faith" by dumping 318 Jews into Switzerland on 21 August 1944 and permitting a further 1,684 to enter that country by train in early December, but the Becher talks with Saly Mayer, representative of the Jewish Joint Distribution Committee in Switzerland, yielded no practical result for the Germans.[19] On the other hand, Becher claimed in connection with the Mayer negotiations to have convinced Himmler in October 1944 to issue orders to Kaltenbrunner and Pohl forbidding any further liquidation of the Jews.[20]

[19] For more detailed accounts of the Becher-Mayer negotiations, see Biss, *Endlösung*, pp. 148-251, 268-270; Höhne, *SS*, pp. 638-641; Hilberg, *Destruction*, pp. 543-545; Reitlinger, *Final Solution*, pp. 472-478, 482; Yehuda Bauer, "The Negotiations between Saly Mayer and the Representatives of the SS in 1944-1945," in *Rescue Attempts during the Holocaust* (Jerusalem: Yad Vashem, 1977), pp. 5-45.

[20] Affidavit of Becher, 8 March 1946, 3762-PS, IMT xxxiii, pp. 68-70. There is still considerable confusion as to the exact date of the alleged Himmler order, which itself has not come to light. Becher testified that the order came in September or October, but Rezsö Kasztner, one of the leaders of the Jewish Rescue Committee in Budapest, maintained that Becher had shown him a written order to halt the extermination of the Jews—dated 25 November 1944. Affidavit of Kasztner, 13 September 1945, 2605-PS, IMT xxxi, p. 13. Raul Hilberg (*Destruction*, p. 631) has accepted this date, though not Becher's influence in bringing about the order. Andreas Biss, a close collaborator of Kasztner, reported (*Endlösung*, pp. 178, 236-237) that SS-Hauptsturmführer Otto Clages, chief of the SD office in Budapest, informed him on 30 September 1944 that Himmler was prepared to halt the gassings at Auschwitz. Biss learned from

Kaltenbrunner knew of the Himmler-Becher initiatives at least by the end of August, for the chief of the SD office in Budapest, SS-Hauptsturmführer Otto Clages, who had contact with the Jewish Rescue Committee in Budapest, reported regularly to Höttl, the chief of the Hungary desk in the SD-Ausland office. That the RSHA chief passively cooperated with Himmler in this dubious enterprise at least until November 1944 is evident from the fact that the RSHA informed puzzled Foreign Office officials on 9 November not only that 318 Jews had been permitted to leave Germany for Switzerland in August 1944 in exchange for vital war materiel, but also that a transaction involving a further 1,000 Jews was in preparation. But neither Kaltenbrunner nor his subordinates, Schellenberg and Höttl, could endure the fact that Himmler was bypassing them—the leaders of the Reich intelligence service—and using the interloper Becher to forge a contact with the West. In Kaltenbrunner's case it is also possible that he questioned the point in allowing "dangerous enemies" of the Reich to escape, for his ideological makeup was not as subtly flexible as that of Himmler. At any rate, in mid-November, the RSHA chief denounced the Becher-Himmler operation to Hitler. Surprisingly (and no doubt to Kaltenbrunner's dismay), the Führer did not react. Neither Himmler nor Becher was punished or reprimanded in any way. Thus excluded, Kaltenbrunner determined henceforth to sabotage any peace initiatives coming from Himmler that did not provide him with a major but protected role. His claim at Nuremberg that the gassings at Auschwitz were halted by a Hitler order issued on his (Kaltenbrunner's) advice in October 1944 is absurd.[21]

Walter Schellenberg was also irritated by Becher's negotiations with the Joint Distribution Committee in Switzerland, for he feared that such efforts would interfere with his own operation. In late 1943, the SD-Ausland chief had established contact with the Swiss conservative politician Jean-Marie Musy, who had close contacts with Rabbi Isaac Sternbuch of the Union of Orthodox Rabbis in the United States. Like Becher, Schellenberg believed that World Jewry could somehow be induced to intercede on behalf of the dying Reich; and, after long, arduous negotiations, he arranged a Himmler-Musy meeting in October 1944. Musy promised to speak to Jewish leaders

---

Becher, however, that a written order to this effect was issued only on 18 November. If mid-November was its actual time, the order appears less as a token of good faith than as a military necessity, for, in mid-November, Himmler also ordered the destruction of the gas chambers themselves so that they would not fall into Soviet hands. See Reitlinger, *Final Solution*, p. 497.

[21] On Kaltenbrunner information to the Foreign Office, see memorandum of Thadden, 5 October 1944, T-120/1757/E025316-E025317, NA; memorandum of Wagner, 9 November 1944, ibid., E025322-E025323. On denunciation of Becher, see testimony of Kaltenbrunner, IMT xi, pp. 335-336.

in Switzerland if Himmler would release a number of prominent Jews and Frenchmen. Though the Reichsführer SS accepted this deal, he feared Hitler too much to carry out his side, and Gestapo chief Müller was able to delay the releases indefinitely.

A few weeks later, Musy wrote Himmler and informed him that through contacts with the Union of Orthodox Rabbis, he had arranged that a fund of twenty million Swiss francs be established to pay for the liberation of all Jews remaining in German hands. Advising Himmler to act quickly in order to secure the most favorable press, he offered to set up another meeting. Himmler, however, still waiting in vain for results from the Becher negotiations and at the same time renewing his loyalty to Hitler as commander in chief of Army Group Upper Rhine, dawdled until the turn of the year. Finally, on 12 January 1945, he met Musy at Wildbad in the Black Forest and, under the patient persuasion of Musy and Schellenberg, agreed to ship twelve hundred Jews to Switzerland by train every two weeks. For each Jew a sum of $1,000 for the purchase of trucks and war materiel would be deposited into a Swiss account under Musy's name. Musy expressed his delight and skillfully led Himmler to believe that the solution of the Jewish question was merely a side issue "through which a larger development could be introduced." On 6 February 1945, the first shipment of Jews, all chosen from Theresienstadt, arrived in Switzerland and five million francs were duly deposited in the account controlled by Musy.[22]

Though perhaps unaware of the exact details, Kaltenbrunner had heard of the Schellenberg-Musy contact; there is even some suspicion that he helped Schellenberg to discredit Becher's operation before finally denouncing it to Hitler. Yet, his hatred and jealousy were aroused by Schellenberg's success in excluding him from the Musy negotiations, which he sought an excuse to denounce. In mid-February 1945, his agents intercepted a telegram from one of General de Gaulle's intelligence centers in Spain alleging that Himmler and Schellenberg had negotiated with Musy about asylum for 250 Nazi leaders in Switzerland. Kaltenbrunner made sure that this message and numerous copies of press reports describing the arrival in Switzerland of the first transport of Jews were presented to Hitler. The Führer then declared

---

[22] On first Himmler-Musy meeting, see Schellenberg, *Secret Service*, p. 370. On intense Schellenberg-Becher rivalry, see Schellenberg to Hilel Storch [representative of the World Jewish Congress in New York], 17 June 1945, in Schellenberg, *Memoiren*, pp. 392-394. On second Himmler-Musy meeting, see Musy to Himmler, 18 November 1944, T-175/118/2643521-2643523, NA; report initialed by Himmler, 18 January 1945, ibid., 2643519-2643520; Schellenberg, *Secret Service*, p. 371. On first shipment of Jews, see Reitlinger, *Final Solution*, p. 502. Though Himmler and Musy negotiated in dollar amounts at Wildbad, Swiss francs were deposited in the blocked account in Musy's name.

that any German who helped a Jew escape would be executed on the spot. In a panic, Himmler called off the transports.[23]

Kaltenbrunner's hostility toward the Himmler-Musy negotiations may have been prompted by the fact that they conflicted with other efforts to ransom off the surviving Jews in Germany in which he himself hoped to play a major role. On 20 September 1944, Peter Kleist had conferred secretly with Hilel Storch, a representative of the World Jewish Congress in New York, in a Stockholm hotel. Storch, who had contacted Kleist through the indefatigable Edgar Clauss, said he was prepared to offer the SS $500,000 per head for the lives of some forty-five hundred Czech, Dutch, and Belgian Jews interned in Tallinn and Kretinga. Although Kleist had had few moral scruples about joining an organization and serving a system that had murdered millions of human beings, he was "highly indignant" that Storch would assume that he or any "half-civilized Central European" would be willing to participate in "such filthy traffic in human beings." When Storch, however, who was obviously bluffing for time, intimated that President Roosevelt himself was willing to negotiate for the lives of all Jews remaining in German captivity, Kleist's scruples evaporated; and when Storch declared that Roosevelt would offer a political solution to the war in return for the lives of some 1.5 million Jews believed to be interned in Germany, Kleist hurried back to Berlin to inform Kaltenbrunner. Though intrigued at the offer, Kaltenbrunner felt compelled to inform Himmler. Kleist was told to go home and sit tight.

A few days later, Kaltenbrunner summoned Kleist. Himmler's reaction had apparently been favorable, for the RSHA chief remarked that the Reich had 2.5 million Jews to offer and that Kleist himself would be sent to Stockholm immediately to handle the negotiations. As a token of good faith, two thousand Jews would accompany the new emissary to the Swedish capital. In early October, however, Kaltenbrunner summoned Kleist again and told him that the Stockholm contact would not be pursued. Apparently Schellenberg had convinced Himmler to dump Kleist, neutralize Kaltenbrunner, and send out his own feelers to the World Jewish Congress.[24] In addition, the Musy negotiations, Schellenberg's own pet project, had just gotten under way. It is thus not surprising that Kaltenbrunner was hostile to them.

After the collapse of the Musy "action," Himmler transferred his hopes to another potential mediator, Count Folke Bernadotte, vice-president of the Swedish Red Cross. During the fall of 1944, the Swedes had come under

---

[23] On possible Schellenberg-Kaltenbrunner collaboration against Becher, see Rezsö Kasztner, "Der Bericht des jüdischen Rettungskomitees aus Budapest 1942-1945," 1946, p. 159, Eichmann Document 900, EPD, IfZ Munich. On Kaltenbrunner's role in the Musy negotiations, see Schellenberg, *Secret Service*, p. 371; testimony of Kaltenbrunner, IMT xi, pp. 279-280.

[24] Kleist, *Tragödie*, pp. 217-221.

increasing Allied pressure to enter the war against Germany. Preferring not to do so, the Swedish government opted instead to sponsor a rescue action on behalf of Scandinavian internees in Germany. Through the services of Himmler's masseur, Felix Kersten, the Swedish government induced Himmler on 8 December 1944 to agree to concentrate all Scandinavian internees in the camp Neuengamme near Hamburg, where they would be cared for by the Swedish Red Cross. Himmler also consented to release from Ravens-brück twenty-eight hundred women of various nationalities.[25] The Swedes offered to provide transport, but Himmler was in no hurry to carry out his part of the agreement, perhaps because he had greater hopes for the Musy action. The breakdown of this action, however, coincided with the arrival of the Swedish Red Cross representative, Count Bernadotte, in Berlin on 16 February 1945.

Though the purpose of Bernadotte's trip was to settle the details for the transfers and releases agreed to on 8 December 1944, Schellenberg and Kersten hoped that the count would convince Himmler to make a final break with Hitler and to initiate peace and/or surrender negotiations with the Western Allies via agreements on concentration-camp prisoners. When Bernadotte arrived, however, Himmler turned timid, isolated himself at his headquarters, and ordered Kaltenbrunner to receive the count. Making a virtue out of the necessity, Schellenberg hoped that Kaltenbrunner's inclusion would neutralize his potential opposition. Kaltenbrunner himself, who felt somewhat exposed, phoned Hitler's headquarters to learn the Führer's attitude to Bernadotte's mission. According to Himmler's liaison officer at Hitler's headquarters, SS-Brigadeführer Hermann Fegelein, the dictator had declared, "One cannot accomplish anything with this sort of nonsense in a total war."[26]

Nevertheless, Kaltenbrunner received Bernadotte on 17 February. Offering Chesterfield cigarettes and Dubonnet, the RSHA chief politely asked his guest the purpose of his visit. Though Bernadotte was reluctant to talk to anyone but Himmler, he finally expressed his hope that the Swedish Red Cross would be permitted to work in the internment camp for Scandinavian prisoners. Kaltenbrunner nodded his agreement, but pushed responsibility for such a measure onto Himmler. After the count had left Kaltenbrunner's office, Schellenberg further softened the RSHA chief with the unctuous statement that Kaltenbrunner handled the Bernadotte interview "in the best traditions of the old Austrian school of diplomacy." Kaltenbrunner's enthusiasm for the Bernadotte contact quickly evaporated, however, when Himm-

---

[25] Felix Kersten, *The Kersten Memoirs, 1940-1945* (New York: Macmillan, 1957), pp. 226-232; Höhne, *SS*, pp. 642-643.

[26] Schellenberg, *Secret Service*, pp. 374-375.

ler, who only with great difficulty could be persuaded to see Bernadotte at all, insisted that the RSHA chief be excluded from the talks.[27]

Bernadotte saw Himmler in Schellenberg's presence on 19 February 1945 at Hohenlychen sanitarium, where the Reichsführer SS spent most of his time as chief of Army Group Vistula. The count proposed the transfer of all Scandinavian internees in Germany to Sweden, but Schellenberg and Himmler insisted on adhering to the Neuengamme plan of 8 December. While Bernadotte returned to Sweden with mixed feelings, Schellenberg passed Himmler's orders to assemble the Scandinavians at Neuengamme to Kaltenbrunner and Müller. Both objected that Neuengamme was insufficiently equipped to receive such a large influx of prisoners and that there were no trucks for transport. Kaltenbrunner bluntly revealed his attitude toward the project to Bernadotte during the count's second visit to Berlin on 5 March, saying that no support could be expected from him.[28] As for the prisoners, they were finally transported to Neuengamme on Swedish Red Cross trucks in April 1945.

With the advantage of hindsight, such feeble efforts at negotiations seem ludicrous. Each SS leader saw himself alone as the savior of Germany and was desperately jealous of all others with similar ambitions. Moreover, on

[27] On the Bernadotte-Kaltenbrunner talk, see Bernadotte, *Curtain*, pp. 25-30. On Schellenberg's flattery and Kaltenbrunner's exclusion from the talks, see Schellenberg, *Secret Service*, pp. 375-376.

[28] On Bernadotte-Himmler meeting, see Bernadotte, *Curtain*, pp. 48-59; Schellenberg, *Secret Service*, pp. 376-377. On Kaltenbrunner's opposition to Bernadotte, see Bernadotte, *Curtain*, p. 66. According to Schellenberg, Kaltenbrunner resisted efforts to release concentration-camp prisoners down to the end of the war. When Schellenberg suggested in late March that Himmler offer the Allies via Musy a four-day truce in order to permit all Jewish and foreign internees to pass through the Allied lines, Himmler told him to ask Kaltenbrunner; the RSHA chief simply inquired whether Schellenberg had gone mad. Kaltenbrunner also blocked Schellenberg's efforts to release the French politicians Edouard Herriot and Paul Reynaud. Finally, when Schellenberg suggested that Himmler receive Hilel Storch in mid-April 1945 to discuss the release of Jewish internees, Himmler allegedly exclaimed: "How am I going to do that with Kaltenbrunner around? I shall be completely at his mercy!" See Schellenberg, *Secret Service*, pp. 371-373; affidavit of Schellenberg, 19 November 1945, 2990-PS, IMT xxxi, pp. 439-441. That Kaltenbrunner was behind these efforts to sabotage Schellenberg's plans is debatable. Schellenberg had practical and personal reasons for painting his rival in the blackest terms; and his allegations are documented by no other source. Moreover, after the Kaltenbrunner-Bernadotte meeting of 5 March 1945, the RSHA chief spent most of his time at his headquarters in Austria, alternately toying with peace projects of his own and fantasies of continued resistance. Finally, the rapid Allied advance after the Americans crossed the Rhine on 7 March accelerated the breakdown of central authority and communications in the Third Reich. After this time, it is unlikely that Kaltenbrunner, from his isolated position in Austria, could have exerted as much influence as Schellenberg suggests. What does seem plausible is not only that Himmler genuinely feared Kaltenbrunner's intervention, but also that Schellenberg mistook (or deliberately distorted) Himmler's own ideological opposition to extensive concessions for fear.

the other side, divisiveness and rivalry were also rampant. The Joint Distribution Committee, its nominal representative Saly Mayer, and the Union of Orthodox Rabbis vied with one another to save the Hungarian Jews; the initiative of the World Jewish Congress was totally uncoordinated with other efforts and hence totally ineffective. Finally, Bernadotte and Kersten fought so bitterly over the credit for the undoubtedly humanitarian action which they helped to implement that Kersten invented a Bernadotte "letter" to Himmler in which the count "stated" that the Jews were not desired in Sweden. While their captors and would-be rescuers wrangled over the honor of saving them, the unfortunate objects of these abortive negotiations died by the hundreds of thousands from hunger and disease in the last two months of the war.[29]

The negotiations failed to bring about any major humanitarian actions on behalf of the concentration-camp prisoners chiefly because neither Himmler nor Kaltenbrunner saw them in this light. Whereas the Jewish organizations and the Red Cross counted on a German collapse and were thus stalling until it developed, Himmler and Kaltenbrunner believed that the only inevitable collapse was that of the Grand Alliance and sought to use their miserable hostages to gain time until events turned to their advantage. In fact, neither Himmler nor Kaltenbrunner had reconciled himself to the possibility of defeat; for parallel to the abortive negotiations, each participated in equally futile measures for the military defense of the Reich.

Though enemy troops crossed the borders of the old Reich in the late summer of 1944, the Nazi leadership clung to the illusion of final victory through the utilization of "wonder weapons" and/or the exploitation of a diplomatic realignment. After all, Hitler had often achieved a dramatic success when times had seemed dark in the past. Final victory depended on the will of the German people to hold out until the miracle could develop; it required ruthlessness and endurance. As early as 7 February 1944, OKW chief Keitel warned military commanders that "capitulation, discontinuation of resistance or retreat do not exist [as options] for fortress and field commanders. For the fortress or field commander, the area entrusted to him is his destiny. The commander of a ship also goes down with it under an unfurled flag. The history of the German soldier knows no other conception." Himmler was not to be left behind in his determination to fight on until the end. When in November 1944 Hitler gave orders to all troop commanders who viewed the military situation as hopeless to relinquish their commands to more determined subordinates, Himmler ordered that

---

[29] For the text of the Bernadotte letter and the story of its invention, see Gerald Fleming, "Die Herkunft des 'Bernadotte-Briefs' an Himmler vom 10. März 1945," VfZ, 26 (October 1978), 571-600. For rivalries in the Jewish camp, see Bauer, "Saly Mayer," pp. 38-41. See ibid., pp. 43-45 for a more favorable assessment of the effect of the negotiations.

copies of the Führer decree be personally presented to officers and noncommissioned officers in the Security Police, the Orpo, and the Waffen SS, and that it be conveyed orally to all soldiers and low-level police officials. The Reichsführer SS exhorted all members of the SS and police to "accept . . . this order with the iron will never to surrender anywhere, regardless of how small the remaining force [of men] is." Kaltenbrunner ordered the decree to be distributed immediately and that he be informed by 15 January 1945 that this had been done.[30] In addition, detailed, fanciful plans for guerrilla warfare on German soil behind enemy lines were submitted to Himmler's office down to the last weeks of the war.[31]

Though few practical steps were taken to implement it in any coordinated fashion, a plan for underground resistance received a great deal of publicity and influenced Allied military strategy toward the end of the war: Operation Werewolf. Concocted by Himmler in late November 1944 at a meeting at Hohenlychen, which included Kaltenbrunner, Schellenberg, Otto Skorzeny (the rescuer of Mussolini), and SS-Obergruppenführer Hans Prützmann, Werewolf foresaw the formation of civilian terrorist bands behind the Allied lines with the double purpose of performing acts of sabotage and murdering German officials who dared to cooperate with the occupying powers. Despite one spectacular exception in Aachen, where the American-appointed mayor, Franz Oppenhoff, was murdered, the Werewolf organization remained a phantom, nourished by the healthy imaginations of officials in the Goebbels Propaganda Ministry.[32]

[30] Circular of Keitel, 7 February 1944, T-175/69/2586319-2586320, NA; decree of Hitler, November 1944, File RSHA, R 58/243, p. 318, BA; circular of Himmler to chiefs of the SS Operations Main Office, the RSHA, and the Hauptamt Orpo, 6 December 1944, ibid., p. 313; circular of Kaltenbrunner to Security Police and SD offices, 18 December 1944, ibid., p. 315.

[31] For examples, see Hildebrandt to Himmler, n.d. [probably December 1944], T-175/219/2757424-2757425, NA; unsigned draft memorandum entitled, "Deutsche Freiheitsbewegung," Berlin, 3 April 1945, T-77/775/5500617-5500621, NA; memorandum of Kreisleiter Kotzler, "Vorschläge zum Aufbau einer Widerstandsbewegung in den von den Bolschewisten besetzten deutschen Ostgebieten," 23 January 1945, T-175/32/2540300-2540302, NA.

[32] On Werewolf, see Otto Skorzeny, Meine Kommandounternehmen: Krieg ohne Fronten (Wiesbaden-Munich: Limes Verlag, 1976), pp. 194-195; Charles Whiting, Hitler's Werewolves: The Story of the Nazi Resistance Movement, 1944-1945 (New York: Stein & Day, 1972), pp. 66-70. On ineffectiveness of Werewolf, see Orlow, Nazi Party, 1933-1945, p. 481; Hermann Meyerhoff, Herne 1933-1945: Die Zeit des Nationalsozialismus (Herne: C. Th. Kartenberg, 1963), p. 142; Hugh R. Trevor-Roper, The Last Days of Hitler, 4th ed. (London: Macmillan, 1971), pp. 50-54; Peter R. Black, "The Resistance that Never Was," unpublished seminar paper, Columbia University, 1973, pp. 1-11. Though few Nazis outside of Goebbels took Werewolf seriously, allied fears of bands of Werewolf fanatics holding out in the Alps helped influence Eisenhower's decision to abandon the chase for Berlin and Prague and to move the bulk of the Anglo-American troops toward the Bavarian and Austrian Alps. Werewolf propaganda also caused some concern on the part of German officials who managed the administration of German cities under Allied occupation. See Karl Stroelin [mayor of Stuttgart] to Hofmann [HSSPF in Baden-Württemberg], 5 April 1945, T-175/223/2760624, NA.

Another phantom to which Kaltenbrunner paid more attention was the so-called Alpine Redoubt (*Alpenfestung*), which was to be established in the Bavarian and Austrian Alps as an impregnable complex for the last stand of the Nazi regime. The idea of a fortress in the Alps, where small, well-trained forces could hold out indefinitely with limited supplies against a technically and numerically superior enemy, had originated with the Swiss, who in 1940-1942 constructed a massive internal fortifications system both as a deterrent to Axis invasion and as a center of continued resistance in the event of such an invasion. In September 1943, when the Italian surrender raised the possibility of a German withdrawal to defensive positions in the southern Alps, German army engineers began to explore the feasibility of a German redoubt; but Nazi faith in total victory excluded any such plans from official consideration. In late May 1944, Himmler, in one of his more practical moods, considered the prospects of fortifications construction in the Alps and even sent a team of geologists to study the region; but by mid-September it was clear that little or nothing had been done in terms of practical measures. It was not until September 1944 that the OKW commissioned an engineering team to prepare a study of proposed areas for defense in the western and southern Austrian Alps. Even this project, owing to inclement weather, was still far from complete in January 1945.[33]

Although in reality there was thus neither any semblance of a fortifications system in the Austro-Bavarian Alps nor any concrete plans to build, equip, and man such a system, the Allied High Command was concerned about the possibility of a Nazi last stand in the mountains, and this concern became known to the SD in the early autumn of 1944. In late September, the SD Branch Office in Bregenz intercepted an American diplomatic report in which it was speculated that the Germans, in the event of a military collapse in the spring of 1945, might hold out for as long as six months from fortified positions in the Alps and that no American commander would take the responsibility for the heavy losses incurred in an assault on the Alpine positions. The chief of the SD office in Bregenz, SS-Sturmbannführer Christian Gontard, forwarded the report on to the RSHA in Berlin, but also sent a copy to the Gauleiter of Tyrol-Vorarlberg, Franz Hofer. After six weeks of hesitation, Hofer wrote a memorandum for the Party Chancellery, suggesting that Hitler give immediate orders for the construction of an Alpine for-

[33] On Swiss Redoubt and Wehrmacht interest, see Jon Kimche, *Spying for Peace: General Guisan and Swiss Neutrality*, 3rd ed. (New York: Roy Publishers, 1962), pp. 27-57; Rodney Minott, *The Fortress That Never Was: The Myth of Hitler's Bavarian Stronghold* (New York–Chicago–San Francisco: Holt, Reinhart & Winston, 1964), pp. 10-14. On Himmler's interest, see staff of Reichsführer SS to Sievers, 5 June 1944, T-175/137/2664687, NA; Himmler to Wolff, 2 June 1944, ibid., 2664726; Hagen, *Geheime Front*, p. 458. On actual lack of serious preparations, see report of General Frattali [officer in the Salò Fascist Republican Army], 12 September 1944, T-175/137/2664685-2664686, NA. On the issue of abortive SS preparations, see Black, "Resistance," p. 13.

tress that would realize the Americans' nightmare. In Berlin, Bormann was too engrossed in his Führer's pipedream of a successful Ardennes offensive to have much interest in the fantasies of others. He suppressed the Hofer memorandum. In January 1945, however, when the failure of the Ardennes offensive had become apparent, Propaganda Minister Goebbels, who had noted in Allied and neutral press clippings the Anglo-American concern about an Alpine campaign, ordered his officials to feed Allied fears by discreetly sending out imaginary material depicting a mountain redoubt stocked with weapons from underground factories and manned by elite troops. In the new atmosphere, Bormann presented Hofer's memorandum to Hitler, who thereupon gave orders to begin construction of defense fortifications at once.[34]

Now that the Führer himself had blessed the idea of an Alpine fortress to frighten the Allies into political concessions, SD officials felt bold enough to indulge in their own illusions concerning the political possibilities of exploiting the Allied concern. Yet, the SD-Ausland was seriously divided on aims and methods. Schellenberg, convinced that only Musy, Bernadotte, or Storch could open the door to the Anglo-American leadership, was indifferent to visions of an Alpine decoy. On the other hand, the Austrian clique (Höttl, Waneck, and Göttsch) hoped to bargain on the basis of the redoubt for an Anglo-American occupation of Austria. They were probably encouraged in this direction by their collaborators from Herzog, Glaise-Horstenau and Neubacher. These Austrian-born dreamers contacted General Alexander Löhr, commander of the German Army Group H on the Austro-Slovenian border, and—later—General Lothar Rendulic, who commanded Army Group E on the Austro-Hungarian border; they came away convinced that both Austrian-born generals would support the plan. In addition, Glaise-Horstenau's contacts on the staffs of Field Marshals Albert Kesselring (Army Group Southwest—Italy), Ferdinand Schörner (Bohemia and Moravia), and Gerd von Rundstedt (commander in chief of the Western Front) assured the support of their commanders for a calculated withdrawal into the Alpine regions in the event that initial negotiations for a separate peace seemed favorable. What the plan lacked, however, was "a personality who could appear as the decisive man within the borders of the territory closed off by the Alpine fortress." This figure had to possess the power and will to make peace and prevent last-ditch destruction plans inspired by the Gauleiter.[35]

[34] Franz Hofer, "Alpen-Reduit," 25 June 1946, in Karl Stuhlpfarrer, *Die Operationszonen "Alpenvorland" und "Adriatisches Küstenland" 1943-1945* (Vienna: Verlag Brüder Hollinek, 1969), pp. 159-166; statement of Gontard, 2 May 1946, in ibid., p. 161. See also ibid., pp. 118-119; Minott, *Fortress*, pp. 18-19. On Hitler's orders, see Hagen, *Bernhard*, pp. 231-232; Minott, *Fortress*, pp. 24-26.

[35] On Schellenberg's attitude, see Höttl Tape, p. 22. On Austrians and contacts with generals, see Hagen, *Geheime Front*, pp. 458-460. On need for decisive personality, see ibid., pp. 459-460.

Höttl could think of only one candidate who possessed the necessary political clout and who at the same time might be won for an "Austrian solution": RSHA chief Ernst Kaltenbrunner. When Kaltenbrunner arrived in the Styrian mountain town of Alt Aussee on 8 March 1945 (presumably on a visit to his mistress, Countess Gisela von Westarp, who had rented a small villa there), Höttl found an opportunity to approach him. How clearly the SD man presented his ideas—which implied capitulation to the Western Allies—is unknown, but, to his great dismay, Kaltenbrunner showed little interest in the "Austrian solution" and instead began to speculate on political options stemming from a determined defense of the Alps. On 15 March Kaltenbrunner summoned Höttl and declared in all seriousness that it would be possible to defend positions in the Tyrol and Vorarlberg. He then called in SS-Brigadeführer Georg Meindl, chief of the armaments department at the headquarters of military district XVII in Vienna and director of the Steyr munitions works in Upper Austria. Meindl said that parts of the Steyr works had already been moved underground and that limited weapons production could begin by 1 May 1945. Kaltenbrunner added that local industrial leaders had assured him that adequate food supplies for both the troops and the Alpine population would be available in the event of a long siege. Later, on another occasion, Kaltenbrunner told Höttl of plans to supply the redoubt with raw materials via courier plane from Spain and to finance the entire system with counterfeit pound notes printed by concentration-camp prisoners. Höttl felt dismayed that Kaltenbrunner was more interested in last-ditch defense plans than in negotiations based on what Höttl considered to be realities.[36]

While he expected that the Alpine fortress threat would bring the Anglo-Americans to the negotiating table, Kaltenbrunner nevertheless felt that he needed Hitler's authorization in advance to carry on the talks, and on 23 March 1945, he traveled to Berlin. On the evening before the journey, he was again visited by Höttl. Indirectly peddling his scheme for negotiations, Höttl urged the RSHA chief to induce Hitler to step down in favor of a moderate government under Reich Finance Minister Count Lutz Schwerin von Krosigk, which would be authorized to conclude peace with the Western Allies while continuing the struggle against the Russians. Kaltenbrunner himself should receive full powers to negotiate with the Allies and to give orders to all military and civilian authorities in Austria and southern Germany. Kaltenbrunner happened to be in a sober, receptive mood, and appeared to be convinced by Höttl's arguments.

Höttl's hopes were dashed during Kaltenbrunner's audience with Hitler on the afternoon of 23 March. The RSHA chief arrived at the Führer's bunker in time for the daily military situation conference and asked Hitler

---

[36] Hagen, *Bernhard*, pp. 250-251, 256-257.

during a pause if he might be granted a private interview after the conclusion of the conference. Hitler assented, adding that he, too, had something to say. When Kaltenbrunner entered Hitler's private quarters, he found the Führer bent over a large-scale model of Linz, where both men had spent much of their childhood and adolescence. Before his guest could speak, Hitler launched into a monologue on the postwar transformation of Linz into a European cultural center and plied Kaltenbrunner with architectural plans and questions about the reaction of the city's inhabitants to various improvements and developments. After a half hour, Hitler suddenly interrupted himself and, summoning all the charisma and sentimentality that he could, announced, "I know, Kaltenbrunner, what you want to say to me. But believe me, if I were not convinced that one day you and I will rebuild the city of Linz according to these plans, I would put a bullet through my head this very day. You need do nothing more than believe! I still have ways and means to conclude the war victoriously!" Hitler's personal architect, Hermann Giesler, who was present at this interchange, reported that Kaltenbrunner wandered out of Hitler's bunker shortly afterward, muttering, "Now a new day of contrasts begins. Sober, harsh reports and undeniable facts are incompatible with the credulous conviction of the Führer."[37]

Kaltenbrunner must have been deeply moved; for when he returned to Alt Aussee a few days later, he told Höttl, "What you're planning is nonsense! All this is unnecessary! We don't need to do anything, the Führer still has means, the war will be won. True, the Führer didn't explain how, but he told me that he would blow his brains out if he didn't know that he would win the war."[38] The incident described above depicts not only Kaltenbrunner's willingness and ability to believe in Hitler despite all the cautions of common sense, but also the magnetic personal power that Hitler could exert on his followers until the last days of his life. In fact, this incident was by no means isolated. One of Hitler's secretaries recounted a virtually identical situation involving Albert Forster, the Gauleiter of Danzig–West Prussia, on his visit to Hitler in mid-March 1945. Upon his arrival at the Reich Chancellery, Forster blustered to the secretaries that this time he would make Hitler see the desperate situation of Danzig. After the interview, he came out a changed man, saying, "The Führer has promised me new divisions for Danzig. I was not at all clear where he would find them, but he has explained to me that he means to save Danzig and that there is no further room for doubt." Another incident involved the HSSPF in Prague, SS-Obergruppenführer Karl Hermann Frank. On 4 April 1945, Frank suggested to Hitler in private that he be permitted to send a Czech delegation (composed of collaborationist industrialists) to negotiate with the Americans

---

[37] Ibid., pp. 251-253, 254; Höttl Tape, pp. 22-23; Hermann Giesler, *Ein anderer Hitler* (Leoni am Starnberger See: Druffel-Verlag, 1977), pp. 21-22.

[38] Hagen, *Bernhard*, pp. 251-253, 254; Höttl Tape, pp. 22-23.

for a separate peace. Hitler refused, and spoke of new weapons and divisions. Frank returned to Prague determined to fight, much to the dismay of his subordinates.[39]

This psychological jockeying between the obvious reality of impending military defeat and the compelling enticement of absolute faith in the Führer's promise of victory proved to be a considerable strain on Kaltenbrunner's nerves in the last months of the war. According to Schellenberg,[40]

> the more desperate the situation became toward the end of the war, the more Kaltenbrunner drank. I would find him in his office at eleven o'clock in the morning, having risen hardly more than a half hour earlier, his small eyes dull and empty. With the joviality of a drunkard he would reach under his desk or bellow, "Orderly!," and pour out a glass of champaign or brandy for me. Then, when he became too obstreperous, I would take a nip or two to pacify him and pour the rest onto the carpet. Usually he did not notice this, but once when he did, the veins in his face became so swollen with rage that I thought he was about to have a stroke.

That Kaltenbrunner, in his more reflective periods, recognized the contradiction between his ideological commitment and his basic common sense is indicated by the above cited remark he made to Giesler outside Hitler's headquarters in 1945.

Though Hitler maintained that victory would be the result of faith alone, Kaltenbrunner continued to cherish hopes of becoming the man who would make the breakthrough to the Western Allies, thus bringing about the diplomatic coup upon which many of the Nazi leaders banked their hopes. Excluded from the Bernadotte negotiations by Himmler and Schellenberg, he nevertheless had the opportunity to deal with the Swiss Red Cross in mid-March 1945. Apparently Himmler had requested a meeting with the president of the International Red Cross, Dr. Carl J. Burckhardt, on the subject of concentration-camp prisoners, but, owing either to fear of denunciation or to loss of interest in the contact, he had then ordered Kaltenbrunner to receive Burckhardt. On 12 March 1945, at the little town of Feldkirch on the Austrian-Liechtenstein border, the RSHA chief and the president of the Red Cross met.

Kaltenbrunner was determined to take no risks. At the outset of the meet-

---

[39] The Forster incident is cited in Bullock, *Hitler*, pp. 697-698. For the incident involving Frank, see Detlef Brandes, *Die Tschechen unter deutschem Protektorat*, Vol. II: *Besatzungspolitik, Kollaboration und Widerstand im Protektorat Böhmen und Mähren von Heydrichs Tod bis zum Prager Aufstand, 1942-1945* (Munich: R. Oldenbourg Verlag, 1975), p. 119.

[40] Schellenberg, *Secret Service*, p. 330. Höttl offered an additional insight into this equivocal relationship between Kaltenbrunner and Schellenberg. He related how Schellenberg, who suffered from a gall bladder ailment, would consume a considerable amount of alcohol at such sessions with Kaltenbrunner, and afterwards would ask Höttl whether he had drunk enough to impress the "chief." See Höttl Tape, p. 16.

ing, he stated that any agreements reached were subject to the approval of Himmler and Ribbentrop. Having thus absolved himself of responsibility to fulfill concessions, he proceeded to make them. First, Red Cross representatives would be permitted entry into the concentration camps on the condition that they remain there until the end of the war—some of the inmates were employed in "war industries" and were thus bearers of "military secrets." Second, medical personnel could enter the camps, but only with a police escort. In addition, several minor agreements on the release or exchange of French and Belgian civilian internees and prisoners of war were concluded. When Burckhardt demanded that the Reich release all Jews remaining in the concentration camps, or, failing this, that Red Cross teams be permitted to care for them, Kaltenbrunner replied that Himmler alone had the authority to grant such concessions. The RSHA chief then added that he thought all the Jews should be released and, as if this statement were a concession in itself, expressed the hope that the Red Cross would intercede with the Allies on Austria's behalf. Burckhardt received these comments in silence and the two men parted.

Ten days passed without confirmation of the concessions. On his own initiative, Burckhardt sent Dr. Hans Meyer of the Swiss Red Cross to Ravensbrück with several truckloads of food and medical supplies and a letter for Kaltenbrunner authorizing Meyer to take custody of 298 French female inmates scheduled for release according to the 12 March agreement. A few days later, on 29 March, the Red Cross president received a letter from the RSHA chief with the following proposals: the RSHA would (1) permit the shipment of provisions and medical supplies to wounded French and Belgian soldiers interned in Germany, but would not yet consent to repatriate them; (2) release a certain number of French civilian internees if German collaborators in Alsace-Lorraine were spared further persecution; (3) exchange individual French civilian internees for individual Reich citizens interned in France; (4) concentrate all French and Belgian civilian internees in a single camp; and (5) permit the hospitalization of women and children captured in the August 1944 Warsaw uprising in return for a concession of "equal value"— e.g., the release by the Anglo-Americans of all German female employees of the Wehrmacht and the German Red Cross. In addition to these relatively meager concessions, Kaltenbrunner advised Burckhardt that he would establish a two-man liaison office in Constance to handle the technical details of the impending releases. Finally, the RSHA chief requested that the Red Cross do something to brighten Germany's reputation in return for future concessions on the Jews.

Meanwhile, Meyer finally succeeded in getting an audience with Kaltenbrunner on 31 March. Flanked by two Foreign Office officials, the RSHA chief agreed to release all French, Belgian, and Dutch inmates at Ravensbrück, but refused to permit the liberation of any Jews from Bergen-Belsen or Theresienstadt. Meyer himself was not able to return to Switzerland with the 298 French women entrusted to his care until 9 April, and it was not until 13 April that Red Cross representatives received the promise of Gestapo chief Heinrich Müller that no more reprisals would be taken against concentration-camp prisoners for whatever reason.[41] Clearly, the SS leaders were being less than generous in their proposals.

After 1 April, Kaltenbrunner appears to have allowed the Red Cross contact to stagnate for a few weeks while he worked on other projects and, since most of the RSHA proposals depended on Allied concessions that the Red Cross had no authority to fulfill, little was done for the concentration-camp prisoners, who in many camps—Bergen-Belsen in particular—were dying of disease and starvation at an appalling rate. Finally, on 22 April, with the military situation hopeless, Kaltenbrunner again contacted Meyer and requested a conference at Innsbruck. At this late stage, he wished to appear more generous. He promised Meyer and Meyer's companion, General Secretary of the Swiss Red Cross Hans Bachmann, that he would intercede with Wehrmacht commanders to facilitate safe passage for all prisoners of war through the front lines; he would also request naval commanders to transport prisoners in northern Germany from Lübeck to Sweden. He requested Red Cross aid for some fourteen thousand Jews interned in a camp at Gunskirchen (near Wels, Upper Austria) and offered to release fifty Allied pilots and some six hundred Jews of Hungarian and Italian nationality from a detention camp at Bolzano in the Italian Alps. Then the RSHA chief launched into a lengthy, detailed defense of National Socialist policies and ideas, which he concluded with the claim that he had done everything possible to avoid bloodshed between the Germans and the Allies in Austria. Kaltenbrunner's two guests became bored and excused themselves after a short while; such was Kaltenbrunner's last personal contact with the Red Cross.

Bachmann and Meyer later testified that in the last days of the the war, the liaison office at Constance was of some importance in facilitating the evacuation of prisoners of war and civilian internees from German-held territory;[42] but such measures became effective much too late and on much too

[41] Testimony of Burckhardt, 17 April 1946, Kaltenbrunner-3, IMT XL, pp. 306-311, 314-318; deposition of Hans Bachmann, 11 April 1946, Kaltenbrunner-5, ibid., pp. 323-325; deposition of Dr. Hans E. A. Meyer, 11 April 1946, Kaltenbrunner-4, ibid., pp. 322-323; excerpts from *Publications on the Activity of the International Red Cross in Favor of Civilian Internees in German Concentration Camps, 1939-1945*, June 1946, p. 101, NO-2620, NA; Reitlinger, *Final Solution*, p. 503.

[42] For this and Innsbruck meeting, see deposition of Bachmann, 11 April 1946, Kaltenbrunner-5, IMT XL, pp. 323-325; deposition of Meyer, 11 April 1946, Kaltenbrunner-4, ibid., p. 322. Kaltenbrunner carried a different impression away from the meetings with the Red Cross officials. He told an interrogator in 1945 that Burckhardt had encouraged his suggestions for an

small a scale to ascribe the saving of many lives to Kaltenbrunner. During his talks with Burckhardt and Meyer in March, he had made few tangible concessions, virtually all of which were tied to Allied concessions on whose implementation the Red Cross had no influence. Given Germany's hopeless military situation, Kaltenbrunner's policy of linking the release of individuals and small groups of political prisoners in Germany to future general political concessions on the part of the Allies seems inflexible at best. In fact, he wished to avoid crucial concessions because he was not yet convinced that Germany would lose the war. He cared nothing for the welfare of concentration-camp inmates; he was interested only in preserving the Nazi regime until the long-predicted collapse of the anti-Hitler coalition permitted it new opportunities to survive and expand. It is true that the Innsbruck concessions were more generous, but their late date gave them the appearance of a clumsy attempt to establish a last-minute alibi.

One specific reason for Kaltenbrunner's reluctance to offer Burckhardt significant concessions at Feldkirch may have been his hope to contact the Western Allies by a more direct route. His target was Allen Dulles, the chief OSS agent in Switzerland. SD leaders had always been optimistic about Dulles's receptivity to peace talks based on a future anti-Bolshevik front, and expected that, with the threat of an Alpine fortress looming on the immediate horizon, Dulles would be willing to talk. It is difficult to know whether Kaltenbrunner himself pursued the contact with Dulles or how much of the effort was made on the initiative of subordinates who were more skeptical of Hitler's optimism. It is known that on 28 February 1945 an Austrian agent, claiming to be Kaltenbrunner's personal representative, approached one of Dulles's men in Switzerland and reported that Kaltenbrunner and Himmler were considering an action to remove Bormann and the "warmongers" around the Führer as an initial step to end the war and that the SS leadership would first like to sound out Allied reactions to such a move. Dulles instructed his agents to make no promises, but nevertheless to encourage such illusions in the hope of stalling fortifications construction in the Alps.[43] At this point, however, Kaltenbrunner—and whoever was urging him on—learned that SS-Obergruppenführer Karl Wolff, highest SS and police leader (*Höchster SS- und Polizeiführer*) and Wehrmacht plenipotentiary general in Italy, had

Austrian "solution" and had closed the meeting with the remark: "I do hope that I shall meet you often." Kaltenbrunner also told his interrogator that he believed he had made a good impression on Bachmann and Meyer. Lennon Report, pp. 43-45.

[43] OSS report to Joint Chiefs of Staff, "Approaches from Austrian and Bavarian Nazis," 27 March 1945, pp. 1-2, CCS 387, Germany 9.21.44, Section 2, Modern Military Records Branch, NA; Allen Dulles, *The Secret Surrender* (New York–Evanston–London: Harper & Row, 1966), pp. 50-51; Bradley F. Smith and Elena Agarossi, *Operation Sunrise: The Secret Surrender* (New York: Basic Books, 1979), p. 62.

contacted Dulles first. The basis of Wolff's feelers, carried on under Himmler's orders, was the price the Allies would pay for a German evacuation of northern Italy. To cover himself, Wolff had informed Hitler and Bormann on a visit to Berlin on 6-7 February 1945 that he would seek contacts with the Allies with a view to bringing Germany out of the war. Either out of fatalistic indifference or sheer laziness, Hitler did not comment, which Wolff interpreted as approval of his efforts.[44]

Wolff, too, hoped that negotiations with the Allies would result in the dissolution of the Grand Alliance, but, in contrast to his rivals, he was willing to talk to the Americans about capitulation. As military plenipotentiary in Italy, he was in a position to dangle the prospect of a German surrender on the Italian Front to OSS men eager for some sort of a political coup. On 8 March, he conferred secretly with Allen Dulles in Zurich and announced his willingness to place himself "and his entire organization [the SS in Italy] at the disposal of the Allies to terminate hostilities." At a second meeting in Ascona on 19 March, which was attended by two Allied military representatives, he confirmed his intention to surrender the German forces— army and SS—in Italy regardless of orders from Berlin.[45]

The disappearance of the German Front in Italy would explode the myth of the Alpine redoubt, for it would permit Allied troops to enter the southern Alpine region, where, of course, they would find no fortress. Kaltenbrunner's pipedream depended on the threat that Field Marshals Schörner, Kesselring, and Rundstedt, and Generals Löhr and Rendulic would withdraw their as yet intact armies into the Alps. Obviously, the surrender of Kesselring's Army Group Southwest would expose the ruse. Kaltenbrunner had been informed in a general way of Wolff's activities through the reports of the chief of the Security Police and the SD in Verona, SS-Brigadeführer Wilhelm Harster. On 9 March he radioed Wolff, demanding that he report to Berlin and explain what was going on. Wolff ignored this, but a Himmler summons brought him to Berlin on 24 March.

That morning Wolff spoke with Kaltenbrunner and Himmler. Whether he revealed all the details of his conversations with Dulles is uncertain. Nevertheless, the revelations were enough to horrify Himmler and elicit bitter reproaches of treason from Kaltenbrunner. Himmler and Kaltenbrun-

[44] Affidavit of Wolff, Spruchgericht Bergedorf, 22 March 1948, ZS-317/II, pp. 35-37, IfZ Munich; Dulles, *Surrender*, pp. 80-81. See also Bormann's notes, entry for 7 February 1945, in Besymenski, *Letzten Notizen*, p. 106. That Wolff felt he could make such a proposition may stem from his good personal relations with Hitler, established while he was Himmler's liaison man to the Führer's headquarters from 1939 to 1943.

[45] On Wolff's motives, see Smith and Agarossi, *Sunrise*, pp. 125-126, 143-144 and passim. On meetings with Dulles, see interrogation of Wolff, 1 December 1947, p. 3, ZS-317/IV, IfZ Munich; Dulles, *Surrender*, pp. 96-100, 115-125; Eugen Dollmann, *Dolmetscher der Diktatoren* (Bayreuth: Hestia-Verlag, 1963), pp. 224-226; Smith and Agarossi, *Sunrise*, pp. 77-100.

ner were prepared to denounce Wolff to Hitler, but an unforeseen event gave them pause. On the morning of 27 March, as a result of the collapse of a Waffen SS offensive in western Hungary under the command of SS-Obergruppenführer Josef (Sepp) Dietrich, Hitler accused the SS troops of cowardice and incompetence and ordered that they be stripped of their armbands. In view of Hitler's verbal laceration of both Dietrich's troops and the SS in general, Himmler and Kaltenbrunner thought it wise not to bring up the delicate matter of Wolff's activities; the SS general returned to Italy.[46]

Suspicions concerning Wolff's initiatives and jealousy of his advanced position probably gave added impetus to the efforts of Kaltenbrunner and Höttl to contact Dulles. Kaltenbrunner had told Höttl in mid-March that he was prepared to go to Switzerland for talks with the OSS man. While Wolff faced Himmler and Kaltenbrunner in Berlin on 24 March, Höttl surfaced in Bern, dropping hints that the SS in Austria was prepared to eliminate the Gauleiter and to "arrange for an orderly transfer of administrative functions [in Austria and southern Germany] to the Western Powers." The SD man further informed OSS agents that the anti-Nazi opposition in Austria was willing to collaborate with the SS; the name of former Social Democratic mayor of Vienna Karl Seitz was mentioned in this context. Höttl accompanied his information with dark references to the rapid pace of fortifications construction in the Alps.[47]

Whether Höttl accurately transmitted Kaltenbrunner's wishes to the OSS or whether he in fact invented proposals and planned to present his chief with a fait accompli in the event of success remains a mystery. Nevertheless, the proposals of Kaltenbrunner (or Höttl) could not compare with the prospects offered by Wolff, and the Höttl initiative was ignored. Kaltenbrunner appears to have sent Höttl to Switzerland again on 15 April with the request for a Dulles-Kaltenbrunner meeting. Dulles sent an agent to hear Höttl's story, but the Austrian's proposals remained vague: an Austrian group under Kaltenbrunner wanted to make a separate settlement with the Allies.[48] This initiative was also ignored.

Kaltenbrunner may have hoped to time Höttl's second trip to Switzerland with Wolff's removal from the Italian scene. On the basis of reports from

[46] Interrogation of Wolff, 1 December 1947, pp. 5-10, ZS-317/IV, IfZ Munich; affidavit of Wolff, Spruchgericht Bergedorf, 22 March 1948, ZS-317/II, pp. 35-37, IfZ Munich; Dulles, *Surrender*, pp. 84, 102, 130; Smith and Agarossi, *Sunrise*, pp. 112-113. On Sepp Dietrich's disgrace, see Goebbels's diary entry for 27 March 1945, in Josef Goebbels, *Final Entries, 1945: The Diaries of Josef Goebbels*, ed. H. R. Trevor-Roper (New York: Avon, 1979), pp. 310-311; Höhne, *SS*, p. 649; John Toland, *The Last 100 Days* (New York: Bantam, 1967), pp. 371-372.

[47] OSS Report, "Approaches," pp. 3-6; affidavit of Höttl, 30 March 1946, p. 5, ZS-429/I, IfZ Munich.

[48] Dulles, *Surrender*, pp. 145, 152.

Verona Security Police chief Harster, who probably suspected the full extent of Wolff's intentions, the RSHA chief persuaded Himmler to recall Wolff on 14 April. The summons came at a particularly crucial moment, for Wolff had just persuaded Kesselring's successor as commander of Army Group Southwest, General Heinrich von Vietinghoff, to consider a capitulation. When the SS general arrived at Hohenlychen on the evening of 17 April, Himmler accused him of treason. Wolff responded that the negotiations had stalled the Allied advance in Italy. Himmler, who himself was scheduled to meet a representative of the World Jewish Congress on 19 April, began to waver under Wolff's arguments. But at this juncture Kaltenbrunner appeared, brandishing an intercepted cable of the Swiss military intelligence service and accusing Wolff of negotiating for a surrender on the Italian Front. The argument went on until three o'clock on the morning of 18 April, at which time Wolff suggested that the matter be brought to Hitler for decision. Himmler turned pale and excused himself, but Kaltenbrunner agreed to go to Berlin. On the way to the capital, Wolff warned Kaltenbrunner to keep his mouth shut or Wolff would reveal what he knew of Kaltenbrunner's own contacts in Switzerland. Unsure of Hitler's reaction, Kaltenbrunner followed Wolff's advice. When Wolff finally saw Hitler at 6:00 A.M. on 18 April, he revealed all but his intention to surrender. The Führer retorted that the Allied demand for unconditional surrender was too steep; "Fortress Italy" was to be held at all costs until the alliance against the Reich collapsed. Only then would Germany accept the best offer that her former enemies might make. To Kaltenbrunner's dismay, Hitler then permitted Wolff to leave, though he asked the latter not to return to Italy.[49]

On 28 April, three days after a last desperate attempt of Höttl to reach Dulles had failed, Gauleiter Franz Hofer approached Kaltenbrunner and informed him that Wolff and Vietinghoff were planning the capitulation of the German armed forces in Italy. Hofer, who had visions of using the Alpine fortress myth to preserve the Tyrol from occupation, violently opposed any plan that would dissolve this fantasy. With his encouragement, Kaltenbrunner sent a telegram to Berlin on 29 April, denouncing Wolff and Vietinghoff, but the message never reached Hitler and wound up instead in the files of the new Reich president, Grand Admiral Karl Dönitz, on 1 May. And though Hofer induced Kesselring to remove Vietinghoff on 29 April, the surrender of the German troops in Italy, dubbed Operation Sunrise by Wolff and Dulles and signed at Caserta by the representatives of Wolff and Vietinghoff on that same 29 April, was carried out as specified on 2 May 1945.[50]

[49] Interrogation of Wolff, 1 December 1947, pp. 10-13, ZS-317/IV, IfZ Munich; interrogation of Wolff, 16 December 1947, pp. 4-5, ibid.; Dulles, *Surrender*, pp. 170-178.

[50] Kaltenbrunner to Hitler, 25 April 1945, T-73/179/3391606-3391607, NA. That Kalten-

Though the two appear to have been opponents in the Sunrise affair, actual relations between Wolff and Kaltenbrunner remained unclear. Up until 1943, the two men were close, with Wolff assuming a father/brother role toward the younger Kaltenbrunner. Shortly after he learned of his appointment to the RSHA, Kaltenbrunner had written to Wolff (who was then chief of Himmler's personal staff) with the request that "you [Wolff] will remain in the future my good friend and adviser, which you have always been and which I need more than ever in my new office." Wolff had responded that Kaltenbrunner could be "assured that I will continue to stand at your side at all times as a friendly adviser insofar as that is possible." More puzzling still is the fact that, while in confinement just after the war, Wolff told a fellow inmate that he had once tried to win Kaltenbrunner's support for Operation Sunrise. Finally, Wolff stated under interrogation that before his interview with Hitler on 18 April, Kaltenbrunner had "prepared" the Führer in a "positive sense" for the interview.[51] If Wolff can be believed, it would appear that Kaltenbrunner's efforts to block Operation Sunrise were not spurred by personal animosity or by the belief that Hitler would repudiate the operation, but by Kaltenbrunner's own belief that the war was not yet lost and that Wolff's surrender would in fact deal an irreparable blow to the German war effort. The loss of the Italian Front would destroy the credibility of Kaltenbrunner's own negotiating stance. As for the "positive" preparation of Hitler, Kaltenbrunner might have been interested in "preparing" Hitler for his own pet schemes.

Kaltenbrunner's impotent intervention in Operation Sunrise on 28-29 April may have been prompted by the concoction of one last mad scheme to avert the inevitable fate of unconditional surrender: the attempt to establish an independent, noncommunist Austria under a government including Nazi and pro-Nazi elements. Kaltenbrunner's attitude toward the idea of an independent Austria while Hitler was still in firm control of the Reich appears unequivocal, despite his later claims at Nuremberg. On 23 October 1944, he signed an order committing one Dr. Felix Hurdes of Vienna to a concentration camp because Hurdes "endangered . . . by his behavior the stability and security of the race and the state in that he was engaged in trea-

---

brunner backdated the telegram is obvious from its mention of Mussolini's execution by partisans. See also Stuhlpfarrer, *Operationszonen*, pp. 132-133; Albert Kesselring, *Soldat bis zum letzten Tag* (Bonn: Athenäum, 1953), pp. 418-419. For the details of the dramatic hours between 29 April and 2 May at Kesselring's headquarters as well as for an analysis of the actual significance of Sunrise, see Smith and Agarossi, *Sunrise*, pp. 158-192. For all of the drama and virtually none of the analysis, see Dulles, *Surrender*, pp. 215-238.

[51] Kaltenbrunner to Wolff, 28 December 1942, Kaltenbrunner SS File, BDC; Wolff to Kaltenbrunner, 22 January 1943, ibid. For Wolff's comments that he had tried to win Kaltenbrunner's support and that Kaltenbrunner had "prepared" Hitler, see Smith and Agarossi, *Sunrise*, p. 212, n. 25; interrogation of Wolff, 16 December 1947, p. 4, ZS-317/IV, IfZ Munich.

sonous activities for a secret organization which had as its goal the reestablishment of an independent Austria."[52] Throughout April 1945, however, Höttl, Neubacher, and the Herzog clique had been urging Kaltenbrunner to lend his support to an anticommunist Austria in its efforts to seek a separate peace with the Western Allies. Höttl was able to tease Kaltenbrunner's interest by reporting that he had heard during his most recent trip to Switzerland (24 March) that the Americans feared strong Soviet influence in postwar Austria. Upon his return to Austria from Berlin on 19 April, Kaltenbrunner accompanied Neubacher on a visit to the commander of Army Group E, General Alexander Löhr, who agreed to pull his troops from Slovenia and northern Croatia back into Carinthia to prevent a "communist uprising" and to maintain intact an "Austrian" army for eventual peace negotiations. During the following week, Kaltenbrunner conferred repeatedly with Neubacher, Glaise-Horstenau, Höttl, Mühlmann, Waneck, and Löhr. By 25 April, the "Austrians" had drawn up a list of ministers whom they hoped the Allies might accept at least as a transitional government in a newly independent Austria. Kaltenbrunner's own role, as he told interrogators, was to lend his "personal prestige" to the government by acting as its adviser and negotiating with the Allies on its behalf.[53]

While the "Austrians" pursued their fantasies, Karl Renner, the Social Democratic chancellor of the First Republic from 1919 to 1920, was hard at work. On 27 April 1945, he proclaimed an independent Austria and established a coalition government in Soviet-occupied Vienna. Proclaimed under the auspices of the Red Army, the Renner government seems to have aroused some mistrust in Anglo-American circles. The examples of Romania and Bulgaria were, after all, quite fresh. Though this suspicion was only temporary, Höttl thought that his hour had finally come and handed his list of ministers to Albrecht Gaiswinkler, whom he took to be a major in the British Secret Intelligence Service, but who in actuality was the leader of the partisan formations in the Alt Aussee region. Höttl later explained to this

---

[52] Protective Custody Order signed by Kaltenbrunner, 23 October 1944, in *Widerstand und Verfolgung in Wien, 1934-1945*, Vol. III (Vienna: Österreichischer Bundesverlag für Unterricht, Wissenschaft und Kunst, 1975), p. 88.

[53] On Austrian plans and visit with Löhr, see Winzer Report. On Höttl, see Robert E. Matteson, "The Last Days of Ernst Kaltenbrunner," *Studies in Intelligence*, 1960, p. A26. Matteson, who had commanded the U.S. infantry unit that captured Kaltenbrunner after the war, wrote this author that he had prepared this report for the Central Intelligence Agency of the United States, in whose employ he was at the time of preparation. See Matteson to the author, 24 July 1978. On the list, see Lennon Report, p. 5; affidavit of Wilhelm Waneck, 15 April 1946, Kaltenbrunner-8, IMT XL, p. 347; conversation with Albrecht Gaiswinkler, Bad Aussee, 12 April 1977. Gaiswinkler was the chief of the local Aussee partisan organization and discussed the "ministers list" with Höttl in the last days of the war. On Kaltenbrunner's role, see Lennon Report, p. 5.

author that the "counter-Renner government" was meant to be a transition government that would on the one hand prevent further useless resistance and on the other hand transfer power in western Austria to a "legitimate" Austrian government. He added that Kaltenbrunner was never seriously interested in the plan, but had been temporarily won over by the suggestion that Kaltenbrunner serve in the new government as state secretary for security.[54] Perhaps Kaltenbrunner did permit himself to share the illusion of his fellow "Austrians" that the counter-Renner government might lead to a political career in postwar Austria; for, while Höttl waited in vain for the "British officer" to contact London and request British recognition of the counter-Renner government, the RSHA chief bestirred himself to make the above-mentioned last effort to sabotage Wolff's surrender negotiations on 28-29 April. By the evening of 29 April, however, he appears to have discarded this fantasy.

Despite the obvious failure of all of his plans, Kaltenbrunner showed no sign of giving up the fight—at least not to his Führer. To the end he pursued the Alpine fortress chimera, expecting it to lead to some kind of political solution by which the Reich's political and military survival could be assured. Shortly after he had parted from Wolff on 18 April, the RSHA chief was summoned by Himmler to Hohenlychen. There he was given full authorization to issue orders in the name of the Reichsführer SS, the Reich minister of the interior, and commander of the Reserve Army in Bavaria, Austria, and the Protectorate of Bohemia and Moravia if Germany were cut in half by the advance of Allied and Soviet troops. On the next day, 19 April, Kaltenbrunner left Berlin for the last time and returned to Austria, setting up temporary headquarters in Salzburg. After organizing a network of liaison officers in all major Austrian and Bavarian cities, he retired to the mountains to see his family (located at Strobl am Wolfgangssee) and to confer with the Höttl clique.[55]

---

[54] The ministers list reportedly included Glaise-Horstenau and Neubacher, former Christian Social leaders Otto Ender, Heinrich Gleissner, and Ludwig Draxler, Bishop Röhracher of Salzburg as the representative of the clergy, and Josef Neumayer, a former salt miner, to represent the Social Democrats. On the Renner government and Allied mistrust, see Hanns Leo Mikoletzky, *Österreichische Zeitgeschichte: Vom Ende der Monarchie bis zum Abschluss des Staatsvertrages, 1955* (Vienna-Munich: Österreichischer Bundesverlag, 1962), p. 452; Goldinger, *Österreich*, pp. 268-269. On Höttl and Gaiswinkler, see Albrecht Gaiswinkler, *Sprung in die Freiheit* (Vienna-Salzburg: Ried Verlag, 1947), pp. 277-299; conversation with Albrecht Gaiswinkler, Bad Aussee, 12 April 1977. On Kaltenbrunner's involvement, see Höttl Tape, pp. 28-29.

[55] Testimony of Kaltenbrunner, IMT XI, p. 296; Lennon Report, pp. 6, 7-8; interrogation of Kaltenbrunner, 19 September 1946, pp. 1-2, ZS-673, IfZ Munich; Walter Huppenkothen, "Verbleib der Angehörigen des Amtes IV [RSHA]," pp. 5-6, Sonderakt Canaris, Aussage Huppenkothen, BDC.

On 29 April, Kaltenbrunner sent off a telegram to the Führer's bunker to warn of Wolff's surrender negotiations and to report on Mussolini's death. Assuring Hitler that orders could still be sent to Salzburg by radio, the RSHA chief reported that while the situation in northern Italy was serious, a new front could be stabilized near the Austrian border. He went on to suggest that specially trained demolition commandos be dispatched to blow up the main roads leading from the Po Valley into the Alpine passes. Two days later, on 1 May, after Hitler's suicide and the succession of Grand Admiral Karl Dönitz as Reich president (events of which Kaltenbrunner was obviously still unaware), the RSHA chief sent one last telegram to Berlin. He had strong praise for the military leadership of General Rendulic, commander of Army Group Southeast (now in western Carinthia and Styria); the efforts of Meindl, the armaments expert of the military district XVII (formerly Vienna), to finance and organize improved munitions production in the underground factories of Salzburg and the East Tyrol; and the strong leadership of the Gau organizations in Salzburg (Gauleiter Scheel) and Carinthia (Gauleiter Rainer). Kaltenbrunner then reported on his orders to increase food deliveries from the Protectorate for storage in the Alpine redoubt and cryptically concluded that the front could only be directed with "the most prompt improvisation."[56]

These last telegrams contained no suggestion that perhaps the war was lost and that only capitulation would spare further unnecessary deaths. Their basic tone reveals serious concern about the military and supply situation, but no inclination to initiate a surrender on the terms of the Allies. Even the concluding remark concerning improvisation on the Southern Front suggests continued efforts to negotiate for terms rather than any solid commitment to end the war. It would seem unlikely that Kaltenbrunner sent these reports in fear of Hitler's wrath, for the Führer—and all potential rivals: Himmler, Bormann, Ribbentrop, and Schellenberg—had long since been cut off in northern Germany. On the other hand, if Kaltenbrunner was seriously considering capitulation, there was no need to write Hitler about anything on 1 May 1945. One can only surmise that Kaltenbrunner still thought in terms of holding out in the Alps until the anti-Hitler coalition collapsed and still felt it necessary to inform Hitler loyally of the military situation. His last illusions were shattered only on 2 May 1945 by the twin blow of Hitler's suicide (the news of which was released only on the evening of 1 May) and the surrender of Army Group Southwest on the afternoon of 2 May.

If Kaltenbrunner shared with Hitler a will to resist until the last possible

[56] Kaltenbrunner to Hitler, 25 April 1945, T-73/179/3391606-3391607, NA. For an explanation of the date discrepancy, see above n. 50. See also Kaltenbrunner to Hitler, 1 May 1945, T-77/864/5611186-5611188, NA.

moment and a dogmatic belief in the dissolution of the Grand Alliance, on another decisive issue he could not bring himself to follow the Führer: he could not see the drama in a wholesale Götterdämmerung, complete with self-destruction. Fanatic supporter of the Nazi regime that he was, he had no desire to pass into oblivion with it. Once the facts had broken his last illusions of military stalemate and political compromise, he was no longer willing to fight for the sake of pure destruction. This seems clear in the case of plans to evacuate the concentration camps in the last week of April 1945.

The cruel policy of evacuating the camps before the arrival of enemy troops had three purposes: (1) to remove potential witnesses who might testify to the inhuman conditions prevailing in labor, detention, and death camps; (2) to preserve for the armaments industry as much of the slave labor force as possible; and (3) to hold hostages for Himmler's negotiations. On 20 July 1944, one day after Soviet troops crossed the River Bug in the direction of L'vov, the commander of the Security Police and the SD in Kraków, SS-Brigadeführer Eberhard Schöngarth, ordered that all inmates of prisons and labor camps in Kraków district be evacuated before capture by the enemy. Those who could not be evacuated for reasons of health or scarcity of transport were to be liquidated, for the "liberation of prisoners or Jews by the enemy . . . must be avoided. Under no circumstances may they fall into the enemy's hands alive."[57] Evacuations were carried out by all possible means; the brutal and deadly marches from Auschwitz and other camps in Poland to the Reich are a horrifying example of the methods used.

As the Allies swept across Germany in February and early March of 1945, two problems beset Himmler's policy of evacuation. First, the enemy was now advancing so quickly that the camps could not be evacuated in time; and, second, given the rapidly shrinking territory under Nazi control, there was no place to go. Though Himmler hoped to surrender the camps to the Allies in return for political concessions, pressure from Hitler and Bormann coupled with the lack of response from the Allied leaders caused him to hesitate. According to one report, Hitler himself, enraged over "reports" that the inmates of Buchenwald had begun to plunder Weimar after the surrender of the camp to the Americans, gave Himmler strict orders on 15 April forbidding the surrender of any concentration camp before it had been evacuated or before its inmates had been liquidated.[58]

---

[57] Reitlinger, *Final Solution*, p. 321. For a similar order in district Radom, see order of the commander of Security Police and SD in Radom, 21 July 1944, L-53, IMT xxxvii, pp. 486-487.

[58] No order to this effect has ever come to light, nor has its existence been confirmed by any source other than Auschwitz camp commandant Rudolf Höss (IMT xi, p. 407) and Kurt Becher (Biss, *Endlösung*, p. 315), who both heard of it verbally from Himmler. More intriguing is Himmler's statement to Norbert Masur of the World Jewish Congress in April 1945 that he

At Nuremberg, the prosecution sought to prove that Kaltenbrunner, as Himmler's deputy, had planned the evacuation and liquidation of inmates of concentration camps in Austria and Bavaria in the last days of the war. Former Munich Gau Staff Office Leader Bertus Gerdes testified that the RSHA chief had ordered the liquidation of all inmates in the labor camps at Landsberg and Mühldorf near Dachau. Franz Ziereis, the commandant at Mauthausen near Linz, testified on his deathbed (he had been mortally wounded while attempting to escape capture) that Kaltenbrunner had given orders to lock the inmates of Mauthausen subcamps Gusen I and Gusen II inside an underground air hangar, which would then be dynamited. Finally, Kurt Becher swore under oath that on 27 April 1945, Ziereis had informed him of a Kaltenbrunner order demanding the liquidation of one thousand Mauthausen inmates each day.[59]

Though the court accepted the prosecution's argument on this point and though Kaltenbrunner was capable of such killings in "defense" of the Reich, this evidence is extremely unreliable. In regard to Landsberg and Mühldorf, the former HSSPF in Munich, SS-Gruppenführer Friedrich Karl Freiherr von Eberstein, swore that all measures for the liquidation of the inmates had been the inspiration of the Gauleiter of Munich-Bavaria, Paul Giesler, while a separate interrogation of Kurt Becher revealed that on 28 April 1945 Becher had received permission from Kaltenbrunner to surrender Dachau and all its inmates to the Americans. As for Mauthausen, Ziereis's evidence is unclear. The Marsalek affidavit indicates that the order for liquidation originated with Himmler, whereas in a separate protocol—not introduced at the trial—Ziereis speaks only of a Himmler order to kill the inmates of Mauthausen. Moreover, a Swiss Red Cross observer named Haefliger reported after the war that the plan to liquidate the inmates of the Mauthausen labor camps in the underground hangar at Gusen I had been the inspiration of Ziereis himself. In a separate interrogation, Becher too had to confess his suspicion that Ziereis had received no orders whatsoever from Himmler or Kaltenbrunner and was preparing to act on his own initiative. In fact, according to Becher, Kaltenbrunner gave orders forbidding the evacuation of

---

(Himmler) had ordered the evacuation of the camps to continue because the Allies were using the camps to foment "hate propaganda" against Germany. See Reitlinger, *Final Solution*, p. 511. This encourages speculation that Hitler never issued the order (though it was in character with the Führer's thinking) in a formal sense and that it was actually a concoction of Himmler, who was still unable to choose between policies of surrender or Götterdämmerung.

[59] Interrogation of Bertus Gerdes, 20 November 1945, 3462-PS, IMT xxxii, pp. 295-300; dying confession of Franz Ziereis, Gusen, 24 May 1945, D-626, NA; affidavit of Hans Marsalek, 8 April 1946, 3870-PS, IMT xxxiii, pp. 279-286; undated letter signed by Kurt Becher, 1946, 3762-PS, IMT xxxiii, pp 68-70. See also arguments of the Nuremberg prosecution, IMT iv, pp. 306-309.

Mauthausen or the liquidation of its inhabitants; this was done at Becher's request on 26 April 1945.[60]

It remains a fact that all major camps in Kaltenbrunner's area of jurisdiction—Mauthausen, Dachau, and the Theresienstadt Ghetto—were surrendered to the Allies intact, while several camps in northern Germany (including Sachsenhausen and Ravensbrück) were evacuated. Without specific proof, it is difficult to assign responsibility for last-minute efforts to evacuate or murder the inmates, for by April 1945 the central SS-Police apparatus, like all other central authorities in Germany, had broken down. Contradictory orders on evacuation and liquidation reached camp commandants and local Party officials as Himmler oscillated between loyalty to Hitler and his fantasies of negotiations with the West. Under the circumstances, camp commandants and local officials seem to have drafted liquidation plans on their own initiative, and, when challenged on them, sought to shift the responsibility to their superiors or to other authorities. Though evacuation orders passed through Kaltenbrunner's office during 1944, his collaboration in such murder schemes during the last days of the war cannot be convincingly proven; on the contrary, he apparently gave orders to surrender Dachau and Mauthausen. As to the reasons for his intervention, it is possible that, in the last days of April, he was seeking to establish a good reputation for the possibility of postwar political activity. Yet, it is more likely that he no longer saw any political advantage in not surrendering the camps. If he had merely been seeking an alibi, he might have shown more initiative in establishing one. But it is clear from Becher's testimony that Kaltenbrunner had to be persuaded with great difficulty to take action. Perhaps, by 26-28 April 1945, he could finally be convinced that the "enemies of the Reich" confined in the camps could no longer cause the Reich any significant harm and at the same time were more useful as living witnesses of his sudden "humanitarianism" than as dead hostages.

Another example of Kaltenbrunner's reluctant participation in efforts to prevent useless destruction was the "salt-mountain art-treasure affair." As the Americans neared Linz, Salzburg, and the Aussee region in late April 1945, Upper Austrian Gauleiter August Eigruber, a hopeless fanatic who was determined to fight until the last breath, made plans to blow up the entrances

---

[60] For judgment of the Tribunal on the evacuation of the concentration camps, see IMT XXII, p. 537. On Landsberg and Mühldorf, see testimony of Eberstein, IMT XX, pp. 307-308; Reitlinger, *Final Solution*, p. 512; interrogation of Becher, 28 March 1946, Eichmann document 827, EPD, IfZ Munich. On Mauthausen, see affidavit of Marsalek, 8 April 1946, 3870-PS, IMT XXXIII, p. 281; "Protokoll des Kommandanten des KZ-Lagers Mauthausen bei Linz, SS-Standartenführer Franz Ziereis," n.d. [23 or 24 May 1945], 1515-PS, pp. 1, 6, NA; interrogation of Becher, 28 March 1946, pp. 2-3, Eichmann document 827, EPD, IfZ Munich; on Haefliger, see Reitlinger, SS, p. 425.

of several abandoned salt tunnels that formed part of the still-active salt mines near Alt Aussee and in which thousands of priceless paintings and other works of art—plundered from all over occupied Europe—had been stored for protection against Allied bombardment. Ignoring the pleas of salt miners and engineers alike that such demolitions would destroy not only the priceless art collection, but many of the active salt tunnels as well, Eigruber was determined that the art treasures should not fall into the hands of "World Jewry" and had nine crates containing undetonated American bombs placed in the tunnel entrances. On 2 May 1945, a coalition of salt miners concerned about their future livelihood, resistance workers concerned with saving the art and foiling Eigruber's plans, and Austrian Nazis adding to their alibis approached Kaltenbrunner, who had arrived in Alt Aussee on 1 May to visit his mistress, Gisela von Westarp. With some difficulty, the RSHA chief was persuaded to countermand Eigruber's orders. Despite the irate Gauleiter's efforts to assert his authority, the bombs were finally removed from the salt tunnels on 5 May on Kaltenbrunner's orders; three days later, the Americans arrived.[61] Again, Kaltenbrunner appears to have been motivated less by overt, self-serving ends than by a distaste for destruction for which he could see no reason; for, if he were only seeking an alibi, it would seem strange that he did not try to exploit this incident at Nuremberg.

Three days after the conclusion of the "salt-mountain art-treasure affair," the German armed forces surrendered unconditionally at Rheims. During the eight months preceding the surrender, Kaltenbrunner had sought peace by following a line that was bound to fail because it sought to reconcile two mutually exclusive concepts. On the one hand, the RSHA chief was dominated by an instinctive loyalty to Hitler and a National Socialist system that refused to countenance the thought of defeat; on the other hand, he realized that Germany could no longer win the war militarily and that a political solution involving considerable sacrifice was essential to the survival of the Reich. Bolstered in the first instance by factors of power and prestige, career, ideological outlook, and psychological make-up, he was encouraged in the second by a naked instinct for self-preservation. The disjointed merger of these two elements resulted in a confused policy combining illusory plans for a die-hard defense of the Reich with equally fantastic schemes for a

---

[61] Max E. Eder, "Die Kunstgutbergungsaktion Salzbergbau, Alt Aussee, Oberösterreich: Kurzer Bericht über deren Anfänge und Verlauf bis zum Eintreffen der U.S. Truppen am 8. Mai 1945," May 1945, File 10.610, DöW. Eder was a chemical engineer employed in the Aussee salt mines. See also Erich Pöchmüller, *Weltkunstschätze in Gefahr* (Salzburg: Pallas Verlag, 1948). Pöchmüller was the general director of the salt mining enterprises in the Aussee region. See also Sepp Plieseis, *Vom Ebro zum Dachstein: Lebenskampf eines österreichischen Arbeiters* (Linz: Verlag "Neuer Zeit," 1946), pp. 370-377. Finally, for a summary of the affair, see Gabriele Hindinger, *Das Kriegsende und der Wiederaufbau demokratischer Verhältnisse in Oberösterreich im Jahre 1945* (Vienna: Verlag Brüder Hollinek, 1968), p. 26.

negotiated peace that would enable the Nazi system to survive. Hitler's inflexible will to save the Reich by military means, the intensity of Kaltenbrunner's own ideological commitment to that will, the limitations placed on his freedom of action by the personal politics of the regime, and finally—and decisively—the Allied determination to destroy the Nazi regime served as key factors in Kaltenbrunner's abortive search for peace and at the same time ensured that it would fail.

Hitler remained convinced virtually until the end that Germany would win the war either through the use of infallible secret weapons or by means of a diplomatic coup exploiting the "inevitable" collapse of the anti-Hitler coalition. He obstinately clung to the illusion that only time, gained by the harshest measures against "traitors" and "weaklings," was needed to permit the expected miracles to unfold. The Führer insisted on faith in victory, for he conceived of defeat only in the most absolute terms. Defeat meant that Providence had deemed the German race unworthy of the lofty role to which she had assigned it; if proven unworthy, the German people might as well die, for it had no future anyway.[62] Any defeat that did not presuppose such drastic consequences could not be discussed, for Hitler did not accept it as a part of the world history that he claimed to represent. While even Goebbels could discard his nihilism long enough to lament that the Führer took no steps to realize his hopes for victory,[63] Hitler preferred to leave the initiative to Providence and expected his followers to believe that "we will conquer because we must conquer, for otherwise world history would have lost its meaning."[64] Given such a philosophy, it was difficult for a convinced Nazi even to contemplate, let alone formulate or implement, a policy based on the possibility of a defeat that was anything less than apocalyptic.

Nevertheless, few of Hitler's supporters could tolerate the negative possibilities determined by his myth world; those who remained ideologically loyal to him preferred to share his fantasies of ultimate victory, despite whatever doubts they had of the outcome. Kaltenbrunner fell into this category. There is no evidence that he ever considered the possibility of capitulation before Hitler's death. His last messages to the Führer contained no hint of despair or reproach, only a will to carry on. As Wilhelm Höttl explained to this author, "Kaltenbrunner remained true to Hitler until the end and believed in him until the last moment despite all personal misgivings that he had and that we [Höttl, Neubacher, etc.] nourished." Parallel to his efforts to negotiate with the Allies, Kaltenbrunner concocted in all seriousness fan-

[62] See citations and discussion in Trevor-Roper, *Last Days*, pp. 53-54; Bullock, *Hitler*, pp. 694-697.

[63] Diary entry for 27 March 1945, in Goebbels, *Final Entries*, p. 309.

[64] Speech of Jodl to Reichsleiter and Gauleiter in Munich, 7 November 1943, L-172, IMT XXXVII, p. 668.

tastic plans to equip and man a mythical Alpine redoubt. And whenever, as Höttl wrote, "it came to pass that he [Kaltenbrunner] recognized the full gravity of the situation, a visit to Hitler, to whom he was a complete slave and whom he believed more than anyone else, brought this to nothing."[65] In fact, Kaltenbrunner's ideological outlook, his personal power, prestige, and fortune were too intimately linked to the doomed Nazi system to permit him to abandon it. Only after the death of his idol and the final collapse of the redoubt myth could he seriously consider means of survivial in a non-Nazi world.

Another obstacle to serious peace feelers lay in the personal politics that continued to characterize Nazi ruling patterns until the day of the regime's collapse. Among the SS leadership alone, six more or less major figures (Himmler, Kaltenbrunner, Wolff, Becher, Schellenberg, and Höttl) competed to find the magic route to the negotiating table, each counting on a dissolution of the anti-Hitler coalition. Though each differed in the degree of his personal loyalty to Hitler himself, all followed the efforts of their rivals with suspicion and jealousy and none hesitated to betray them to Hitler if he thought that his own interests and plans were being undermined by their activities. As we have seen, Schellenberg and Kaltenbrunner worked together to torpedo the Himmler-Becher negotiations in Switzerland, whereupon Kaltenbrunner sought to impede the negotiations of Himmler with Musy and Bernadotte after Himmler and Schellenberg had excluded him from them. Kaltenbrunner and Höttl sought to undermine Wolff's contact with Dulles and to replace it with their own. The supreme threat which rivals used to tie each other's hands was that of denunciation to the Führer. It seems likely that Himmler and Kaltenbrunner feared this most of all, not necessarily because of the threat of physical retribution, but because they did not wish their Führer to think of them as traitors or, worse still, weaklings. For, though many were denounced to him, Hitler took few retributive actions; Becher and Himmler were not punished for their negotiations with the Joint Distribution Committee, nor was Wolff stopped by the revelation of his close contact with Dulles. Hitler did not care. Such individual actions were merely sideshows in the world historical drama that he expected to unfold. He neither forbade nor authorized them, thus increasing the confusion of the would-be peacemakers. The SS leaders—especially Himmler and Kaltenbrunner—continued to fear that, if indeed Hitler's miracle came to pass, the Führer would remember their moment of weakness and draw the consequences; and they remained cautious about making moves which could be denounced by their rivals.

Finally, the peace that Kaltenbrunner sought, a negotiated peace with the

[65] Höttl Tape, p. 24; statement of Wilhelm Höttl, 6 October 1945, 1899-PS, NA.

Western Allies based on the survival of the Nazi system in some form, was, even without the ideological and political handicaps placed on the search from within the Third Reich, unattainable. Roosevelt and Churchill were consistent in their determination that Germany surrender unconditionally and single-minded in their intent to "extirpate" Nazism as a basis for the moral reconstruction of Germany.[66] Roosevelt's announcement on unconditional surrender at Casablanca was in part prompted by misunderstandings surrounding General Dwight D. Eisenhower's controversial negotiations with the commander in chief of the Vichy French forces in North Africa, Admiral François Darlan, in the fall of 1942.[67] The use of Jews otherwise earmarked for annihilation as well as other concentration-camp prisoners as hostages against political concessions could not have appealed to any Allied statesman, given the Allies' general political philosophy. Moreover, none of Himmler's or Kaltenbrunner's contacts—Musy, Bernadotte, Burckhardt, the Jewish Rescue Committee in Budapest, the Joint Distribution Committee, or the World Jewish Congress—had the slightest influence on Anglo-American policy makers, though all exploited Nazi preconceptions that they could wield such an influence. The failure of the Anglo-American authorities to respond to appeals of Jewish and war refugee organizations to bomb the gas chambers in Auschwitz and the railroad lines between Budapest and the notorious death camp was a real and depressing indication of the low priority that Jewish lives had in Allied military and political planning.[68] That efforts of Jewish and Red Cross organizations managed to save any lives at all was owing in large part to the enormous capacity for self-deception on the part of the SS leaders, who believed that "World Jewry" would save them in return for the lives of its brethren.

While the Nazis were certainly correct in predicting the collapse of the Grand Alliance, they underestimated the hostility that Hitler and his policies had aroused among the Western Powers. Thus, only those who were able to convince individuals in the Allied or neutral camps that they had broken

[66] For the Anglo-American attitude on unconditional surrender from Casablanca to Yalta, see Herbert Feis, Churchill, Roosevelt, Stalin: The War They Waged and the Peace They Sought (Princeton: Princeton University Press, 1957), pp. 350-358. See also the discussion in John Wheeler-Bennett and Anthony Nicholls, The Semblance of Peace: The Political Settlement after the Second World War (New York: Norton, 1974), pp. 59-64.

[67] Wheeler-Bennett and Nicholls, Semblance, pp. 53, 59; Smith and Agarossi, Sunrise, p. 13.

[68] Arthur D. Morse, While Six Million Died: A Chronicle of Apathy (New York: Random House, 1968), pp. 358-361 and passim; Walter Laqueur, The Terrible Secret: Suppression of the Truth about Hitler's "Final Solution" (Boston-Toronto: Little, Brown & Co., 1980), passim. On Anglo-American hesitation to aid the Jews of Hungary, see John S. Conway, "Between Apprehension and Indifference: Allied Attitudes to the Destruction of Hungarian Jewry," The Wiener Library Bulletin, 27, n.s., nos. 30/31 (1973/1974), 37-48.

with Hitler before the collapse of the Reich were able to benefit in a personal sense from the dissolution of the anti-Hitler coalition. This is certainly true in the cases of Becher, Schellenberg, and Wolff.[69] Kaltenbrunner, however, had remained true to his Führer until the last possible moment; his attempts to prove otherwise at Nuremberg were futile. He had identified himself so closely with the regime and the worst of its policies that there was little hope that he would escape the full wrath of those who had made great sacrifices to crush it and eradicate its remnants.

On 1 May 1945, Kaltenbrunner left his political headquarters in Salzburg and his family in Strobl and moved to Alt Aussee to stay with his mistress and the infant twins she had borne him six weeks earlier. If the RSHA chief had finally given up on the Alpine fortress, many others had not. On 1 May 1945, Kesselring, the commander of Army Group Southwest, issued orders warning Reich officials to remain at their posts throughout Germany and to stay out of the Alpine area. On the next day, Lieutenant General Winter of the OKW Operations department established a series of checkpoints along the northern foothills of the Alps to prevent a mass retreat of disorganized and ill-trained units of the Wehrmacht and the SS into the Alpine regions. In addition, all civilians not residing in the mountain provinces were to be turned back to north and central Germany.[70] Among the refugees who poured into Alt Aussee searching for instructions were the notorious deportation expert Adolf Eichmann and Paul Blöbel, former Einsatzkommando chief in the USSR. If such unsavory characters had hoped for advice, comfort, or leadership from the top-ranking SS officer in the region, they were disappointed, for Kaltenbrunner "did not himself know what to do."[71] Indeed, the RSHA chief turned them away from his mistress's door and, a few days after the general surrender at Rheims, took off into the mountains.

[69] Wolff was held for interrogation by the Americans but not tried; was acquitted by a British military court in 1949; and was only convicted and sentenced to a prison term in 1962 by a West German court. Schellenberg was a defendant in the famous "Ministries" Case tried before an American military tribunal at Nuremberg in 1949, was convicted, but received only a six-year sentence, four years of which were considered to have been served. Becher was never indicted. The cases of Wolff and Schellenberg were undoubtedly made easier by the Cold War atmosphere of 1949.

[70] Telegram of Kesselring to Gauleiter Hofer, Gauleiter Eigruber, Gauleiter Giesler, Gauleiter Scheel, Gauleiter Uiberreither, Gauleiter Henlein, Reich Minister Lammers, State Secretary Frank, and SS-Obergruppenführer Kaltenbrunner, 1 May 1945, T-77/861/5608155-5608156, NA; decree of Winter, 2 May 1945, ibid., 5608150-5608152.

[71] Höttl Tape, p. 10. On Eichmann's last meeting with Kaltenbrunner, see ibid.; testimony of Höttl, Alt Aussee, 19-21 June 1961, HS 65/61, Eichmann Interrogation Book, pp. 68-69, IfZ Munich; Adolf Eichmann, "Ich transportierte sie zum Schlachten: Eichmanns Geschichte," 1960, pp. 90-94, Eichmann document 1423, EPD, IfZ Munich.

CHAPTER VIII

Ideological Soldier on Trial

SHORTLY after the conclusion of the salt-mountain art-treasure affair, Kaltenbrunner approached Fritz Moser, a local hunter from Alt Aussee, and asked to be guided up to a small hunting cabin situated on the Wildensee in the mountains outside of Alt Aussee. After some hesitation, Moser agreed. Together with another hunter, Sebastian Radauschl, Moser led the former RSHA chief, an adjutant, and two other SS men to the cabin on 7 May 1945. A few days after his return to Alt Ausee, Moser informed a local contact of the Austrian anti-Nazi resistance of Kaltenbrunner's whereabouts. This information was passed on to an agent of the American Counter Intelligence Corps (CIC) on 11 May. Early next morning, led by four guides from Alt Aussee, a small squad of United States infantry commanded by Colonel Robert E. Matteson of the CIC ascended the mountain trails to the hut, where they surprised Kaltenbrunner and his companions in their sleep. The RSHA chief surrendered without a fight, presenting the Americans with identity papers in the name of a Wehrmacht physician named Josef Unterwogen. He was observed to be "completely calm," showing neither fear nor excitement. When the party returned to Alt Aussee, Gisela von Westarp, who had been informed by Matteson and was concerned for her lover's safety, confirmed Kaltenbrunner's identity by impulsively embracing him.[1]

What did Kaltenbrunner intend with this half-hearted effort to escape? The Austrian resistance leaders were and are convinced that he planned to go underground, but the evidence for this is not solid. In conversations with this author, Sebastian Radauschl maintained that the hut's existence and whereabouts were well known to local hunters and the village authorities, and expressed his astonishment that Kaltenbrunner stayed there for more

---

[1] On request to Moser, see conversation with Sebastian Radauschl, Alt Aussee, 13 April 1977; Plieseis, *Vom Ebro zum Daschtein*, pp. 394-396; Plieseis to the editors of the *Neuen Mahnruf* (Vienna), 27 October 1960, File 631, DöW; Gaiswinkler, *Sprung*, pp. 460-461. On capture and reaction of Gisela von Westarp, see conversation with Karl Moser (now mayor of Alt Aussee, then one of Matteson's guides), Alt Aussee, 13 April 1977; Matteson, "The Last Days of Ernst Kaltenbrunner," pp. A20-A25; "Counterintelligence Report on Head of RSHA Kaltenbrunner, Dr. Ernst," Hdqtrs Twelfth Army Group, Mobile Field Interrogation Unit No. 4, 25 May 1945, pp. 1, 4, Folder CIR 4/3, IIR, Modern Military Records Branch, NA; Ralph E. Pearson, *Enroute to the Redoubt: A Soldier's Report as a Regiment Goes to War*, Vol. III (Chicago: Adams Printing Service, 1958), pp. 230-231; Houston, "Kaltenbrunner," pp. 170-172.

than a day. One of the guides who assisted the Americans concurred, declaring that at best the hut offered a temporary refuge. Kaltenbrunner's brother Werner, himself an experienced mountain climber and familiar with the region, speculated in an interview with this author that Kaltenbrunner merely wanted to avoid capture for a few more days. Wilhelm Höttl, who was with Kaltenbrunner in Alt Aussee, has suggested that Kaltenbrunner was "in truth only half-heartedly intent on escape," that he merely "wanted to rest, to sleep, and to think."[2] Escape in any case would have been difficult for the hulking, scar-faced Austrian. He was by no means a nondescript-looking man like Eichmann or Treblinka death-camp commandant Franz Stangl; and, unlike such smaller fry, he was wanted as a major war criminal.

Perhaps Kaltenbrunner's decision to remain at the Wildensee cabin was dictated by lethargy, exhaustion, and depression;[3] yet, another motive also suggests itself. Kaltenbrunner was no advocate of Götterdämmerung and it is likely that, in the first days of May 1945, he still believed the Grand Alliance would dissolve—too late, perhaps, to save the Reich, but still in time to affect his personal fate. Wilhelm Höttl stated that Kaltenbrunner was convinced that the Western Allies would eventually utilize his experience in intelligence and police matters for the coming showdown with Soviet communism and that therefore it was only necessary to hide for a short period. Moreover, the RSHA chief seems to have been miraculously blind to the ugly reputation that he had earned abroad, figuring perhaps that Himmler and Pohl would be blamed for both concentration camps and extermination policies.[4]

Some circumstantial evidence supports this hypothesis. En route to the Wildensee hut, Kaltenbrunner asked one of his guides if he would act as a contact man in Alt Aussee when the Americans arrived. Moreover, in sharp contrast to his later behavior, he appears to have been calm and collected during his initial interrogations. An interrogator remarked that Kaltenbrunner was "neither arrogant nor submissive; he appears straightforward and not unfriendly, a reasonable and well-spoken man with a measure of peasant self-assuredness." Kaltenbrunner reportedly told Otto Skorzeny, with whom he briefly shared a cell in Wiesbaden in June 1945, that he had been interrogated by a British history professor in such a way as to permit some opti-

[2] Plieseis, *Ebro*, pp. 394-396; Gaiswinkler, *Sprung*, pp. 460-461; conversation with Sebastian Radauschl, Alt Aussee, 13 April 1977; conversation with Karl Moser, Alt Aussee, 13 April 1977; interview with Dr. Werner Kaltenbrunner, Vöcklabruck, 25 March 1977; Wilhelm Höttl, *The Secret Front* (New York: Frederick A. Praeger, 1954), p. 313. This English edition of *Geheime Front* is considerably shorter and contains different material.

[3] Sebastian Radauschl remarked that on the way to the hut, Kaltenbrunner's morale was "at the zero point." Conversation with Sebastian Radauschl, Alt Aussee, 13 April 1977.

[4] Interview with Dr. Wilhelm Höttl, Bad Aussee, 14 and 15 April 1977, Höttl Tape, p. 26.

mism for the future. Perhaps Kaltenbrunner indeed permitted himself one last illusion of postwar survival and political importance.[5]

How fanciful such illusions were is indicated by a brief review of Allied plans to deal with the leaders of a defeated Germany. Anglo-American and Soviet representatives had officially announced their intention to punish Nazi war criminals as early as the Moscow conference of foreign ministers in October 1943. At various times between the conferences at Teheran (November 1943) and Yalta (February 1945), Stalin, Roosevelt, and Churchill all thought in terms of summary executions; only after the Yalta conference did each unequivocally opt for a trial. On 8 August 1945, the Allies established an International Military Tribunal that would try twenty-four individual defendants and six organizations on a four-count indictment: (1) participation in a common conspiracy to wage "aggressive war," commit war crimes, and commit crimes against humanity; (2) planning, initiating, and waging aggressive war; (3) perpetration of war crimes; and (4) perpetration of crimes against humanity.[6] On 20 November 1945, after six months of feverish interrogation, document classification, and legal analysis, the trial opened at the Palace of Justice in Nuremberg.

Kaltenbrunner had been featured on every Allied list of major war criminals since April 1944; his name also appeared on the preliminary list of ten defendants for the major trial drawn up by the British in June 1945. Though he was correct in his bitterly expressed contention that he was in Nuremberg merely as a substitute for Himmler, it is difficult to imagine how the prosecution could have passed him over, for, given the deaths of Himmler and Heydrich, he was clearly the highest-ranking SS officer whose responsibilities linked him to the Gestapo, the SD, the Einsatzgruppen in the USSR, and the horrors in the concentration camps. Moreover, the prosecution had drafted its lists with an eye to the six organizations (SS, Gestapo, SD, Reich cabinet, Nazi Party political leadership, and the OKW and German General Staff) which were to be tried as collective entities; the individual defendants were chosen as representatives of the accused organizations.[7]

Kaltenbrunner was thus the obvious choice to represent the SS, the Gestapo and the SD; his nearest significant rival, former SS-Obergruppenführer Oswald Pohl, chief of the SS Economic and Administrative Main Office

---

[5] Conversation with Sebastian Radauschl, Alt Aussee, 13 April 1977; "Counterintelligence Report on Head of RSHA," 25 May 1945, p. 9, NA; Skorzeny, *Geheimkommando*, p. 376.

[6] Wheeler-Bennett and Nicholls, *Semblance*, pp. 119, 153, 224, 391, 397-398, 402-403; Smith, *Judgment*, pp. 23-24, 29-30, 35-36; Werner Maser, *Nürnberg: Tribunal der Sieger* (Düsseldorf-Vienna: Econ Verlag, 1977), p. 34.

[7] On Kaltenbrunner on lists and prosecution methods in drafting lists, see Smith, *Judgment*, pp. 28, 48-49, 60-61, 64, 166-167, 187. On Kaltenbrunner's reaction to the indictment, see Gilbert, *Nuremberg Diary*, p. 11; testimony of Kaltenbrunner, IMT xi, p. 232.

(WVHA), to which the concentration-camp administrations were subordinated, had no authority over or direct connection to the Gestapo and the SD, while Kaltenbrunner was directly linked to Pohl's area of responsibility by virtue of the Gestapo's authority to ship individuals and groups to concentration or extermination camps for incarceration or liquidation.

If Kaltenbrunner harbored any illusions concerning the good will of his captors, these were quickly shattered. After ten weeks of confinement and rigorous interrogation in London, he was brought to Nuremberg in September 1945; on 19 October, he was served an indictment charging him with perpetration of war crimes and crimes against humanity and participation in a conspiracy to commit such crimes (counts 1, 3, and 4). Although there is no hard evidence that he had been physically mishandled in London, he found the psychological strain of the interrogations difficult to endure, for he arrived at Nuremberg a broken man.[8] When served the indictment, he began to sob, moaning that no one would defend him; while in consultation with a court assistant concerning the appointment of defense counsel, he "was in an emotional state and wept during part of the interview." The prison psychiatrist reported that the former RSHA chief was deeply depressed, that he repeatedly broke down and wept, crying that he would not receive a fair trial.[9] On 17 November 1945, three days before the trial was to begin, Kaltenbrunner was rushed to the hospital with what was later diagnosed to be a spontaneous subarachnoid hemorrhage, which, as the prison psychiatrist later speculated, might have been induced by rising blood pressure owing to Kaltenbrunner's tension and agitation about the impending trial.[10] He was unable to appear in court to plead until mid-December and

[8] Otto Skorzeny claimed that Kaltenbrunner had been locked in the Tower of London and tortured daily, but had no evidence for this. Significantly, he did not mention Kaltenbrunner's mistreatment in the earlier version of his memoirs. See Skorzeny, *Kommandounternehmen*, p. 403. Wilhelm Höttl, who, like Skorzeny, had contact with Kaltenbrunner in the Nuremberg prison, reported that Kaltenbrunner never spoke of physical torture, though he had emphasized that the experience in London was "miserable." See Höttl Tape, p. 27. Other defendants and potential witnesses were reportedly beaten, though evidence for this is restricted to their own complaints and those of their families. See Oswald Pohl, "Erlebnisse und Erfahrungen in englischen und amerikanischen Gefängnissen und Gerichten," June 1948, ZS-567/II, IfZ Munich; affidavit of Karl Wolff, 25 August 1947, pp. 3-6, ZS-317/II, IfZ Munich; interrogation of Kurt Lindow, 19 April 1950, pp. 4-6, Landgericht Frankfurt/Main, 54 Js 344/50, ZS-583, IfZ Munich; Maser, *Nürnberg*, pp. 70, 80-82.

[9] Airey Neave, *On Trial at Nuremberg* (Boston-Toronto: Little, Brown & Co., 1978), pp. 126, 130, 222; Kelley, *22 Cells*, p. 134.

[10] A subarachnoid hemorrhage, caused by the rupture of a tiny blood vessel located in the membrane covering the brain, can be fatal. On condition and speculation about it, see Kelley, *22 Cells*, p. 134; Burton C. Andrus, *I Was the Nuremberg Jailer* (New York: Coward-McCann, 1969), pp. 112, 115-116. This author has also been advised by Dr. Victor Risch of Baltimore and Dr. Robert Ettinger of Columbia, South Carolina, that such a condition most frequently

thereafter suffered another hemorrhage, which kept him hospitalized throughout January.

Was this merely the behavior of an abject coward, afraid that he would hang? Certainly, Kaltenbrunner feared for his life; many of the defendants viewed the indictment as a death sentence that would be preceded by a show trial.[11] Yet, his behavior contrasts so sharply with his later deportment on the stand and after his conviction that one must seek deeper psychological factors. Kaltenbrunner had fallen from a high position of power in which he believed himself to have been playing a vital, historic role in the defense and development of the German nation. Under the physical rigors and psychological pressures of confinement, he not only witnessed his own descent to the status of a criminal, but was also forced to contemplate the ruin of everything he had stood for. He had believed he was making history, but was now forced to consider that he had been committing crimes.[12] Moreover, he had lived for so long in a world dominated by the Hitler myth, which justified the acts for which he was now being held responsible as historical necessities, that confrontation with the reality of what he had done may have been, at least temporarily, too unbearable a strain for his psyche to support.[13] This is not to say that he regretted any of his actions, but rather that he was frightened that history might not judge them correctly. Such ruminations, coupled with the physical stress of imprisonment (including forced withdrawal from excessive alcohol and tobacco habits) may have had much more of an impact on Kaltenbrunner's behavior before the trial than simple fear for his life, for he appears to have accepted his verdict, sentence, and impending execution stoically.

---

occurs after a physical blow to the head, and that it is unlikely to occur solely as a result of tension. Although it seems improbable that the prison guards would have mistreated Kaltenbrunner in the Nuremberg prison because of the adverse publicity which might have resulted, it is possible that Kaltenbrunner either accidently or deliberately injured himself in such a way as to precipitate the hemorrhage.

[11] For interpretation of Kaltenbrunner as a coward, see Kelley, 22 *Cells*, p. 134; Andrus, *Jailer*, p. 116; Neave, *On Trial*, p. 223. On defendants' belief that Nuremberg was a show trial, see Neave, *On Trial*, p. 138. Neave had the task of serving the Nuremberg indictments and arranging with the defendants for the appointment of defense counsel. For a specific example, see Baldur von Schirach, *Ich glaubte an Hitler* (Hamburg: Mosaik Verlag, 1967), pp. 320-321.

[12] When an interrogator at Nuremberg pressed Kaltenbrunner on the question of whether Hitler had given orders that could be considered criminal, the former RSHA chief admitted that this might be so, but then snapped irrelevantly: "I don't think I can make history as a prisoner." See interrogation of Kaltenbrunner, 9 October 1945, NCA, Supplement B, p. 1308.

[13] Other defendants were under similar emotional stress and did not break down, but with the possible exceptions of Göring (who tried to assume the role of the Nazi regime's principal defender), Frank (who sought refuge in an almost frantically vibrant Catholicism), and Ribbentrop (who himself was near breakdown throughout the trial), none was so totally immersed in Hitler's myth world and at the same time so intimately linked with its most hideous aspects.

At some point between his return to court in February 1946 and his turn on the stand in April, Kaltenbrunner marshaled his strength and prepared a determined fight for his life. The basic points of his defense were: (1) that he was appointed chief of the RSHA solely to reorganize the political intelligence service of the Reich and to amalgamate it with the military intelligence department; (2) that Himmler retained actual control over the police executive (Gestapo and Kripo); (3) that therefore Himmler (dead), Pohl (in custody), Müller (missing), Nebe (dead), and Eichmann (missing) were responsible for the atrocities and crimes for which the Allies sought to judge him guilty; (4) that he had remained RSHA chief after gradually learning of these policies solely out of a sense of duty to his fatherland and in the hope of ameliorating them; and (5) that through his protestations to Hitler, his stand against the regime's anticlerical policies, and his negotiations with the Swiss Red Cross and Allen Dulles, he not only actively sought to end the war, but saved many lives in the process.[14] When confronted with incriminating affidavits on the stand, he denied their validity, demanding a confrontation with the witness. When handed Security Police orders issued from central or local Gestapo offices, he branded them as the inspiration of Himmler or Müller and claimed to have no knowledge of their origins or effects. Finally, when the prosecution submitted to him documents bearing his own signature, he tried to explain them away by every possible stratagem; if this failed, he simply denied having signed them. The high point in this flood of denials was his refusal to acknowledge his own handwritten signature on a letter to Vienna mayor Hanns Blaschke stating that Jews diverted to Strasshof en route from Budapest to Auschwitz would be subject to a "special action"; the original was signed in ink: "Dein Kaltenbrunner."[15]

During his cross-examination, Kaltenbrunner was able to embarrass the prosecution on occasion. When Colonel John Harlan Amen, representing the American prosecution, presented him with the affidavit of an RSHA official concerning "special treatment" (*Sonderbehandlung*) at camps "Walzertraum" and "Winzerstube," Kaltenbrunner explained to the amusement of the court that "Walzertraum" was the most fashionable Alpine hotel in Germany, and "Winzerstube" was a famous hotel in Bad Godesberg where privileged prisoners were kept. And yes, he *had* been involved in this type

[14] Testimony of Kaltenbrunner, IMT XI, pp. 232-386; Kaltenbrunner to Kauffmann, 1 July 1946, Kaltenbrunner File; Kaltenbrunner's final plea, 31 August 1946, IMT XXII, pp. 378-381. In the author's Kaltenbrunner File is a typed draft of the plea signed in pencil by Kaltenbrunner. It is virtually identical to the text read into the trial transcript. Points 1, 2, and 3 were also heavily stressed in Kaltenbrunner's "memoir" to his children. See E. Kaltenbrunner, "Memoir," Nuremberg, July-August 1946, pp. 53-54, Kaltenbrunner File.

[15] Testimony of Kaltenbrunner, IMT XI, pp. 346-348. As a result of this incident, Kaltenbrunner was dubbed "the man without a signature." See Haensel, *Gericht*, p. 158.

of special treatment! On another occasion, Kaltenbrunner was confronted with the affidavit of another RSHA official, who had been told by one of his colleagues that Kaltenbrunner had made decisions concerning the liquidation of prisoners incarcerated in Gestapo prisons in Berlin before he moved south into the Alps. Kaltenbrunner hotly denounced such evidence as hearsay and inadmissible; the tribunal had to agree.[16] Nevertheless, such rare successes on the stand could hardly outweigh the mass of evidence against him, nor have documents uncovered since the trial been very helpful in relation to his defense.

Though his story was greeted with general disbelief, Kaltenbrunner's vigorous defense surprised several in the courtroom, including one or two of the judges. Carl Haensel, defense counsel for the SS and the SD, depicted Kaltenbrunner on the stand in terms of "a beast of prey, a fox or a polecat that jumps from the shadows for the throat of its prey. When the fury erupts from Kaltenbrunner, you believe that you can smell fumes of sulphur. At this time, he has grown tall and stately. . . . When he becomes distorted with rage, he looks like the gargoyles on Gothic cathedrals." The more sober-minded Viktor Freiherr von der Lippe, an assistant to Raeder's defense lawyer, noted in his diary that Kaltenbrunner was "surprisingly quick-witted" and that "a part of the audience is impressed by his mental abilities. . . . The court follows [the proceedings] with interest, even with a sort of respect for Kaltenbrunner's cold-blooded dialectic." As if to confirm Lippe, Norman Birkett, the British alternate on the bench, wrote:

> Kaltenbrunner . . . was an interesting figure on the witness stand. [He] . . . is making a vigorous defense, denying his signature to documents of a most incriminating nature, endeavoring to show that he was really without power or influence. He is a fluent speaker and speaks with great animation and uses much gesture. In some matters he is no doubt right and it is then that he grows animated. Some of the things attributed to him are no doubt exaggerated, but it is impossible to think of the position occupied by Kaltenbrunner and, at the same time, to believe that he was ignorant of so many matters.

American tribunal judge Francis Biddle was also convinced that several minor points in the case against Kaltenbrunner could not be substantiated.[17]

---

[16] On special treatment, see testimony of Kaltenbrunner, IMT xi, pp. 338-339; affidavit of Josef Spacil, 9 November 1945, 3839-PS, IMT xxxiii, pp. 197-199. On amusement in the court, see Viktor Freiherr von der Lippe, *Nürnberger Tagebuchnotizen, November 1945 bis Oktober 1946* (Frankfurt am Main: Verlag Fritz Knapp, 1951), p. 220. For documentary proof of Kaltenbrunner's statements concerning Winzerstube, see Pohl to Himmler, 14 June 1944, T-175/19/2522891-2522893, NA, which includes the amounts of food rationed to the inmates of Winzerstube. On heresay evidence, see testimony of Kaltenbrunner, IMT xi, pp. 340-341; affidavit of Martin Sandberger, 19 November 1945, 3838-PS, IMT xxxiii, pp. 195-196.

[17] Haensel, *Gericht*, p. 151; Lippe, *Tagebuchnotizen*, p. 219; H. Montgomery Hyde, *The*

Two questions might be raised here. Why did Kaltenbrunner follow a line of consistent denial, virtually impossible to substantiate in view of the evidence against him? And how did he achieve such a personal transformation from weeping wreck to determined adversary on the stand? The answer to the first reflects a curious mixture of motives arising from the desire for self-preservation and a contempt for the tribunal as an enemy court. On the one hand, when the indictments were not followed immediately by the expected convictions and death sentences, Kaltenbrunner may have taken heart and begun to hope that he would emerge from the trial with his neck intact. When one of the defense attorneys indignantly asked why he did not shoulder the responsibility for SS crimes and thus protect individual SS men who were innocent of them, the former RSHA chief had sneered, "A trial is a game . . . and everybody plays to win." On the other hand, Kaltenbrunner was certain that he was being tried by an enemy court dominated by an alien ideology and determined to see him hang. To his children he complained that no person had ever found himself in such an unjust situation, but that "the world must have its revenge and justice does not coincide with politics and propaganda."[18]

Kaltenbrunner appears to have reasoned that since a court comprised of Anglo-American "liberals" and Russian "bolsheviks" could never view his actions or the Nazi regime itself in the light of National Socialist ideological precepts, his only available defense was denial of participation in or knowledge of acts that the court had defined as crimes. He thus hoped that he could avoid the noose by playing the game within the confines of the enemy's ideological rules. Hence a statement that he had "always been of the opinion that a man's liberty must be counted among his highest privileges and that only a judgment of a court, firmly rooted in a constitution, should be allowed to infringe on that liberty"[19] was not necessarily desperate groveling but rather calculated hypocrisy prepared for the ears of the (Western) judges. Though such tactics seemed absurd, exasperated the prosecution, disgusted Kaltenbrunner's own defense lawyer, and infuriated some of his codefendents, it is clear that, given the weight of the evidence against him, his own view of the tribunal as a kangaroo court and his albeit slim hopes for survival, Kaltenbrunner had no other defense.[20] Predictably, the court

---

Life and Times of Lord Birkett of Ulverston (New York: Random House, 1965), p. 514; Smith, *Judgment*, p. 188.

[18] Haensel, *Gericht*, p. 167; Smith, *Judgment*, p. 112; E. Kaltenbrunner, "Memoir," pp. 42, 54.

[19] Testimony of Kaltenbrunner, IMT xi, p. 244.

[20] For disgust of other defendants, see Gilbert, *Nuremberg Diary*, pp. 235, 237, 239-240, 241-242; Schirach, *Ich glaubte*, p. 324. On Kaltenbrunner with no other defense, see Davidson, *Trial*, p. 327; Houston, "Kaltenbrunner," p. 178.

did not accept it; the judges pronounced his guilt on counts 3 and 4 (war crimes and crimes against humanity) and sentenced him to death by hanging.[21]

The second question, that of Kaltenbrunner's psychological transformation between his arrival at Nuremberg and his vigorous defense on the stand, is far more difficult to answer. Indeed, no explanation at all would have been possible had it not been for the bitter enmity which arose between Kaltenbrunner and his defense counsel, Kurt Kauffmann, during the course of the trial and which was reflected most sharply in an argument over the presentation of the final plea in Kaltenbrunner's defense. For, in his sharp emotional reaction to Kauffmann, Kaltenbrunner left for posterity some indication of his political-psychological character as it was molded and modified in the Nuremberg cell. These emotional outpourings, laced with deceit, cynicism, and hypocrisy, offer one plausible if somewhat speculative explanation not only of the inconsistencies in Kaltenbrunner's personality, but also of the nature of his National Socialist faith.

Although the immediate cause of Kaltenbrunner's vindictive verbal assault on Kauffmann concerned Kauffmann's treatment of Kaltenbrunner's case, beneath the technical disputes lay a fundamental abhorrence of each man for the other on the basis of his ideological convictions. Kauffmann was a devout and profoundly conservative Catholic with a strong attachment to the antirationalist, ultramontane trend in Catholic intellectual thought during the mid- and late nineteenth century.[22] He bemoaned the "humiliation of God" and the "deification of Man" implicit in the French revolutionary tradition and bringing in their wake "as an inevitable consequence and punishment" a "chaos" that had "afflicted mankind with wars, revolution, famine, and despair." He astutely recognized that Hitler and Nazism were not solely the result of Versailles and economic hardship, but claimed that they were a culmination of the flight from God begun in the Renaissance and the Reformation. Liberalism, the child of seventeenth- and eighteenth-century rationalism in England and France, was the evil that had brought the Hitler catastrophe upon Germany and the world: "The real and last root of these calamitous modern movements which threaten state, society, and Christianity, is rootless Liberalism in the meaning of that anthropocentric

---

[21] The legal arguments in Kaltenbrunner's case turned on the controversial conspiracy charge (count 1). Here Kaltenbrunner was acquitted. See Smith, *Judgment*, p. 189. On the verdict and the sentence, see IMT xxII, pp. 538-588.

[22] Kauffmann was fond of quoting and referring to Juan Francisco Maria de la Donoso Cortes, Spanish diplomat, politician, and court adviser in the years before, during, and after the 1848 revolutions. Originally a liberal, Donoso Cortes later renounced his views and became a fanatical defender of ultramontane doctrines. He was an intimate friend of ultramontane Catholicism's most eloquent champion, Louis Veuillot. See entry in *The Catholic Encyclopedia*, vol. xv (New York: Encyclopedia Press, 1913), p. 132.

humanism. . . . Man and his autonomous reason became the criterion of everything. . . . Two world wars, with revolutions in their wake, are never an accidental development but rather a predetermined evolution of the human race founded on some intellectual-religious error."[23]

Kauffmann loathed National Socialism as much as he did liberalism, rationalism or, for that matter, bolshevism; and he quickly came to despise Kaltenbrunner as a living example of its worst excesses. Virtually alone of all his colleagues, he never developed the slightest respect or sympathy for his client. When Kaltenbrunner appeared in court on 10 December 1945 to plead, Kauffman demonstratively refused to shake his hand in greeting. The defense lawyer found the denial tactic of his client distasteful and did not hesitate to make his attitude known to the court. He even conceded Kaltenbrunner's guilt to the tribunal and sought to fashion his arguments around the theme of separating that obvious culpability from the nebulous and, to him, unjust accusation of the German people implicit in the charges against the organizations.[24]

Kaltenbrunner's contempt and loathing for Kauffmann was equally intense. The former RSHA chief confided to codefendant Alfred Jodl that his defense lawyer was a "petty" and "cowardly" "arch-Catholic"; Kaltenbrunner's children were told of a "fanatical political opponent." Kaltenbrunner smuggled a copy of the final plea draft out of prison to his brother Roland in Linz to show him that "I not only had to defend myself against the prosecution, but also against the defense." Perhaps this contempt and hatred for Kauffmann—and the defense lawyers in general—was best typified by his outburst during a recess: "You defense lawyers . . . are like little rabbits paralyzed by the serpent's gaze of the prosecution!"[25]

It seems likely that this enmity toward Kauffmann induced Kaltenbrunner not only to attempt a rebuttal of Kauffmann's disparaging remarks on the Nazi regime and its police chief, but also to write a memoir of his life in order to explain himself to his children. Though Kaltenbrunner probably hoped that these documents would be released when history was rewritten in his favor and thus colored them to his best advantage, some of his com-

---

[23] Draft of Final Plea by Kurt Kauffmann, June 1946, p. 12, Nachlass Roland Kaltenbrunner. See also IMT xviii, p. 48. For other examples of Kauffmann's thinking, see Kauffmann Draft, pp. 1-2, 8, 9, 11, 13-14; IMT xviii, pp. 40, 45-46, 48, 49.

[24] On Kauffmann's hatred of Kaltenbrunner as exception, see Luise Jodl, *Jenseits des Endes: Leben und Sterben des Generaloberst Alfred Jodl* (Vienna-Zurich-Munich: Verlag Fritz Molden, 1976), p. 231. On Kauffmann's treatment of Kaltenbrunner in the courtroom and his concessions of Kaltenbrunner's guilt, see Gilbert, *Nuremberg Diary*, p. 63; Final Plea, IMT xviii, pp. 51, 54, 63, 68.

[25] Kaltenbrunner to Jodl, 24 June 1946, Kaltenbrunner File; E. Kaltenbrunner, "Memoir," p. 42; handwritten note of Kaltenbrunner, n.d., attached to Kauffmann Draft, Nachlass Roland Kaltenbrunner; Haensel, *Gericht*, p. 166.

ments on National Socialism are not only indicative of his cynicism and lack of remorse, but also reveal—in however distorted a form—a little of the world in which he lived.

Kaltenbrunner was especially stung by Kauffmann's critique of National Socialism as the monster-child of eighteenth-century rationalism and nineteenth-century liberalism, as the culmination of egoistic nonbelief in a being or concept superior to man. Moreover, he was particularly enraged by Kauffmann's belief that Catholicism had avoided such spiritual pitfalls. If, in his final plea, Kauffmann were going to disparage the offspring of Liberalism, Kaltenbrunner reasoned, he would do better to direct his attack "above all against Americanism and bolshevism. . . . For basically American automat-civilization [*Zivilisationsschablone*] and bolshevist mass materialism are the *extreme forms of nonbelief* and the *hubris* of the self-laudatory human spirit" (emphasis in the original). National Socialism, on the other hand, was not a child of but a "reaction to Liberalism and the atomization of the human community conjured up by Liberalism." For National Socialism, "as we saw it, sought to guide men out of the irresponsible rootlessness that had arisen [out of Liberalism] once more into relationships based on duty." As this could no longer be achieved by religious confessions or political parties, a political-metaphysical alternative had to be found. This was provided by National Socialism, which "sought the impulses [*Impulse*] that [would] make it possible to again dissolve the spiritual and social divisions which had resulted from the French Revolution; i.e., that impulse, to be awakened in every individual, which would give him the will and the ability to overcome his own individualism for the benefit of a higher community and responsibility." In order to understand National Socialism properly, in order that it withstand "the critique of history," it must be stated (i.e., by Kauffman to the court) that Nazism, unlike Liberalism, did not have as its "point of departure . . . the demand to be without responsibilities [*Fessellosigkeit*], but the search for organic unity and responsibility."[26] In short, Kaltenbrunner, drawing on the century-old traditions of völkisch mysticism, sought to present National Socialism as an organic (i.e., living) substance (i.e., faith), supplanting both church and state in cementing and defining natural relationships between men and ordering their existence within a "divinely ordained" framework of duty and responsibility. If he believed what he was writing here, it is reasonable to suggest that his personal response to National Socialism took on a religious hue, definable under Hans Buchheim's concept of a *Religionsersatz*,[27] a modernized substitute for the medieval concept

[26] Kaltenbrunner to Kauffmann, 24 June 1946, pp. 12, 13, 14, Kaltenbrunner File.
[27] Buchheim, *Glaubenskrise.*

of the union of church (spiritual life) and state (political life), which transcended the traditional limits of both spheres.

For Kaltenbrunner, the symbol and substance of this new force, which, replacing both God and state, would determine the relationships between men on earth, was the "racial community" (*völkische Gemeinschaft*). He insisted that National Socialism proposed only to be a function of "the law of divine creation [in that it] accepted race as the basic value [*Grundwert*] and the races as the divinely inspired building blocks [*Bausteine*] of mankind." For man did not exist as an individual entity; his identity was marked by his race and his "spiritual-intellectual quintessence" (*das Bild des vergeistigten Menschen*) was not the reflection of "racial mixture," but of "racial individuality," which had forged the "generally valid principles of humanity."[28] He explained to his children in more simplified and romanticized terms that he "loved" in National Socialism "the program for which we joined; the noble motif of its sense of sacrifice; its goal, to bring the estates [*Stände*] together once again, to honor service to Mother Nature in the labor service [*Arbeitsdienst*], to secure the eternal youth of our race through a land inheritance law [*Erbhofgesetz*]; to allow the workers to share the profits; to reward performance and not heritage; the Winter Relief as the symbol of comradeship binding upon all; in short, the consciousness of our own [i.e., those of the German race] strengths [*die Besinnung auf eigene Kräfte*]." At one point, Kaltenbrunner became so carried away that he expressed a hope that if his children were lucky enough to have friends, those friends would be "people whom National Socialism taught brotherly love."[29] With this improbable combination of lopsided Herder, values purloined from the Judeo-Christian moral ethic, and a heavy dose of pseudosocialism fastened together by a tenuous völkisch mysticism, Kaltenbrunner wished to define the "true" essence of National Socialism for the unbeliever (Kauffmann), the potential believers (his children), and posterity.

But what of the dark side, the frightful legacy of National Socialism: the war unleashed and lost, the physical destruction and dismemberment of Germany, the mass murder of millions of innocent people, the fiendish system of the concentration camps, and the brutal exploitation of Europe's natural, cultural, and human resources against a backdrop of violent conquest and oppression—how did Kaltenbrunner propose to explain away such ugly blots on the landscape of his National Socialist paradise? This he did, however unconvincingly, in typical National Socialist style. Ignoring the fact that such policies were logical and practical (if not exactly inevitable) outgrowths of the racial theory that was intrinsic to the very existence of Na-

---

[28] Kaltenbrunner to Kauffmann, 24 June 1946, p. 13.
[29] E. Kaltenbrunner, "Memoir," pp. 16-17.

tional Socialism, he swept aside the horrifying realities, separating them from what he insisted was still a pure, unsullied ideal. The atrocities committed by the Nazis were "deviations" (*Entartungen*) forced upon them by the war and encouraged by men of bad faith who thereby betrayed the revolution. As a National Socialist, *he*, Kaltenbrunner, had nothing to do with such atrocious crimes, was not a harbinger of the amoral chaos in which they could be committed, and could not be accused of not having striven "in an idealistic youth for maturity and ethical goals [*sittliche Reife und Ziele*]." Moreover, neither such deviations ("which were not influenced or foreseen by me") nor the fact of National Socialism's political defeat invalidated the fundamental truth of the Nazi ideology. This, Kaltenbrunner insisted, had not been refuted or even conquered by another morally superior creed, but rather had been overwhelmed by a "materially superior combination of powers" whose representatives now sought to judge Nazism by virtue of their position as conquerors. But Nazism could not be judged on the basis of its political fate: "What with Hitler was perhaps ideologically correct, could have been politically incorrect; that is, a political attitude [i.e., decision] of Hitler's could be proven false by default of success without justifying repudiation on ideological grounds." Therefore, "from the complete failure and defeat of Adolf Hitler as 'World Politician' we can make no conclusions about the viability of ideas represented but not originated by him."[30] Hitler transgressed not against any moral ethic of politics, but rather against a "natural philosophy of politics" in which only the physical dimensions of time, space, and force had validity. His regime could not be judged by conditions prevailing in Germany in 1939 or 1945 because his work had been interrupted "prematurely" by the war. Though the Führer was dead, it was a "fully open question whether the ideas that he represented have died with him."[31]

The denial of the effects of the National Socialist system coupled with flimsy and intellectually banal attempts to preserve an untarnished ideal reflect in part the efforts of a cynic seeking any excuse to escape hanging, and in part the mental gyrations of a fanatical believer seeking not only his life, but moral justification for his actions, if not from the world then at least from the tenets of his faith. Simplifying his arguments for his children, Kaltenbrunner attributed the failure of National Socialism to realize its "noble" ideals to traitors and incompetents (excluding Hitler, of course) in the Reich leadership (a tiresome theme in Nazi explanations of German military

---

[30] Kaltenbrunner sardonically added for Kauffmann's benefit that Catholics should be happy that the validity of an idea was not dependent on the political fate of its adherents, for otherwise the political failures and excesses of the Church would mean a weakening of the Catholic idea. See Kaltenbrunner to Kauffmann, 24 June 1946, p. 8.

[31] Ibid., pp. 8, 13.

and political defeats—and of extra importance since the Jews could not be blamed this time!), who permitted the outbreak of the war and thus "rendered in vain all our sacrifices for the construction of the fatherland, which we had made with such difficulty and yet so willingly." Fallible individuals had "sinned" (*versündigt*) so deeply against "our idea that today total incompetents believe that they can speak of a debased National Socialism." They had made "mistakes which can accompany every revolutionary development, but which should not have been permitted to happen . . . above all not through a war in the first stages of the newly created Reich." But National Socialism was not "debased," Kaltenbrunner declared. Its mistakes and excesses resulted from the failures of individuals; and there had been "no one present who could have fixed [those individuals] for good in time."[32]

Kaltenbrunner was vague on what actually constituted such "mistakes" and "deviations," other than the unleashing of the war. Even here one is not certain, for he was obviously referring only to the war against England and the United States; he "considered a showdown with bolshevism unavoidable for us Germans." Sooner or later, such a struggle had to come as long as this "insidious doctrine" did not "renounce its penetration of the European-Occidental cultural sphere, whose defender and justified leader was and is our race [*Volk*]."[33] Moreover, his astonishing silence on the question of the Jews leads one to suspect that, for him, the "deviations" of the Nazi system did not include the mass extermination of this people—perhaps another "unavoidable" development—but rather consisted of "nonideological" corruption and sadism in the camps and in Gestapo prisons. He may indeed have thought the "Jewish Question" too delicate a topic to take up with his children, whom he suspected would grow up in a world which at least in principle would reject the idea that an individual's value is determined by his membership in a race and would certainly condemn in unequivocal terms extermination policies carried out in application of such principles.

Most remarkable in Kaltenbrunner's prison writings is the absence of any guilt, remorse, or even reflection on the millions of innocent people who had been murdered by the regime that he served or who had died as a result of its policies. On the contrary, he appears to have been convinced that he had always done right, that his actions had been necessary, and that "history" would someday prove this. In his memoir to his children, he expressed the desire to be buried with the many peasants who died at the battle of Emmlinger Moos (during the Upper Austrian peasant wars in the seventeenth century) "in the consciousness that I too served a good cause." But,

[32] E. Kaltenbrunner, "Memoir," pp. 41, 52.
[33] Ibid., p. 33.

as he assured his children, history "will someday be written differently" and would show that "we wanted what was just and best"; when the "truth" was again spoken, they could be "proud of your Daddy as a man who sacrificed all for the greater good." His only guilt, he declared, was "of a purely personal nature"; no one except his wife Elisabeth could sit in judgment over him for this. If he could only speak to her once more, he "would be free." Finally, as he sneeringly wrote Kauffmann, he would not take "so tragically" what was said of him in view of how much or little weight words "spoken today" would have in ten or more years: "we must think and speak in view of eternity [*für uns gilt wohl, sub specie aeternitatis zu denken und sprechen*]; this court has already rendered itself sufficiently ridiculous."[34]

Such appalling insensitivity toward the millions of deaths and widespread carnage left in the wake of the Nazi system may have been bolstered by a psychological reconstruction of the totalitarian myth world in which Kaltenbrunner had lived for much of his adult life. During the first months of his incarceration, he appears to have lost this ideological security blanket that both justified his actions and absolved him of responsibility for them. Without it, he broke down, partly in fear for his life, but more fundamentally in the fear that his actions—the revolting crimes to which he was an accessory—might not find justification in the light of "history"; for he must have possessed some slim remnant of that which the Nazis contemptuously labeled bourgeois morality so as to psychologically require higher justification for murder. Then, during the winter months of the trial, he appears to have reconstructed the myth world, for cynical as his denials of responsibility might be, his unconvincing defense of National Socialism as an ideology seems to be aimed not only at his children and his lawyer, but also at himself. If this assumption is valid, it offers one explanation for the sudden change in Kaltenbrunner's behavior during the trial. He had been "rehabilitated" in the light of a mythical verdict of history, and could now face the verdict of the court, which no longer mattered, with fortitude if not serenity.[35]

Kaltenbrunner also took comfort in the nihilistic element of völkisch thought, in the concept of his role as combatant fighting in perpetual, historical struggle against an archetypal enemy. Such thinking was reinforced by the SS conception of ideological soldierhood, which claimed as virtues contempt for the weak and glory in battle. Even though the struggle had been lost, Kaltenbrunner sought solace in the fact that he had been a part of it and felt contempt for those who had not. This perverted elitism, rooted

[34] Ibid., pp. 23, 42, 44; Kaltenbrunner to Kauffmann, 24 June 1946, p. 15.

[35] See the eyewitness description of journalist and authoress Rebecca West, who cannot be suspected of harboring sympathy for the Nazis. Rebecca West, *A Train of Powder* (New York: Viking, 1955), pp. 59-60.

in the concept of glorious and necessary struggle, is particularly evident in Kaltenbrunner's outburst at the defense lawyers during a recess at the trial:[36]

> You didn't bring out [in the trial] at all what really happened. Everything was at the end, we stood at the end; and we tried once more to set up a dam against the flood from the East. Admittedly, we built it with blood and living bodies, but there was no other possibility. . . . We defended ourselves, tried to defend ourselves. The result shows that we were unsuccessful. We were still too weak. People like you slipped through our fingers and escaped us [*sind uns durchgerutscht und durchgekommen*].

To Alfred Jodl, in whom he thought to have found a soulmate, Kaltenbrunner wrote of his contempt for Kauffmann and of his satisfaction at having had the opportunity to participate in the struggle:[37]

> How much you are to be envied that you have two such distinguished defense counsel, so conscious of their duty. Nevertheless, we expect nothing, and no one will find us weak! What a splendid feeling [it is] to have lived a life that demanded and found danger and readiness for action. This intellectual [Kauffmann] can maneuver all he wants with his Donoso Cortes. He will never find that in life which we experienced. Respect and enthusiasm for the mountains in nature and for that which is greatest, love!

Though such statements reflect a certain bravado as part of mental preparation for death, they also seem indicative of the philosophy of an unrepentant ideological soldier, willing whenever and wherever in his perpetual restlessness to struggle against enemies defined in the stark terms of his artificially simplified world. The same ideology that had provided justification for murder now provided comfort for impending death.

On 1 October 1946, the International Military Tribunal pronounced Kaltenbrunner guilty of committing war crimes and crimes against humanity and sentenced him to death. It is difficult to quarrel with the verdict. The tribunal which handed it down has since been widely criticized and justified from all possible angles;[38] and, while a searching analysis of the political,

---

[36] Haensel, *Gericht*, p. 166.

[37] Kaltenbrunner to Jodl, 24 June 1946, Kaltenbrunner File.

[38] Several of the Nuremberg defense counsel have criticized the trial on legal and moral grounds, though most of these concur that, given the circumstances prevailing in 1945-1946, the proceedings were fair. See Carl Haensel, "The Nuremberg Trial Revisited," *DePaul Law Review*, 13 (spr.-sum. 1964), 248-259; Otto Kranzbuehler, "Nuremberg Eighteen Years Afterwards," ibid., 14 (spr.-sum. 1965), 333-347; Otto Pannenbecker, "The Nuremberg War Crimes Trial," ibid., pp. 348-358. Most critical of the trial is Herbert Krauss, "The Nuremberg Trial of the Major War Criminals: Reflections after Seventeen Years," ibid., 13 (spr.-sum. 1964), 233-247. The most recent broadside leveled against the tribunal is that of Werner Maser, *Nürnberg*. For an analysis of American attitudes for and against the trial, see William J. Bosch, *Judgment on Nuremberg: American Attitudes towards the Major German War Crimes Trials*

moral, psychological, and legal value of the Nuremberg Trial would exceed the scope of this work, a few remarks might be helpful in assessing its role in judging Kaltenbrunner.

The bulk of the critique leveled against the tribunal centers around the following points: the legal viability of the charge of conspiracy (count 1) and the definition of "aggressive" war (count 2); the questionable impartiality of a tribunal composed only of the victors in World War II; the problem of Allied and Soviet participation in war crimes during World War II (count 3); and the failure of the tribunal to establish or define a viable legal structure, let alone apparatus, for the prosecution of future crimes such as those that were dealt with at Nuremberg. Although the conspiracy charge and the definition of aggressive war were tenuous in a legal sense, it must be noted as a symbol of the tribunal's recognition of this situation that only one of the twenty-two defendants (Hess) was sentenced solely as a result of conviction on these two counts. Furthermore, no one convicted of waging aggressive war at Nuremberg was hanged for conviction on this count alone. The "Tribunal of Victors" critique has a certain validity, for the court was undoubtedly influenced by political factors. Nevertheless, apart from Bradley Smith's study of how the judges sought to overcome or at least mitigate such influences,[39] it is unlikely that a court of neutrals—particularly European or South American neutrals—or of Germans would *not* have been influenced by political considerations (e.g., fear of reprisal by a revived Germany or sympathy with fascism). The tu quoque argument has validity not only with respect to war crimes (count 3), but also to crimes against humanity (count 4). Hiroshima, Nagasaki, Dresden, Hamburg and British commando instructions could have been defined as criminal acts under the charter of the International Military Tribunal; the murder of some ten thousand Polish officers in Katyn Forest can qualify as a crime against humanity. It can be argued that the Soviet extermination of the "kulak" class and the political purges of the 1930s qualify as crimes against humanity in the same way as does the Nazi extermination of the Jews. Yet Stalin's purges of the 1930s were conducted internally and were as little subject to prosecution by an international court as was the Röhm purge in 1934, the Kristallnacht brutalities of 1938 or the American internment of Nisei Japanese in 1941-42. Through their attempt to conquer Europe by force of arms, the Nazis brought

(Chapel Hill: University of North Carolina Press, 1970). The most convincing defenders of the trial on moral, political, practical and, with certain reservations, legal grounds are: Smith, *Judgment*, especially pp. 300-306; Davidson, *Trial*, pp. 586-594; John Mendelsohn, "Trial by Document: The Problem of Due Process for War Criminals at Nuremberg," *Prologue*, 7 (Winter 1975), 227-234.

[39] Smith, *Judgment*, *passim*.

their uniquely genocidal aims and methods into the international arena and thus into the reach of an international tribunal.

Finally, the argument that Nuremberg neither prevented the victors (or, for that matter, anyone else) from committing acts that could have been prosecuted under the charter of the International Military Tribunal, nor established a system for the efficient, just prosecution of such crimes is tragically valid. Yet this indicates a failure to live up to (or to try to live up to) the ideals and potential symbolized by the Nuremberg Trial rather than a conclusive indictment of the tribunal itself. Beset by legal and moral pitfalls as it was, the tribunal still attempted to provide the twenty-two defendants with a fair trial. Given the state of political and psychological shock and exhaustion prevalent in war-devastated Europe in the summer of 1945, the general moral revulsion at the crimes committed by the Nazis, and the bitter hatred of Germany and Germans that had been building up in occupied Europe during the war, the trial seems in retrospect to have been a political and psychological necessity. It prevented the full wrath of the victor and liberated nations from exploding upon the German people by its efforts to distinguish in a legal sense between the guilty and the innocent. In view of the widespread sentiment for summary retaliation against both the Nazi leaders and the German people, it is to the credit of the victors that they voluntarily sought to limit the punishment to verdicts arrived at in a series of trials by law, in which the defendants could hope for acquittal if they were proven innocent of the charges brought against them. The acquittals of Papen, Schacht, and Fritzsche were not mere cynical gestures geared to provide a facade of respectability to a kangaroo court. They were rather the result of a deliberate weighing of the evidence during which the judges, disregarding their political prejudices, found that these men, whatever their moral responsibility for what had happened, were legally innocent of the crimes for which they had been charged.[40]

Kaltenbrunner's conviction and sentence were not unjustified then, in view of what he had done and what had been proven in court. The former RSHA chief could not have been defended (let alone exonerated) unless one were either to accept his denials of knowledge and responsibility despite overwhelming evidence to the contrary or to adopt the principles of the Nazi myth world in toto and cease to define his crimes as crimes, but rather as "necessary military measures." Kaltenbrunner himself lacked the gall to assert the latter openly and sought refuge in the former as part of a calculated attempt to insure his own personal survival. In his more lucid moments, he realized that his case was hopeless unless tried within a Nazi framework. There was thus little justification for his complaints of victimization by con-

[40] Ibid., pp. 266-268.

queror's justice. Given his role in the murder and mistreatment of hundreds of thousands of people, it is difficult to imagine his acquittal in any court anywhere in 1946 or since.

After conviction and sentence, Kaltenbrunner settled down to wait stoically for death. One eyewitness noted in his diary on 2 October that the former RSHA chief seemed "calm and controlled, now that he had given up the fight."[41] Though it has been suggested that he derived his inner strength from a return to his boyhood Catholicism,[42] this is clearly a fairy tale; if anything, the revival of his Nazi faith afforded him strength and stubbornness to face the final ordeal. In September, shortly before judgment, he had had an opportunity to see his wife and apparently arrived at a reconciliation with her concerning whatever discord his extramarital affairs might have incited.[43] On 6 October, one of his mistresses (possibly Gisela von Westarp) was able to visit him on the intervention of the Catholic chaplain. Three days later, he wrote to his children for the last time, explaining that they should look after their mother, "since I can no longer come home to you from the great war." He wrote to his wife on the evening of his death, again begging forgiveness and insisting that he would die "in the belief that I wanted the best and did my duty."[44] Ninety-six minutes after midnight on the night of 15-16 October 1946, he ascended the scaffold. Reportedly, he took thirteen minutes to die. His body, along with the bodies of ten of his codefendants, was transported by train to Munich, where it was cremated. The ashes were strewn into the Isar River, running through the suburb of Munich-Solln.[45]

[41] Lippe, *Tagebuchnotizen*, p. 526.

[42] Hagen, *Geheime Front*, pp. 35-36; Houston, "Kaltenbrunner," pp. 182-183. Kaltenbrunner's participation in the prison masses conducted by Catholic chaplain Sixtus O'Connor had little to do with spiritual enlightenment or comfort in a religious sense. O'Connor apparently permitted his flock to converse with one another briefly (which was otherwise strictly forbidden) before the services began. Kaltenbrunner spent much of this time talking to Höttl, Seyss-Inquart, and Hans Frank about his defense. See Höttl Tape, p. 27; handwritten note of Kaltenbrunner attached to Kauffmann Draft, n.d., Nachlass Roland Kaltenbrunner. Nevertheless, Kaltenbrunner must have derived some comfort from O'Connor's presence, for this puzzling character was the only person at Nuremberg who believed his denials without question and who "never ceased to insist that those who threw doubt on . . . his statements were doing [him] . . . an injustice." See Fritzsche, *Sword in the Scales*, p. 186.

[43] On 3 October 1946, Kaltenbrunner wrote to his father-in-law: "Lisl has forgiven me for what I have done wrong in my life and I believe to have gathered from her words that she was happy as my wife." Kaltenbrunner to Karl Eder, 3 October 1946, possession of Elisabeth Kaltenbrunner.

[44] Haensel, *Gericht*, p. 167; Lippe, *Tagebuchnotizen*, p. 535; Kaltenbrunner to Hansjörg (12), Gertrud (9), and Barbara (2) Kaltenbrunner, 9 October 1946, Kaltenbrunner Family Records; Kaltenbrunner to Elisabeth Kaltenbrunner, 15 October 1946, possession of Elisabeth Kaltenbrunner.

[45] Houston, "Kaltenbrunner," p. 179; Maser, *Nürnberg*, pp. 1-2, 507.

Conclusions

THOUGH Kaltenbrunner has been dead for thirty-five years, his image as a ruthless, criminally insane, almost demonic monster persists to the present. Historians have gradually discarded the simplistic Nuremberg picture of the Nazis and the SS as conspiratorial criminals striving for selfish ends, but efforts are still made to reassure us that since the Nazis were not "psychologically normal and healthy individuals," only criminally deranged misfits are capable of doing what they did.[1] Yet George Browder, referring to the personnel of the Security Police and the SD, writes that this image does not satisfy and is even dangerous;[2] it implies that we can recognize and combat future outbursts of Nazi-like criminality merely by curbing the activities of the emotionally imbalanced or the criminally insane. This, of course, was just one of the fundamental misunderstandings about Hitler and the Nazi movement during and after its rise to power.

Despite superficial appearances, which his callous denials did nothing to dispel, Kaltenbrunner does not fit easily into the monster-criminal-psychopath category established at Nuremberg. This study has unearthed no evidence from his pre-Nazi career that might suggest that his was an aberrant personality prone to criminality and that he would one day supervise an apparatus entrusted with the murder and torture of millions of people.[3] Born into a respectable middle-class family that already had made the painful transition from the traditional artisan class to the nineteenth-century bourgeoisie, he enjoyed a secure childhood and early adolescence, the full social and professional benefits of university life, and an opportunity to work in the field for which he had been trained. Before he joined the Heimwehr in 1929, he had been employed in a Linz law firm, and, with the passions of the Burschenschaft behind him, he seemed ripe for responsible integration into postwar Austrian middle-class society. Sixteen years later he stood in the dock at Nuremberg, representing the most monstrous and repulsive aspects of the Nazi regime.

What happened? First, that middle-class society which the young Kaltenbrunner had been on the verge of entering lacked a stable, cohesive structure. The proud self-image of the Austrian professional had been shattered

---

[1] Miale and Selzer, *Mind*. On discarding the Nuremberg picture, see Höhne, *SS*; Arendt, *Eichmann*; Fest, *Face*; Browder, "Sipo and SD."

[2] Browder, "Sipo and SD," pp. 416-417.

[3] See similar conclusions on Himmler's pre-Nazi career in Bradley F. Smith, *Himmler*, p. 170.

by the psychological shock and the economic consequences both of the dissolution of the Habsburg Monarchy and of the catastrophic inflation of the postwar years; the younger generation developed a chronic anxiety about financial security, social status, and career opportunity. This was the case in Germany too,[4] but in Austria the situation was aggravated economically and psychologically by the painful transition from empire to tiny Balkanized republic. Trapped by political defeat, economic disaster, and cultural despair, the Austrian middle classes confronted what they perceived to be their disintegration as a cohesive social, cultural, and national unit. For Kaltenbrunner and others of his generation, integration into this society seemed tantamount to tying a living body to a decomposing corpse.

Völkisch nationalism swept into this social and cultural vacuum with tremendous force. With its obsessive suspicion of "foreign" influence—personified in the Jew and manifesting itself in socialism, liberalism, capitalism, Freemasonry, Czechs, Slovenes, Italians, France, and Soviet Russia—the völkisch creed provided many insecure would-be doctors, lawyers, teachers, scientists, and engineers with concrete enemies to whom their social, economic, and psychological distress could be attributed. Simultaneously, it offered the utopian prospect of a unified, racially pure German Reich in which their elite status and professional security would be guaranteed.

In Austria, the "bulwark" (*Hort*) of such ideas and hopes lay in the German nationalist fraternities at the universities. Since the mid-1880s, the overwhelming majority of the dueling fraternities, symbols of elite status to those not granted such by birth, were völkisch in orientation. Hugo Kaltenbrunner and his son Ernst were both captivated by the enthusiasm of the völkisch crusade; but, whereas Hugo found a place in a proud and secure adult society that blunted the sharp edges of his youthful exuberance, no such security was available to young Ernst. Unmitigated by positive activity in a complicated modern society, his youthful ideals remained intact until the Nazi movement gave them a practical basis for implementation. Moreover, the unique conditions in Central Europe after World War I had a devastating impact on the revolt of the younger generation, otherwise so prevalent in modern society and characteristic of student movements. Bruno Bettelheim has perceptively noted that young dissidents in postwar Germany and Austria soon discovered that the parental establishment against which they rebeled was itself in a state of collapse and could not offer the expected resistance. Deprived of solid values by or against which they could assert themselves and facilitate their "anxious moves into semi-adult independence,"[5] many postwar students clung all the more tenaciously to the secure

[4] On Himmler's fears, see ibid., pp. 84-85, 103-104, 127-128, 138-140.

[5] Bruno Bettelheim, *The Informed Heart: Autonomy in a Mass Age* (New York: Avon, 1971), p. 13.

mythical paradise provided for them by völkisch influences at the universities and, later, by the Nazis.

Like others in his generation, Kaltenbrunner never adjusted to postwar life in Austria. Unable to confront the complicated and often dismal realities of twentieth-century mass society, he eagerly responded to the Nazi offer of a simpler world in which he could feel at home. Moreover, membership in the SS satisfied an urge, springing from his middle-class background and his fraternity experience, to retain some sense of elite status within a modern mass movement.

If we can thus explain Kaltenbrunner's attraction to Nazism and the SS as a means of asserting his adulthood or attaining status, we have still to resolve the question of why he assisted in the implementation of the Nazi program of racial extermination. While thousands were murdered daily, he was able to remain "normal" in his off hours and was seen as a kind father by his children, an attractive lover by his mistresses, and a good comrade by his friends; indeed, he seems to have developed that split personality in regard to his actions and his human relations that Joachim Fest has analyzed.[6] Was he then merely a "commonplace, run-of-the-mill chap who ended his life as a convicted war criminal . . . an example of the horrible banality of evil"?[7] Was he a "man from the crowd,"[8] who drifted into mass murder because it happened to be part of the job to which he had been assigned? This picture, too, does not satisfy, for it neglects—at least in Kaltenbrunner's case—the key factor of personal initiative and implies a way of absolving responsibility for the consequences of individual career decisions. Despite Arendt's and Fest's gruesome visions of mindless robots herding human beings into gas chambers, one remains confronted with the fact that at every stage of his career, Kaltenbrunner voluntarily and knowingly placed himself in a position where he would be expected to carry out such orders. In 1929 he left the Lasser firm to join the paramilitary Heimwehr. Two years later he joined the SS, which was sworn to obey any commands that the Führer might issue; and, after the executions of Röhm, Strasser, and Schleicher in 1934, it was clear that such orders included extralegal murder. When Kaltenbrunner actively sought a pivotal police post in Austria in 1938, he knew that the Nazi police specialized in persecuting enemies of the regime. Finally, despite his knowledge of conditions in Mauthausen, deportations of Austrian Jews to Poland, and Einsatzgruppen activities in the USSR, he agreed to take over the RSHA when the position was offered. Though one might argue that the diplomat, the local policemen, or the railroad official was the epitome of banality, drawn into criminal activity as the re-

[6] Fest, *Face*, p. 302.
[7] Houston, "Kaltenbrunner," p. 190.
[8] Fest, *Face*, p. 276, in reference to Rudolf Höss.

gime radicalized its policies, such arguments are untenable in the cases of SS main office leaders and HSSPFs in the field who placed themselves voluntarily and absolutely at the disposal of the regime from the start. Kaltenbrunner certainly rose from the crowd, but it is evident that he, not the crowd, became chief of the RSHA.[9]

Why? First, the impact of völkisch ideas on young Kaltenbrunner was paramount and consistent. Like Hitler, he was born and raised in the German borderlands of the Habsburg Empire, where the proximity of German and Slav, the uncertainty concerning national identity within the multinational state, and the fear of submersion into alien cultures (Slavic, Jewish, Catholic) combined to produce a particularly virulent brand of völkisch nationalism attractive to the German-Austrian middle and lower-middle classes and already apparent in Schönerer's pan-Germanism. The definition and dehumanization of Germandom's enemies and the vision of a political union with Germany based on racial purity were widespread among middle-class, anticlerical German-Austrian professionals of Hugo Kaltenbrunner's generation; young Ernst was exposed to these concepts first in the home and later, in a more radical form, at the Realgymnasium in Linz.

The role of the fraternity experience in Graz in the formation of Kaltenbrunner's political character cannot be underestimated. Not only did it confirm and reinforce the adolescent political views that the young man had acquired in Raab and Linz, but it also anchored them in the uncompromising spirit of the university student movement. The fraternity students went beyond the mere definition of Germany's enemies to call for their elimination as a prerequisite for realizing the vision of a racially (and thus culturally) superior Germanic utopia in which, of course, they would hold secure positions in academia, medicine, business, or the state bureaucracy. Perhaps even more crucial for Kaltenbrunner's future development was the social atmosphere of fraternity life, which fostered the consciousness of membership in an elite destined by education and character to play a significant role in adult society. In addition to academic achievement, characteristics deemed essential for leadership were harshness toward oneself and others as expressed in the dueling ritual, a sense of arrogant superiority toward "unworthy" types as reflected in the rules regarding the ability to give

[9] Full biographies of the two prime examples of the banality thesis, Adolf Eichmann and Rudolf Höss, do not yet exist. Most of the material on Höss stems from his autobiography, which, like Kaltenbrunner's "memoir," was written in prison while he was awaiting his execution, and oozes with self-pity. The current view of Eichmann comes from the trial report of Hannah Arendt, which, despite her warnings, is still often taken for a definitive biography. See Höss, *Kommandant in Auschwitz*; Arendt, *Eichmann*; Fest, *Face*, pp. 276-287. Studies of these individuals based on primary and contemporary sources might raise questions about the validity of the banality thesis similar to those raised by this study of Kaltenbrunner.

satisfaction, and an absolute identification with the elite, manifest in the festivals, demonstrations, and drinking bouts. While it would be a gross exaggeration to assert that convictions and social mores held in 1926 lead in a direct line to mass murder in 1943, such habits of thought, formed early and undiluted by the moderating force of a stable career in a stable society, nevertheless created a psychological climate in which Kaltenbrunner would be prepared to accept such orders when they became necessary, and—more important—to grasp their ideological significance.

As an elite within the Nazi Party, the SS confirmed and reinforced the völkisch ideology and the mores instilled by the fraternity. As a member of the SS, Kaltenbrunner could take his place in a political and racial elite imbued with a sense of special mission and providing a ready-made society of like-minded companions. At the same time, the SS harnessed his völkisch enthusiasm to its own concept of the ideological soldier whose battle code was loyalty (*Treue*) to the concept of the Führer, much as Ignatius Loyola harnessed the fanatical faith of his followers to the cause of Pope, Emperor, and Counterreformation. In Himmler's Black Order, Kaltenbrunner could prove beyond all doubt his dedication to the German Volk by executing the most difficult tasks necessary to protect it.

The SS and its special tasks also fulfilled his need for action to reinforce continually the foundations of the totalitarian myth world. Kaltenbrunner's intellect could tolerate neither ambiguity nor uncertainty;[10] his restless nature was equally incapable of adjusting to the drudgery of everyday life. As a lawyer's apprentice in Salzburg and Linz bereft of the political and social atmosphere of the fraternity, he was bored and lonely, drifting in and out of local taverns until the Heimwehr and the Nazis offered him a new combination of political mission and relentless action. Again in 1938, after a period of political excitement in the Nazi underground and the loss of executive power as HSSPF in Austria, he lapsed into restless boredom, reflected in hard drinking and sexual adventurism. The 1943 RSHA appointment was welcome because it promised not only action and responsibilities of the most vital importance for the defense of Reich and Volk but also an opportunity to conquer and wield real personal power and to enjoy the excitement of playing spymaster. That his new job included the extermination of human beings among its duties did not detract from Kaltenbrunner's eagerness, for like many of the Gestapo and SD men he commanded, he developed no criminal self-image, but rather viewed himself as a loyal soldier commanding a sector of the internal front against the enemy. Indeed, his only solace at Nuremberg was the memory of the excitement of "battle"[11] in service of

[10] Miale and Selzer, *Mind*, p. 125.
[11] Kaltenbrunner to Jodl, 24 June 1946, Kaltenbrunner File.

the ideal of unity based on racial purity. In this connection his careerism cannot be overlooked; but he was that type Hitler prized most: a man who linked his own advancement so intimately to the general idea that neither career nor commitment could be separated from one another.[12]

Through it all, Kaltenbrunner's individual character remains opaque, masked by the emotional ardor of his ideology. In 1977, his brother, Werner, recalled Kaltenbrunner as taciturn and reserved (*verschlossen*), though careful to preserve an optimistic face. Kaltenbrunner's subordinates and comrades, looking back, saw him as a good sport and devoted comrade, but offer little of what he might really have thought or felt.[13] His love for his wife, children, and mistresses seems real enough, but even here his need for variety suggests an inability to sustain emotional commitment to individuals. All of his emotional energy, indeed, his very identity as an adult, was tied up with National Socialism. Like Himmler, he resolved his personal identity crisis through commitment to the völkisch ideology and its most able political exponent: National Socialism.[14] Against the general instability of adult society in postwar Central Europe, identification with the Nazi creed permitted him to make the transition to adulthood. Without it (as his behavior at Nuremberg graphically demonstrated), he was left paralyzed by the fear not only of death, but of the meaninglessness of his adult life.

If Kaltenbrunner's personality defies easy classification among the current theories of the National Socialist mind, his career is an example of how the combination of ideological commitment and agility in personal politics promoted career advancement and the acquisition of personal power in the Third Reich. Kaltenbrunner was not an "old fighter," nor did he have personal access to Hitler before 1943-1944; yet, from total obscurity he rose to become one of the most powerful men in Nazi Germany. How can this success in gaining and retaining political power be explained?

First, did Kaltenbrunner's Austrian origins have an effect on his career? No doubt a particularly virulent strain of völkisch nationalism infected Kaltenbrunner as a member of the German-Austrian middle class in the Habsburg state. Hitler himself carried the disease whose most obvious symptoms

---

[12] Rauschning, *Gespräche mit Hitler*, p. 256.

[13] Interview with Dr. Werner Kaltenbrunner, Vöcklabruck, 25 March 1977; interview with Dr. Wilhelm Höttl, Bad Aussee, 14 and 15 April 1977, Höttl Tape; interview with Leopold Tavs, Vienna, 21 January 1977, Tavs Tape; letters of Alfred Eduard Frauenfeld (19 December 1976), Franz Peterseil (17 May 1977), and Hans Christian Seiler (17 May 1977) to the author; interview with Otto Holzinger, Ried im Innkreis, 10 June 1977, Holzinger Tape.

[14] Smith, *Himmler*, p. 172. National Socialism gave meaning to Goebbels's adult existence as well. Robert Herzstein has written that "young Dr. Goebbels was a failure in life, in his own eyes, until he found National Socialism." Robert Edwin Herzstein, *The War that Hitler Won: The Most Infamous Propaganda Campaign in History* (London: Hamish Hamilton, 1979), p. 41.

were racial nationalism, anti-Semitism, and Slavophobia. Moreover, since Hitler was an Austrian, one might conclude that he would have encouraged the rise of ideologically loyal countrymen. Finally, the tension arising from the underground struggle against the Schuschnigg regime reinforced the radicalism of the Austrian Nazis and prepared them temperamentally for future tasks in service of the Reich. Evidence for the advantages of Austrian birth appears present in the number and prominence of Germans born in the Habsburg borderlands who took part in the Nazi occupation of Europe and committed themselves to Nazi extermination policies. Alfred Frauenfeld and Otto Wächter served as general commissars in the Crimea and Galicia. Arthur Seyss-Inquart was Reich commissar in the Netherlands. Hermann Neubacher was Hitler's special plenipotentiary in the Balkans. August Meyszner earned a special order of notoriety for his fanatical brutality in Serbia, as did Hanns Rauter in Holland and Karl Hermann Frank in Bohemia and Moravia. Odilo Globocnik and Hans Höfle managed "Action Reinhard," the slaughter of Polish Jewry. Franz Stangl commanded the death camp at Treblinka. Eduard Roschmann and Franz Murer commanded the SS units guarding the ghettos in Riga and Vilnius; while nearly a third of the members of the Eichmann commando, four times the percentage of Austrians in the Reich (8.5 percent), either had been born or grew up in Austria (Eichmann himself, Franz Novak, Alois and Anton Brunner, Erich Rajakowitsch).[15]

Yet, despite exceptional cases of regional cronyism (by no means peculiar to the National Socialist system), Austrians (or other borderland Germans) did not rise in the Nazi power structure because they were Austrians, but rather, like their Reich German counterparts, because they were ideologically reliable and tactically competent. Though Hitler displayed some sentiment for Linz, there is no evidence that he had any for Austrians as individuals; Bormann and Himmler, chiefs of the Nazi Party and the SS, respectively, certainly had none. Nevertheless, it was precisely to Himmler that Kaltenbrunner owed his spectacular rise; not because he was an Austrian, but because he was personally loyal, ideologically reliable, and at the same time able to carry out Himmler's instructions despite obstacles created by political and personal intrigues. As a provincial SS leader, Kaltenbrunner came to Himmler's attention because of his personal contacts in the influential Upper Austrian Nazi organization. He won Himmler's respect and favor through his personal loyalty and his ability to restrain the Austrian SS from participation in the strife that fragmented the Austrian Nazi underground. Kaltenbrunner demonstrated his political acumen by bringing the SS gradually onto the Seyss-Inquart/Rainer line, which not only kept its members out of jail, but conformed to Hitler's adamant demand for an

---

[15] Steiner, *Power Politics*, pp. 70, 247-248; Luža, *Anschluss Era*, pp. 226-227.

official hands-off policy in Austria. In the scar-faced Austrian, Himmler had a man whose leadership enabled him to conceal his (Himmler's) direct control of the Austrian SS organization and to insure that the disastrous putsch attempt of 25 July 1934 would not be repeated. The Reichsführer SS rewarded his faithful minion with a police appointment in Austria; and, when he needed a replacement for Heydrich, he again chose Kaltenbrunner for his proven loyalty, ideological reliability (i.e., preparedness to assume responsibility for the "difficult tasks" of the Security Police), and political skill in dealing with potential rivals. Though Kaltenbrunner's Austrian origins certainly contributed to the development of his ideological reliability, his rise in the SS until 1943 differed little in its causes from the successful careers of Reich Germans like Reinhard Heydrich, Friedrich Wilhelm Krüger, and Karl Wolff.

Both his subordinates in the RSHA and postwar historians have characterized the style and effect of Kaltenbrunner's rule at the RSHA with respect to inventiveness, dynamism, and ruthless decisiveness, as inferior to that of the first RSHA chief, Reinhard Heydrich. Wilhelm Höttl reflected that Kaltenbrunner lacked both the "unfathomable malice" and the "personal importance" of his predecessor; Walter Schellenberg maintained that Himmler was able to curtail Kaltenbrunner's authority in the RSHA by cultivating direct contacts with the RSHA department chiefs; journalist Heinz Höhne dismissed Kaltenbrunner as a "second-rater" installed only to prevent the rise of another Heydrich.[16] Although Kaltenbrunner was less inventive and dynamic than his infamous predecessor, the corollary that he was a less effective security chief for Hitler's Reich does not follow. In fact, Heydrich and Kaltenbrunner complemented one another in maintaining the RSHA as a decisive and efficient instrument for the implementation of Nazi security and racial policies within the Reich and throughout Europe. If in his correspondence and decrees Heydrich appears as the visionary, peering into and preparing for the perceived distant future of the Nazi regime, Kaltenbrunner's correspondence dealt with specific problems of the day and rarely took philosophical leaps into the future. The RSHA was Heydrich's (and—one must not forget—Himmler's) ideological and administrative inspiration; its first chief delegated the details of Security Police and SD operations to his department chiefs in order to reserve the energy and opportunity to develop basic ideological and structural guidelines for the future of police rule in the Reich. Kaltenbrunner, on the other hand, was an ideological bureaucrat who immersed himself in legal debate concerning the disposal of the property of deported Jews or provisions on the treatment of pregnant foreign

---

[16] Hagen, *Geheime Front*, p. 84; Schellenberg, *Secret Service*, pp. 329-330; Höhne, *SS*, p. 624.

workers, in the practical details of constructing a Reich foreign intelligence service, and in exposing the anatomy of the 20 July 1944 conspiracy. Heydrich's superiority to Kaltenbrunner lay less in Heydrich's aptitude for running the RSHA than in his ability to combine efficient administration with the innovative spirit of a visionary. His application of the Nazi ideology was marked by a creative streak and a personal decisiveness that Kaltenbrunner did not always display.

In all fairness to Kaltenbrunner, it must be noted that Heydrich developed his talents in an atmosphere congenial to experimentation. From 1934, the first RSHA chief had operated from Berlin, the seat of Nazi political power. To develop the SS and police apparatus in Germany and occupied Europe, he had five years of peace, three years of spectacular military success and, perhaps most important, the constant and considerably less divided attention, supervision, and participation of Himmler, whose key role in the development of SS and police power was underestimated both by subordinates under the spell of Heydrich's personal magnetism and, later, by historians and journalists peering at the development of the RSHA through the eyes of these subordinates. Heydrich's well-known experiment in occupation policy in Bohemia and Moravia and his plans for pacifying occupied France were conceived in the years of Hitler's greatest military triumphs, when the battle fronts were still distant, Allied aerial bombardment still insignificant, and local resistance movements still divided and disorganized. His death on 4 June 1942—on the eve of the great summer offensives that would carry the armed forces of the Reich to their farthest geographical limit of expansion—prevented Heydrich from outliving the era of confidence that the Nazi system would dominate Europe for a thousand years.

Kaltenbrunner operated under outside constraints to which Heydrich had not been subject. When he came to Berlin in January 1943, he had not much more than two years to familiarize himself with a complex series of contacts and power relationships that Heydrich had developed over eight years. Moreover, Himmler, whose SS interests had diversified considerably from the initial security function of the early 1930s, no longer had the time or opportunity to provide Kaltenbrunner with either the guidance or the effective support that Heydrich had enjoyed prior to the outbreak of the war. Finally, Kaltenbrunner occupied his office in the RSHA on the eve of the Stalingrad surrender, at a time in which the security problems of the Nazi state had a genuine as well as an ideological foundation. Instead of combatting unarmed political opponents and mythical racial opponents whose real representatives did not understand that a war of annihilation was being waged against them until large numbers of their fellows had been exterminated, the Nazi security apparatus faced well-armed and organized resistance movements. As resistance to Nazi rule in occupied Europe intensified, Germany suffered catastrophic military defeats on the battle fronts and devastating bombardment from the air. As quickly as it had expanded during Heydrich's day, the Reich contracted while Kaltenbrunner sat in the Prinz-Albrecht-Strasse (the location of the RSHA). These factors undoubtedly influenced the style of Kaltenbrunner's rule, though the RSHA was no less effective an instrument of Nazi rule under Kaltenbrunner than it had been under Heydrich. Kaltenbrunner's concern for the present rather than the future as RSHA chief can be traced therefore not only to his relative lack of decisiveness and Heydrich's greater innovative ability, but also to the rapidly contracting world in which Kaltenbrunner replaced Heydrich.

Kaltenbrunner's success as chief of the RSHA can perhaps best be explained by comparing him to four other Nazi leaders, who could be considered the most powerful men in the Third Reich in 1942-45: Martin Bormann, Heinrich Himmler, Josef Goebbels, and Albert Speer.[17] Like Kaltenbrunner, all were born close to the turn of the century: Goebbels (1897), Himmler and Bormann (1900), and Speer (1905). All except Bormann came from solid middle-class families, missed World War I because of youth or physical handicap, and completed a university degree. Like Kaltenbrunner, Himmler and Goebbels had been students during part of the tumultuous five years following the collapse of the Central European empires. Bormann, Goebbels, Himmler, and Kaltenbrunner joined the Nazi Party or a kindred organization before the world depression of the 1930s, though only Goebbels was prominent in the movement when it gained power in 1933. Speer, Bormann, and Kaltenbrunner remained unknown until the second half of World War II. Finally, all received significant appointments during the crisis years of 1942-44 as a symbol of Hitler's faith in them: Speer as minister of armaments and war production (February 1942); Kaltenbrunner as chief of the RSHA (January 1943); Bormann as secretary of the Führer (April 1943); Himmler as minister of the interior (August 1943) and commander in chief of the Reserve Army (July 1944); and Goebbels as Reich plenipotentiary for total war (July 1944).

These men gained and retained power on the basis of their personal loyalty, indeed devotion, to Hitler. Each, even Speer, saw in Hitler the incarnation of Germany and its destiny; each identified him with the realization of his personal-political utopia: Goebbels and Bormann in their single-minded pursuit of power; Himmler and Kaltenbrunner in their vision of a dominant

[17] Wulf, *Bormann*; Lang, *Sekretär*; Smith, *Himmler*; Manvell and Fraenkel, *Himmler*; Josef Wulf, *Heinrich Himmler* (Berlin: Arani Verlag, 1960); Heiber, *Goebbels*; Goebbels, *Diaries*; Speer, *Inside*; Gregor Janssen, *Das Ministerium Speer: Deutschlands Rüstung im Krieg* (Frankfurt-Berlin: Ullstein Verlag, 1968); Matthias Schmidt, *Albert Speer: Das Ende eines Mythos* (Bern-Munich: Scherz, 1982); portraits in Fest, *Face*, pp. 83-97, 111-124, 125-135, 198-208.

Germanic racial elite; Speer in his "architectural megalomania."[18] Each surrendered himself to the dictator's charisma. Goebbels, writes Fest, "submitted himself, his whole existence, to his attachment to the Fuehrer, to whom he subordinated himself in a positively pathological manner."[19] Himmler made loyalty to Hitler not only the motto of his SS, but also the measure of his own personal self-value. Bormann followed his Führer around like a faithful dog, recording every word, fulfilling every whim, removing every bothersome administrative difficulty. Kaltenbrunner's faith was so complete that a mere hour with Hitler in the ruins of Berlin could convince him that final victory was inevitable. Even Speer could never cut his emotional ties to Hitler. Despite his disgust at the Führer's order to destroy Germany's natural and industrial resources in the spring of 1945 (an order he ultimately disobeyed), Speer was still "confused and emotionally shaken" when he met the dictator for the last time on 23 April 1945.[20] Hitler was instinctively aware of such sentiments and rightly interpreted them as a sign that these men would follow him anywhere; thus he endowed their persons and positions with the charismatic legitimacy of his own personality. He chose his servants well, for none save Speer—and even he not happily—deserted.

Loyalty to Hitler and his recognition of that loyalty, though representing the essence of ideological commitment in the Third Reich, was not the only basis for the career success these men enjoyed, for such reciprocal loyalty also characterized the positions of men like Ley and Göring, Ribbentrop and Rosenberg, yet did not prevent their becoming powerless. The practical, as opposed to ideological, basis of political and personal power in the Third Reich was rooted in responsibility for carrying out that which Hitler deemed essential and in possession of either the technical skill or the political muscle to carry it out effectively. Speer kept the war machine functioning, thus prolonging the survival of the Reich in the struggle against its enemies from without. Himmler's SS had the responsibility of protecting the dictator and the regime from the enemies within. Kaltenbrunner operated the apparatus that physically eliminated both types of enemies. Bormann codified the dictator's ramblings and relieved him of all the tiresome administrative and personal details of his rule. Finally, Goebbels managed, with astounding success, the delicate task of selling the bankrupt regime to the German people until the day of Hitler's death. It is significant that of the five, four carried out "ideological" tasks; and all in their success became as indispensable to Hitler as he was to them.

Nevertheless, as the generals, old-school diplomats, jurists, and administrators discovered to their dismay, competence in the execution of appointed

---

[18] Speer, *Inside*, p. 50.
[19] Fest, *Face*, p. 190.
[20] Speer, *Inside*, p. 480.

tasks still had to be linked to a special direct or indirect personal relationship to the dictator to insure career success and actual political power in the Third Reich. The power of Speer, Bormann, and Goebbels was based not on their official titles but on their personal indispensability to Hitler. Although Himmler and Kaltenbrunner commanded an apparatus of power, their access to Hitler in the last years of the war was less frequent; but the "vital nature" of their ideological tasks was so closely tied to Hitler's personal fears and manias that they could effectively use his ideology to advance their personal and political aims in the jungle of conflicting ambitions and jurisdictions. Ideological commitment, political adeptness in overcoming rivals, and technical competence in getting the job done were thus inextricably intertwined in their contribution to political career building in the Third Reich.

Yet the rise of such men ultimately signaled the oncoming catastrophe. By 1942-1943, those in power knew that Hitler had tied Germany's fate to his own and that, unless one chose to depart from the scene, one had to either follow him to the end or overthrow him. In this final crisis, the reins of power could no longer be entrusted to those who were not personally committed to Hitler and ideologically committed to the regime. Bormann, Himmler, Kaltenbrunner, Goebbels, Speer, and others like them on the middle and lower levels of power knew that they were riding the "last wave" of Hitler's leadership; they were the ideological bureaucrats, the technicians of power, who surfaced or (in Goebbels's case) resurfaced at the moment when the Nazi state, through its aggressive and criminal acts, had finally conjured up a real coalition of enemies determined to destroy the German Reich. National Socialism is unthinkable without them and they without it. Of the five, three committed suicide in May 1945; another was hanged seventeen months later. Only Speer (who disobeyed) survived the war and its aftermath; but even he remained linked to the Nazi era in that he made his postwar fortune from the proceeds of his memoirs.

OBSERVING Adolf Eichmann on the stand at his trial in Jerusalem, Hannah Arendt was struck by the fact that "the only notable characteristic" that she could detect "in his past behavior as well as in his behavior during the trial and throughout the pre-trial police examination was something entirely negative: it was not stupidity but *thoughtlessness*" (emphasis in the original).[21] Albert Speer once wrote that in his decision to join the Nazi Party, his "inclination to be relieved of having to *think*, particularly about unpleasant facts, helped to sway the balance" (emphasis added).[22] If Arendt was correct

[21] Hannah Arendt, *The Life of the Mind*, Vol. I: *Thinking* (New York–London: Harcourt, Brace, Jovanovich, 1978), p. 4. See also Arendt, *Eichmann*, pp. 287-288.

[22] Speer, *Inside*, p. 20. See also p. 345.

in her assumption that thinking, or the quest for meaning, "relentlessly dissolves and examines anew all accepted doctrines and rules," that it is "equally dangerous to all creeds," we might wonder as she did whether the "activity of thinking as such . . . could . . . be among the conditions that make men abstain from evildoing or even actually 'condition' them against it."[23] During the Hitler regime and the generations that preceded it, the greater part of a nation not only ceased thinking, but refused to think, indeed sought desperate flight from the mere possibility of having to think. In a period of rapid technological development and cataclysmic economic and social change which, compounded in their psychological effects by political defeat and revolution, tore apart the foundations of old value structures, a society ruled according to a fixed system of ideas and values was called for and embraced. In the state of "mass thoughtlessness" that resulted, shocking crimes were committed.

Since the nineteenth century, humanity has been gradually losing the protection offered in traditional values defined by both divine and natural laws. Like their later totalitarian counterparts, these laws also offered people relief from the *need* to think; but unlike the totalitarian model, the natural-divine laws managed to give the individual's life intrinsic meaning through the implicit power to choose, and to preserve one's dignity and uniqueness ("inalienable rights"). However, systems based on concepts of humanity's creation in the divine image or of one's innate "rights" to liberty, equality, and the pursuit of happiness wear thin in the nuclear age. Indeed, today one might sneer with the nineteenth-century racist, Georges Vacher de Lapouge: "Every man is related to all men and all living creatures. Therefore there are no human rights any more than there are . . . rights of the armadillo. As soon as man loses his right to be a separate entity in the image of God, he no longer had any more right than any other mammal. The idea of justice is an illusion. Nothing exists but violence."[24]

The Nazi experience demonstrated with shocking clarity this "void of violence" left by the gradual loss of principles confirming the sanctity of human life and the absence of a "thinking" population. A new system was imposed in which disregard for human life became a virtue and murder a moral duty. Not only were the Nazis able to impose the antihuman principle in the void of violence; other organized populations have succeeded as well if not as thoroughly in doing the same. The history of the world since 1945 is replete with examples.

But can the process of thinking prevent such evildoing? Arendt warned that thinking in itself did not create values but rather "dissolved accepted

[23] Arendt, *Thinking*, pp. 5, 176.
[24] Quoted in Ernst Nolte, *Three Faces of Fascism* (New York: Mentor, 1969), p. 357.

rules of conduct."[25] If she was correct, would her "thinking" not deepen the void of meaninglessness brought about by technological advancement, economic insecurity, and social change? Would not an unthinking, hedonistic thrust toward wealth and power or yet more insatiable craving for all-inclusive systems of thought be thereby encouraged? Refusal to think for fear of the void, however, cannot exorcise that fear. Those who drown their principles in blood so that they might convince themselves and others of their validity cannot hope to be successful, for the process of thinking will continue to dissolve them until all thinkers (or, following the logic of the idea, all potential thinkers, or human beings) are exterminated.

To paper over the void (i.e., the possibility that human life has no intrinsic meaning) with an inflexible Weltanschauung offering for mass consumption easily digestible answers to cosmic questions would ultimately subordinate the individual to the system and cut one off from the only genuine links to others: one's uniqueness and autonomy. The acceptance of fixed systems, therefore, risks treating man as a means and not as an end and endangers the unique self by submerging it into a mass identity—be it nation or class, generation or sex, ethnic group or political ideology. National Socialism represents only the most extreme but by no means isolated example of the results of such unthinking identification.

If the possibility of meaninglessness cannot be denied without lethal consequences for individual uniqueness, it is possible to accept the presence of the void, to overcome the fear of it, to develop an inner ability for internal self-government linked to a "conscientious search for meaning despite the realization that, as far as we know, there is no purpose to one's life."[26] To this search must be linked a consciousness that not only the life of the human race but also individual human life is priceless. Such a stance is not merely a matter of theoretical morality but also of practical survival, for a price placed on one life implies that all lives can be similarly priced; and murderers by virtue of their act create an implicit justification for their own murder by others.

The search for meaning in the presence of the void is frightening, for success is always uncertain and answers are neither simple nor absolute. Each individual must face the crisis alone and can not expect that today's rational guidelines will be valid tomorrow. One can take comfort only in the fact that one's fellows face the same crisis. In a search for truth and meaning, Ernst Nolte stated that "indisputable and basic to all truth is the fact of differentiation itself, and this structure of existence may more properly be called transcendence."[27] To cope with such differentiation of truth, hu-

[25] Arendt, *Thinking*, p. 192.
[26] Bettelheim, *Informed Heart*, p. 75.
[27] Nolte, *Three Faces*, p. 540.

mankind must think—even at the risk of dissolving the systems it creates and meeting the void head on—and, on the basis of that thought, "judge" (Kant's "peculiar talent which can be practiced only and cannot be taught")[28] the difference between right and wrong in each individual situation.

Fascism, and especially National Socialism, was only the most extreme form of a vicious but also desperate revolt against having to think in the face of the pressures of undertaking such an uncertain venture in a time of economic, social, and psychological crisis. Ernst Kaltenbrunner's life symbolizes a frantic effort to escape the threat of the void by denying its existence, an angry refusal to think in a world that had lost all meaning. By subordinating himself to the Nazi ideology and disappearing into the Germanic "racial elite," he denied his own humanity to the point where murder no longer presented a moral issue if sanctioned by the Nazi creed. Thus, he was in fact partially responsible for his transformation into the monster that shocked and disgusted observers at Nuremberg. He had chosen extreme methods to cope with the crisis that faced him in the early twentieth century and that, under varying local conditions, still confronts the thinking individual at the threshold of the twenty-first. To illustrate what can happen if a nonthinking stance toward crisis is adopted, the effort to "rehumanize" Kaltenbrunner is possible and useful. Arendt's question, Can thinking prevent evildoing?, is answered by Nolte's observation that "when . . . thought has become the friend of man—only then can man be said to have finally crossed the border into a post-fascist era."[29] In the more than three decades since Kaltenbrunner's execution, events throughout the world have indicated that the crossing remains problematic.

[28] Arendt, *Thinking*, p. 215.
[29] Nolte, *Three Faces*, p. 567.

APPENDIX A

Equivalent Ranks of Officers in German, British, and American Military Services

SS	German Army (to 1945)	British Army	U.S. Army	German Police
Reichsführer	Generalfeldmarschall	Field Marshal	General of the Army	—
Oberstgruppenführer	Generaloberst	—	—	Generaloberst der Polizei
Obergruppenführer	General	General	General	General der Polizei
Gruppenführer	Generalleutnant	Lieutenant General	Lieutenant General	Generalleutnant der Polizei
Brigadeführer	Generalmajor	Major General	Major General	Generalmajor der Polizei
Oberführer	Oberst	Brigadier	Brigadier General	Oberst der Schutzpolizei Reichskriminaldirektor

SOURCE: Helmut Krausnick et al., *Anatomy of the SS State* (New York: Walker, 1968), pp. 576-577.

(Continued on next page)

Appendix A—continued

SS	German Army (to 1945)	British Army	U.S. Army	German Police
Standartenführer	Oberst	Colonel	Colonel	Oberst der Schutzpolizei Reichskriminaldirektor
Obersturmbannführer	Oberstleutnant	Lieutenant Colonel	Lieutenant Colonel	Oberstleutnant der Schutzpolizei Oberregierungs- und Kriminalrat
Sturmbannführer	Major	Major	Major	Major der Schutzpolizei Regierungs- und Kriminalrat
Hauptsturmführer	Hauptmann	Captain	Captain	Hauptmann der Schutzpolizei Kriminalrat
Obersturmführer	Oberleutnant	Lieutenant	First Lieutenant	Oberleutnant der Schutzpolizei Kriminalkommissar
Untersturmführer	Leutnant	Second Lieutenant	Second Lieutenant	Leutnant der Schupo Kriminalsekretär

Chain of Command for the Higher SS and Police Leaders, 1940

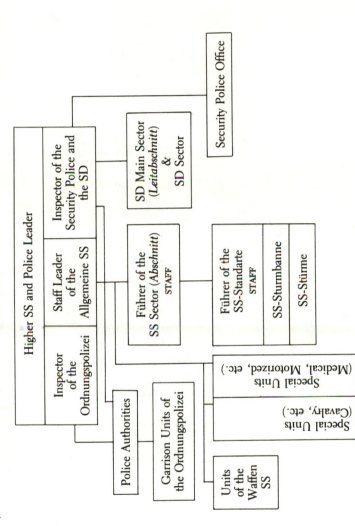

SOURCES: Ermenhild Neusüss-Hunkel, *Die SS* (Frankfurt: Norddeutsche Verlagsanstalt, 1956), p. 141; citing from Werner Best, *Die deutsche Polizei* (Darmstadt: L. C. Wittich, 1940), p. 102.

SS Main Offices, 1944

Reichsführer SS and Chief
of German Police (RFSS)
Heinrich Himmler

Personal Staff
Reichsführer SS
SS-Obergruf.
Karl Wolff

SS-Hauptamt (SS-HA)
SS-Obergruf.
Gottlob Berger

SS-Führungshauptamt
(SSFHA) SS-Obergruf.
Hans Jüttner

Rasse- und Siedlungs-
hauptamt (RuSHA)
SS-Obergruf.
Richard Hildebrandt

Hauptamt SS-Gericht
SS-Obergruf.
Franz Breithaupt

SS-Personalhauptamt
SS-Obergruf.
Maximilian von Herff

Reichssicherheitshauptamt
(RSHA) SS-Obergruf.
Ernst Kaltenbrunner

Hauptamt Ordnungspolizei
(HA-Orpo) SS-Oberstgruf.
Kurt Daluege

Wirtschafts- und Verwaltungshauptamt (WVHA) SS-Obergruf.
Oswald Pohl

Hauptamt Volksdeutsche
Mittelstelle (HA-Vomi)
SS-Obergruf.
Werner Lorenz

RKF Hauptamt (Reichs-
kommissar für die Festigung
deutschen Volkstums, RKFDV)
SS-Obergruf.
Ulrich Greifelt

SOURCE: Heinz Höhne, *The Order of the Death's Head: The Story of Hitler's SS* (New York: Ballantine, 1971), fold-out flap between pp. 530-531.

APPENDIX D

The RSHA, 1944

The Chief of the Security Police and SD
Reich Security Main Office

Amt I	*Amt II*	*Amt III*	*Amt IV*
Training, Personnel, Organization (SS-Standartenf. Erich Ehrlinger)	Budget & Economy (SS-Standartenf. Josef Spacil)	SD-Inland (SS-Brigadef. Otto Ohlendorf)	Gestapo (SS-Gruppenf. Heinrich Müller)
I Org: General Organization	II A: Budget, Salary	III A: Racial and Legal Regulation (SS-Oberstubaf. Höppner)	IV A: Opponents, Sabotage, Protective Service (SS-Gruppenf. H. Müller)
I A: Personnel	II B: Economic & Institutional Affairs	III B: Nationality (SS-Standartenf. Ehlich)	IV B: Political Churches, Sects, and Jews (SS-Ostubaf. Lischka)
I B: Education, Training	II C: Technical Affairs	III C: Research, Culture, Public Means of Leadership (SS-Standartenf. Spengler)	IV C: Personnel Files, Protective Custody, Press, and Party (SS-Oberf. Somann)
I Mil: Personnel		III D: Economy (SS-Standartenf. Seibert)	IV D: Greater German Spheres of Influence
		III E: "Society" Intelligence Service (SS-Sturmbannf. Wegener)	IV E: Counterespionage (SS-Standartenf. Walter Huppenkothen)
			IV F: Ports and Foreign Police

(Continued on next page)

Appendix D—*continued*

The Chief of the Security Police and SD
Reich Security Main Office

Amt V	*Amt VI*

Kriminalpolizei (SS-Gruppenf. Artur Nebe, later SS-Oberf. Friedrich Panzinger)

SD-Ausland (SS-Brigadef. Walter Schellenberg)

V A: Criminal Policy & Prevention

V B: Employment (SS-Standartenf. Werner)

V C: Investigations, Intelligence Service & Information (SS-Oberstubaf. Schulze)

V D: Criminal, Technical & Biological Institutes (SS-Standartenf. Heess)

V Wi: Economy (Economic crime) (SS-Oberstubaf. Filbert)

VI A: Administration & Organization (SS-Standartenf. Martin Sandberger)

VI B: West Europe, West Africa (SS-Standartenf. Steimle)

VI C: Russia and Near East (SS-Oberstubaf. Rapp)

VI D: West (Britain, U.S.A., South America, Scandinavia) (SS-Oberstubaf. Paeffgen)

VI E: Southeast Europe (SS-Oberstubaf. Wilhelm Waneck)

VI F: Technical Apparatus (Oberstleutnant Boening)

VI G: Methodical Scientific Research Service (SS-Stubaf. Krallert)

VI S: Sabotage (SS-Oberstubaf. Otto Skorzeny)

VI Wi: Economy (SS-Standartenf. Schmied)

(Continued on next page)

The Chief of the Security Police and SD
Reich Security Main Office

Amt Mil	Amt VII	Amt N	Amt San
Military Intelligence (Oberst Georg Hansen, later SS-Brigadef. Walter Schellenberg)	Ideological Research (SS-Oberstubaf. Dittel)	Communication Affairs (SS-Standartenf. Sansoni)	Medical Affairs (SS-Oberstubaf. Strohschneider)
Mil A: Administration (SS-Standartenf. Martin Sandberger)	VII A: Material Comprehension (SS-Stubaf. Burmeister)	N/Fe: Teletype (SS-Stubaf. Walther)	*Amtsgruppe Polizei-Attachés*
Mil B: West Europe (SS-Standartenf. Steimle)	VII B: Evaluation (SS-Stubaf. Muehler)	N/Fu: Radio (SS-Hauptstuf. Marks)	
Mil C: East Europe (Major Ohletz)	VII C: Archives, Museums, Special Tasks (SS-Stubaf. Richter)		Police Attachés (SS-Standartenf. Zindel)
Mil D: Sabotage (SS-Oberstubaf. Otto Skorzeny)			
Mil E: Technical (Oberstleutnant Boening)			
Mil F: Front Reconnaissance (Oberst Buntrock)			

SOURCES: Organization of the Security Police and the SD, 1943-1945, 2346-PS, NCA, VIII, back flap; report of Wilhelm Höttl, "The SD and the RSHA," 9 July 1945, ZS-429/II, IfZ Munich; Geschäftsverteilungsplan, Amt III [RSHA], 15 September 1944, File RSHA, R 58/Folder 792, BA.

Local Organization of the Security Police
and the SD 1939-1945

Old Reich, Austria,
Protectorate of
Bohemia and Moravia

Occupied Territories

Old Reich side

Reichsführer SS and
Chief of German Police

Reich Security
Main Office

Inspector of Security
Police and SD

Higher SS and
Police Leaders

SD Main
Sectors
(SD-Leitabschnitte)

Criminal
Police
Offices
(Kripoleitstellen)

Gestapo
Offices
(Stapoleitstellen)

SD-Sectors
(SD-Abschnitte)

Criminal
Police Offices
(Kripostellen)

Gestapo Offices
(Stapostellen)

Occupied Territories side

Reichsführer SS and
Chief of German Police

Higher SS and   Reich Security
Police Leaders   Main Office

Commander (Befehlshaber)
of Security Police and SD
(In regions directly behind
the front, Commander of
Einsatzgruppe of the
Security Police and SD)

Commanders (Kommandeure) of
Security Police and SD (In
regions directly behind the
front, Commanders of
Einsatzkommandos of the
Security Police and the SD)

Sonderkommandos and
Teilkommandos of the
Security Police and SD

SOURCE: "Organization of the Security Police and the SD, 1943-1945," 2346-PS, NCA, VIII, inside flap of back cover.
NOTE: Solid lines indicate direct chain of command. Broken lines show indirect chain of command, with direct having precedence.

Bibliography

I. ARCHIVAL AIDS

Guides to German Records Microfilmed at Alexandria, Va. 79 vols. Washington: National Archives, 1958-1983 (mimeographed).

II. PRIMARY SOURCES

A. ARCHIVAL RECORDS

National Archives, Washington, D.C.
    Nuremberg Trial Documents (series NG, NI, NO, NOKW, PS).
    Records of the Reich Ministry of Armaments and War Production, T-73, Roll 179.
    Records of Headquarters, German Armed Forces High Command, T-77, Rolls 775, 861, 864, 900.
    Records of Headquarters, German Army High Command, T-78, Roll 497.
    Records of the National Socialist German Workers' Party, T-81, Roll 5.
    Miscellaneous German Records Collection, T-84, Rolls 13, 14, 16, 22, 150.
    Records of the German Foreign Office, T-120, Rolls 354, 751, 1757.
    Records of the Reichsführer SS and Chief of German Police, T-175, Rolls 19, 22, 31, 32, 33, 38, 53, 57, 58, 59, 62, 66, 68, 69, 75, 103, 117, 119, 122, 123, 124, 126, 128, 137, 155, 199, 219, 223, 232, 240, R256, 267, 281, 355, 403, 428, 429, 458, 486, 574, 657.
    Records of Private German Individuals, T-253, Roll 22.
    Records of the Reich Ministry for the Occupied Eastern Territories, T-454, Roll 75.
    Records of the Berlin Document Center, T-580, Rolls 62, 72.
    Poole Team Interrogations, M-679, Rolls 1, 2, 3.
    NSDAP Personnel Records, Roll 490, Record Group 242, Modern Military Records Branch.
    CG, US Third Army, Interrogation Report No. 10, 21 June 1945, Modern Military Records Branch.
    "Counterintelligence Report on Head of RSHA Kaltenbrunner, Dr. Ernst," Hdqtrs. Twelfth Army Group, Mobile Field Interrogation Unit No. 4, 25 May 1945, CIR 4/3, IIR, Modern Military Records Branch.

Lennon, Harry F., "Intermediate Interrogation Report," 28 June 1945, CIR 4/3, IIR, Modern Military Records Branch (Lennon Report).

OSS Report to Joint Chiefs of Staff, "Approaches from Austrian and Bavarian Nazis," 27 March 1945, CCS 387, Germany 9.21.44, Section 2, Modern Military Records Branch.

Winzer, 1st Lt. George, Intermediate Interrogation Report on Hermann Neubacher, 29 January 1946, Folder CI-IIR, no. 36, Modern Military Records Branch (Winzer Report).

International Law Library, Columbia University, New York City.

United States v. Weizsäcker et al. (mimeographed proceedings).

YIVO Institute for Jewish Research, New York City.

Kaltenbrunner to Goebbels, 1 April 1944, Berlin Collection, Occ E (RA)— 2.

Berlin Document Center, West Berlin.

Personnel Files:

H. Becker (SS).

H. Böhme (SS).

E. Ehrlinger (SS).

E. Kaltenbrunner (SS).

R. Kaltenbrunner (RuS/Sippenamt).

W. Kaltenbrunner (SS).

W. Keppler (SS).

H. Klausner (SS).

F. Rainer (SS).

H. Rauter (SS).

E. Spaarmann (SS).

B. Streckenbach (SS).

K. Taus (SS).

Aktenmappe Österreich, Ordner 303.

Aktenmappe RSHA, Ordner 457.

Aktenmappe SA, Ordner 414/415.

Aktenmappe SS, Ordner 304/6.

Aktenmappe SS und Kirche, Ordner 245.

Aktenmappe SOEG, Ordner 364.

SS-Hang Ordner, 2277, 2293, 2297.

SS-Sammelliste, vols. 43, 69.

Sonderakt Canaris:

Huppenkothen, W., "Canaris und Abwehr."

Bundesarchiv, Koblenz.

Records of the Hauptamt Ordnungspolizei, R 19, folder 401.

Records of the Reich Chancellery, R 43 II, folder 678a.

Records of the Reich Security Main Office, R 58, folders 239, 243, 280, 441, 486, 801, 1225, 1280.

Records of the Southeast Europe Society (SOEG), R 63, folders 35, 63, 206.

Records of the General Commissar in Minsk, R 93, folder 20.

Records of the Race and Settlement Main Office, NS 2, folder 78.

Records of the Adjutantur des Führers, NS 10, folder 50.

Nachlass Arthur Seyss-Inquart, folders 1, 3, 8, 23, 39, 56, 60.

Institut für Zeitgeschichte, Munich.

Personal Files:

>G. Berger (ZS-427).

>W. Höttl (ZS-429).

>W. Huppenkothen (ZS-249).

>E. Kaltenbrunner (ZS-673).

>K. Lindow (ZS-583).

>R. Mildner (ZS-431).

>O. Ohlendorf (ZS-278).

>O. Pohl (ZS-567).

>W. Schellenberg (ZS-291).

>A. Seyss-Inquart (ZS-300).

>G. Steengracht von Moyland (ZS-1546).

>E. von Thadden (ZS-359).

>E. Veesenmayer (ZS-1554).

>H. Wagner (ZS-1574).

>W. Waneck (ZS-1579).

>K. Wolff (ZS-317).

Eichmann Trial Prosecution Documents (EPD), nos. 674, 816, 817, 827, 856, 900, 1423, 1492.

Eichmann Vernehmungsbuch (Eichmann Interrogation Book—affidavits collected for the Eichmann Trial), 2904/62.

Himmler, Heinrich. Log of telephone conversations, 16 September 1941–17 August 1943, F 37/2.

Hueber, Franz. Testimony, Landgericht Salzburg, 11 June 1947, G 13.

Kaltenbrunner, Ernst. "Lebenslauf." Nuremberg, 1945, F 190.

Mittelstaedt, Kurt. "Die Unrechtsbekaempfung in Konzentrationslagern und aehnlichen Einrichtungen durch SS-Richter." Oberursel, 1945-1946, F 65.

Morgen, Konrad. Affidavit, 28 December 1945, F 65.

Allgemeines Verwaltungsarchiv, Vienna.
  Files of the Ministry of the Interior in the Federal Chancellor's Office
    (Bka-Inneres):
  22/general, Boxes 4913, 4914, 4972.
  22/Oberösterreich, Boxes 5102, 5103, 5104, 5111, 5112, 5113.
  Papers of Büro Glaise-Horstenau, Box 39/10.

Neues Politisches Archiv des österreichischen Staatsarchivs, Vienna.
  Boxes 305, 307, 308.

Dokumentationsarchiv des österreichischen Widerstandes, Vienna.
  Eder, Max E. "Die Kunstgutbergungsaktion Salzbergbau, Alt Aussee,
    Oberösterreich: Kurzer Bericht über deren Anfänge und Verlauf bis
    zum Eintreffen der U.S. Truppen am 8. Mai 1945." May 1945, 10.610.
  Persche, Alfred. "Hauptmann Leopold: Der Abschnitt 1936-1938 der
    Geschichte der nationalsozialistischen Machtergreifung in Österreich."
    N.d., 1460/1.
  Plieseis to editors of Neuen Mahnruf (Vienna), 27 October 1960, 631.
  Scharizer to Kaltenbrunner, 20 March 1941, 1456.

Österreichisches Institut für Zeitgeschichte, Vienna.
  Personal Files:
    W. Höttl.

Landgericht Linz, Linz.
  Investigation of Hugo Flatz, KMS 56/44.

Stadtarchiv, Linz.
  Linzer Tagblatt. Jahrgang 17, nos. 122, 123, 28 and 29 May 1932.
  Linzer Tagespost. no. 122, 28 May 1932.
  Linzer Volksstimme. Jahrgang 9, Folge 4, 24 January 1931; Jahrgang 10,
    Folge 23, 4 June 1932.

B. DOCUMENTS IN PRIVATE HANDS

Kaltenbrunner Family Records (possession of Dr. Hansjörg Kaltenbrunner,
    Gramastetten, Austria).
  Birth and baptismal certificates for Hugo Kaltenbrunner.
  Grade reports and professional certificates for Hugo Kaltenbrunner.
  Announcement of Hugo Kaltenbrunner's entry into the Beurle Law Firm,
    1 December 1918.

Kaltenbrunner File (originals in the possession of Dr. Hansjörg Kaltenbrun-
    ner, Gramastetten, Austria; copies in the possession of this author).
  Kaltenbrunner to Jodl, 24 June 1946.
  Kaltenbrunner to Kauffmann, 24 June, 1 and 5 July 1946.

Kaltenbrunner, Ernst. "Memoir," Nuremberg, July-August 1946.
Kaltenbrunner, Hansjörg. "Persönliche Eindrücke über meinen Vater von meiner Kindheit." Gramastetten, 11 June 1977.
"Der Lebenslauf Carl Adam Kaltenbrunners." 1905 (mimeographed).
Mistlbacher, Carl. "Ahnentafel." 12 October 1936–13 March 1938.

Nachlass Roland Kaltenbrunner (originals in the possession of Dr. Hansjörg Kaltenbrunner, Gramastetten, Austria; copies in possession of this author).
"Der obere Absang oder Saganger, später Unterhaindl oder untere Kaltenbrunner Werkstatt genannt, zum Marktgerichte Kirchdorf hörig."1863.
Letters of Carl Adam Kaltenbrunner to Karl Kaltenbrunner, 1857-1863.
Draft of Final Plea (at the Nuremberg Trial) by Dr. Kurt Kauffmann, June 1946, with handwritten note of Kaltenbrunner attached.

Possession of Frau Elisabeth Kaltenbrunner, Linz.
Kaltenbrunner to Karl Eder, 3 October 1946.
Kaltenbrunner to Elisabeth Kaltenbrunner, 15 October 1946.

Possession of Dr. Hansjörg Kaltenbrunner, Gramastetten.
Kaltenbrunner to Hansjörg, Gertrud, and Barbara Kaltenbrunner, 9 October 1946.

C. INTERVIEWS AND CORRESPONDENCE

Bart, Richard. Conversation, Linz, 31 January 1977.
Frauenfeld, Alfred Eduard. Letters to the author of 19 December 1976 and 20 February 1977.
Gaiswinkler, Albrecht. Conversation, Bad Aussee, 12 April 1977.
Gleissner, Heinrich. Letter to the author of 13 December 1976.
Holzinger, Otto. Interview, Ried im Innkreis, 10 June 1977; and letter to the author of 10 May 1977.
Höttl, Wilhelm. Interview, Bad Aussee, 14 and 15 April 1977; and letters to the author of 15 June 1977 and 9 November 1979.
Kaltenbrunner, Elisabeth. Interview, Linz, 25 March 1977.
Kaltenbrunner, Hansjörg. Conversations, Gramastetten, 25 and 26 March 1977.
Kaltenbrunner, Werner. Interview, Vöcklabruck, 25 March 1977.
Koref, Ernst. Letter to the author of 9 December 1976; and verbal information, Linz, 1 February 1977.
Latzel-Lasser, Irmfried. Letter to the author of 11 January 1977.
Matteson, Robert E. Letter to the author of 24 July 1978.
Mayrhofer, Franz. Letter to the author of 27 April 1977.
Moser, Karl. Conversation, Alt Aussee, 13 April 1977.

Peterseil, Franz. Letter to the author of 17 May 1977.

Picha, Otto. Interview, Vienna, 26 January 1977; and letter to the author of 17 February 1976.

Pöschl, Wilhelm. Letter to the author of 24 May 1977.

Radauschl, Sebastian. Conversation, Alt Aussee, 13 April 1977.

Rodenbücher, Alfred. Letter to the author of 13 March 1977.

Seiler, Hans Christian. Letter to the author of 17 May 1977.

Tavs, Leopold. Interview, Vienna, 21 January 1977.

Thanner, Erich. Letter to the author of 12 April 1977.

Trunkel, Father (Roman Catholic Pfarramt, Alt Aussee). Letter to the author of 10 January 1977.

D. PUBLISHED DOCUMENTS

Bericht der Historischen Kommission des Reichsführers SS. *Die Erhebung der österreichischen Nationalsozialisten im Juli 1934: Akten der Historischen Kommission des Reichsführers SS.* Edited by Fritz Klenner, Hans Oprecht, and Erich Pogats. Vienna-Frankfurt-Zurich: Europa Verlag, 1965.

Boberach, Heinz, ed. *Meldungen aus dem Reich: Auswahl aus den geheimen Lageberichten des Sicherheitsdienstes der SS, 1939-1944.* Munich: Deutscher Taschenbuch Verlag, 1968.

Braham, Randolph L., ed. *The Destruction of Hungarian Jewry: A Documentary Account.* 2 vols. New York: World Federation of Hungarian Jews, 1963.

Documents on German Foreign Policy, 1918-1945. Series C. Vols. I, II, III. Series D. Vols. I, II, III. Washington: U.S. Government Printing Office, 1949-1958.

Domarus, Max, ed. *Hitler: Reden und Proklamationen, 1932-1945.* 2 vols. Munich: Süddeutscher Verlag, 1965.

Heiber, Helmut, ed. *Reichsführer! Briefe an und von Himmler.* Munich: Deutscher Taschenbuch Verlag, 1970.

Der Hochverratsprozess gegen Dr. Guido Schmidt vor dem Wiener Volksgericht. Vienna: Druck und Verlag der österreichischen Staatsdruckerei, 1947.

International Military Tribunal. *Trial of the Major War Criminals Before the International Military Tribunal.* 42 vols. Nuremberg: Secretariat of the Military Tribunal, 1947-1949.

Kotze, Hildegard von, ed. *Heeresadjutant bei Hitler 1938-1943: Aufzeichnungen des Major Engel.* Stuttgart: Deutsche Verlags-Anstalt, 1974.

Noakes, Jeremy, and Pridham, Geoffrey, eds. *Documents on Nazism, 1919-1945.* New York: Viking, 1975.

Oberösterreichischer Amtskalender. *Der Oberösterreicher*. Linz: Verlag von Vinzenz Fink, 1906. Linz: Wimmer Verlag, 1919, 1930, 1932, 1933.

Office of the U.S. Chief of Counsel for the Prosecution of Axis Criminality. *Nazi Conspiracy and Aggression*. 8 vols. and 2 supplements. Washington: U.S. Government Printing Office, 1946-1948.

Peter, Karl Heinrich ed. *Spiegelbild einer Verschwörung: Die Kaltenbrunner-Berichte an Bormann und Hitler über das Attentat vom 20. Juli 1944. Geheime Dokumente aus dem ehemaligen Reichssicherheitshauptamt*. Stuttgart: Seewald Verlag, 1961.

Slapnicka, Harry. *Oberösterreich 1917-1977: Karten und Zahlen*. Linz: Oberösterreichischer Landesverlag, 1977.

Trevor-Roper, H. R., ed. *The Bormann Letters*. London: Weidenfeld & Nicolson, 1954.

Trials of War Criminals Before the Nuremberg Military Tribunals. 15 vols. Washington: U.S. Government Printing Office, 1949-1954.

Widerstand und Verfolgung in Wien, 1934-1945. 3 vols. Vienna: Österreichischer Bundesverlag für Unterricht, Wissenschaft und Kunst, 1975.

E. Partisan Books and Pamphlets

Best, Werner. *Die deutsche Polizei*. Darmstadt: L. C. Wittich, 1940.

Heimatschutz in Österreich. Vienna: Verlag Zoller, 1935.

Jung, Rudolf. *Der nationale Sozialismus: Seine Grundlagen, sein Werdegang und seine Ziele*. 3rd ed. Munich: Deutscher Volksverlag, 1922.

Moschner, Richard. *Kärnten—Grenzland im Süden*. Berlin: Junker und Dünnhaupt Verlag, 1940.

Spann, Othmar. *Der wahre Staat—Vorlesungen über Abbruch und Neubau der Gesellschaft gehalten im Sommersemester 1920 an der Universität Wien*. Leipzig: Quelle, 1921.

F. Memoirs, Diaries, Apologia

Andrus, Burton C. *I Was the Nuremberg Jailer*. New York: Coward-McCann, 1969.

Bazna, Elyesa. *I Was Cicero*. London: André Deutsch, 1962.

Bernadotte, Count Folke. *The Curtain Falls: The Last Days of the Third Reich*. New York: Alfred A. Knopf, 1945.

Biss, Andreas. *Der Stopp der Endlösung: Kampf gegen Himmler und Eichmann in Budapest*. Stuttgart: Seewald Verlag, 1966.

Boldt, Gerhard. *Hitler: The Last Ten Days*. New York: Berkeley Medallion, 1973.

Dollmann, Eugen. *Dolmetscher der Diktatoren*. Bayreuth: Hestia-Verlag, 1963.

Dulles, Allen. *The Secret Surrender*. New York–Evanston–London: Harper & Row, 1966.

Fritzsche, Hans. *The Sword in the Scales*. London: Allan Wingate, 1953.

Gaiswinkler, Albrecht. *Sprung in die Freiheit*. Vienna-Salzburg: Ried Verlag, 1947.

Giesler, Hermann. *Ein anderer Hitler*. Leoni am Starnberger See: Druffel-Verlag, 1977.

Gilbert, G. M. *Nuremberg Diary*. New York: Signet, 1961.

Gisevius, Hans Bernd. *Wo ist Nebe? Erinnerungen an Hitlers Reichskriminaldirektor*. Zurich: Droemer, 1966.

Goebbels, Josef. *Final Entries 1945: The Diaries of Josef Goebbels*. Ed. H. R. Trevor-Roper. New York: Avon, 1979.

———. *The Goebbels Diaries, 1942-1943*. Ed. Louis P. Lochner. New York: Doubleday, 1948.

Haensel, Carl. *Das Gericht vertagt sich*. Hamburg: Claasen Verlag, 1950.

Hagen, Walter (pseudonym for Wilhelm Höttl). *Die geheime Front: Organisation, Personen und Aktionen des deutschen Geheimdienstes*. Linz-Vienna: Nibelungen Verlag, 1950.

———. *Unternehmen Bernhard: Ein historischer Tatsachenbericht über die grösste Geldfälschungsaktion aller Zeiten*. Wels-Starnberg: Verlag Welsermühl, 1955.

Hitler, Adolf. *Mein Kampf*. Trans. Ralph Mannheim. Boston: Houghton Mifflin, 1943.

Höss, Rudolf. *Kommandant in Auschwitz: Autobiographische Aufzeichnungen*. Ed. Martin Broszat. Munich: Deutscher Taschenbuch Verlag, 1981.

Höttl, Wilhelm. *The Secret Front*. New York: Frederick A. Praeger, 1954.

Jodl, Luise. *Jenseits des Endes: Leben und Sterben des Generaloberst Alfred Jodl*. Vienna-Munich-Zurich: Verlag Fritz Molden, 1976.

Kelley, Douglas M. *22 Cells in Nuremberg: A Psychiatrist Examines the Nazi War Criminals*. New York: Greenberg, 1947.

Kersten, Felix. *The Kersten Memoirs, 1940-1945*. New York: Macmillan, 1957.

———. *Totenkopf und Treue: Heinrich Himmler ohne Uniform*. Hamburg: Robert Mölich Verlag, n.d.

Kesselring, Albert. *Soldat bis zum letzten Tag*. Bonn: Athenäum, 1953.

Kleist, Peter. *Die europäische Tragödie*. Göttingen: Verlag K. W. Schütz, 1971.

———. *Zwischen Hitler und Stalin, 1939-1945: Aufzeichnungen*. Bonn: Athenäum, 1950.

Langoth, Franz. *Kampf um Österreich: Erinnerungen eines Politikers*. Wels: Verlag Welsermühl, 1951.

Leverkuehn, Paul. *German Military Intelligence.* London: Weidenfeld & Nicolson, 1954.

Lippe, Viktor Freiherr von der. *Nürnberger Tagebuchnotizen, November 1945 bis Oktober 1946.* Frankfurt am Main: Verlag Fritz Knapp, 1951.

Moyzisch, L. C. *Operation Cicero.* New York: Coward-McCann, 1950.

Neave, Airey. *On Trial at Nuremberg.* Boston-Toronto: Little, Brown & Co., 1978.

Orb, Heinrich. *Nationalsozialismus: 13 Jahre Machtrausch.* Olten: Verlag Otto Walter, 1945.

Papen, Franz von. *Memoirs.* New York: E. P. Dutton, 1953.

Pearson, Ralph E. *Enroute to the Redoubt: A Soldier's Report as a Regiment Goes to War.* Vol. III. Chicago: Adams Printing Service, 1958.

Plieseis, Sepp. *Vom Ebro zum Dachstein: Lebenskampf eines österreichischen Arbeiters.* Linz: Verlag "Neue Zeit," 1946.

Pöchmüller, Erich. *Weltkunstschätze in Gefahr.* Salzburg: Pallas Verlag, 1948.

Rauschning, Hermann. *Gespräche mit Hitler.* Vienna: Europa Verlag, 1973.

Ribbentrop, Joachim von. *Zwischen London und Moskau: Erinnerungen und letzte Aufzeichnungen.* Ed. Annelies von Ribbentrop. Leoni am Starnberger See: Druffel-Verlag, 1954.

Rintelen, Anton von. *Erinnerungen an Österreichs Weg: Versailles—Berchtesgaden—Grossdeutschland.* Munich: Verlag F. Bruckmann, 1941.

Schellenberg, Walter. *Hitler's Secret Service.* New York: Pyramid, 1971.

————. *Memoiren.* Cologne: Verlag für Politik und Wirtschaft, 1959.

Schirach, Baldur von. *Ich glaubte an Hitler.* Hamburg: Mosaik Verlag, 1967.

Schuschnigg, Kurt von. *My Austria.* New York: Alfred A. Knopf, 1938.

Skorzeny, Otto. *Geheimkommando Skorzeny.* Hamburg: Hansa Verlag Josef Toth, 1950.

————. *Meine Kommandounternehmen: Krieg ohne Fronten.* Wiesbaden-Munich: Limes Verlag, 1976.

Speer, Albert. *Inside the Third Reich.* New York: Macmillan, 1970.

————. *Spandau: The Secret Diaries.* New York: Pocket Books, 1977.

Starhemberg, Ernst Rüdiger. *Memoiren.* Vienna-Munich: Amalthea Verlag, 1971.

Streeruwitz, Ernst Streer Ritter von. *Springflut über Österreich: Erinnerungen, Erlebnisse, und Gedanken aus bewegter Zeit, 1914-1929.* Vienna-Leipzig: Bernina, 1937.

Waugh, Evelyn. *The Diaries of Evelyn Waugh.* Ed. Michael Davie. Boston-Toronto: Little, Brown & Co., 1976.

West, Rebecca. *A Train of Powder.* New York: Viking, 1955.

Winkler, Franz. *Die Diktatur in Österreich.* Zurich-Leipzig: Orell Füssli Verlag, 1935.

Zernatto, Guido. *Die Wahrheit über Österreich*. New York: Longmans, Green & Co., 1939.

III. SECONDARY SOURCES

A. Unpublished Material

Bernbaum, John A. "Nazi Control in Austria: The Creation of the Ostmark, 1938-1940." Doctoral dissertation, University of Maryland, 1972.

Black, Peter R. "The Austrian National Socialists and the Destruction of the Austrian State, 1933-1938." Master's thesis, Columbia University, 1973.

————. "The Resistance that Never Was." Unpublished seminar paper, Columbia University, 1973.

Browder, George Clark. "Sipo and SD, 1931-1940: Formation of an Instrument of Power." Doctoral dissertation, University of Wisconsin, Madison, 1968.

Houston, Wendell Robert. "Ernst Kaltenbrunner: A Study of an Austrian SS and Police Leader." Doctoral dissertation, Rice University, 1972.

Schmier, Louis. "Martin Bormann and the Nazi Party, 1941-1945." Doctoral dissertation, University of North Carolina, 1968.

B. Books

Abshagen, Karl Heinz. *Canaris, Patriot und Weltbürger*. Stuttgart: Union Deutsche Verlagsgesellschaft, 1950.

Adam, Uwe Dietrich, *Judenpolitik im Dritten Reich*. Düsseldorf: Droste Verlag, 1972.

Adorno, T. W. et al. *The Authoritarian Personality*. New York: Harper & Bros. 1950.

Arendt, Hannah. *Eichmann in Jerusalem: A Report on the Banality of Evil*. Rev. ed. New York: Viking, 1965.

————. *The Life of the Mind*. Vol. I: *Thinking*. New York–London: Harcourt, Brace, Jovanovich, 1978.

————. *The Origins of Totalitarianism*. 2nd ed. New York: Meridan, 1958.

Aronson, Shlomo. *Beginnings of the Gestapo System: The Bavarian Model in 1933*. Jerusalem: Israel Universities Press, 1969.

Ball, M. Margaret. *Post-War German-Austrian Relations: The Anschluss Movement, 1918-1936*. Stanford: Stanford University Press, 1937.

Bärnthaler, Irmgard. *Die Vaterländische Front: Geschichte und Organisation*. Vienna-Frankfurt-Zurich: Europa Verlag, 1971.

Bayle, François. *Psychologie et Ethique du National-Socialisme: Etude anthropologique des dirigeants SS*. Paris: Presses Universitaires de France, 1953.

Becke, Karl. *Die Wiener Burschenschaft Albia: 1870 bis 1930.* Vienna: F. Hammann, 1930.

Besymenski, Lew. *Die letzten Notizen von Martin Bormann: Ein Dokument und sein Verfasser.* Stuttgart: Deutsche Verlags-Anstalt, 1974.

Bettelheim, Bruno. *The Informed Heart: Autonomy in a Mass Age.* New York: Avon, 1971.

Biddiss, Michael D., ed. *Gobineau: Selected Political Writings.* London: Jonathan Cape, 1970.

Bilger, Ferdinand. *Die Wiener Burschenschaft Silesia von 1860 bis 1870 und ihre Bedeutung für die Anfänge der deutschnationalen Bewegung in Österreich.* Heidelberg: Karl Winters, 1911.

Borkenau, Franz. *Austria and After.* London: Faber & Faber, 1939.

Bosch, William J. *Judgment on Nuremberg: American Attitudes towards the Major German War Crimes Trials.* Chapel Hill: University of North Carolina Press, 1970.

Botz, Gerhard. *Gewalt in der Politik: Attentate, Zusammenstösse, Putschversuche, Unruhen in Österreich, 1918-1934.* Munich: Wilhelm Fink Verlag, 1976.

Bracher, Karl Dietrich. *The German Dictatorship: The Origins, Structure, and Effects of National Socialism.* New York: Praeger, 1970.

Braham, Randolph L. *The Politics of Genocide: The Holocaust in Hungary.* 2 vols. New York: Columbia University Press, 1981.

Brandes, Detlev. *Die Tschechen unter deutschem Protektorat.* Vol. II: *Besatzungspolitik, Kollaboration und Widerstand im Protektorat Böhmen und Mähren von Heydrichs Tod bis zum Prager Aufstand, 1942-1945.* Munich: R. Oldenbourg, 1975.

Brissaud, André. *Canaris.* New York: Grosset & Dunlap, 1974.

Broszat, Martin. *Nationalsozialistische Polenpolitik, 1939-1945.* Frankfurt-Hamburg: Fischer Bücherei, 1965.

Buchheim, Hans. *Glaubenskrise im Dritten Reich: Drei Kapitel nationalsozialistischer Religionspolitik.* Stuttgart: Deutsche Verlags-Anstalt, 1953.

————. *SS und Polizei im NS-Staat.* Duisdorf: Selbstverlag der Studiengesellschaft für Zeitprobleme, 1964.

Buchheit, Gerd. *Der deutsche Geheimdienst: Geschichte der militärischen Abwehr.* Munich: Paul List Verlag, 1966.

————. *Richter in roter Robe: Freisler, Präsident des Volksgerichtshofes.* Munich: Paul List Verlag, 1968.

Bullock, Alan. *Hitler: A Study in Tyranny.* New York: Bantam, 1961.

Burschofsky, Ferdinand. *Beiträge zur Geschichte der Deutsch-Nationalen Arbeiterbewegung.* 2 vols. Hohenstadt: Im Selbstverlag, 1907.

Carsten, F. L. *Fascist Movements in Austria: From Schönerer to Hitler.* London-Beverly Hills: Sage, 1977.

Carsten, F. L. *Revolution in Central Europe, 1918-1919*. Berkeley–Los Angeles: University of California Press, 1972.

Chary, Frederick B. *The Bulgarian Jews and the Final Solution, 1940-1944*. Pittsburgh: University of Pittsburgh Press, 1972.

Colvin Ian. *Chief of Intelligence*. London: Gollancz, 1951.

Conway, J. S. *The Nazi Persecution of the Churches, 1933-1945*. New York: Basic Books, 1968.

Davidson, Eugene. *The Trial of the Germans: An Account of the Twenty-two Defendants Before the International Military Tribunal at Nuremberg*. New York: Collier Books, 1972.

Dawidowicz, Lucy S. *The War Against the Jews, 1933-1945*. New York: Bantam, 1976.

Delarue, Jacques. *The Gestapo: A History of Horror*. New York: Dell, 1965.

Diamant, Alfred. *Austrian Catholics and the First Republic: Democracy, Capitalism, and the Social Order, 1918-1934*. Princeton: Princeton University Press, 1960.

Edmondson, C. Earl. *The Heimwehr and Austrian Politics, 1918-1936*. Athens: University of Georgia Press, 1978.

Ehrlicher, Klaus-Eckart, and Leitinger, Reinhart. *1868-1968, Ein Hort deutschen Fühlens: Die Grazer akademische Burschenschaft Arminia im Wandel der Zeiten*. Radkersburg: Grenzlanddruckerei Ernst Huallenz, 1970.

Eichstädt, Ulrich. *Von Dollfuss zu Hitler: Geschichte des Anschlusses Österreichs, 1933-1938*. Wiesbaden: Franz Steiner Verlag, 1955.

Erikson, Erik H. *Childhood and Society*. 2nd ed. New York: W. W. Norton, 1963.

Feis, Herbert. *Churchill, Roosevelt, Stalin: The War They Waged and the Peace They Sought*. Princeton: Princeton University Press, 1957.

Fenyo, Mario D. *Hitler, Horthy, and Hungary: German-Hungarian Relations, 1941-1944*. New Haven: Yale University Press, 1972.

Fest, Joachim C. *The Face of the Third Reich: Portraits of the Nazi Leadership*. New York: Pantheon, 1970.

Festschrift zum 60. jährigen Stiftungsfest der Grazer akademischen Burschenschaft "Arminia": 1868-1928. Graz: Verlag der Grazer akademischen Burschenschaft "Arminia," n.d.

Feuer, Lewis S. *The Conflict of the Generations: The Character and Significance of Student Movements*. New York: Basic Books, 1969.

Fischer, Alexander. *Sowjetische Deutschlandpolitik im Zweiten Weltkrieg, 1941-1945*. Stuttgart: Deutsche Verlags-Anstalt, 1975.

Fromm, Erich. *Escape from Freedom*. New York: Avon, 1965.

Gehl, Jürgen. *Austria, Germany, and the Anschluss, 1931-1938*. London: Oxford University Press, 1963.

Genschel, Helmut. *Die Verdrängung der Juden aus der Wirtschaft im Dritten Reich.* Göttingen: Musterschmidt Verlag, 1966.

Gilbert, G. M. *The Psychology of Dictatorship.* New York: Ronald Press, 1950.

Goldinger, Walter. *Geschichte der Republik Österreich.* Vienna: Verlag für Geschichte und Politik, 1962.

Gulick, Charles A. *Austria: From Habsburg to Hitler.* 2 vols. Berkeley–Los Angeles: University of California Press, 1948.

Heiber, Helmut. *Josef Goebbels.* Munich: Deutscher Taschenbuch Verlag, 1974.

Herzstein, Robert Edwin. *The War that Hitler Won: The Most Infamous Propaganda Campaign in History.* London: Hamish Hamilton, 1979.

Hilberg, Raul. *The Destruction of the European Jews.* Chicago: Quadrangle, 1967.

Hindinger, Gabriele. *Das Kriegsende und der Wiederaufbau demokratischer Verhältnisse in Oberösterreich im Jahre 1945.* Vienna: Brüder Hollinek, 1968.

Hoensch, Jörg K. *Die Slowakei und Hitlers Ostpolitik: Hlinkas Slowakische Volkspartei zwischen Autonomie und Separation, 1938-1939.* Cologne-Graz: Böhlau Verlag, 1965.

Hoffmann, Peter. *The History of the German Resistance, 1933-1945.* Cambridge: MIT Press, 1977.

Hofmann, Josef. *Der Pfrimer-Putsch: Der steirische Heimwehrprozess des Jahres 1931.* Vienna-Graz: Stiasny Verlag, 1965.

Höhne, Heinz. *Canaris: Patriot im Zwielicht.* Munich: Wilhelm Goldmann Verlag, 1978.

——. *The Order of the Death's Head: The Story of Hitler's SS.* New York: Ballantine, 1971.

Holldack, Heinz. *Was wirklich geschah: Die diplomatischen Hintergründe der deutschen Kriegspolitik.* Munich: Nymphenburger Verlagshandlung, 1949.

Horn, Wolfgang. *Führerideologie und Parteiorganisation in der NSDAP, 1919-1933.* Düsseldorf: Droste Verlag, 1972.

Hüttenberger, Peter. *Die Gauleiter: Studie zum Wandel des Machtgefüges in der NSDAP.* Stuttgart: Deutsche Verlags-Anstalt, 1969.

Hyde, H. Montgomery. *The Life and Times of Lord Birkett of Ulverston.* New York: Random House, 1965.

Jagschitz, Gerhard. *Der Putsch: Die Nationalsozialisten 1934 in Österreich.* Graz-Vienna-Cologne: Verlag Styria, 1976.

Janssen, Gregor. *Das Ministerium Speer: Deutschlands Rüstung im Krieg.* Frankfurt-Berlin: Ullstein Verlag, 1968.

Jarausch, Konrad H. *Students, Society, and Politics in Imperial Germany: The Rise of Academic Illiberalism.* Princeton: Princeton University Press, 1982.

Jedlicka, Ludwig. *Ein Heer im Schatten der Parteien: Die militärpolitische Lage Österreichs, 1918-1938.* Graz-Cologne: Verlag Hermann Böhlaus, 1955.

————. *Der 20. Juli 1944 in Österreich.* 2nd ed. Vienna-Munich: Verlag Herold, 1966.

Jenks, William A. *Austria under the Iron Ring.* Charlottesville: University Press of Virginia, 1965.

Kahn, David. *Hitler's Spies: German Military Intelligence in World War II.* New York: Macmillan, 1978.

Kann, Robert A. A *History of the Habsburg Empire, 1526-1918.* Berkeley–Los Angeles–London: University of California Press, 1977.

Kater, Michael H. *Studentenschaft und Rechtsradikalismus in Deutschland, 1918-1933: Eine sozialgeschichtliche Studie zur Bildungskrise in der Weimarer Republik.* Hamburg: Hoffmann und Campe Verlag, 1975.

Kimche, Jon. *Spying for Peace: General Guisan and Swiss Neutrality.* 3rd edition. New York: Roy Publishers, 1962.

Klemperer, Klemens von. *Ignaz Seipel: Christian Statesman in a Time of Crisis.* Princeton: Princeton University Press, 1972.

Knoll, Kurt. *Geschichte der Grazer akademischen Burschenschaft Stiria.* Graz: Stiria, 1912.

————. *Die Geschichte der wehrhaften Vereine deutscher Studenten in der Ostmark.* Vienna: Reinholt, 1924.

Koch, H. W. *The Hitler Youth: Origins and Development, 1922–1945.* New York: Stein & Day, 1976.

Koehl, Robert L. *RKFDV: German Resettlement and Population Policy, 1939-1945.* Cambridge: Harvard University Press, 1957.

Kogon, Eugen. *Der SS-Staat: Das System der deutschen Konzentrationslager.* Frankfurt am Main: Verlag der Frankfurter Hefte, 1946.

Kohn, Hans. *The Mind of Germany: The Education of a Nation.* New York: Harper Torch, 1965.

Krausnick, Helmut et al. *Anatomy of the SS State.* New York: Walker & Co., 1968.

Kwiet, Konrad. *Reichskommissariat Niederlände: Versuch und Scheitern nationalsozialistischer Neuordnung.* Stuttgart: Deutsche Verlags-Anstalt, 1968.

Lang, Jochen von. *Der Sekretär: Martin Bormann, der Mann, der Hitler beherrschte.* Stuttgart: Deutsche Verlags-Anstalt, 1977.

Laqueur, Walter. *The Terrible Secret: Suppression of the Truth about Hitler's "Final Solution."* Boston-Toronto: Little, Brown & Co., 1980.

————. *Young Germany: A History of the German Youth Movement*. London: Routledge & Kegan Paul, 1962.

Luža, Radomír. *Austro-German Relations in the Anschluss Era*. Princeton: Princeton University Press, 1975.

Macartney, C. A. *The Habsburg Empire, 1790-1918*. New York: Macmillan, 1969.

Manvell, Roger, and Fraenkel, Heinrich. *The Canaris Conspiracy*. New York: Pinnacle, 1972.

————. *Himmler*. New York: Paperback Library, 1968.

Maser, Werner. *Nürnberg: Tribunal der Sieger*. Düsseldorf-Vienna: Econ Verlag, 1977.

May, Arthur. *The Hapsburg Monarchy, 1867-1914*. New York: Norton, 1968.

Meyerhoff, Hermann. *Herne 1933-1945: Die Zeit des Nationalsozialismus.*. Herne: C. Th. Kartenberg, 1963.

Miale, Florence, and Selzer, Michael. *The Nuremberg Mind: The Psychology of the Nazi Leaders*. New York: Quadrangle, 1975.

Mikoletzky, Hanns Leo. *Österreichische Zeitgeschichte: Vom Ende' der Monarchie bis zum Abschluss des Staatsvertrages, 1955*. Vienna-Munich: Österreichischer Bundesverlag, 1962.

Milgram, Stanley. *Obedience to Authority: An Experimental View*. New York: Harper & Row, 1974.

Minott, Rodney. *The Fortress that Never Was: The Myth of Hitler's Bavarian Stronghold*. New York-Chicago-San Francisco: Holt, Rinehart & Winston, 1964.

Molisch, Paul. *Geschichte der deutschnationalen Bewegung in Österreich von ihren Anfängen bis zum Zerfall der Monarchie*. Jena: Verlag von Gustav Fischer, 1926.

————. *Politische Geschichte der deutschen Hochschulen in Österreich von 1848 bis 1918*. 2nd ed. Vienna-Leipzig: Wilhelm Braumüller, 1939.

Morse, Arthur D. *While Six Million Died: A Chronicle of American Apathy*. New York: Random House, 1968.

Moser, Jonny. *Die Judenverfolgung in Österreich, 1938-1945*. Vienna: Europa Verlag, 1966.

Mosse, George L. *The Crisis of German Ideology: Intellectual Origins of the Third Reich*. New York: Grosset & Dunlap, 1964.

————. *Toward the Final Solution: A History of European Racism*. New York: Harper & Row, 1980.

Neumann, Franz. *Behemoth: The Structure and Practice of National Socialism, 1933-1944*. Toronto–New York–London: Oxford University Press, 1944.

Neusüss-Hunkel, Ermenhild. *Die SS*. Hannover-Frankfurt: Norddeutsche Verlagsanstalt, 1956.

315

Nolte, Ernst. *Three Faces of Fascism: Action Française, Italian Fascism, National Socialism*. New York: Mentor, 1969.

Nusser, Horst G. W. *Konservative Wehrverbände in Bayern, Preussen und Österreich, 1918-1933*. Munich: Nusser Verlag, 1973.

Nyomarkay, Joseph. *Charisma and Factionalism in the Nazi Party*. Minneapolis: University of Minnesota Press, 1967.

Orlow, Dietrich. *The History of the Nazi Party, 1919-1933*. Pittsburgh: University of Pittsburgh Press, 1969.

———. *The History of the Nazi Party, 1933-1945*. Pittsburgh: University of Pittsburgh Press, 1973.

———. *The Nazis in the Balkans: A Case Study of Totalitarian Politics*. Pittsburgh: University of Pittsburgh Press, 1968.

Pauley, Bruce F. *Hahnenschwanz und Hakenkreuz: Der steirische Heimatschutz und der österreichische Nationalsozialismus, 1918-1934*. Vienna: Europa Verlag, 1972.

———. *Hitler and the Forgotten Nazis: A History of Austrian National Socialism*. Chapel Hill: University of North Carolina Press, 1981.

Peterson, Edward N. *The Limits of Hitler's Power*. Princeton: Princeton University Press, 1969.

Pichl, Eduard Herwig. *Georg Schönerer und die Entwicklung des Alldeutschtums in der Ostmark*, 3rd ed. 6 vols. Oldenburg-Berlin: Gerhard Stalling, 1938.

Pulzer, P.G.J. *The Rise of Political Anti-Semitism in Germany and Austria*. New York: John Wiley & Sons, 1964.

Reitlinger, Gerald. *The Final Solution: The Attempt to Exterminate the Jews of Europe, 1939-1945*. 2nd ed. London: Vallentine, Mitchell, 1968.

———. *The SS: Alibi of a Nation, 1922-1945*. New York: Viking, 1968.

Ritter, Gerhard. *Carl Goerdeler und die deutsche Widerstandsbewegung*. Stuttgart: Deutsche Verlags-Anstalt, 1954.

Rosar, Wolfgang. *Deutsche Gemeinschaft: Seyss-Inquart und der Anschluss*. Vienna-Frankfurt-Zurich: Europa Verlag, 1971.

Ross, Dieter. *Hitler und Dollfuss*. Hamburg: Leibnitz Verlag, 1966.

Scheuer, Oskar. *Die geschichtliche Entwicklung des deutschen Studententums in Österreich*. Vienna: Schemann, 1910.

Schmidt, Matthias, *Albert Speer: Das Ende eines Mythos*. Bern-Munich: Scherz, 1982.

Schorske, Carl E. *Fin-de-Siècle Vienna: Politics and Culture*. New York: Alfred A. Knopf, 1980.

Seabury, Paul. *The Wilhelmstrasse: A Study of German Diplomats under the Nazi Regime*. Berkeley–Los Angeles: University of California Press, 1954.

Slapnicka, Harry. *Oberösterreich—als es "Oberdonau" hiess, 1938-1945.* Linz: Oberösterreichischer Landesverlag, 1978.

———. *Oberösterreich—Zwischen Bürgerkrieg und Anschluss, 1927-1938.* Linz: Oberösterreichischer Landesverlag, 1975.

Smith, Bradley F. *Heinrich Himmler: A Nazi in the Making, 1900-1926.* Stanford: Hoover Institute Press, 1971.

———. *Reaching Judgment at Nuremberg.* New York: Basic Books, 1977.

Smith, Bradley F., and Agarossi, Elena. *Operation Sunrise: The Secret Surrender.* New York: Basic Books, 1979.

Smyth, Howard McGaw. *Secrets of the Fascist Era: How Uncle Sam Obtained Some of the Top-Level Documents of Mussolini's Period.* Carbondale-Edwardsville: Southern Illinois University Press, 1975.

Stadler, Karl R. *Austria.* New York-Washington: Praeger Publishers, 1971.

———. *The Birth of the Austrian Republic, 1918-1921.* Leiden: A. W. Sijthoff, 1966.

Steinberg, Michael Stephen. *Sabers and Brownshirts: The German Students' Path to National Socialism, 1918-1935.* Chicago: University of Chicago Press, 1973.

Steiner, John M. *Power Politics and Social Change in National Socialist Germany: A Process of Escalation into Mass Destruction.* The Hague–Paris: Mouton Publishers, 1976.

Stern, Fritz. *The Politics of Cultural Despair: A Study in the Rise of the Germanic Ideology.* New York: Anchor, 1965.

Stuhlpfarrer, Karl. *Die Operationszonen "Alpenvorland" und "Adriatisches Küstenland" 1943-1945.* Vienna: Verlag Brüder Hollinek, 1969.

Suval, Stanley. *The Anschluss Question in the Weimar Era: A Study of Nationalism in Germany and Austria, 1918-1932.* Baltimore-London: Johns Hopkins University Press, 1974.

Sydnor, Charles W., Jr. *Soldiers of Destruction: The SS Death's Head Division, 1933-1945.* Princeton: Princeton University Press, 1977.

Taylor, A.J.P. *The Habsburg Monarchy, 1809-1918: A History of the Austrian Empire and Austria-Hungary.* New York: Harper Torch, 1965.

Toland, John. *The Last 100 Days.* New York: Bantam, 1967.

Trevor-Roper, Hugh R. *The Last Days of Hitler.* 4th ed. London: Macmillan, 1971.

Waite, Robert G. L. *The Psychopathic God: Adolf Hitler.* New York: Signet, 1978.

Weber, Max. *The Theory of Social and Economic Organization.* New York: Oxford, 1947.

Weinberg, Gerhard L. *The Foreign Policy of Hitler's Germany: Starting World War II, 1937-1939.* Chicago: University of Chicago Press, 1980.

Wheeler-Bennett, John. *The Nemesis of Power: The German Army in Politics, 1918-1945.* New York: St. Martin's Press, 1954.

Wheeler-Bennett, John, and Nicholls, Anthony. *The Semblance of Peace: The Political Settlement after the Second World War.* New York: Norton, 1974.

Whiteside, Andrew G. *Austrian National Socialism Before 1918.* The Hague: Martinus Nijhoff, 1962.

————. *The Socialism of Fools: Georg Ritter von Schönerer and Austrian Pan-Germanism.* Berkeley–Los Angeles: University of California Press, 1975.

Whiting, Charles. *Hitler's Werewolves: The Story of the Nazi Resistance Movement, 1944-1945.* New York: Stein & Day, 1972.

Wolf, Walter. *Faschismus in der Schweiz: Die Geschichte der Frontenbewegung in der deutschen Schweiz, 1930-1945.* Zurich: Flamberg Verlag, 1969.

Wulf, Josef. *Heinrich Himmler.* Berlin: Arani Verlag, 1960.

————. *Martin Bormann—Hitlers Schatten.* Gütersloh: Siegbert Mohn Verlag, 1962.

Zeller, Eberhard. *Geist der Freiheit: Der zwanzigste Juli 1944.* Munich: Hermann Rinn, 1952.

C. Articles

Bauer, Yehuda. "The Negotiations between Saly Mayer and the Representatives of the SS in 1944-1945." In *Rescue Attempts during the Holocaust,* pp. 5-45. Jerusalem: Yad Vashem, 1977.

Braham, Randolph L. "The Rightists, Horthy and the Germans: Factors Underlying the Destruction of Hungarian Jewry." In *Jews and Non-Jews in Eastern Europe, 1918-1945,* ed. George Mosse and Bela Vago, pp. 137-156. New York–Toronto: John Wiley & Sons, 1974.

Browning, Christopher R. "Unterstaatssekretaer Martin Luther and the Ribbentrop Foreign Office." *Journal of Contemporary History,* 12 (April 1977), 313-344.

Buchheim, Hans. "Die Höheren SS- und Polizeiführer." *Vierteljahrshefte für Zeitgeschichte,* 11 (October 1963), 362-391.

————. "The Position of the SS in the Third Reich." In *Republic to Reich: The Making of the Nazi Revolution,* ed. Hajo Holborn, pp. 251-297. New York: Pantheon, 1972.

Burin, Frederick S. "Bureaucracy and National Socialism: Reconsideration of Weberian Theory." In *Reader in Bureaucracy,* ed. Robert K. Merton et al., pp. 33-47. Glencoe, Illinois: The Free Press, 1952.

Cerwinka, Günter. "Ernst Kaltenbrunner und Südtirol: Zur Gründung einer italienischen Studentengruppe im Jahre 1923 in Graz." *Blätter für Heimatkunde*, 50, Heft 4 (1976), 173-177.

Conway, J. S. "Between Apprehension and Indifference: Allied Attitudes to the Destruction of Hungarian Jewry." *The Wiener Library Bulletin*, 27, nos. 30/31 (1973/1974), 37-48.

Fleming, Gerald. "Die Herkunft des 'Bernadotte-Briefs' an Himmler vom 10. März 1945." *Vierteljahrshefte für Zeitgeschichte*, 26 (October 1978), 571-600.

Gerth, Hans H. "The Nazi Party: Its Leadership and Composition." In *Reader in Bureaucracy*, ed. Robert K. Merton et al., pp. 100-113. Glencoe, Illinois: The Free Press, 1952.

Gilg, Peter, and Gruner, Erich. "Nationale Erneuerungsbewegungen in der Schweiz, 1925-1940." *Vierteljahrshefte für Zeitgeschichte*, 14 (January 1966), 1-25.

Goldhagen, Erich. "Weltanschauung und Endlösung: Zum Antisemitismus der nationalsozialistischen Führungsschicht." *Vierteljahrshefte für Zeitgeschichte*, 24 (October 1976), 379-405.

Gross, Nachum Th. "Die Stellung der Habsburgermonarchie in der Weltwirtschaft." In *Die Habsburgermonarchie 1848-1918*, Vol I: *Die wirtschaftliche Entwicklung*, ed. Alois Brusatti, pp. 1-28. Vienna: Verlag der österreichischen Akademie der Wissenschaften, 1973.

Haag, John. "Othmar Spann and the Quest for a 'True State.' " *Austrian History Yearbook*, 12-13 (1976-1977), 227-250.

Haensel, Carl. "The Nuremberg Trial Revisited." *DePaul Law Review*, 13 (spr.-sum. 1964), 248-259.

Jagschitz, Gerhard. "Die Anhaltelager in Österreich." In *Vom Justizpalast zum Heldenplatz: Studien und Dokumentationen*, 1927-1938, ed. Ludwig Jedlicka and Rudolf Neck, pp. 128-151. Vienna: Druck und Verlag der österreichischen Staatsdruckerei, 1975.

———. "Zwischen Befriedung und Konfrontation: Zur Lage der NSDAP in Österreich 1934 bis 1936." In *Das Juliabkommen von 1936: Vorgeschichte, Hintergründe und Folgen*, pp. 156-187. Vienna: Verlag für Geschichte und Politik, 1977.

Jedlicka, Ludwig. "The Austrian Heimwehr." In *Journal of Contemporary History*, Vol. I: *International Fascism, 1920-1945*, ed. George Mosse and Walter Laqueur, pp. 127-144. New York: Harper Torch, 1966.

———. "Gauleiter Josef Leopold, 1889-1941." In *Geschichte und Gesellschaft: Festschrift für Karl R. Stadler zum 60. Geburtstag*, pp. 143-161. Vienna: 1974.

Klemperer, Klemens von. "Chancellor Seipel and the Crisis of Democracy in Austria." *Journal of Central European Affairs*, 22 (January 1963), 468-478.

Koehl, Robert. "The Character of the Nazi SS." *Journal of Modern History*, 34 (September 1962), 275-283.

———. "Feudal Aspects of National Socialism." *American Political Science Review*, 54 (December 1960), 921-933.

———. "Toward an SS Typology: Social Engineers." *American Journal of Economics and Sociology*, 18 (January 1959), 113-126.

Kotze, Hildegard von. "Hitlers Sicherheitsdienst im Ausland." *Politische Meinung*, 8 (July-August 1963), 75-80.

Kranzbuehler, Otto. "Nuremberg Eighteen Years Afterwards." *DePaul Law Review*, 14 (spr.-sum. 1965), 333-347.

Krauss, Herbert. "The Nuremberg Trial of the Major War Criminals: Reflections after Seventeen Years." *DePaul Law Review*, 13 (spr.-sum. 1964), 233-247.

Lerner, Daniel. "The Nazi Elite." In *World Revolutionary Elites: Studies in Coercive Ideological Movements*, ed. Harold D. Lasswell and Daniel Lerner, pp. 194-318. Cambridge: MIT Press, 1965.

Matteson, Robert E. "The Last Days of Ernst Kaltenbrunner." *Studies in Intelligence*, 1960 (copy in possession of this author).

Mastny, Vojtech. "Stalin and the Prospects of a Separate Peace in World War II." *American Historical Review*, 77 (December 1972), 1365-1388.

McGrath, William J. "Student Radicalism in Vienna." In *Journal of Contemporary History*, Vol. VI: *Education and Social Structure in the 20th Century*, ed. Walter Laqueur and George Mosse, pp. 183-201. New York: Harper Torch, 1967.

Meier, Hedwig. "Die SS und der 20. Juli 1944." *Vierteljahrshefte für Zeitgeschichte*, 14 (July 1966), 299-316.

Mendelsohn, John. "Trial by Document: The Problem of Due Process for War Criminals at Nuremberg." *Prologue*, 7 (Winter 1975), 227-234.

Paetel, Karl O. "Die SS: Ein Beitrag zur Soziologie des Nationalsozialismus." *Vierteljahrshefte für Zeitgeschichte*, 2 (January 1954), 1-33.

Pannenbecker, Otto. "The Nuremberg War Crimes Trial." *DePaul Law Review*, 14 (spr.-sum. 1965), 348-358.

Pauley, Bruce F. "A Case Study in Fascism: The Styrian Heimatschutz and Austrian National Socialism." *Austrian History Yearbook*, 12-13, Part 1 (1976-1977), 251-273.

Ritter, Harry R. "Hermann Neubacher and the Austrian Anschluss Movement, 1918-1940." *Central European History*, 8 (December 1975), 348-369.

Rosenkranz, Herbert. "The Anschluss and the Tragedy of Austrian Jewry, 1938-1945." In *The Jews of Austria: Essays on Their Life, History, and Destruction*, ed. Josef Fraenkel, pp. 479-546. London: Vallentine-Mitchell, 1967.

Shils, Edward. "Charisma, Order and Status." *American Sociological Review*, 30 (April 1965), 199-213.

Skilling, H. Gordon. "Austrian Origins of National Socialism." *University of Toronto Quarterly*, 10 (July 1941), 482-492.

Stadler, Karl R. "Austria." In *European Fascism*, ed. S. J. Woolf, pp. 88-110. New York: Vintage, 1969.

Index

Library of Congress Cataloging in Publication Data

Black, Peter R.
Ernst Kaltenbrunner, ideological soldier of
the Third Reich.

Bibliography: p.   Includes index.
1. Kaltenbrunner, Ernst. 2. National socialism—
Biography. 3. Austria—History—1918-1938. 4. Germany—
History—1933-1945. 5. Nationalsozialistische Deutsche
Arbeiter-Partei. Schutzstaffel—History. I. Title.
DD247.K28B56 1984   943.086'092'4 [B]   83-42550
ISBN 0-691-05397-9

PETER R. BLACK is a historian in the Office of
Special Investigations, United States Department of Justice.
This is his first book.